GEORGE MACDONALD AND THE LATE GREAT HELL DEBATE

Rethinking the Core Foundations of Evangelical Theology

by

Michael Phillips and George MacDonald

In these days, when men are so gladly hearing afresh that "in Him is no darkness at all;" that God therefore could not have created any man if He knew that he must live in torture to all eternity; and that his hatred to evil cannot be expressed by injustice; itself the one essence of evil,—for certainly it would be nothing less than injustice to punish infinitely what was finitely committed, no sinner being capable of understanding the abstract enormity of what he does,—in these days has arisen another falsehood—less, yet very perilous: thousands of half-thinkers imagine that, since…hell is not everlasting, there is then no hell at all. To such folly I for one have never given enticement or shelter, I see no hope for many, no way for the divine love to reach them, save through a very ghastly hell. Men have got to repent; there is no other escape for them, and no escape from that.

—*George MacDonald,* from the Preface to
Letters From Hell by Valdemar Thisted, 1885

.
Published 2013 by Yellowood House, an imprint of Sunrise Books

ISBN: 9780940652897

Contents

PART 3—Jonathan Edwards Redux:
Sinners in the Hands of an Angry God: *Unlocking the Truth About Hell*

For these are the words of the Lord God: Now I myself will ask after my sheep and go in search of them. As a shepherd goes in search of his sheep when his flock is dispersed all around him, so I will go in search of my sheep and rescue them, no matter where they were scattered...I will bring them out...gather them in from other lands, and lead them home.

Ezekiel 34:11-13 (New English Bible)

LOVE'S CONSUMING FIRE

For those readers unfamiliar with the two names on the cover of this book, some brief introductions are probably in order.

I am Michael Phillips (1946-), a Christian writer mostly known for my works of fiction. In the 1970's I discovered the writings of obscure Victorian Scotsman George MacDonald (1824-1905), the man whose books were instrumental in leading C.S. Lewis out of atheism into Christianity, and whom Lewis considered a spiritual mentor for the rest of his life. Eventually MacDonald's perspectives on the Fatherhood of God became as life-changing for me as they were for Lewis. As a result, I embarked on a campaign to reintroduce MacDonald's work to the 20th century reading public through newly published editions of his books. This effort was carried out in the 1980s and 1990s. [1]

As author of more than fifty books during the latter half of the 19th century, George MacDonald's reputation through the years has rested primarily on his realistic fiction, imaginative works, short stories, literary essays, poetry, and fairy tales. Little known among the general reading public, however, have been five volumes of non-fiction treatises on the Bible through which MacDonald articulated an uncommon vision of God and his work among men. (MacDonald was originally a preacher by profession. He pastored only one church early in his life before turning to writing full-time.) Aspects of his vision of an eternally loving Fatherhood, and a childship of obedience through which his sons and daughters fulfill their relation to that Fatherhood, are sprinkled like radiant literary gems through all MacDonald's novels. It is most powerfully illuminated, however, in his volumes of "unspoken sermons." In these remarkable essays, as throughout his fiction, MacDonald hints at purposes that may lay in God's heart to accomplish in the afterlife beyond what was considered "orthodox" by the 19th century church. Of particular interest to MacDonald was his conviction that the "consuming fire" of Hebrews 12:29 was in fact not the fire of a tormenting hell of retribution, but was in fact a fire of consuming *Love* born in the heart of God for the purification and perfection of saint and sinner alike.

Because of such writings, all his life George MacDonald lay open to the charge of "universalism," or as it is more accurately termed for our purposes *universal reconciliation*, a clear heresy to fundamentalist Christians of his time, as to many in our own. Though MacDonald never stated a definite opinion on the possibility whether all men would ultimately be saved through the purifying fires of a redeeming hell, this criticism has followed him to this day.

That's where I come in. As MacDonald's biographer and as the one who has introduced readers to MacDonald through my editions of his works, many have looked to me, for lack of a better term, to "interpret" and clarify MacDonald's perspectives on this highly controversial topic. Innumerable have been the letters and whispered conversations through the years as readers have come to me with their questions, asking me also what conclusions my own scriptural research has yielded.

At length, in 1998, specifically to address this need, I compiled and privately printed a few hundred copies of a small booklet entitled *Universal Reconciliation: A Brief Selection of Pertinent Quotations.* [2] Our purpose was to provide a resource for individuals interested in the afterlife, particularly readers of George MacDonald who had contacted us about his views.

In the fifteen years since, interest in universal reconciliation has grown. Many more books about this controversial subject have been published. And an awareness of George MacDonald's singular contribution to Christian thought has begun to spread into the Christian mainstream. The objective of *George MacDonald and the Late Great Hell Debate* is to shine the light of MacDonald's thought on some of these difficult and admittedly controversial directions. It will serve as an adjunct to and expansion upon that earlier compilation.

One of the most important features of a study of this kind will always be the passages of Scripture upon which it is based. Foundational to the volume *Universal Reconciliation* was the section entitled "Scriptural Evidences." It listed dozens of passages that form the scriptural underpinnings to a perspective of the afterlife that explores beyond the confines of the traditional orthodoxy. That list should be considered foundational to all that follows.

Similarly, my Introduction to *Universal Reconciliation,* though written more than fifteen years ago, remains a clear statement of my own growth. It stresses what remains my firm conviction that this journey of exploration into the high purposes of God is primarily a personal and private quest. I earnestly hope and pray that you who come to this new book will read that Introduction and prayerfully heed its exhortation against controversy and divisiveness.

Several factors have prompted this more public articulation of ideas than I have felt it appropriate to offer in the past. The publication earlier this year of the fantasy *Hell and Beyond* suddenly thrust my perspectives into the limelight. It has seemed that a follow-up offering more specificity about the ideas raised in *Hell and Beyond* is now required. Additionally, the recent publication of several best-selling books has opened more doors of interest in the public consciousness than has been the case for years. Along with this has been a steadily burgeoning awareness of the theological impact of the writings of George MacDonald greater than anything seen since his own lifetime. It seems that the time has come for a more thorough treatment of George MacDonald's ideas about redemption, salvation, the atonement, and the purpose of hell.

These factors together have prompted a hunger within the hearts and minds of thousands of Christian men and women for a deeper, consistent, well-reasoned, and scriptural discussion on the subject of hell, the afterlife, and God's eternal purposes. It is to those hungry, growing souls that this book is dedicated. If you are such a one, this book is for *you*.

I would make abundantly clear at the outset what this book *is*, and what it is *not*. In reverse order, it is *not* intended as a persuasional tool for or against any doctrinal idea. With MacDonald, I will not be a spokesman for any doctrine. I care not, as he did not, who may agree or disagree with the theological perspectives presented here. Debate and persuasion are an anathema to me as they were to MacDonald. Though it is obvious that I am attempting to "make a case" for universal reconciliation, I do not place myself in the position of judge or jury telling anyone what conclusions they should or should not draw. I merely hope to lay out the evidence for objective consideration. While I may not be an entirely neutral observer, my *conclusions* remain uncertain. I do not profess to know what God will accomplish in eternity. My answer to the great questions raised by the scriptural conundrum of how expansive salvation might ultimately be is a resounding, *I don't know.*

I am in the position of an attorney doing my best for my client. That client is George MacDonald. I hope to fairly and accurately represent him. But in the final analysis, you will be jury to your own conclusions.

However, I am far from an impartial attorney. The writings of George MacDonald have been formative in my spiritual development, along with those of his protégé C.S. Lewis, in more ways than I can enumerate. I have been absorbing the ideas, words, and outlook of these two men, at the time of this writing, for close to forty-five years. Their perspectives of God's nature and being, his purposes in the universe, and what constitutes life as a Christian son or daughter of God have become so intrinsic to the root system of my beliefs that I cannot separate my own perspectives from theirs. As Lewis said that he had never written a book in which he did not quote from MacDonald (by which he meant that MacDonald's entire outlook had permeated his own faith at every point), I would say the same. MacDonald's vision of the Fatherhood of God has permeated so deeply into my being that I cannot say where MacDonald's influence leaves off and my perspectives as a Christian man and communicator and student of Scripture have developed in their own directions.

It is important to make the following point in order to clarify the nature of this book. There have been dozens, perhaps hundreds of books written about the high themes we will consider here. Why add another to the list? Precisely because we will *not* here be trying to persuade or convince or proselytize to any theologic point of view. We will be attempting to probe the heart of George MacDonald as *he* probed the heart of God. Our goal is to illuminate the message that comes through in George MacDonald's books with greater clarity. This book is not primarily about a theological doctrine, it is about a man's vision of God.

In probing MacDonald's heart, it cannot be helped that my own perspectives—in many cases perhaps inseparable from his—will be part of the mix. I will at times be speaking on my own behalf, at other times specifically on MacDonald's behalf. If the two intermingle in a way that makes them indistinguishable, I'm not sure that can be helped. If you find that ambiguity troublesome, perhaps this book will not be for you. At this stage of my life, however, there is really no way around it. If I am MacDonald's attorney, I have also taken my own stand alongside him and can no longer separate his defense from my own. In the words of Martin Luther, alongside MacDonald I will say, "Here I, too, stand."

This deepening fusion of my spiritual root system into the hundredfold good soil of MacDonald's transformative vision of Fatherhood, as I say, has been a long process of more than forty years. These perspectives are not merely "learned." They penetrate slowly over years of quiet, expanding growth as the Spirit of God works within our hearts to make us who we are. I have steeped myself in these ideas, in MacDonald's sermons, in the gospels, in the commands of Jesus, in the epistles of Paul—reading them over and over and over, praying and seeking the Father's heart, allowing Jesus' words and Paul's insights and MacDonald's wisdom all to shine the light of truth from different angles of the same prism into my brain and heart and spiritual consciousness.

I have walked the streets of Aberdeen and corridors at King's College that MacDonald walked, stood where he stood, listened in my spirit to his heart and to that of his characters Robert Falconer and Hugh Sutherland. I have walked and prayed through the streets of Huntly and the rooms and halls of the Farm where MacDonald grew up, listening and trying to absorb the vision of this man who knew God's heart. I have walked along the banks of Scotland's Don and Dee, Bogie and Deveron. I have climbed the highlands of Glencoe with MacDonald's descendents, and up the hills deep in the Grampians on the slopes of the fictional Glashgar where Gibbie searched for the legacy of his father—that wonderful image of mankind's quest for the Father heart of God—and where he and Donal came to know that Fatherhood. I have sat in my imagination with Lady Euphra as she listened with tearful indignation to the sermon about Jesus protecting us from the wrath of God. Judy and I have walked the streets and shorelines of Cullen with Malcolm, marveling at his courage and his own tumultuous journey to discover both fatherhood and Fatherhood, imaginatively participating in his formative discussions with Sandy Graham. Late into the night I have sat with Thomas Wingfold listening to Polwarth illuminate God's heart, shared in the childlike prayers of Andrew, Dawtie, and Sandy from MacDonald's *The Elect Lady* and asked the same questions that drove Barbara Wylder toward the God of truth.

In all these ways, through the reality of MacDonald's fictional characters and the power of his sermons, as well as through the pain and learning curve of my own ineffective and faltering earthly fatherhood, I have come to feel what I pray in some small way is the pulse of God's heart. Most importantly, I have tried to allow that transforming vision into the depths of my being. Through such experiences, it has been my mission not only to participate in Gibbie's, Malcolm's, Falconer's, Cosmo's, Wingfold's, Barbara's, and Euphra's inner journeys, but also to *share* them with the world, and thus also more deeply to share with hungry hearts the good news of the Consuming Love of God that has been so obscured by the modern church.

To make public the outcome of this deeply personal pilgrimage of the last forty years is the purpose of this book.

As George MacDonald's "interpretive attorney," so to speak, I have long maintained a position of what I have called "public neutrality." Perhaps that is not an entirely accurate representation of my perspective at this point. I *hope* that God has within his eternal purpose a plan by which to draw all creation into the home of his heart. I am not neutral in desire and motive, though perhaps I would still say I am neutral of conclusion.

My position might be described as a very interested fan at a football game. I may yell and cheer and stand up and shout. If someone sitting beside me turns and asks, "Do you know who's going to win?" my answer would be, "No." But it is obvious which team I am rooting for.

I make no secret of my allegiance, nor of which team I am rooting for in the eternal contest for the souls of humanity. I don't know how everything will turn out in the end. In the meantime, however, I will energetically and forcefully produce the arguments why I *think* the game will turn out as I hope it will.

The end of all this is simply that I am scripturally and prayerfully intrigued about what God may accomplish in the afterlife. My position on the question whether all will ultimately be saved is one of hopeful uncertainty.

Do I believe that all will ultimately be reconciled to God: *I don't know*. Do I believe that some will suffer in hell to eternity because of their refusal to repent: *I don't know*.

I maintain no dogmatic position of "belief" at either point. I do not know what will be the eternal outcome.

I would not presume to say I know. I do not need to know.

God *may* have the means to save all in the end. Some *may* refuse those means to all eternity. I believe that free will remains, and will remain, intrinsic to the equation between God and man. Repentance and the redemptive power of the cross will always be the necessary door to God. Some may forever refuse to walk through that door.

Knowing that I do not know, and *cannot* know, I choose not to hazard a *belief* one way or the other. I am a mortal. My eyes cannot penetrate the veil. I believe in the Father's eternal love and forgiveness. I trust him.

For those who want a statement of belief, I will repeat now what I said in the 1998 Introduction to *Universal Reconciliation:*

*I believe that the Fatherhood of God is universal. I believe that God is the Father of every created being. I believe that the love, goodness, forgiveness, and trustworthiness of the Father of Jesus Christ are infinite. Therefore, I trust HIM completely. Though he slay me, yet will I trust him, and so may all creation likewise trust him. He is a GOOD Father, so all he does **must** be good and can only be good. His essential nature is LOVE, so everything that proceeds out of his divine will must reflect that love. It is in his heart to FORGIVE infinitely. Jesus told us so. Therefore...we may TRUST him, and trusting him, may trust him for ALL things, for ALL men, for ALL possibilities. What is in the heart of God the Father to do will be full of love, full of goodness, and full of forgiveness. In those foundational and infinite truths of his essential nature and character I rest. In those foundational truths of his essential nature and character are all my questions swallowed up. I am at peace...for I TRUST Him.*

Beyond that, I care not to go. I am fascinated to explore beyond the boundaries of traditional thought concerning what might be in God's heart to accomplish. I find no need within myself to formulate a "systematic theology" of his reconciliatory purposes. I trust *God* far more than I trust in *my* capacity to understand the infinity of his loving purpose. But make no mistake...I am rooting for the God team!

And with this as my opening statement, I will now proceed to make the case on behalf of my client.

Michael Phillips, 2013

THE CURIOUS CASE OF CHRISTIANS AT FUNERALS

by
Michael Phillips

I attended a funeral several years ago for a man not known for spiritual faith. The ceremony, however, was conducted by a Christian minister and I was curious what words of "comfort" he would offer the family and friends who had gathered.

There are die-hard fundamentalists, even in such circumstances, who don't mind calling it like they see it. The "comfort" they see appropriate is to urge salvation upon those who remain while there is yet time, so that *they* won't go to hell themselves like the recently departed loved one. To speak of eternal damnation at the time of death seems extraordinarily callous to most of our sensibilities. But I have known individuals who perceive such as their duty, speaking up for truth and warning those who are alive before it is too late.

At this funeral, however, the minister did not preach of hellfire. He spoke rather of Jesus' words of consolation, reminding us that he is the resurrection and the life. His tribute was so hopeful that a bystander would assume the man in the coffin to have been a saint who had served God for fifty years.

Is this not usually the case—that our most "hopeful" thoughts about God and the afterlife emerge at the time of death? Is it because at such times the "better angels of our nature," as Abraham Lincoln called them, rise up to overpower the low theologies we have been taught? Whatever harsh views about hell and God's judgment one holds, they often cannot withstand the intense scrutiny of reality when death comes close.

Suddenly the innate goodness of our humanity cries out, "Whatever his faults, whatever his beliefs, whatever his sin…I cannot bring myself to condemn this man. And if I cannot, surely God will…"

Most leave the sentence unfinished.

They don't know what to do with the glaring dichotomy in their hearts between a theology of belief (non-Christians will burn forever in hell) and the unexpected compassion they feel when standing at the graveside of an unbeliever.

Was the minister just being nice for the sake of the bereaved? Is all the talk about eternal life—when we know good and well that the man or woman in the casket had no faith in Jesus whatever—just a lie? And if we *are* lying, what does that make of us?

I don't think we are lying.

Something very profound is going on at those times that possibly strikes to the heart of the meaning of the universe. There will always be those whose doctrines are stronger than their humanity, those who are able to shut out such hopeful thoughts and say to themselves, "That poor sinner is burning in hell right now. All these people ought to wise up and get their hearts right with God or the same will happen to them."

The majority of Christians are not quite so heartless. Most men and women feel more compassion and mercy even than their hardest theologies ascribe to God.

It was while I stood in that cemetery a number of years ago that a realization struck me: At funerals most Christians become temporary universalists.

In our deepest hearts, we truly struggle at such times to find a way to believe that God's love will vanquish even the unbelief of the most unbelieving and unrepentant sinner.

Hope rises within us. That hope may be a greater indicator of truth than we realize.

Not long after the funeral, the mother of a close friend died. A lifelong evangelical, our friend was suddenly confronted with the horrifying thought that her mother, an avowed *non*-Christian—if the doctrine of evangelical belief was true—was burning in hell, and would continue to do so for all eternity.

It wasn't mere wishful thinking that caused her to turn with revulsion from the idea. At that moment, I think a germ of Truth rose up from deeper within her heart than anyplace she knew existed. That spark challenged the veracity of a doctrine she had believed all her life. Suddenly her *heart* spoke. And her *brain*, with all its learned dogma, had no answer to give.

I can still hear the poignant, confused, grieving, yet hopeful tone of her voice as she said, "I know my mom had no faith, but...but I just...I just can't believe...I can't believe that God would..."

She could not finish the sentence either.

Her belief in a hell of torment for unbelievers could not withstand the moment when eternity suddenly stared her in the face. If she loved her mother, surely God would...

Her unformed human confusion could only dissolve into despairing perplexity. Doctrine had deserted her.

What *would* God do? She didn't even know what questions to ask. The doctrines of her belief system did not intersect with the reality of life as she suddenly had to confront it. Not only did those doctrines have no *answers* to give, they even forbade the *questions*.

I had never mentioned the idea of universal reconciliation to this friend. Until the moment of her mother's death the doctrines she had been taught were satisfactory. All at once her heart was hungry to explore depths in God's being she had never considered before.

In response to her tearful confusion, therefore, I gently posed the possibility, "You know, God may have more in mind for your mother than either you or she ever realized. He may not be through with her yet."

After the brief discussion of that day, I have not again spoken about it with her. The matter is between our friend and God now. These are not truths to be pushed or urged upon others by force. They are possibilities to be quietly *absorbed* by the heart ready, willing, and hungry to know the Father of Jesus Christ more intimately. Suffering opens the heart toward higher regions that touch God's eternal sympathy with the groaning and travailing of his creation.

Such seasons of prayer and spiritual exploration come differently for us all. Some, whose curiosity and spiritual hunger in these areas have been aroused, can think of nothing else until the conundrum is satisfactorily resolved. They want to read everything they can get their hands on. Others are not interested.

Some individuals, therefore, have given a great deal of thought and prayer to their beliefs about the afterlife and what those beliefs imply about the character of God. Others have given little thought to it. Circumstances have not yet made it a priority in their lives.

What the great hell debate really boils down to is a modest and straightforward question:

Who is God?

To resolve the question of hell demands that we look at the nature and character of God himself.

But these are turbulent waters. Diverging from tradition is considered dangerous. The quest to grapple with the afterlife lands us in the midst of a controversy that has bubbled beneath the surface of Christendom for 1800 years.

And yet...*is* the idea of an encompassing salvation really a "dangerous doctrine?" Many Christians earnestly think so. You will encounter them in your spiritual odyssey. The higher the questions you ask of God, the more their proof-textual artillery will take aim straight between your eyes.

This highlights why my words on these topics are often misunderstood. In emphasizing my attempt to remain open to a diversity of viewpoints, I say that I loathe doctrinal argumentation. Yet I have a greater aversion to formularistic, rote, non-thinking on the part of Christians who allow themselves to believe the most hideous things of God. Toward such, I fear, I have little patience. Jesus got angry when people spoke untruths about his Father. I see no inconsistency in our doing so as well. Therefore, my avowed uncertainty of conclusion on *doctrine* implies no neutrality toward *sloppy thinking* that demeans God's character. When I encounter mindless pat answers of proof-textual response, righteous indignation rises within me to hear the illogical things otherwise good people say of the Father of Jesus Christ, especially when they base their conclusions on erroneous, shallow, and inconsistent interpretations of Scripture. Perhaps some will find this dichotomy difficult to balance as we progress together. I don't suppose it can be helped that this dual perspective will become blurred for some readers. If from time to time indignation spills over and my words cause offense, I beg your forgiveness. I simply ask in such instances that you attempt to discern *why* I occasionally speak forcefully, and whether there are certain things Christians *ought* to get angry about. Doctrine is not one of them. Wrong thinking about the character of God is.

All this is a roundabout way of warning you that reading this book could be hazardous to your health.

Actually, that's not true. It will probably be *good* for your spiritual health—invigorating, stimulating, life-producing. But it could prove dangerous for your relationships, your reputation, and your standing in your church.

Therefore...count the cost. Turning the next page may begin a journey from which there is no turning back...and which could change your life in ways you neither expect nor can imagine.

PART 1

HEY, CHRISTIAN—WHAT DO YOU BELIEVE?

Why We Must Confront Hell Squarely

ONE

GOD'S SIGNATURE TUNE:
THE ETERNAL SYMPHONY OF UNITY

What the Doctrine of Punitive Hell
Says of God's Nature

by
Michael Phillips

E very musician, artist, and writer has his or her "signature tunes"—
themes and modes of communication, ways of expressing himself
unique to the particular stirrings of creative life inside him.

It does not take an expert to recognize the difference between Wagner
and Mozart, Debussy and Handel, Monet and Michelangelo, or between
Dickens and MacDonald. Style is part of it of course. But more important
are the thematic undercurrents that drive their artistry, and the deep truths
they are attempting to communicate through their work. These emerge as
artistic "melodies," so to speak, whether conveyed by musical notes,
colors on canvas, or words on a page.

I have spent most of my adult life trying to accurately identify those
melodies in George MacDonald's work. In the process many themes have
emerged in my own writing. I never set out to compose new music,
merely to exhume MacDonald's symphonic works from history's
archives. As I began, I often felt like a schoolboy barely learning his
scales trying to conduct an orchestra and choir performing Handel's
Messiah! Yet as time has passed, the role of conductor of MacDonald's
masterpieces has led to my own compositions. They have had fewer
complex harmonies and less sweeping grandeur—mere string quartets
alongside MacDonald's symphonies—yet hopefully have built upon some
of the same melodies.

THE FAR-OFF MUSIC OF ETERNITY

One of the enormously curious aspects of this process is that the "tune" I have most strenuously tried to *avoid* allowing to become a signature tune of my own, and that I have avoided emphasizing in my work with MacDonald, continues to exert its pervading influence. It was not an intended signature tune for MacDonald either. Yet its melody runs through his work from top to bottom. Every time I pick up one of his books, every time I set my own pen to paper, its far-off strains beckon— the symphony that rises above the other symphonies, the melody of which all other tunes are but faint and broken echoes.

It is the melody that swallows up all questions, all anxieties, all fears, all uncertainties, all scriptural perplexities.

I encountered it in the second or third book by George MacDonald I ever read. Something pierced deep into my soul. Immediately I hungered to know more. Thus began a long adventure of learning to hear what I now believe is nothing less than *God's* signature tune. It is the music, as I read it back then, of North Wind speaking of pain and death, and the unanswerable questions of life.

"I will tell you how I am able to bear it, Diamond: I am always hearing, through every noise...the sound of a far-off song. I do not exactly know where it is or what it means; and I don't hear much of it, only the odour of its music...but what I do hear, is quite enough...Somehow, I can't say how, it tells me that all is right; that it is coming to swallow up all cries."

Like little Diamond, don't we all react at first with question? Death and hell rise to assert themselves out of what we have been taught, attempting even as we first begin to detect its strains, to drown out the high music. But North Wind continues, reassuring even in terror of the wonderfully strange new possibilities she hints at, to set even such seemingly insurmountable anxieties to rest.

"It wouldn't be the song it seems to be if it did not swallow up all their fear and pain too, and set them singing it themselves with the rest. I know it will. And do you know...that song has been coming nearer and nearer. Only I must say it was some thousand years before I heard it." [3]

I am thankful to God that it did not take George MacDonald a thousand years. He began hearing it at an early age. It took me longer, but thankfully not a thousand years either. We are thick-headed and stubborn creatures, but God persists in trying to get the truth of his high music through to us. I am so grateful for the many ways he has found to get it into my brain...and even more for the ways he has found to get it into my heart. When MacDonald wrote the words of North Wind he was still a relatively young man of forty-five, though by then reaching his height as one of God's prophetic spokesmen of the nineteenth century. He had begun to illuminate God's signature tune a few years earlier in his masterpiece *Robert Falconer*. In the years that followed he would discern that music with increasing clarity, and deftly express its soaring melody by the power of his pen. In my own case, I think I began hearing the wondrous music of reconciliation somewhere around my twenty-fourth year.

It has been there ever since. It is just as North Wind says, though I take the liberty of paraphrasing her words into my own circumstances: *I am always hearing, through every doctrine, through every passage of Scripture, sometimes obscured by church teaching and tradition, the sound of a far-off song. It tells me that all is right, and that He is coming and will one day swallow up all the world's pain and grief and unbelief and sin, and set the universe singing the symphony of unity in the whole creation.*

I might try not to emphasize it, but the high melody of God's eternal purpose and man's ultimate destiny is always there, informing and giving meaning to everything else.

WE *MUST* HEAR THE MUSIC

I am finally recognizing that it *must* be so. This particular symphony rises above all other tunes—high above all ideas and doctrines and theologies. It rises above all the music of life because it is music we are intended to hear.

It tells us that God is going to make things right with his creation, that his victory will be complete, that his love and forgiveness will triumph over *all* sin, *all* rebellion, and *all* that is contrary to his will.

It is the symphony that tells us who God is! Thus it is music we *must* learn to hear.

None of life's lesser tunes—be they religious or secular—can reach their fulfillment until we learn to hear the One song aright. All else proceeds out of the One song, points toward it, and will one day be swallowed back up into that majestic symphony of eternity that is continually trying to get through to us.

This "must" explains why I have decided to focus on a few of the overtones and harmonics of the "far-off song" with the publication of this book. For it is not simply one song among many for Christians. We may one day come to realize that it was *the* Song of all songs.

And if it is God's signature tune, *the* Song above all songs, it must eventually be sung in God's Church—though the theologians of that church have done their best to prevent its being heard for 1900 years.

AN UNHEARD SYMPHONY

Many never learn to hear this music. Many *Christians* never learn to hear it. Mistaking dissonant melodies (which they call doctrines, and which they have learned from pastors, priests, and teachers), their ears grow incapable of taking in God's grand symphonic masterpiece. They are not trained in the right kind of spiritual music.

Even after I began to hear North Wind's song, for years I downplayed this highest of all symphonies in my writing because of the controversy surrounding it. I did so in an honest attempt to follow George MacDonald's example.

Yet I always wondered, if God himself composed this symphony of eternity, why his own people did not make a greater effort to hear it. *Why* is it controversial? *Why* is it not eagerly embraced by Christ's followers? *Why* are its proponents, like MacDonald and his mentor, English pastor and theologian F.D. Maurice, branded as heretics—as ridiculous a charge as can be imagined? *Why* is it not preached from pulpits across the land as mighty "good news?" These are among history's enduring perplexities.

It seems a sad fact of religious life that its ecclesiastical leaders— from ancient Judaism to fifteenth-century Catholicism to contemporary Evangelicalism—expend great effort to insure that their flocks hear only the music composed in the hallowed rooms of their own institutional hierarchies. Evil names are given to music that chances to get through from outside.

Thus God cannot make his melodies heard in the very churches and cathedrals where his name is honored. These assemblies are sadly filled with multitudes whose ears have grown dull from listening to man's doctrinal dirges rather than God's high celestial anthems.

ILLOGICAL INCONSISTENCIES BLOCK TRUE KNOWING OF GOD

One of my own lesser signature tunes has been an emphasis on what I call implicational thinking.

If A...then B.

Because Christians are not trained in implicational thinking, most do not pause to consider the logical consequences of their ideas. They maintain their doctrinal beliefs in a vacuum. They do not ask if they make sense. They blindly accept what they have been taught without question, and call it "faith."

The most significant belief where implicational thinking is absolutely required concerns the nature of God. MacDonald explores this most pointedly in his novel *There and Back* where he says what I paraphrase as, "Everything depends on what kind of God one believes in." [4]

It is impossible to understate the importance of this truth. Wrong belief about God makes us incapable of hearing his universal music.

Not subjecting their beliefs to the rigors of implicational thinking, most Christians spend their energies listening to the doctrinal compositions of men. The inconsistencies of these compositions are reasoned away with unbelievably contorted explanations. All the while the people in the pews rarely pause to ask whether the theological emperor behind the pulpit is wearing any clothes.

The disconnect between such doctrines and the character of God implied by them is stunning. The very men and women who should be sharing the symphony of heaven with the world seem themselves oblivious to its most elemental strains.

THE PREVENTATIVE TO ETERNITY'S MUSIC—A HYPOCRITICAL GOD

Obviously nothing can be so important for a Christian than the nature and character of God. Yet what do most Christians believe about him? It is a question whose enormous implications do not become clear until one confronts Christianity's most glaring conundrum.

Any inquiry into the nature of God plunges us straight into the dichotomy posed by the existence of hell.

When one stares hell in the face, and asks, "Who is this God that would eternally torment those who do not believe in him? What kind of God would *do* that!" at last the raw horrifying implications of traditional Christianity come into focus.

All lesser doctrines suddenly pale in comparison. The doctrine of hell, as no other component of Christian orthodoxy, determines the nature of the God we believe in.

Is he, or is he not, a God who could, a God who would, a God who *will* send sinners to everlasting torment because they do not believe in him or in his Son?

In the world's eyes, nothing else matters. This is *the* issue upon which the Christian message rises or falls.

Even in the midst of modernity, humanism, and secularism, people do not have so serious a problem with miracle and supernaturalism as one might suppose. Indeed, in their heart of hearts most men and women *want* to believe.

But they *do* have a problem with hypocrisy. Nothing angers people more than pretended righteousness.

Yet that is what Christianity has been presenting to the world for some 1800-1900 years—a hypocritical, self-righteous God.

I truly believe that the world would not find the incarnation and the resurrection difficult to believe if the doctrine of hell were not looming behind them as the great Hypocrisy of the universe.

The cross may indeed be a stumbling block to some. But I disagree with the implication many draw from Paul's words, that it is *the* major stumbling block to faith. Perhaps it was in Paul's time, but I do not perceive it so in ours.

People can believe in Jesus walking on the water, in his raising Lazarus from the dead, even in his dying for our sins and rising from the grave. The world has always been willing to believe in Jesus.

But it *cannot* believe in a God who would send a majority of creation to eternity in hell.

Hell is the great stumbling block to right belief about God. If Christians understood the music of eternity, the world would be far more receptive to the *true* message of the cross.

The implications of eternal punitive hell are too enormous, positively too staggering for unbelievers to cope with. They *should* be too staggering, as taught, for Christians to cope with. If the doctrine of hell as commonly taught is true, the God it portrays is nothing short of a monster. No theological double-talk can get rid of that fact. If that is our god, let us say, with MacDonald: "There is no God. Let us neither eat nor drink, that we may die! For lo, this is not our God!" [5]

Andrew Jukes says that we become what we worship.[6] If indeed we worship a false god, a hypocritical god, a self-righteous and vengeful god, what positively dreadful implications this has for the state of the Church.

CHRISTIAN RESPONSES

The question for Christians, then, is how do we respond?

Obviously truth is not gauged by the world's reaction. Because the world doesn't like the idea of hell (one must admit that many Christians don't like it either), does not mean it isn't true. But perhaps the apparent inconsistency involved within the divine character ought to give us pause to take a closer look at what centuries of tradition have taught us.

What if the doctrine *isn't* true? What if it isn't as scriptural as we have been led to believe? What if the world's reaction is not only justifiable but a very proper response to a hideous untruth?

Three responses surface to such queries:

1) Some Christians in essence say, *Too bad.* The Bible warns sinners of the wages of sin. If they don't want to burn forever, they should repent and accept Christ. The Bible is clear in its teaching of everlasting hell. The words are rarely quite so callous, but follow what they say to the end and it amounts to the same thing.

Numerous proof texts usually follow, in the interpretation of which the bold prayerful *thought* involved is roughly zero.

2) Others don't want to face the glaring dichotomy, and ignore it.

3) Still others—like F.D. Maurice and George MacDonald and William Law and Hannah Hurnard and Andrew Jukes and A.R. Symonds and Thomas Allin and William Barclay and others who have courageously raised their prophetic voices through the years in spite of criticism and rebuke, along with increasing thousands in our own time—probe the Scriptures and the character of God to find out whether the things said of him by the elder-traditions can really be true and whether they are supported by the Bible.

CHRISTENDOM'S DREADFUL HISTORICAL RECORD

Certainly those who feel an inner disquiet with the implications of traditional theology cannot forever ignore it. Eventually the sense of unease comes calling—What can it be but the Holy Spirit speaking, deep calling to deep?—and inquiring men and women begin casting their gaze about for something more worthy to believe of their God.

Their sense of unease turns to outright horror as they listen aghast to the appalling things that have been said by some of the most revered saints of Christendom.

Consider the following questionable sentiments from those who have been commissioned to carry God's *love* into the world:

> *"The bliss of the saved may please them more, and they may render more abundant thanks to God...that they are permitted to gaze on the punishment of the wicked."* (St. Thomas Aquinas) [7]

> *"The elect, while they see the unspeakable sufferings of the ungodly, shall not be affected with grief, but rather satiated with joy at the sight, and give thanks to God for their own salvation."* (Peter Lombard) [8]

> *"Though infants departing from the body without baptism will be in the mildest damnation...he greatly deceives and is deceived who preaches that they will not be in damnation."* (St. Augustine) [9]

> *"It is the highest degree of faith to believe that God is merciful, who saves so few and damns so many; to believe him just, who of His own will makes us necessarily damnable."* (Martin Luther) [10]

> *"The world will probably be converted into a great lake or liquid globe of fire...in which the wicked shall be overwhelmed...their heads, their eyes, their tongues, their hands,*

their feet, their loins, their vitals shall for ever be full of glowing, melting fire...they shall be full of...torments; not for one minute, not for one day, nor for one age, nor for two ages, nor for a thousand ages...but for ever and ever, without any end at all, and never, never be delivered...The view of the misery of the damned will double the ardour of the love and gratitude of the saints in heaven. " (that saint of Calvinism, Jonathan Edwards)[11]

Can it be any wonder that George MacDonald said that from such an image of God he turned with loathing? [12]

And more recently the highly esteemed John Piper maintains that God will take *pleasure* in the punishment of the wicked:

God is grieved in one sense by the death of the wicked, and pleased in another...when a rebellious, wicked, unbelieving person is judged...God delights in...the exaltation of truth and righteousness, and the vindication of his own honor and glory... God and the saints in heaven will be happy in heaven for all eternity knowing that many millions of people are suffering in hell forever...the vindication of God's infinite holiness is cherished so deeply. [13]

Are there Christians who think that the saints in heaven, and God himself, will actually *enjoy* the torments of the damned? I find it hard to imagine. Yet this too has been intrinsic to the prevailing theology.

What else can one do upon reading these words than cry out: *What kind of God did and do these men worship!*

I fear that millions in our own day *do* believe such things, and worse, without the slightest compunction.

Thank God that there are those of the Church, perhaps few in number, who are appalled to believe such atrocious things of their God. For them the faint strains of the far-off symphony are beginning to be heard.

THE BIG QUESTION

If something is amiss in the traditional teaching, does it not behoove us to investigate? Any Christian who cares to correctly understand the character of God, must eventually ask the big question:

Is the commonly taught view of eternal damnation consistent with the Father of Jesus Christ?

It is the pivotal query of Christianity.

It is ingrained into us to read the foundations of our faith through the lens of Christology—the incarnation, the trinity, the atonement, and the death and resurrection of Jesus Christ. As pivotal as Christ's role is,

however—obviously no Christianity exists apart from him—a deeper
magic exists from before the dawn of time (*before* the incarnation, *before*
the atonement, *before* the resurrection)—a yet *more* fundamental pillar of
belief than Jesus.

That is the character and nature of God himself.

The Christology of Christianity is built on the foundation of God's
being. We cannot understand Jesus or his work unless we understand the
Fatherhood that gave rise to the Sonship. The incarnation, the trinity, the
atonement, and the death and resurrection of Jesus all emerge out of the
character of God. Jesus is our Elder Brother, our Savior, our Lord, our
Master, our Redeemer. But our life comes from Jesus Christ's Father,
because he is *our* Father.

We know these things because Jesus told us so. To worship the Son
above the Father is to disobey Jesus himself. To worship the Father
through our worship of the Son is to honor both Father and Son in proper
balance, and to take Jesus' example unto ourselves.

To know Jesus truly, we must know his Father as he is, not as he has
been characterized by small-seeing theologians from Dante to Calvin to
Edwards to Piper.

Do we believe in a God *capable* of eternally tormenting large
numbers of beings he himself created…or do we believe him *incapable* of
such cruelty. "Punishment" is a far different thing. God *may* punish that
he might redeem. But is he a God capable of pure, purposeless, unending
cruelty?

How and *why* such a state of affairs comes to pass (theological
explanations notwithstanding about sin, free will, God's not condemning
but man freely choosing his eternal state, and so on) begs the fundamental
question:

Is God capable of such a thing…*however* it comes to be?

Note the words of Martin Luther, that founding saint of
Protestantism, just quoted. In his view, it is *God* who does the damning. It
is *God* "who saves so few and damns so many." It is God *himself*, "who of
His own will makes us necessarily damnable."

In George MacDonald's words:

Very God forbid! [14]

Luther's words are a direct falsehood against the word and character
of God. They are a slap in the face and an affront to Jesus himself. Let us
no longer ignore the implications of a theology we have for so long
allowed to be perpetuated as an insidious cancer in our midst.

Pretending that God is powerless to change man's free choice of sin
is to torture out of certain passages of the Bible a meaning that may never
have been intended by God.

Such explanations do not alter the stark implications of the question:

Is God one whose intrinsic nature makes him *capable* of sanctioning eternal torment as the ultimate solution for sin?

Even if it is man's fault, would God *allow* man to suffer in hell forever? Even if man chooses it, even if man says, "I *want* hell as my final reward," would God not step in and say, "You may want it, but you are my creation and I will not *allow* it. You do not know what is for your best. I am your Father. My love compels me to do the best for you that you are too selfish and sinful to want for yourself."

We must all face these questions and decide for ourselves what manner of "God" we worship.

INFINITE LOVE OR DIVINE HYPOCRISY

It is true that Christianity does not rise or fall on the question of hell. It rises and falls on the character of God first, then on the commands and resurrection of Christ. But insofar as Christianity is presented to the world and is understood by the world—hell is the pivotal question. In the world's eyes hell looms larger than the cross and is the great stumbling block of the gospel.

For years I was myself one of those who tried to convince myself that God was loving and trustworthy even if sinners were doomed to an eternity in hell. Even after I began to move toward a more neutral position of *I don't know*, I remained convinced that unity was a higher truth than hell. (And that remains my position.) I failed to fully recognize, however, the implications of what belief in an eternal punitive hell says about the nature of the God one worships. I did not yet recognize that the entire divine character was at stake:

Infinite Love vs. Divine Hypocrisy.

I still believe that unity is a higher truth than correctness of doctrine. It has been many years since God began stirring me toward the higher melodies of North Wind. And now, in my seventh decade of life, I have come to the conclusion that the question of hell and what it says of the divine character is a conundrum all Christians must confront sooner or later. Not only is it the pivotal issue insofar as how the world perceives Christianity, it is the pivotal issue for Christians.

We *must* know who God is.

We cannot adequately know him without asking what eternal punitive hell says of God's character.

The spectre of hell prevents North Wind's song from coming through. The doctrine gets in the way.

But God wants us to hear the high Logos song of the great coming right of all things, coming right because he is at the heart of them. As long as we hold on to belief in evil things of God, and call those evil things by holy names, such wrong knowing and the calling of evil good will prevent a *right* knowing of the Father of Jesus Christ as we must know him.

A PRIVATE QUEST

Unity is the highest tune in God's eternal symphony, pointing toward the harmony and reconciliation of all things. Unity is the truth toward which everything points. The incarnation, the trinity, the atonement, and the resurrection are all melodies that will be drawn up together in the grand sweeping symphony that will culminate in the unity of God's creation.

These high matters, however, are not ones about which the debate and discussion can yet fruitfully be public. Perhaps the time for a widespread inquiry may come, but it is not yet. The Church at large is not ready for it. The church is too theologically immature and scripturally ignorant. Humility is one of the most necessary components of the needful discussion. At present, however, the Evangelical wing of the Church is far too self-righteously pleased with itself for such a discussion to take place. Yet that day may be hastening toward us.

Some disagree in this, but I perceive that the quest needed at present is an inward, private, prayerful one. Like MacDonald, I write not to those who would debate the issue. Indeed, I will *not* debate it. As long as men and women are satisfied to believe low things of God, let them be so satisfied. Their belief is its own reward. Like my spiritual and literary mentor, I write for those for whom the so-called orthodox view has become burdensome, to help the hungry heart sift and sort and think through his or her own prayerful journey. As I emphasized earlier, I do not care to persuade or convince to any doctrine, only perhaps to shed a little light on what can be a lonely path. I *do* care to persuade Christians toward bold thinking in their faith, and about what doctrines they choose to believe. Toward such bold thinking Christianity, I am anything but neutral. [15] I consider it one of the most urgent necessities of our faith. Toward such boldness of thought I will speak as forcefully as I am able.

This sole attempt at persuasion would urge this final imperative upon us all, once we rise from the knees of our inquiry—with tear stained faces it may be: Let us not content ourselves to theorize, let us obey in doing what God puts before us to do, loving our brethren of differing perspectives on this and all matters doctrinal.

That I care not to persuade removes nothing from my earnest conviction that these are matters every Christian must eventually wrestle through in the prayer closets of their hearts. If we do not face them here, we will have to face them there. It may be that it will not be St. Peter or Mary or even Jesus himself who will meet us at the gates of heaven (I speak foolishly to get a point across!), but the Father himself. The question he asks may not be, "Who died for your sins?" but rather:

"How could you *possibly* believe such monstrosities of me! Why did you not love me enough to get to know me better? Why did you not summon the courage to question the theological absurdities your pastors and teachers taught? They have much to answer for…but *you* should have known better, especially after all my Son told you about me."

Hell is therefore a doctrine above all doctrines that Christ's followers must face if they are to know the Father he came to reveal. How else will they hear the highest melodies of all, the music of the spheres, the anthem of eternity that God's heavenly hosts are singing even now—the symphony of eternal love, unity, and victorious reconciliation.

Two

THE TRUTH IN JESUS

by
George MacDonald

From *Unspoken Sermons, Second Series*
as reprinted in *The Truth in Jesus* [16]

Edited by Michael Phillips [17]

But ye did not so learn Christ; if so be that ye heard him, and were taught in him,
even as truth, is in Jesus: that ye put away, as concerning your former manner of life,
the old man, which waxeth corrupt after the lusts of deceit.
[That is, "which is still going to ruin through the love of the lie."]
—Eph. 4:20-22

How have we learned Christ? It ought to be a startling thought that we may have learned him wrong.

That is a far worse thing than not to have learned him at all, for his place in our minds is occupied by a false Christ that is hard to exorcize. The point is whether we have learned Christ as he taught himself, or as *men* who thought they understood, but did not understand him, have taught us about him. Do we only think we know him—with fleshly notions that come from low mean human fancies and explanations. Or do we truly know him—after the spirit, in our limited measure, in the same way as God knows him?

HAVE WE LEARNED JESUS HIMSELF OR ONLY ABOUT HIM?

Throughout its history, the Christian faith has been open to more corrupt misrepresentation than the Jewish could ever be. As it is higher and wider, so must it yield larger scope to corruption. Have we learned of Christ in false statements and corrupted lessons about him, or have we learned *himself*? Nay, true or false, is our brain only full of things concerning him, or does he dwell himself in our hearts, a learnt, and ever being learnt lesson, the power of our life?

I have been led to what I am about to say, by a certain statement made by one who is in the front rank of those who assert that man can know and ascertain nothing about the existence of an infinite higher Power from whom all things proceed. His statement is this:

"The visiting on Adam's descendants through hundreds of generations dreadful penalties for a small transgression which they did not commit; the damning of all men who do not avail themselves of an alleged mode of obtaining forgiveness, which most men have never heard of; and the effecting a reconciliation by sacrificing a son who was perfectly innocent, to satisfy the assumed necessity for a propitiatory victim; are modes of action which, ascribed to a human ruler, would call forth expressions of abhorrence; and the ascription of them to the Ultimate Cause of things, even now felt to be full of difficulties, must become impossible."

I do not quote the passage with the design of opposing it for I entirely agree with it. Indeed, it almost feels an absurdity to say so. Neither do I propose addressing a word to the writer of it or to any who agree with his belief in man's incapacity to know God. My purpose here is altogether differently directed.

One of my earliest recollections is of beginning to be at strife with the false system here assailed. Such paganism I scorn as heartily in the name of Christ, as I scorn it in the name of righteousness. Rather than believe a single point involving its spirit, even with the assurance thereby of such salvation as the system offers, I would join the ranks of those who "know nothing," and set myself with hopeless heart to what I am now trying with an infinite hope in the help of the pure originating One—to get rid of my miserable mean self, comforted only by the chance that death would either leave me with no more thought, or else might reveal something of the Ultimate Cause which it would not be an insult to him, or a dishonor to his creature, to hold concerning him. Even such a chance alone might enable one to live.

WHY DO MEN NOT ENQUIRE MORE DEEPLY INTO MATTERS OF BELIEF?

I will not now enquire how it comes that the writer of the passage quoted seems to put forward these so-called beliefs as representing Christianity. Nor will I ask why he would think such a creed representative of those who call themselves Christians, seeing that many—some of them of higher rank in literature than himself—believe in

Christ with true hearts, and hold to not one of such things as he has set down. He would doubtless be surprised at how many sincere Christians hold them in at least as great abhorrence as he.

His answer would probably be that, even had he been aware of such fact that his statement was not an accurate reflection of the beliefs of *all* Christians, what he had been trying to deal with was the forming and ruling notions of religious society. He would insist that such *are* the views held by the bulk of both educated and uneducated calling themselves Christians, even though some of them may vainly think by an explanatory clause here and there to lessen the disgracefulness of their falsehood. And sadly, that such are the things so held, I am, alas! unable to deny.

It helps nothing, I repeat, that some—thinking seriously very little on the matter—use *quasi* mitigated forms to express their doctrines, and imagine that so they indicate a different class of ideas. It would require but a brief examination to be convinced that they are not merely analogous—they are ultimately identical.

But were I to address the writer, I should ask why he had not examined the matter in greater depth. Why is it that, refusing these dogmas as abominable and in themselves plainly false, yet knowing that they are attributed to men whose Christian teaching has done more to civilize the world than that of any other belief or religion, and if such ideas as he represents could not have done so—why has he not taken such pains of enquiry as must surely have satisfied a man of his intelligence that they were *not* the teaching of such men? I would ask him to consider whether the reason for this may not lie in the fact that their beliefs were actually so *different*, and so *good*, that even the forced companionship of such horrible lies as those he has recounted, has been unable to destroy their regenerative power throughout history.

I suppose he will allow that there was a man named Jesus who died for the truth he taught. Can he believe that he died for such alleged truth as he has set down? Would it not be well, I would ask him, to enquire what he did *really* teach, according to the primary sources of our knowledge of him?

If he answered that the question was uninteresting to him, I should have no more to say. Nor did I now start to speak of him except with the object of making my position plain to those to whom I would speak—not unbelievers such as himself, but those, namely, who *do* call themselves Christians.

If I should ask those, as I said, who call themselves Christians, "How has it come about that such opinions as the above writer has set down are actually held concerning the Holy One, whose ways you take upon you to set forth?" most of them would answer, "Those are the things he tells us himself in his word. We have learned them from the Scriptures."

Many also would set forth explanations which appear to explain the things in such a way that makes them no longer seem so villainous. Still others would remark that better ideas, though largely held by individuals within Christendom, had not yet had time to show themselves as the belief of the religious leaders and thinkers of the nation.

WHAT ARE WE CONVEYING TO OUR GENERATION—OPINION OR TRUTH

Of those whose presentation of Christian doctrine is represented in the quotation above, there are two classes—those who are *content* it should be so, and those to whom such doctrines are *grievous*, but who do not see how to get rid of them.

To the latter it may be some little comfort to have one who has studied the New Testament for many years and loves it beyond the power of speech can express, declare to them his conviction that there is not an atom of such teaching in the whole lovely, divine utterance. I declare further that such an explanation of essential Christian doctrine is all and altogether the invention of men—honest invention, in part at least, I grant, but still false.

Thank God, we are not bound to accept any man's explanation of God's ways and God's doings, however good the man may be, if it does not commend itself to our conscience. The man's conscience may be a better conscience than ours, and his judgment clearer. Yet still we cannot accept that which we cannot see to be good. To do so would be to sin.

But it is by no means my object to set forth what I believe or do not believe. A time may come for that. My design is now very different indeed. I desire to address those who call themselves Christians, and expostulate with them thus:—

Whatever be your *opinions* on the greatest of all subjects, is it well that the impression with regard to Christianity made upon your generation should be that of mere opinion, or should it not come from something beyond opinion?

Is Christianity even capable of being represented by *opinion*, even the best of opinion? If it were, how many of us are such as God would choose to represent his thoughts and intents by *our* opinions concerning them? Who is there of his friends whom any thoughtful man would depute to represent his thoughts to his fellows?

If you answer, "The opinions I hold and by which I represent Christianity are those of the Bible," I reply that none can understand, still less represent, the opinions of another, but such as are of the same mind with him. Certainly no one who *mistakes* his whole scope and intent, so far as in supposing *opinion* to be the object of any writer in the Bible, could be capable of accurately representing such writer.

Is Christianity a system of articles of belief, even if they are correct as language can give them? Never.

I am so far from believing it that I would rather that a man held, as numbers of you do, what seem to me the most obnoxious untruths, opinions the most irreverent and gross, if at the same time he *lived* in the faith of the Son of God—that is, trusted in God as the Son of God trusted in him—than I would have a man hold formulas of belief that coincided at every point with my own, if he knew nothing of a daily life and walk with God. The one, holding doctrines of devils, is yet a child of God. The other, holding the doctrines of Christ and his Apostles, is of the world, yea, of the devil.

What!—a man hold the doctrine of devils and yet be of God?

Yes—for to hold a thing with the intellect is not to believe it. A man's real belief is that which he lives by. And if a man lives by the love of God and obedience to his law so far as he has recognized it, even if he holds, as I say, to certain hideous doctrines, those false beliefs are actually outside of him. He *thinks* they are inside, but no matter. They are not true and cannot really be inside any good man. They are sadly against him, for he cannot love to dwell upon any of those supposed characteristics of his God. He acts and lives nevertheless in a measure like the true God.

What a man believes, is the thing he *does*. A good man would shrink with loathing from actions such as he thinks God justified in doing. Like God, he loves and helps and saves. Will the living God let such a man's opinions damn him? No more than he will let the correct opinions of another, who lives for himself, save him. The best salvation even the latter could give would be but damnation.

What I come to and insist upon is, that, supposing your theories right, even suppose they contain all that is to be believed, yet those theories are not what makes you Christians, if Christians indeed you are. On the contrary, they are, with not a few of you, just what *keeps* you from being Christians.

PLANS OF SALVATION OFFER NO SALVATION

For when you say that, to be saved, a man must hold this or that, then you are forsaking the living God and his will, and putting trust in some notion *about* him or his will. To make my meaning clearer: Some of you say that we must trust in the finished work of Christ. Or you say that our faith must be in the merits of Christ—in the atonement he has made—in the blood he has shed.

All these statements are a simple repudiation of the living Lord, *in whom* we are told to believe. It is his presence with and in us, and our obedience to him, that lifts us out of darkness into light, and leads us from the kingdom of Satan into the glorious liberty of the sons of God. No manner or amount of belief *about him* is the faith of the New Testament.

With such teaching I have had a lifelong acquaintance, and I declare it most miserably false. But I do not now mean to dispute against it. Except the light of the knowledge of the glory of God in the face of Christ Jesus make a man sick of his opinions, he may hold them to doomsday for me.

No opinion, I repeat, is Christianity, and no preaching of any plan of salvation is the preaching of the glorious gospel of the living God. Even if your plan, your theories, were absolutely true, the holding of them with sincerity, the trusting in this or that about Christ, or in anything he did or could do—the trusting in anything but himself, his own living self—is still a delusion.

Many will grant this heartily. And yet the moment you come to talk with them, you find they insist that to believe in Christ is to believe in the atonement, meaning by that only and altogether their special theory about the atonement. And when you say we must believe in the atoning Christ, and cannot possibly believe *in* any theory concerning the atonement, they go away and denounce you, saying, "He does not believe in the atonement!"

If I explain the atonement otherwise than they explain it, they assert that I deny the atonement, and count it of no consequence that I say I believe in the atoner with my whole heart, and soul, and strength, and mind. This they call *contending for the truth!*

Because I refuse an explanation which is not in the New Testament, though they believe it *is* because they can think of no other—an explanation which seems to me as false in logic as detestable in morals, not to say that there is no spirituality in it whatever—therefore they say I am not a Christian!

Small wonder that men such as I quoted at the beginning refuse the Christianity they suppose such "believers" to represent!

I do not say that this sad folly may not mingle with it a potent faith in the Lord himself. But I do say that the importance they place on theory is even more sadly obstructive to true faith than such theories themselves. While the mind is occupied in enquiring, "Do I believe or feel this thing right?"—the true question is forgotten: "Have I left all to follow him?"

To the man who gives himself to the living Lord, every belief will necessarily come right. The Lord himself will see that his disciple believe aright concerning him. If a man cannot trust him for this, what claim can he make to faith in him? It is because he has little or no faith that he is left clinging to preposterous and dishonouring ideas, holding onto the traditions of men concerning his Father rather than his own teaching or that of his apostles.

The living Christ is to them but a shadow. No soul can thoroughly believe in the all but obliterated Christ of their theories. The disciple of such a Christ rests on his work, or his merits, or his atonement!

FAITH IN CHRIST—DOING WHAT HE SAID

What I insist upon is that a man's faith shall be in the living, loving, ruling, helping Christ, devoted to us as much as ever he was, and devoted with all the powers of the Godhead to the salvation of his brethren. It is not faith that he did this, that his work wrought that—it is faith in the man who did and is doing everything for us that will save him. Without this he cannot work to heal spiritually, any more than he would heal physically when he was present to the eyes of men.

Do you ask, "What is faith in him?"

I answer, The leaving of your way, your objects, your self, and the taking of his and him. It is the leaving of your trust in men, in money, in opinion, in character, in atonement itself, *and doing as he tells you.*

I can find no words strong enough to serve for the weight of this necessity—this obedience. It is the one terrible heresy of the church, that it has always been presenting something else than obedience as faith in Christ. The work of Christ is not the Working Christ, any more than the clothing of Christ is the body of Christ. If the woman who touched the hem of his garment had trusted in the garment and not in him who wore it, would she have been healed? The reason that so many who believe *about* Christ rather than in him, get the comfort they do, is that, touching thus the mere hem of his garment, they cannot help believing a little in the live man inside the garment.

It is not to be wondered at that such believers should so often be miserable. They lay themselves down to sleep with nothing but the skirt of his robe in their hand—a robe too, I say, that never was his, they only suppose it his—when they might sleep in peace with the living Lord in their hearts.

Instead of so knowing Christ that they have him in them saving them, they lie wasting themselves in soul-sickening self-examination as to whether they are believers, whether they are really trusting in the atonement, whether they are truly sorry for their sins—the way to madness of the brain and despair of the heart. Some even ponder the imponderable—whether they are of the elect, whether they have an interest in the blood shed for sin, whether theirs is a saving faith—when all the time the man who died for them is waiting to begin to save them from every evil—and first from this self which is consuming them with trouble about its salvation.

He will set them free and take them home to the bosom of the Father—if only they will mind what he says to them—which is the beginning, middle, and end of faith. If, instead of searching into the mysteries of corruption in their own charnelhouses, they would but awake and arise from the dead, and come out into the light which Christ is waiting to give them, he would begin at once to fill them with the fulness of God.

IT *IS* OBEDIENCE

"But I do not know how to awake and arise."

I will tell you:—Get up, and do something the master tells you. In such a manner you will make yourself his disciple at once. Instead of asking whether you believe or not, ask yourself whether you have this day done one thing because he said, *Do it*, or once abstained because he said, *Do not do it.*

It is simply absurd to say you believe, or even want to believe in him, if you do not do anything he tells you. If you can think of nothing he ever said as having had an atom of influence on your *doing* or *not doing,* you have no good ground to consider yourself a disciple of his. Do not, I implore you, worse than waste your time in trying to convince yourself that you *are* his disciple and that for this reason or that you can be sure that you believe in him. Even though you might be able to succeed in persuading yourself to absolute certainty that you are his disciple, what difference will it make if one day he says to you, "Why did you not do the things I told you? Depart from me—I do not know you!"

Do not try to persuade yourself. If the thing be true you can make it truer. If it be not true, you can begin at once to make it true, to *be* a disciple of the Living One—by obeying him in the first thing you can think of in which you are not obeying him.

We must learn to obey him in everything, and so must begin somewhere. Let it be at once, and in the very next thing that lies at the door of our conscience!

Oh fools and slow of heart, if you think of nothing but Christ, and do not set yourselves to do his words! You but build your houses on the sand. What will the religious teachers have to answer for who have turned your regard away from the direct words of the Lord himself, which are spirit and life, to contemplate instead various plans of salvation tortured out of the words of his apostles, even if those plans were as true as they are actually false! There is but one plan of salvation, and that is to believe in the Lord Jesus Christ—that is, to take him for what he is, our master, and his words as if he meant them, which assuredly he did.

To do his words is to enter into vital relation with him. To obey him is the only way to be one with him. The relation between him and us is an absolute one. It can begin to *live* no way but in obedience. It *is* obedience.

There can be no truth, no reality, in any initiation of at-one-ment with him, that is not obedience.

Will one with even the poorest notion of a God dare think of entering into relations with him and ignore the very first principle of such relationship, which is: *What he says I will do*? The thing is eternally absurd, and comes of the father of lies.

I know what he whispers to those of you to whom my words are distasteful: "He is teaching the doctrine of works!"

But one word of the Lord humbly heard and received will suffice to send all the demons of false theology into the abyss. He says the man that does not do the things he tells him, builds his house to fall in utter ruin. He instructs his messengers to go and baptize all nations, "teaching them to observe all things whatsoever I have commanded you."

Tell me it is faith he requires—I know it! And is not faith the highest act of which the human mind is capable? But faith in what? Faith in what he is, in what he says—a faith which can have no existence except in obedience—a faith which *is* obedience. To do what he wishes is to put forth faith in him.

WHAT IS TRUE FAITH?

For this the teaching of men has substituted this or that belief *about* him, faith in this or that supposed design of his manifestation in the flesh. It was himself, and God in him that he manifested. But faith in him and his father thus manifested, they make altogether secondary to acceptance of the paltry contrivance of a juggling morality, which they attribute to God and his Christ, imagining it the atonement, and "the plan of salvation."

"Do you put faith in *him*," I ask, "or in the doctrines and commandments of men?"

If you say "In him," then I return with this question: "Is it possible that you do not see that, above all things and all thoughts, you are bound to obey him?" Do you not express longing to trust in him more, but find it too hard? Too hard it is for you, and too hard it will remain while the things he tells you to do—the things you can do—even those you will not try!

How should you be capable of trusting in the true one while you are not true to him? How are you to believe he will do his part by you, while you are not such as to do your part by him? How are you to believe while you are not faithful? How, I say, should you be capable of trusting in him?

The very thing that will make you able to trust in him, and thus able to receive all things from him, you turn your back upon. Obedience you decline, or at least neglect.

You say you do not refuse to obey him? I care not whether you refuse or not, while you do not obey. Remember the parable: "I go, sir, and went not." What have you done *this day* because it was the will of Christ? Have you once dismissed an anxious thought for the morrow? Have you ministered to any needy soul or body and kept your right hand from knowing what your left hand did? Have you begun to leave all and follow him? Did you set yourself to judge righteous judgment? Are you being wary of covetousness? Have you forgiven your enemy? Are you seeking the kingdom of God and his righteousness before all other things? Are you hungering and thirsting after righteousness? Have you given to someone that asked of you? Tell me something that you have done, are doing, or are trying to do because he told you.

If you do nothing that he says, it is no wonder that you cannot trust in him, and are therefore driven to seek refuge in the atonement, as if something he had done, and not he himself in his doing were the atonement.

Is that not how you understand it? What does it matter how you understand, or what you understand, so long as you are not of one mind with the Truth, so long as you and God are not *at one*, do not atone together? How should you understand? Knowing that you do not heed his word, why should I heed your explanation of it? You do not his will, and so you cannot understand him. You do not know him, that is why you cannot trust in him. You think your common sense enough to let you know what he means? Your common sense ought to be enough to know itself unequal to the task. It is the heart of the child that alone can understand the Father.

Would you have me think you guilty of the sin against the Holy Ghost—that you *understand* Jesus Christ and yet will not obey him? That would be too dreadful. I believe you do not understand him. No man can do yet what he tells him aright—but are you trying? Obedience is not perfection, but trying.

You count him a hard master, and will not stir. Do you suppose he ever gave a commandment knowing it was of no use for it could not be done? He tells us a thing knowing that we must do it, or be lost. He knows that not even his Father himself could save us but by getting us at length to do everything he commands. There is no other way we can know life or learn the holy secret of divine being.

He knows that you can try, and that in your trying and failing he will be able to help you, until at length you shall do the will of God even as he does it himself. He takes the will in the imperfect deed, and makes the deed at last perfect.

Correctest notions without obedience are worthless. The doing of the will of God is the way to oneness with God, which alone is salvation. Sitting at the gate of heaven, sitting on the footstool of the throne itself— yea, clasping the very knees of the Father—you could not be at peace, except in their every vital movement, in their smallest point of consciousness, your heart, your soul, your mind, your brain, your body, were one with the living God.

If you had one brooding thought that was not a joy in him, you would not be at peace. If you had one desire you could not leave absolutely to his will you would not be at peace. You would not be saved, therefore could not feel saved. God, all and in all, ours to the fulfilling of our very being, is the religion of the perfect, son-hearted Lord Christ.

PAGANISM PERSISTS IN LOW INTERPRETATIONS OF GOD'S WAYS

Of course I know it is faith that saves us. But it is not faith in any work of God—it is faith in God himself. If I did not believe God is as good as the tenderest human heart—as good as the fairest, purest, most unselfish human heart could imagine him, yea, an infinitude better, higher than we as the heavens are higher than the earth, believe it, not as a mere theory or proposition, or even as a thing I was intellectually convinced of, but with the responsive condition and being of my whole nature—then what would faith really mean? If I did not feel every fibre of heart and brain and body safe with him because he is the Father who made me as I am—I would not be saved. For this faith is salvation. It is God and the man as one. God and man together, the vital energy flowing unchecked from the creator into his creature—that is the salvation of the creature.

But the poorest faith in the living God, the God revealed in Christ Jesus—if it be vital and true, that is obedient—is the beginning of the way to know him. And to know him is eternal life. If you mean by faith anything of a different kind, that faith will not save you. A faith, for instance, that God does not forgive me because he loves me, but because he loves Jesus Christ, cannot save me. It is a falsehood against God. If the thing were true, such a gospel would be the preaching of a God that was not love, therefore in whom was no salvation, a God to know whom could not be eternal life. Such a faith would damn, not save a man, for it would bind him to a God who was anything but perfect.

Such assertions going by the name of Christianity, are nothing but the poor remnants of paganism. It is only with that part of our nature not yet Christian that we are able to believe them, so far indeed as it is possible a lie should be believed at all.

We must forsake all our fears and distrusts for Christ. We must receive his teaching heartily, and not let the interpretation of it attributed to his apostles make us turn aside from it. I say *interpretation* attributed to them, for what they teach is never against what Christ taught, though very often the exposition of it is. This comes from no fault in the apostles, but from the grievous fault of those who would understand, and even explain, rather than obey.

We may be sure of this, that no man will be condemned for any sin that is past. If he be condemned it will be because he would not come to the light when the light came to him, because he would not cease to do evil and learn to do well. The only things that will be held against him will be that he hid his unbelief in the garment of a false faith and would not obey, that he imputed to himself a righteousness that was not his, that he preferred imagining himself a worthy person to confessing himself everywhere in the wrong and repenting.

We may be sure also of this, that, if a man becomes the disciple of Christ, the Lord will not leave him in ignorance as to what he has to believe. He shall know the truth of everything it is needful for him to understand. If we do what he tells us, his light will go up in our hearts. Till then we could not understand even if he explained to us. If you cannot trust him to let you know what is right, but think you must hold this or that doctrine before you can come to him, then your occasional doubts probably give rise to what are actually your best times spiritually, in which you come nearest to the truth—those, namely, in which you fear you have no faith.

So long as a man will not set himself to obey the word spoken, the word written, the word printed, the word read, of the Lord Christ, I would not take the trouble to convince him concerning the most obnoxious doctrines that they are false as hell. It is those who want to believe but who are hindered from true belief by such doctrines, whom I would help. Disputation about things but hides the living Christ who alone can teach the truth, who is the truth, and the knowledge of whom is life.

I write for the sake of those driven away from God by false teaching that claims to be true. And well it might drive them away, for the God so taught by some of those doctrines is not a God worthy to be believed in. A stick, or a stone, or a devil, is all that some of our brethren of mankind have to believe in. He who believes in a God not altogether unselfish and good, a God who does not do all he can for his creatures, belongs to the same class. His is not the God who made the heaven and the earth and the sea and the fountains of water—not the God revealed in Christ.

If a man see in God any darkness at all, and especially if he defend that darkness according to his contorted theologies, attempting to justify it by saying that he is one who respects the person of God, I cannot but think his blindness must follow his mockery of *"Lord! Lord!"* Surely, if he had been strenuously obeying Jesus, he would before now have received the truth that God is light, and in him is no darkness—a truth which is not acknowledged by calling the darkness attributed to him light, and the candle of the Lord in the soul of man darkness. It is one thing to believe that God can do nothing wrong, quite another to call whatever presumption may attribute to him right.

ONLY AS WE DO CAN WE KNOW

The whole secret of progress is the doing of the thing we know. There is no other way of progress in the spiritual life, no other way of progress in the understanding of that life. Only as we *do*, can we *know*.

Is there then anything you will not leave for Christ? You cannot know him—and yet he is the Truth, the one thing alone that can be known!

Do you not care that you are imperfect? Would you rather keep this or that imperfection than part with it to be perfect? You cannot know Christ, for the very principle of his life was the simple absolute relation of realities—his one idea was to be a perfect child to his Father.

He who will not part with all for Christ is not worthy of him, and cannot know him. The Lord is true and cannot acknowledge such a one. How could he receive to his house, as one of his kind, a man who prefers something to his Father, a man who is not wholly *for* God, a man who will strike a bargain with God and say, "I will give up so much, if you will spare me."

Such a man or woman counts it too much to yield all to him who has only made us and given us everything, yea his very self by life and by death. His conduct says, "I never asked you to do so much for me, and I cannot make the return you demand." He will have to be left to himself. He must find what it is to be without God!

Those, on the other hand, who *do* know God—or have but begun to catch a far-off glimmer of his gloriousness, of what he is—regard life as insupportable except that God be the All in all, the first and the last.

HOW THE WORLD WOULD BE CHANGED IF WE ONLY OBEYED!

To let their light shine, not to force on them their interpretations of God's designs, is the duty of Christians towards their fellows.

If you who set yourselves to explain the theory of Christianity had set yourselves instead to do the will of the Master, the one object for which the Gospel was preached to you, how different would now be the condition of that portion of the world with which you come into contact! Had you given yourselves to the understanding of his word that you might do it, and not to the quarrying from it of material wherewith to buttress your systems, in many a heart by this time would the name of the Lord be loved where now it remains unknown.

The word of life would then have been held out to a hungry world indeed!

Attracted by your behaviour and undeterred by your explanations of Christianity—for you would not be forcing them on their acceptance—men and women would be saying to each other, as Moses said to himself when he saw the bush that burned with fire and was not consumed, "I will now turn aside and see this great sight!"

All around you they would be drawing nigh to behold how these Christians loved one another!

They would see how just and fair Christians were to every one that had to do with them. They would take note that their goods were the best, their weight surest, their prices most reasonable, their word most certain. They would see in their families neither jealousy nor emulation, that mammon was not worshipped, that in their homes selfishness was neither the hidden nor the openly ruling principle. They would see that their children were as diligently taught to share as some are to save or to spend upon self. They would see that their mothers were more anxious lest a child should hoard than lest he should squander. They would see that in no Christian house was religion one thing while in the practice of daily life another, and that among them the ecclesiastic did not think first of his church nor the peer of his privileges.

FALSE FAITH AND TRUE FAITH

What do I hear you say in objection?—*"How could the world go on if people lived so?"*

The Lord's world will go on, and perhaps without you. The devil's world will go on too, and may include you. Your objection is but another and overwhelming proof of your unbelief. Either you do not believe the word the Lord spoke—that, if we seek first the kingdom of God and his righteousness, all things we need will be added to us—or what he undertakes does not satisfy you. It is not enough. You want more. You prefer the offers of Mammon.

You are in no way anxious to be saved from the snare of *too-much.* You want what you call a fortune—the freedom of the world. You do not want to live under such restrictions as the Lord might choose to lay upon you if he saw that something might be made of you precious in his sight! You want to inherit the earth, but not by meekness. You want to have the comforts of the life of this world, come what may of life eternal, the life that God shares with you. Whatever will happen with regard to that you would gladly let God look after, if only you might be sure of not sharing the fate of the rich man when you die.

But you find that, unable to trust him for this world, neither can you trust him for the world to come. Refusing to obey him in your life, how can you trust him for your life? Hence the various substitutes you seek for faith in him.

You would hold him to his word, bind him by his promises, appeal to the atonement, to the satisfaction made to his justice, as you call it. But all the while you take no trouble to fulfill the morally and spiritually imperative condition—the condition and means in one—on which he gives life to those who believe in, that is, obey, him. Only through this absolutely reasonable and necessary condition can he offer you deliverance from the burden of life into the strength and glory of life— that you shall be true, and to him obedient children.

You say "Christ has satisfied the law," but you will not satisfy him!

He says, "Come unto me," and you will not rise and go to him.

You say, "Lord I believe; help mine unbelief." But when he says, "Leave everything behind you, and be as I am towards God, and you shall have peace and rest," you turn away, muttering about *figurative language*.

If you had been true, had been living *the* life, had been Christians indeed, you would, however little, have drawn the world after you. In your churches you would be receiving truest nourishment, yea strength to live—thinking far less of serving God on the Sunday, and far more of serving your neighbour during the week. The sociable vile, the masterful rich, the deceitful trader, the ambitious poor, whom you have attracted to your communities with the offer of a salvation other than deliverance from sin, would not be lording it over them and dragging those neighbours down. Your churches would be the cleaner and the stronger for their absence.

Meanwhile, the publicans and sinners would have been drawn instead, and turned into true men and women. And the Israelite indeed, who is yet more repelled by your general worldliness than by your misrepresentations of God that show him selfish like yourselves rather than the purity of creation—the Israelite in whom is no guile would have hastened to the company of the loving men and true, eager to learn what it was that made them so good, so happy, so unselfish, so free of care, so ready to die, so willing to live, so hopeful, so helpful, so careless to possess, so undeferential to possession.

Finding you to hold—from the traditional force of false teaching— such things as you do, he would have said, "No—such beliefs can never account for such mighty results!"

You would have answered, "Search the Scriptures and see."

He would have searched, and found—not indeed the things you imagine there, but things infinitely better and higher, things that indeed account for the result he marveled at. He would have found such truth as he who has found will hold forever as the only gladness of his being. There you would have had your reward for being true Christians in spite of the evil doctrines you had been taught and teaching. You would have been taught in return the truth of the matter by him whom your true Christianity had enticed to itself, and sent to the fountainhead free of the prejudices that disabled your judgment.

Thus delivered from the false notions which could not fail to have stunted your growth hitherto, how rapid would it not have become!

IN DOING RIGHT WILL WE THINK RIGHT

If any of you tell me my doctrine is presumptuous, that it is contrary to what is taught in the New Testament and what the best of theologians have always believed, I will not therefore proceed to defend my beliefs and these principles on which I try to live. How much less will I defend my opinions!

I appeal to you instead by asking whether or not I have spoken the truth concerning our paramount obligation to *do* the word of Christ.

If you answer that I have not, I have nothing more to say. There is no other ground on which we can meet. But if you agree that it *is* a prime—even if you do not allow it *the* prime duty—then what I insist upon is that you should do it. Thus and not on any other basis, may we recommend the knowledge of him.

I do not attempt to change your opinions. If they are wrong, the obedience alone on which I insist can enable you to set them right. I only urge you to obey, and assert that thus only can you fit yourselves for understanding the mind of Christ.

I say none but he who does right can think right. You cannot *know* Christ to be right until you do as he does and as he tells you to do. Neither can you set him forth to others until you know him as he means himself to be known—that is, as he is.

If you are serving and trusting in Mammon, how can you know the living God, the source of life, who is alone to be trusted in? If you do not admit that it is the duty of a man to do the word of Christ, or if, admitting the duty, you yet do not care to perform it, why should I care to convince you that my doctrine is right?

What is it to any true man what you think of his doctrine? What does it matter what you think of any doctrine? If I could convince the judgment of your intellects, your hearts remaining as they are, I should but add to your condemnation.

The true heart must see at once, that, however wrong I may or may not be in other things, at least I am right in this—that Jesus must be obeyed, and obeyed immediately, in the things he did say. The true heart will not long imagine to obey him in things he did not say. If a man do what is unpleasing to Christ, believing it his will, he shall yet gain thereby, for it gives the Lord a hold of him, which he will use. But before he can reach liberty, he must be delivered from that falsehood.

For him who does not choose to see that Christ must be obeyed, he must be left to the teaching of the Father, who brings all that hear and learn of him to Christ, that they may learn what he is who has taught them and brought them. He will leave no man to his own way, however much he may prefer it.

The Lord did not die to provide a man with the wretched heaven he may invent for himself, or accept invented for him by others. He died to give him life, and bring him to the heaven of the Father's peace. The children must share in the essential bliss of the Father and the Son.

This is and has been the Father's work from the beginning—to bring us into the home of his heart, where he shares the glories of life with the Living One, in whom was born life to light men back to the original life. This is our destiny. And however a man may refuse, he will find it hard to fight with God—useless to kick against the goads of his love. For the Father is goading him, or will goad him, if needful, into life by unrest and trouble. Hell-fire itself will have its turn if less will not do.

Can any need it more than such as will neither enter the kingdom of heaven themselves, nor allow those who would to enter it? The old race of the Pharisees is by no means extinct. They were St. Paul's great trouble, and are yet to be found in every religious community under the sun.

WHEN WE WALK IN LIGHT, TRUTH WILL GROW

The only thing that will truly reconcile all differences is this: To walk in the light. So St. Paul teaches us in his epistle to the Philippians, the third chapter and sixteenth verse.

After setting forth the loftiest idea of human endeavour in declaring the summit of his own aspiration, he does not say, "This must be your endeavour also, or you cannot be saved." Rather he says, "If in anything ye be otherwise minded, God shall reveal even this unto you. Nevertheless whereto we have already attained, let us walk by that same."

Observe what widest conceivable scope is given by the apostle to honest opinion, even in things of grandest import!—the one only essential point with him is, that whereto we have attained, what we have seen to be true, *we walk by that.* In such walking, and in such walking only, love will grow and truth will grow. The soul, then first in its genuine element and true relation towards God, will see into reality what was before but a blank to it. And he who has promised to teach, will teach abundantly.

Faster and faster will the glory of the Lord dawn upon the hearts and minds of his people so walking. Then they will be his people indeed! Fast and far will the knowledge of him spread. Truth of action, both preceding and following truth of word, will prepare the way before him.

The man who walks in that to which he has attained—that truth he has been shown—will be able to think aright. The man who does not think right *cannot* think right because he has not been walking right. Only when he begins to do the thing he knows will he begin to think aright. Then God will come to him in a new and higher way, and work along with the spirit he has created. Without its heaven above its head, without its life-breath around it, without its love-treasure in its heart, without its origin one with it and bound up in it, without its true self and originating life, no human soul can think to any real purpose—nor ever could to all eternity.

When man joins with God, then is all impotence and discord cast out. Until then, there can be but disharmony. God is constantly working against the gates of hell that open in the heart of man. He can but hold his own as long as the man contests against him. But when the man *joins* God in the battle, then is Satan foiled. For then, for the first time, nature receives her necessity—no such necessity does she have so fundamental as this law of all laws—that God and man are one. Until they begin to be one in the *reality* as they have always been in the divine Idea—in the flower as in the root, in the finishing as in the issuing creation—nothing can go right with the man, and God can have no rest from his labour in him.

As the greatest orbs in heaven are drawn by the least, God himself must be held in divine disquiet until every one of his family be brought home to his heart. There they will become one with him in a unity too absolute, profound, far-reaching, fine, and intense, to be understood by any but the God from whom such unity comes. Such a high reconciliation is to be guessed at, however, by the soul from the unspeakableness of its delight when at length it is with the *only* that can be its own, the one that it can possess, the One that can possess it.

For God is the heritage of the soul in the *ownness* of origin. Man is the offspring of his making will, of his life. God himself is his birthplace. God is the self that makes the soul able to say. *I too, I myself.* This absolute unspeakable bliss of the creature is that for which the Son died, for which the Father suffered with him. Then only is life itself. Then only is it right, is it one. Then only is it as designed and necessitated by the eternal life-outgiving Life.

Whereto then we have attained let us *walk* by that same!

THREE

LAYING CLAIM TO A PERFECT FATHERHOOD

The staggering implications of Matthew 5:48

by
Michael Phillips

My wife Judy and I owned and operated a Christian bookstore for thirty-five years between 1970 and 2004. During that time, we witnessed enormous changes taking place within the body of Christ, some hopeful, others which caused us grave concern. Books on hell were always popular, the more gory the better. A number of widely popular books were released about hell in our final years—several basing their authenticity on visions God had supposedly given the authors, including the most ghastly depictions of the sufferings of unbelievers.

The sadness I felt to see my own and George MacDonald's books languishing on the shelves, gathering dust and going out of print, while many of these horrific and questionable accounts zoomed to the top of best seller lists, was puzzling. What sort of appetite in the Christian mind, I wondered, were these books feeding—written in juvenile fashion, luring to the surface what I can only call a base lust for horror and suffering? What could account for their widespread appeal, the feverish enthusiasm (wide-eyed, excited, anxious to pass them out like candy...*Have you read this!*) about the future torments of the wicked? Our customers actually *enjoyed* it! They ate it up! Place a George MacDonald book and one of these contemporary hell-vision books side by side in any Christian bookstore, and 99 out of 100 people pick up the book on hell without hesitation.

It may be important to assess why these trends exist. What does a morbid fascination with the suffering of sinners (as one particular factor in what I would submit is a much larger problem) tell us? Something more far-reaching is at stake than merely what books sell in Christian bookstores. If we can look into this quandary with *seeing* spiritual eyes, it may reveal some telling insights about why the orthodox doctrine of punitive hell has found such fruitful soil in the Christian church.

DISBELIEF OR HOPE

It would seem that there are only two legitimate responses on the part of serious, thinking, sensitive, scripturally astute Christians to the doctrine of punitive eternal hell—outright disbelief, or an uncertain hope in something more.

Many, of course, will lambaste those who come to the first conclusion. But right or wrong, a rejection of the orthodox view is a *legitimate* conclusion for an individual to draw.

The second and, in my view, *only* legitimate alternative response is the "hope" that the doctrine is untrue, but, if it is, weeping grief.

I can thus respect those on both sides of this scriptural conundrum who say either:

"I cannot bring myself to believe it is true."

Or:

"I *hope* with all my heart that God has in his power to save all men...but if some are indeed doomed to an eternity in hell, then may God be merciful to us, for we are all sinners together."

I see no other options.

Indeed, my own perspective of what I call an open-minded uncertainty is not so very different: I *hope* universal reconciliation is true, but whatever is in God's heart to accomplish, I trust him more than I trust in any doctrine that attempts to explain his ways.

The third alternative, however,—eager and enthusiastic belief in a tormenting punitive hell—I find a complete perversion, an embarrassment at the heart of the church, an affront to all Jesus taught about his Father. Too Many Christians are cheering for the wrong team! If one feels compelled to believe in the orthodox position, it should be with tears in the eyes. It should be a sad, regretful belief, certainly not an enthusiastic one. The fascination with a Jonathan Edwards perspective of hell's torments that I have witnessed among evangelical Christians indicates, to my thinking, something very, very wrong. All men and women should *hope* in universal salvation. No Christian can be excused for *wanting* eternal punishment to remain an intrinsic element of his or her creed.

Not to hope for universal salvation is to deny the work of Jesus Christ himself. We may not know every final eternal outcome. But we ought to know whose side we are rooting for—God's or Satan's.

THE FLESH RELISHES IN HELL

It must sadly be admitted, however, that the large percentage of fundamental Christians do *not* hope for universal salvation. Indeed, they are afraid to hope for it. At the same time, many seem to feel a gleeful righteousness to envision the miseries of the lost.

I find this delight indicative of a serious cancer in the church. I think we must ask why this fascination exists. Why do the very people who have been commissioned to take the good news of Fatherhood into the world, reject the high and perfect and infinitely forgiving Fatherhood of God?

The answer lies in each of our hearts. The flesh relishes in vengeance. We do not *want* to relinquish belief in hell. We do not *want* to let it die into a grander belief in a loving God whose final victory will be gloriously complete. To do so requires relinquishing the final vestige of unforgiveness within ourselves. We resist. We don't want to forgive *completely*. We *enjoy* unforgiveness. Fanning the flames of hell's fire enables us to nurture our own sin nature under the guise of correct doctrine.

The story is told of one of George MacDonald's Calvinist in-laws who vowed that she could never lie comfortable in bed at night if she did not believe in hellfire and everlasting pains for the unrepentant. [18]

Jonathan Edwards said, "The view of the misery of the damned will double the ardour of the love and gratitude of the saints in heaven." [19]

We should recoil at the very thought of an everlasting, God-designed torment—recoil because it is a blasphemy against the character of God.

Our response should be as Moses', "No, Lord, it is not worthy of you!" [20]

With the prophet Amos, we should say, "Sovereign Lord, forgive! Sovereign Lord, I beg you, stop!" [21]

These old men of God had the courage to doubt what was said of God that was unworthy of his love.

But we don't possess their courage. We do just the opposite. With Jonathan Edwards, there are those who actually delight in it.

We spiritualize this latent vengeance of the old man by directing these unconverted corners of self at impersonal "evil," or at Satan himself. We spiritualize it with platitudes about "loving the sinner but hating the sin." But I doubt we love the sinner near as much as we claim to hate the sin. Our theology doesn't require us to forgive *everything*. So unforgiveness itself remains.

NURTURING SELF-RIGHTEOUSNESS

What is the spirit behind our fascination with everlasting torment? Unbelievably, why do Christians seemingly delight in it more than non-Christians? Why do we cling so tenaciously to such a repellant doctrine?

Because at a foundational human level it appeals to the self-righteousness which resides in the heart of every man and every woman.

Our very doctrines of salvation allow "the elect" to cherish the illusion (however deeply hidden from the eyes of the conscious self) that they are more spiritually responsive than others of our kind.

Whatever we *say* to the contrary, Christians feel a meritorious virtue in their salvation. They pay lip service to the truth that it comes from no merit of their own. But the unspoken corollary is that it is noble to have chosen to accept that salvation. We are, and we allow ourselves to take pride in the fact, the "chosen" people.

Self-righteousness, however, is self-delusionary and self-blinding. Those most in need of apprehending its subtleties are least likely to perceive them.

About our delight in hell, George MacDonald asks:

"Why do we feel this satisfaction? Because we hate wrong, but, not being righteous ourselves, we more or less hate the wronger as well as his wrong. Hence, we are not only righteously pleased to behold the law's disapproval proclaimed in his punishment, but unrighteously pleased with his suffering, because of the impact upon us of his wrong. In this way the inborn justice of our nature passes over to evil." [22]

GOD'S PERFECT FORGIVENESS

In only one place in Scripture are we commanded to be perfect. Jesus gives the command, not in reference to righteousness, but in reference to forgiveness of our enemies. God's perfect, complete, infinite forgiveness is our example of what the *perfection* of God is, and what forgiveness is to be. Jesus says that we are to be perfect in the same way—perfect in *forgiveness*, because *God* is perfect in forgiveness.

Does humanity's latent fleshly vengeance explain why Christians so thoroughly miss the astounding point of the last eleven verses of Matthew 5?

Vengeance, revenge, and punishment, says the Son of God, are things of the past. *Forgiveness must now be total and complete.*

The Father's forgiveness covers all mankind just as do the sun and the rain—they encompass everybody. No one is excluded. The words could not be more clear. Jesus simply says, the Father forgives *all*.

By such forgiveness will our own childship be measured. The love and forgiveness of the Father extends to the good *and* the evil! The message of Matthew 5:44-45 is unmistakable—God's forgiveness extends to *all*.

Not mere *potential* forgiveness. Not mere forgiveness that is *available* if only man will receive it. Not mere forgiveness which God *offers* but which most reject.

Our theologies have manufactured these limitations to constrict God's forgiveness. Those limitations, however, do not originate in Scripture. Jesus was no Calvinist who *limited* the extent of God's love and forgiveness. (Can there be any more odious expression of our faith than the "*limited* atonement" of Calvinism's TULIP belief system? [23] The very idea is an affront to God's omnipotence, and a contradiction at the heart of God's character.)

The astounding point of Matthew 5:48 is that God forgives even his enemies perfectly. Those who hate him, those who reject him, those who curse him. God forgives *all*. He forgives them perfectly.

Then the command of conclusion: *Be perfect, therefore, as your heavenly Father is perfect.*

Is it possible that there will remain souls *unforgiven* to all eternity, when God's is a perfect forgiveness? Is it a *perfect* forgiveness which merely offers forgiveness, but finds that forgiveness rejected? Such a one-way forgiveness might be many things, but it hardly seems fitting to call it a *perfect* forgiveness.

Be perfect, as your heavenly Father is perfect.

HOW FAR ARE WE WILLING TO FORGIVE?

So then comes the question that probes yet deeper: How far are *we* willing to carry obedience to that command?

Laying doctrine aside, in quiet prayerfulness, how would you and I respond if the Lord said, "I want you to forgive Satan for the evil he has caused in the world. I want you to forgive him, because I may someday want to save him too."

Do we shrink from the thought? Does the suggestion fill us with anger?

"What...forgive Satan? Never!"

Perhaps such will never be required of us. I propose it only as an exercise to uncover our attitude toward *infinite* forgiveness.

How far are we *willing* to forgive?

If the Lord told me to forgive Satan, I hope I would fall on my knees, not arguing the theological implications, but asking for his help to obey the command.

God would have us put *all* hatred to death...except our hatred of lingering evil within our *own* selves.

Are such questions too huge? Admittedly they peer into regions far beyond the vision of our natural eyes.

But am I *willing*?

Do I want to be *fully* the son of a *perfect* Father?

THE GREAT EQUILIZER

If God's victory over sin will be a triumph without reservation, distinction, or qualification, if indeed mankind is *one*...then the basis for pride is dead altogether.

With God's complete victory comes death of self, death of anger, death of vengeance—the complete laying down of any hope for thinking oneself more worthy than anyone else.

"He causes his sun to rise...he sends his rain on the righteous and the unrighteous."

He wants us to reach for perfection in ourselves, by claiming it also in our ideal view of his own divine and perfect Fatherhood!

In his sermon entitled "The Voice of Job," George MacDonald makes an astonishing assertion. He says not only that God has claims upon us as our Creator, but that *we* likewise have claims upon *him*. It is our birthright to claim him as our Father—our *perfect* Father.

"What would he have," MacDonald writes, "but that his children should claim their father?...The child has, and must have, a claim on the father, a claim which it is the joy of the father's heart to acknowledge...Right gloriously he meets the claims of his child!" [24]

With Jesus, we can lay claim to the perfect Fatherhood of God!

Can we lay aside the *limited* atonements of man's theologies and say with Jesus, "God, you are *perfect* in forgiveness. Give me your mind and heart."

Are you and I *willing* to forgive...infinitely, whomever and to whatever heights and depths that forgiveness takes us?

Are we *willing* to lay down every vestige of anger and unforgiveness, all vengeance from within the hidden places of our hearts? Are we willing to forgive...all?

Are we *willing* to undergo the fires of purification ourselves, that all the dross of self and the impurities of the flesh may be burned out of us forever, that we may reflect the image and character of the Father's perfect Son?

Let us then fall on our faces before the Father and beg him to send the fire of his purifying love into the uttermost depths of our own hearts and minds and souls!

Let us then rise and look upon his face, and let us declare to the world that we have a Father who loves to the uttermost, and who will love us into the becoming of his *perfect* sons and daughters!

FOUR

THE DREADED BOOGIEMAN CALLED UNIVERSALISM

The Confusing Terminology of a New Paradigm

by
Michael Phillips

There are, as the saying goes, heresies...and then there are heresies. It will come as no surprise to anyone reading this book that the debate swirling around the ancient theological conundrum whether all men and women will ultimately be saved involves one of the most dreaded "heresies" ever to rear its head in Christ's church—in the eyes of those who oppose such a perspective. Perhaps not surprisingly, those who are convinced that the Bible teaches precisely such an inclusive view of eternity and God's ultimate victory hail it as one of the great truths of Scripture and a hidden mystery of the ages.

Obviously the debate between the two views—heresy or truth—is heated. No doubt every one of us has encountered the intense passions that boil on both sides.

There also exist imaginary heresies. Such is the more accurate perspective in this case. A belief in the potential salvation of all men is *not* a true heresy. It does not lie outside the framework of biblical teaching. It conflicts with one particular *interpretation* of the afterlife. But it does not lie outside the Bible itself. We must establish that fact clearly before this discussion proceeds.

There are two reasons why we need to dismiss the notion of "heresy." One, abundant scriptural evidence exists pointing to the possibility that all men will ultimately be saved. Of course those who oppose this view interpret such scriptural evidence through another lens, arguing vehemently that Scripture does *not* teach the universality of salvation. There will always be different ways to read most passages in the Bible.

51

These amount to differences of viewpoint, not heresy. You and I may read *James* and *Galatians* and arrive at different conclusions about the role of faith and works in the life of the Christian. But that makes neither of us heretics.

Another reason why believing that all men may ultimately be saved does not constitute heresy is that many reputable Christians have held to such a belief through the centuries, including many highly respected teachers, pastors, priests, and writers. A case can be made that Paul held this view, even Jesus himself. A number of such individuals of repute and stature are quoted and referenced in the book *Universal Reconciliation: A Brief Selection of Pertinent Quotations* mentioned earlier.

Removing the word "heresy" from the discussion immediately clears the fog so that we can investigate these scriptural possibilities with open minds. We can do so without anger and hostility toward those with whom we disagree. We may continue to draw differing conclusions as we read, study, and interpret various passages of Scripture. But at least we can do so maintaining the Spirit of Christ between us.

However, there are other more serious impediments to objectivity. These usually stem from the terminology we use. Words not only carry meaning, they carry *implications*. These implications may be just as important to a discussion as the technical meaning of a word. Furthermore, what I *mean* when I use a certain term may be quite different than the meaning that goes into your head when you hear what I say, and vice-versa.

One reason George MacDonald's writing occasionally requires editing is to help us get to the meaning he intended. When editing one of his sermons some years ago, I encountered the word "car." My senses were jarred immediately. MacDonald had written this sermon twenty years before the invention of the automobile! How curious, I thought. So in editing MacDonald's original, how was I to render the construction of this particular sentence to avoid it carrying a completely *inaccurate* implication into the minds of readers? If my job was to help people understand MacDonald's intended *meaning*, how was I best to do that?

We observe examples of this around us every day. One of the great frustrations of communication is embodied in the simple phrase we use all the time, "But that's not what I *meant*."

This problem of meaning and implication, and potential inaccuracies that go into our brains as we listen to one another, is amplified a hundredfold when we are talking about matters of belief. These are extremely difficult concepts for words to communicate accurately.

The term "universalism" is one of the worst. It conveys a myriad of potential meanings, about which cluster implications of heresy for many who hear it. Every one of these possible meanings raises even more implications, both accurate and inaccurate. The instant you or I hear the word, a string of assumptions a mile long leaps into our brains. What do I mean when I say it...what do you mean when *you* say it? They may be very different. The word *Universalism*, and dozens of connotations that come in its wake, represents one of the great Boogiemen of Christendom.

When *Hell and Beyond* was released, my agent said to me, "Under no circumstances use the word *universalism*. Don't even say 'universal.' People will draw negative inferences by implication. Don't give them anything that can lead to your being branded a universalist. Keep away from the conversation if people start talking about universal health care."

That's how deep is fear of this boogieman in the evangelical church. "Don't even discuss the *universe*," he added. "If the subject comes up, talk about creation."

So the term "Universalism" is one we will do best to avoid. It too readily conveys the notion of a peaches-and-cream eternity where everyone goes to heaven, sin is never dealt with, the cross and death of Christ are of no importance, atonement means nothing, Jesus is not greater than Buddha, Christianity is no different than Islam or Hinduism. There are no judgments, no accountings, no reckonings. I call "universalism" as the term commonly suggests, *Cotton Candy Heaven.*

An equally serious flaw in this commonly held perspective of what "universalism" means to most is that hell is a myth. Since hell doesn't exist, and since everyone goes to heaven, and since everything will have a happy ending, nothing matters now. Live large, live for yourself, and do whatever feels good because everyone will live happily ever after in the end.

Nothing could be further from what I believe. Nothing could be further from what George MacDonald believed.

Anyone who has read either of our writings knows clearly enough that we both view the afterlife from an entirely different perspective. We believe that hell plays a vital and intrinsic role in how God intends to accomplish his eternal purposes.

Cotton-candy, simplistic "universalism," therefore, is a false and inaccurate expression of the possible truth that all men and women may one day come to salvation in Christ.

It is also a poor word choice because of its historical meaning. In the 19th century, "Universalism" was a denominational designation associated with the Unitarian Church. This meaning, too, has carried through into our own time. In 1961 a merger took place between two historically Christian denominations, the Universalist Church of America and the American Unitarian Association. The new denomination *Unitarian Universalism,* which now retains very little "Christian" teaching, further blurs the term in the public mind. For some, therefore, "universalism" does not imply a set of theological ideas about the afterlife, but rather a church system with its accompanying doctrines.

Universalism thus carries too many inaccurate connotations to be a useful term. Whenever I hear it, I know that clarification is needed before fruitful discussion can begin. Where does one place the fires of purifying hell into the lazy cotton-candy universalism of modernism?

When people ask me, "Was George MacDonald a universalist?" or, "Are you a universalist?" I always answer with either, "Absolutely not," or "Not as you probably mean the term."

If we are not going to use the word "universalism," therefore, what term do we attach to the ideas we are discussing here? I read an article recently about so-called "universalism" that used nearly a dozen different words and phrases to describe various hybrids and offshoots of the central concept. Most I had never heard of. These included oneness universalism, Calvinist universalism, soteriological universalism, God is love universalism, covenant universalism, pluralistic universalism, philosophical universalism. This confusing terminology illustrates what we are up against in trying to accurately understand the perspectives of George MacDonald.

Many useful alternate terms have been employed through the years.

The Larger Hope.
Universal Salvation.
The Unity of All Things.
Apocatastasis (the Greek terms for universal salvation)
Universal Restoration.
Final Restitution.
Universal Repentance.
Restitution of All Things.
God's Complete Victory.
Ultimate Reconciliation.
Infinite Grace.

I usually use the term *Universal Reconciliation,* which will appear most often here. My wife and I are also fond of the phrase *Universal Opportunity* in order to convey the truth that, while we do not claim to know the final outcome, our conviction is that God will never turn his back on any saint or sinner of his creation, and that "opportunity" for repentance will never end. Perhaps this is something like what C.S. Lewis tried to illustrate in *The Great Divorce*.

In the end, it matters little by what terms you and I convey our beliefs and convictions, so long as we take every precaution to insure that what we *say* and what others *hear* are substantially the same. We must also insure that what we hear when others are speaking is faithful to the meaning that *they* intend.

FIVE

LIGHT

by
George MacDonald

From *Unspoken Sermons, Third Series*
as reprinted in *The Truth in Jesus* [25]

Edited by Michael Phillips

This then is the message which we have heard of him, and declare unto you,
that God is light, and in him is no darkness at all.
—1 John i. 5
And this is the condemnation, that light is come into the world,
and men loved darkness rather than light, because their deeds were evil.
—John iii. 19

We call the story of Jesus, told so differently yet to my mind so
consistently by four narrators, *the gospel.*

What makes this tale *the good news?*

Is everything in the story of Christ's life on earth good news? Is it
good news that the one and only good man ever to have lived was served
by his fellow-men as Jesus was—cast out of the world in torture and
shame? Is it good news that he came to his own, and his own received him
not?

What makes it fit, I repeat, to call the tale *good news?*

THAT CALLED A "GOSPEL" WHICH IS THE OPPOSITE OF GOOD NEWS

If we asked this or that theologian, in so far as he was a true man and
answered from his own heart and not from the tradition of the elders, we
should understand what he saw in it that made it good news to him,

though it might involve what would be anything but good news to some of us.

The so-called "deliverance" some think it brings might be founded on such notions of God as to not a few of us contain as little of good as of news. To share in the deliverance which some men find in what they call the gospel—for all do not apply the word to the tale itself, but to certain deductions made from the epistles and their own consciousness of evil—we should have to believe such things of God as would be the opposite of an evangel to us. Indeed, it would be a message from hell itself.

To believe such things, we should have to imagine possibilities worse than any evil from which their "good news" might offer us deliverance. We would first have to believe in an unjust God from whom we have to seek refuge. True, he is called "just" by those holding to such theologies. But at the same time they say he does that which seems to the best in me the essence of *injustice.*

Hearing such a statement, they will tell me that I judge after the flesh.

I answer, "Is it then to the flesh the Lord appeals when he says, *Yea, and why even of yourselves judge ye not what is right?* Is he not the light that lighteth every man that cometh into the world?"

They tell me I was born in sin, and I know it to be true. They tell me also that I am judged with the same severity as if I had been born in righteousness, and that I know to be false. They make it a consequence of the purity and justice of God that he will judge us—born in evil, and for which birth we were not accountable—by our sinfulness instead of by our guilt.

They tell me, or at least give me to understand, that every wrong thing I have done makes me subject to be treated as if I had done that thing with the free will of one who had in him no taint of evil, even though at the time I may not have recognized the thing as evil, or seen it only in the vaguest fashion.

Is there any gospel in telling me that God is unjust, but that there is a way of deliverance from him? Show me my God unjust, and you wake in me a damnation from which no power can deliver me—least of all God himself. It may be "good news" to such as are content to have a God capable of unrighteousness, if only he be on *their* side!

THE LORD IS THE GOSPEL

Who would not rejoice to hear from Matthew, Mark, or Luke, what he meant by the word *gospel*—or rather, what in the story of Jesus made him call it *good news!* Each would probably give a different answer to the question, all the answers consistent, and each a germ from which the others might be reasoned. But in the case of John, we do have his answer to the question. He gives us in one sentence of two parts, not indeed the gospel according to John, but the gospel according to Jesus Christ himself.

He had often told the story of Jesus, the good news of what he was, did, and said. What in it did John look upon as the essence of the goodness of its news? In his gospel he now tells us what in it makes it good news—and tells us the very goodness of that good news. It is not his own message about Jesus, but the soul of that message which makes it gospel. It is the news Jesus brought *concerning the Father.* That is the message he gave to the disciples to deliver to men.

Throughout the story, in all he does and is, and says, Jesus is telling the news concerning his father. This he was sent to give to John and his companions, that they might hand it on to their brothers. But here, in so many words, John tells us what he himself has heard from The Word— what he has gathered from Jesus as the message he has to declare. He has received it in no systematic form. It is what a life, *the* life, what a man, *the* man, has taught him, The Word is the Lord. The Lord is the gospel. The good news is no fagot of sticks of man's gathering on the Sabbath.

Every man must read the Word for himself. One may read it in one shape, another in another. All will be right if it be indeed the Word they read, and if they read it by the lamp of obedience. He who is willing to do the will of the Father shall know the truth of the teaching of Jesus. The spirit is "given to them that obey him."

Let us hear how John reads the Word in his version of the gospel.

"This then is the message," he says, "which we have heard of him, and declare unto you, that God is light, and in him is no darkness at all."

Ah, my heart, this is indeed the good news! This is a gospel!

If God be light, what more, what else can I seek than God, than God himself! Away with your doctrines! Away with your salvation from the "justice" of a God whom it is a horror to imagine! Away with your iron cages of false metaphysics! I am saved—for God is light!

My God, I come to thee. That thou shouldst be thyself is enough for time and eternity, for my soul and all its endless need.

GOD IS LIGHT!

Whatever seems to me darkness, that I will not believe of my God. If I should mistake, and call that darkness which is light, will he not reveal the matter to me, setting it in the light that lighteth every man, showing me that I saw but the husk of the thing, not the kernel? Will he not break open the shell for me, and let the truth of it, his thought, stream out upon me?

He will not let it hurt me to mistake the light for darkness as long as I do not take it and call darkness light. The one comes from blindness of the intellect, the other from blindness of heart and will. I love the light, and will not, at the word of any man or upon the conviction of any man, believe that that which seems to me darkness can exist in God.

Where would the good news be if John said, "God is light, but you cannot see his light. You cannot tell, you have no notion, what light is. What God means by light, is not what you mean by light. What God calls light may be horrible darkness to you, for you are of another nature from him!"

Where, I say, would be the good news of that?

It is true that the light of God may be so bright that we see nothing. But that is not darkness, it is infinite hope of light. It is true also that to the wicked "the day of the Lord is darkness, and not light." But is that because the conscience of the wicked man judges good and evil oppositely to the conscience of the good man? I think not. When he says, "Evil, be thou my good" he means by *evil* the same thing that God means by evil, and by *good* he means *pleasure*. He cannot make the meanings change places.

To say that what our deepest conscience calls darkness may be light to God, is blasphemy. To say that light in God and light in man are of differing kinds, is to speak against the spirit of light. God is light far beyond what we can see, but what we mean by light, God also means by light. What is light to God is light to us, or would be light to us if we saw it, and will be light to us when we do see it.

God means us to be jubilant in the fact that he is light—that he is what his children, made in his image, mean when they say *light*. He wants us to rejoice that what we perceive as darkness in him only seems dark by excess of glory, by too much cause of jubilation. However dark it may be to our eyes, it is in fact light, and light as we mean it, light for our eyes and souls and hearts to take in the moment they are enough of eyes, enough of souls, enough of hearts, to receive it in its very being.

Living Light, thou wilt not have me believe anything dark of thee! Thou wilt have me so sure of thee as to dare to say that what I see as dark and unlike the Master cannot be of thee! If I am not honest enough, if the eye in me be not single enough to see thy light, thou wilt punish me, I thank thee, and purge my eyes from their darkness. Then they may be capable of letting the light in, and so shall I become an inheritor, with thy other children, of that light which is thy Godhead, and makes thy creatures need to worship thee. "In thy light we shall see light."

All men will not, in our present imperfection, see the same light. But light is light notwithstanding. And what each does see is his safety if he obeys it. In proportion as we have the image of Christ mirrored in us, we shall know what is and is not light. But never will anything prove to be light that is not of the same kind with that which we mean by light, with that in a thing which makes us call it light. The darkness yet left in us makes us sometimes doubt whether certain things be light or darkness. But when the eye is single, the whole body will be full of light.

AN EVER-ENLARGING ENOUGH

To fear the light is to be untrue, or at least it comes of untruth. No being needs fear the light of God, either for himself or another. Nothing in light can be hostile to our nature, which is of God, or inimical to anything in us that is worthy. All fear of the light, all dread lest there should be something dangerous in it, comes of the darkness still in those of us who do not love the truth with all our heart. It will vanish as we are more and more interpenetrated with the light.

In a word, there is no way of thought or action which we count admirable in man, in which God is not altogether adorable. There is no loveliness, nothing that makes man dear to his brother man, that is not also in God, only it is infinitely better in God.

He is God our saviour. Jesus is our saviour because God is our saviour. He is the God of comfort and consolation. He will soothe and satisfy his children better than any mother her infant.

The only thing he will not give them is—permission to stay in the dark, If a child cry, "I want the darkness," and complain that he will not give it, he will continue not to give it. He gives what his child *needs*—often by refusing what he *asks*.

If his child say, "I will not be good. I prefer to die—let me die!" his dealing with that child will be as if he said— "No. I have the right to make you content, not by giving you your own will but mine. That is your one good. You shall not die. You shall live to thank me that I would not hear your prayer. You know what you ask, but not what you refuse."

There are good things God must delay giving until his child has a pocket to hold them—till he gets his child to make that pocket. He must first make him fit to receive and to have. There is no part of our nature that shall not be satisfied—and satisfied not by lessening it, but by enlarging it to embrace an ever-enlarging enough.

Come to God, then, my brother, my sister, with all your desires and instincts, all your lofty ideals, all your longing for purity and unselfishness, all your yearning to love and be true, all your aspirations after self-forgetfulness and child-life in the breath of the Father. Come to him with all your weaknesses, all your shames, all your futilities, all your helplessness over your own thoughts, all your failure, even with the sick sense of having missed the tide of true affairs. Come to him with all your doubts, fears, dishonesties, meannesses, paltrinesses, misjudgments, wearinesses, disappointments, and stalenesses. He will take you and all your miserable brood, whether of draggle-winged angels, or covert-seeking snakes, into his care—the angels for life, the snakes for death—and yourself for liberty in his limitless heart!

INTERPRETATIONS OF DARKNESS ARE THE WORK OF THE ENEMY

For he is light, and in him is no darkness at all. If he were a king, a governor, if the only name that described him were *The Almighty*, you might well doubt whether there could be light enough in him for you and your darkness. But he is your father, and more your father than the word can mean in any lips but his who said, "my father and your father, my God and your God."

And such a father *is* light, an infinite, perfect light. If he were any less or any other than he is, and you could yet go on growing, you must at length come to the point where you would be dissatisfied with him. But he is light, and in him is no darkness at all.

If anything seems to be in him that you cannot be content with, be sure that the ripening of your love to your fellows and to him, the source of your being, will make you at length know that anything else than just what he is would have been to you an endless loss.

Do not be afraid to build upon the rock Christ, as if your holy imagination might build too high and heavy for that rock, thinking it will give way and crumble beneath the weight of your divine idea. Let no one persuade you that there is a little darkness in him because of something he has said which his creature interprets as darkness. The interpretation is the work of the enemy—a handful of tares of darkness sown in the light.

Neither let your cowardly conscience receive any word as light because another calls it light, while it looks to you dark. Say either that the thing is not what it seems, or that God never said or did it.

Of all evils, to misinterpret what God does, and then say the thing as interpreted must be right because God does it, is of the devil. Do not try to believe anything that affects you as darkness. Even if you mistake and fail to see something true thereby, you will do less wrong to Christ by such an omission than you would by accepting as his what you can see only as darkness.

It is impossible you are seeing a true and real thing—seeing it as it is, I mean—if it looks to you darkness. But let your words be few, lest you say with your tongue what you will afterward repent with your heart.

Above all things *believe* in the light, that it is what you call light, though the darkness in you may give you occasional cause to doubt whether you are accurately seeing the light.

"But there is another side to the matter: God is light indeed, but darkness *does* exist. Darkness is death, and men are in it."

"Yes," I answer, "—darkness is surely death, but not death to him that comes out of it."

It may sound paradoxical, but no man is condemned for anything he has done. He is condemned for continuing to do wrong. He is condemned for not coming out of the darkness, for not coming to the light, the living God, who sent the light, his son, into the world to guide him home.

GOD GIVES TIME

Let us hear what John says about the darkness.

For here also we have, I think, the word of the apostle himself. He begins at the 13th verse, I think, to speak in his own person. In the 19th verse he says, "And this is the condemnation,"—not that men are sinners—not that they have done that which, even at the moment, they were ashamed of—not that they have committed murder, not that they have betrayed man or woman, not that they have ground the faces of the poor, making money by the groans of their fellows—not for any hideous thing are they condemned, *but that they will not leave such doings behind, and do them no more.*

This is the condemnation, that light is come into the world, and men would not come out of the darkness to the light, but "loved darkness rather than light, because their deeds were evil." Choosing evil, clinging to evil, loving the darkness because it fits with their deeds, therefore turning their backs on the inbreaking light...If God be true, if he be light, and darkness be alien to him, how can they but be condemned? Whatever of honesty is in man, whatever of judgment is left in the world, must allow that their condemnation is in the very nature of things. It must rest on them, and remain so long as the conditions necessitating it remain.

But if one happens to speak some individual truth which another man has made into one of the cogs of his system, he is in danger of being supposed to accept all the toothed wheels and their relations in that system. I therefore go on to say that it does not follow, because light has come into the world, that it has fallen upon this or that man. He has his portion of the light that lighteth every man, but the revelation of God in Christ may not yet have reached him.

A man might see and pass the Lord in a crowd, and not be to blame like the Jews of Jerusalem for not knowing him. A man like Nathanael might have started and stopped at the merest glimpse of him, but all growing men are not yet like him without guile. Everyone who has not yet come to the light is not necessarily keeping his face turned away from it.

We dare not say that this or that man would not have come to the light had he seen it. We do not know that he will not come to the light the moment he does see it.

God gives every man time. There is a light that lightens sage and savage, but the glory of God in the face of Jesus may not have shined on this particular sage or that particular savage. The condemnation falls, rather, on those who, having seen Jesus, *refuse* to come to him, or *pretend* to come to him but *do not* the things he says. They have all sorts of excuses at hand. But as soon as a man begins to make excuse, the time has come when he might be doing that from which he excuses himself.

How many are there not who, believing there is something somewhere with the claim of light upon them, go on and on to get more out of the darkness! This consciousness, all neglected by them, gives broad ground for the expostulation of the Lord—*Ye will not come unto me that ye might have life!*

THAT WHICH CANNOT BE FORGIVEN

"All manner of sin and blasphemy," the Lord said, "shall be forgiven unto men; but the blasphemy against the spirit shall not be forgiven."

God speaks, as it were, in this manner: "I forgive you everything," he says. "Not a word more shall be said about your sins—only come out of them. Come out of the darkness of your exile. Come into the light of your home, of your birthright, and do evil no more. Lie no more, cheat no more, oppress no more, slander no more, envy no more, be neither greedy nor vain. Love your neighbour as I love you. Be my good child. Trust in your father. I am light—come to me and you shall see things as I see them, and hate the evil thing. I will make you love the thing which now you call good and love not. I forgive all the past."

"I thank thee, Lord, for forgiving me," some say, "but I prefer staying in the darkness. Forgive me that too."

"No," replies God, "that I cannot do. That is the one thing that cannot be forgiven—the sin of choosing to be evil and refusing deliverance. It is impossible to forgive that sin. It would be to take part in it. To side with wrong against right, with murder against life, cannot be forgiven. The thing that is past I pass. But he who goes on doing the same, annihilates this my forgiveness. He makes it of no effect. Let a man have committed any sin whatever, I forgive him. But to choose to *go on* sinning—how can I forgive that? It would be to nourish and cherish evil. It would be to let my creation go to ruin.

"Shall I keep you alive to do things hateful in the sight of all true men? If a man refuse to come out of his sin, he must suffer the vengeance of a love that would be no love if it left him there. Shall I allow my creature to be the thing my soul hates?"

THREE FORMS OF PUNISHMENT

There is no excuse for this refusal. If we were punished for every fault, there would be no end, no respite—we should have no quiet wherein to repent. But God passes by all he can. He passes by and forgets a thousand sins, yea, tens of thousands, forgiving them all—only we must begin to be good, begin to do evil no more.

He who refuses must be punished and punished—punished through all the ages—punished until he gives way, yields, and comes to the light, that his deeds may be seen by himself to be what they are, and be by himself reproved, and the Father at last have his child again. For the man who in this world resists to the full, there may be, perhaps, a whole age or era in the history of the universe during which his sin shall not be forgiven. But *never* can it be forgiven until he repents. How can they who will not repent be forgiven, except in the sense that God does and will do all he can to make them repent. Who knows but such sin may need for this cure the continuous punishment of an aeon?

There are three conceivable kinds of punishment.

First, that of mere retribution, which I take to be entirely and only human. Therefore, indeed, it would more properly be called *inhuman*, for that which is not divine is not essential to humanity, and is of evil, and an intrusion upon the human.

Second, punishment which works repentance.

And finally, there is that punishment which refines and purifies, working for holiness. But the punishment that falls on those whom the Lord loves because they have repented, is a very different thing from the punishment that falls on those whom he loves indeed but cannot forgive because they hold fast by their sins.

DIFFERENT FORMS OF FORGIVENESS

There are also various ways in which the word forgive can be used.

A man might say to his son—"My boy, I forgive you, but I must punish you, for you have done the same thing several times, and I must make you remember."

Or, again, he might say—"I am seriously angry with you. I cannot forgive you. I must punish you severely. The thing was too shameful! I cannot pass it by."

Or, once more, he might say—"Unless you alter your ways entirely, I shall have nothing more to do with you. You need not come to me. I will not take the responsibility of anything you do. So far from answering for you, I shall feel bound in honesty to warn my friends not to put confidence in you. Never, never, till I see a greater difference in you than I dare hope to see in this world, will I forgive you. I can no more regard you as one of the family. I would die to save you, but I cannot forgive you. There is nothing in you now on which to rest forgiveness. To say, I forgive you, would be to say, *Do anything you like, I do not care what you do.*"

So God may forgive and punish. And he may punish and not forgive, that he may rescue. To forgive the sin against the holy spirit would be to damn the universe to the pit of lies, to render it impossible for a man so forgiven ever to be saved. He cannot forgive the man who will not come to the light because his deeds are evil. We must become as little children.

SIX

WHAT DID THE SCOTSMAN REALLY BELIEVE?

George MacDonald and Universal Reconciliation

by
Michael Phillips

E ver since I began introducing people to the books and ideas of George
MacDonald, *one* issue has dominated the theological landscape
surrounding the beliefs of the 19th century Scotsman. The question *most*
frequently posed to me about MacDonald is to clarify his position on
universal reconciliation.

Because of its potential divisiveness, and the enormity of
misunderstanding about it prevalent within evangelicalism, this is not a
question I am usually eager to address.

At one of the first instances in which I was asked to speak about my
work with George MacDonald, it was with fear and trembling that I
opened the meeting for questions, hoping no one would ask "the big
question" I was unprepared to answer. No sooner had I invited responses
from the floor, however, than the question shot at me point blank:

"Was George MacDonald a universalist?"

That was some twenty years ago.

At last I am prepared to give an answer.

The purpose of this book is to present, along with my own
perspectives, an interpretive analysis of George MacDonald's outlook on
salvation and the afterlife as I have come to view them after four decades
reading, studying, and reflecting on his work.

WHY THIS ANALYSIS OF MACDONALD'S VIEWS

I do not presume to speak *for* George MacDonald—his own words
will have to speak for themselves. To assist us, therefore, as we have

already begun, we will also present selections from his writings to illuminate his thoughts in certain areas in which his work was at once so groundbreaking and controversial.

The single highest goal of my professional life has been to correctly and accurately grasp George MacDonald's perspectives and then to represent them faithfully to our generation. It has been the highest aim of my *spiritual* life to correctly and accurately understand the nature and character of the God MacDonald served, and likewise to serve and obey him.

My prayerful priority has been to lay hold of MacDonald's *heart*. The myriad details of MacDonald's biography, and the intellectual analysis of his imaginative and mythical contributions, are of less concern to me than to know his thoughts and feelings as he sought to understand God's character, and then communicate to the world what he discovered. There has been much analysis and discussion through the years of MacDonald's writings. Ninety percent of it, in my opinion, misses this essential significance of George MacDonald's life. Such analysis is not necessarily inaccurate. MacDonald's writings offer a full smorgasbord of interpretive possibilities. Much in these studies is fascinating. Yet a great deal of it aims wide of the bull's eye.

If MacDonald's words speak for themselves, it may be asked why an interpretive perspective of his view of universal reconciliation is necessary?

For the simple reason that MacDonald never divulged in so many words exactly what he believed. To my knowledge the words "universalism" or "universal reconciliation" never once appear in his writings.

MacDonald's curious indefiniteness about this topic that so interested him, and that has intrigued his readers for a century and a half, makes it the single most enduring puzzle in MacDonald's biography. It insures that enigma and controversy will follow him as long as his books are read.

Illumination is needed beyond MacDonald's words themselves for the simple reason that people want to know what MacDonald thought. I hope, therefore, to help a few readers understand more clearly the ideas presented (cryptically it may occasionally be) in MacDonald's books.

Our starting point in this inquiry must surely be the perplexing question,

Why did George MacDonald never address universal salvation directly?

Was the idea unimportant to him? Were Christians of his day uninterested in universal reconciliation?

We know just the opposite to be the case. The debate over "universalism" in MacDonald's day was vigorous and heated.

Late nineteenth century Great Britain was an intellectual greenhouse for new concepts, in every field, from politics to science to theology. Liberal trends were pushing beyond boundaries inconceivable a hundred years earlier. Scientific advances were changing the way people viewed the natural world. Darwin had already proposed an evolutionary foundation for the animal kingdom. Within the first decade of the twentieth century Einstein would propose his theory of special relativity.

This surge of new ideas brought with it rapid and enormous change. Some of it was for the better, some was not. It could be argued that most of the *social* change proved generally beneficial to people and culture, while many of the new *philosophical* ideas of the times produced a deviation from traditional and biblical truth.

This environment of change and new ideas caused a reevaluation of traditional norms in every discipline and walk of life—science, society, business, politics, industry, art, music, and religion. The debate between God and science, and evolution and creation, was at the forefront in this newly expanding intellectual climate.

This reevaluating, questioning outlook was evident in the church of the nineteenth century as well as throughout society in general. Whereas the debate over evolution took place for the most part between the conservative church and the scientific community, no more divisive point of contention existed *within* the church of Great Britain than the theological controversy over the potentiality of *universal reconciliation.* It was a conflict that raged furiously in all denominations and seminaries, split churches, and resulted in the publication of multitudes of books and pamphlets, and thousands of parlor debates throughout England and Scotland. As is true today, a belief in universal reconciliation was considered heresy in some circles, enlightened thinking in others.

MACDONALD'S CHOSEN SILENCE

In this wide open climate of debate and discussion, MacDonald's silence on universal reconciliation is particularly curious. It has roots in a principle of paramount importance for all who would follow, not merely MacDonald's ideas but the example of his life. It is my firm conviction that he made a conscious and purposeful decision not to address the doctrine specifically. He so valued unity and so recognized the divisiveness of this issue that he did not want to add more fuel for division to the body of Christ by "taking sides." He would write about God. But he would not write about his personal doctrinal position.

"The one main fault in the Christian Church," said MacDonald from the pulpit in 1879, "is separation, repulsion, recoil between the component particles of the Lord's body...Who said you were to be of one opinion? It is the Lord who asks you to be of one *heart*....If there is one role I hate, it is that of the proselytizer...Not for a moment would I endeavor by argument to convince another of...my opinion. If it be true, it is God's work to show it, for logic cannot." [26]

A few years later, he furthered this perspective with the powerful assertion: "I write with no desire to provoke controversy, which I loathe, but with some hope of presenting to the minds of those capable of seeing it the glory of the truth of the Father and the Son...I am as indifferent to a reputation for orthodoxy as I despise the championship of novelty." [27]

And finally, later in that same year of 1889, in speaking of the atonement, he added: "I have passed through no change of opinion concerning it since first I began to write or speak; but I have written little and spoken less about it, because I would preach no mere negation. My work was not to destroy the false, except as it came in the way of building the true. Therefore I sought to speak but what I believed, saying little concerning what I did not believe...and shunning dispute. Neither will I now enter any theological lists to be the champion for or against mere doctrine. I have no desire to change the opinion of man or woman." [28]

MY OWN PUBLIC NEUTRALITY

MacDonald's example is one I personally try to follow. I have steadfastly refused to doctrinalize my own view into a yes-or-no, black-and-white position. I have long identified my outlook as an intrigued, open-minded, perhaps even enthusiastic neutrality...cheering on the sidelines without yet knowing how the game will end.

Many through the years on all sides of various debative doctrinal fences have objected to that stance. They say that I fear to commit myself, that I refuse to show my true colors. However, such it must remain. MacDonald's example is not only dear, but imperatively important to me. If he is a spiritual mentor, what can I do but seek to follow his example.

When people ask me, therefore, "Do you believe that all will ultimately be reconciled to God in heaven?" in all sincerity I answer, "I honestly do not know. There is much scriptural evidence to support such a view. I am intrigued by the possibility. But I feel it would be wrong to doctrinalize my thoughts into a position. I have studied enough to see that many passages in the Bible support universal salvation. But when it comes to formulating a categoric answer, Scripture remains puzzlingly and frustratingly vague. Therefore I remain open to whatever God will do, and however he will do it. I believe that he will conquer and eliminate sin. How he will do so lays beyond the finite purview of man's mind to comprehend. I simply trust that God's infinite love will be victorious in the end, and will swallow up all our questions, all our doctrines, and all our uncertainties. In that I rest."

This position of what I call a public "neutrality" or "uncertainty" stems from my conviction that I am not sure God *intends* us to know everything about what he will ultimately accomplish and how he will accomplish it.

My own views on the matter are still fluid. My scriptural research is ongoing. I consider an *open* attitude of prayer and inquiry to be the most truly scriptural position for me in good conscience to hold. I think honesty requires the admission that scriptural evidence points in many directions.

This uncertainty stems from no lack of conviction on my part, but from years of prayerful study. God has shown us many possibilities. But he has not revealed *full* truth to us on this and many difficult topics. My views may change as God continues to carry out his work in my heart and mind. That is where I presently stand. Honesty requires me also to say that I am probably growing *less* neutral as the years go by.

Finally, I will add this: *Whatever* may be God's ultimate purpose to accomplish in eternity, I find that the scriptural and prayerful inquiry into such matters has immeasurably enriched my faith, my walk, and my knowledge of the heart of God. I believe it *healthy* to consider such things. Prayerful study of scriptural unknowns keeps one's faith from becoming stagnant and drifting into a dependence on proof-texts, dogma, formula, and pious clichés.

Whether this represents George MacDonald's position, I do not know. His reasons for taking no public stand may differ from my own. I have arrived at *my* position of public neutrality by following what I perceive as George MacDonald's *example*, even if not every specific of his point of view.

We who study and seek to uncover George MacDonald's ideas and understand them must do so with sober minds, realizing that we are in a sense going against MacDonald's own wishes. If he had wanted his position unambiguously spelled out, he would have done so himself. But he did *not*. And for good reason. He would not add fuel to a doctrinal debate.

Therefore, whatever we unearth here, in my opinion, will serve the kingdom of God most effectively if it remains between ourselves and God, even between ourselves and George MacDonald. Others feel it their duty to champion the truths they feel they have discovered. However, I refuse to participate in that attempt and the ongoing disputation that is necessarily part of it. MacDonald wrote: "I do not attempt to change your opinions. If they are wrong, the obedience alone on which I insist can enable you to set them right. I only urge you to obey...I will not therefore proceed to defend my beliefs and these principles on which I try to live. How much less will I defend my opinions!" [29]

Even in the quest to understand him, we must be faithful to what MacDonald stood for. He did not, he *would* not dispute about universal reconciliation. Neither should we. The moment we engage in debate about it, especially the particularly odious form of debate that leads to controversy, we stain the legacy of MacDonald's name.

With these priorities in mind, our goal here together will be to isolate several key areas in MacDonald's writings that, taken together, give us a picture of his perspective of God's eternal purposes. Some of what follows may be expressed in the negative, in point-counterpoint terminology, as an inevitable consequence of MacDonald's reaction against the Calvinist doctrine of his upbringing. The traditional views of 16th century Reformed theology remain deeply ingrained today, even in the non-Christian world. In some cases there is no clearer way to get at what we are focusing on than to say what it is not.

Having not only been reading MacDonald, but also studying and praying regarding these matters for forty years or more, my own ideas and MacDonald's have become an enormous intertwined tapestry within my spiritual consciousness. It is one which gives a generally uniform picture of God and his work, but whose individual threads have become impossible to isolate apart from the whole.

In what follows, then, it cannot be helped that my own ideas and perspectives are melded with his. In most cases, I can no longer distinguish them. Though the intent here is to represent MacDonald, I know of no other way to thoroughly explain his perspective than through the lens of my *own* spiritual outlook—in other words, attempting to be faithful to MacDonald, to try to explain the vision I perceive when I look at the entire tapestry. Some of these ideas come directly from MacDonald's books, others from my own writings which, though not directly traceable to MacDonald, yet help illuminate his thought.

Analysis of the letter seems generally to be the method employed for religious study on most topics. George MacDonald's approach was different. His perspectives cannot be got at by letter of doctrine.

While it is true that analysis has its place, and while I occasionally benefit from such studies, MacDonald's progression toward truth was rooted instead in the character of God. Raw analysis always fades in the overpowering light of the two questions that for MacDonald loomed as gigantic beacons of light pointing toward Truth: "What is God like...what do our hearts tell us?"

In penetrating the depths of what follows, therefore, we have to break through to a more personal level than the intellect alone. We will thus continue to shine light on those two all important considerations:

What is God like?
What do our hearts tell us?

SEVEN

THE CONSUMING FIRE

by
George MacDonald

From *Unspoken Sermons, First Series* [30]

Edited by Michael Phillips

Our God is a consuming fire.
—Hebrews 12:29

Nothing is inexorable but love. Love is one, and love is changeless. God will not yield to selfish prayer. To do so is not true Love. Love which will yield to prayer is imperfect and poor. If it did, it would not be love that yields, but its alloy. For if at the voice of entreaty love conquers displeasure, it is love asserting itself, not love yielding its claims. It is not love that grants a gift unwillingly. Still less is it love that answers a prayer to the wrong and hurt of him who prays.

LOVING UNTO PERFECTION

Love loves unto purity. Love has ever in view the absolute loveliness of that which it beholds. Where loveliness is incomplete, and love cannot love its fill of loving, it spends itself to make more lovely, that it may love more.

Love strives for perfection, even that its own love may be perfected—not in itself, but in the object. As it was Love that first created humanity, so even human love, in proportion to God's divine love, will go on creating the beautiful for its own outpouring. There is nothing eternal but that which loves and can be loved. Love is ever climbing towards the consummation when such shall encompass the entire universe, imperishable, divine.

Therefore all that is not beautiful in the beloved, all that comes between and is not of Love's kind, must be destroyed.

And our God is a consuming fire.

If this be hard to understand, it is as the simple, absolute truth is hard to understand. It may be centuries of ages before a man comes to see a truth—ages of strife, effort, aspiration. But when once he does see it, it is so plain that he wonders he could have lived without seeing it. That he did not understand it sooner was simply and only that he did not see it.

To see a truth, to know what it is, to understand it, and to love it, are all one. There is many a motion towards truth, many a misery for lack of it, many a cry of the conscience against the neglect of it, many a dim longing for it as an unknown need before at length the eyes come awake, and the darkness of the dreamful night yields to the light of the sun of truth. But once beheld it is forever. To see one divine fact is to stand face to face with essential eternal life.

For this vision of truth God has been working for ages of ages. For this simple condition, this apex of life, upon which a man wonders like a child that he cannot make other men see as he sees, the whole labour of God's science, history, and poetry has been evolving truth upon truth in lovely vision. From the time when the earth gathered itself into a lonely drop of fire from the red rim of the driving sun-wheel until now, the truth of inexorable love has been growing. And for this will the patience of God labour while there is yet a human soul whose eyes have not been opened, whose child-heart has not yet been born in him.

For this one condition of humanity, this simple beholding of love, has all the outthinking of God flowed in forms innumerable and changeful from the foundation of the world. And for this too has the divine destruction been going forth, that his life might be our life, that in us, too, might dwell that same consuming fire which is essential love.

ABSOLUTE PURITY—A LOVELY TERROR

Let us look at the utterance of the apostle which is crowned with this lovely terror: "Our God is a consuming fire."

"Wherefore, we receiving a kingdom which cannot be moved, let us have grace, whereby we may serve God acceptable with reverence and godly fear, for our God is a consuming fire."

We have received a kingdom that cannot be moved—whose nature is immovable. Let us have grace to serve the Consuming Fire, our God, with divine fear—not with a fear that cringes and craves, but with the bowing down of all thoughts, delights, and loves before him who is the life of them all—bowing to him in knowing that he will have them all pure. The kingdom he has given us cannot be moved because it has nothing weak in it. It is of the eternal world, the world of being, of truth. Therefore, we must worship him with a fear pure as the kingdom is unshakeable. He will shake heaven and earth, that only the unshakeable may remain (*verse 27*). He is a consuming fire, that only that which cannot be consumed may stand forth eternal.

The nature of God is so terribly pure that it destroys all that is not pure as fire. His nature demands like purity in our worship. He will have purity.

It is not that the fire will burn us if we do not worship thus, but that the fire will burn us until we worship thus. Yea, it will go on burning within us after all that is foreign to it has yielded to its force, no longer with pain and consuming, but as the highest consciousness of life, the presence of God.

When evil, which alone is consumable, shall have passed away in his fire from the dwellers in the immovable kingdom, the nature of man shall look the nature of God in the face, and his fear shall then be pure. For a holy and eternal fear must spring from a knowledge of the nature, not from a sense of the power. But that which cannot be consumed must be one within itself, a simple existence. Therefore in such a soul the fear towards God will be one with the homeliest love. Yea, the fear of God will cause a man to flee, not from him, but from himself—not from him, but *to* him, the Father of himself, in terror lest he should do Him wrong or his neighbour wrong.

And the first words which follow for the setting forth of that grace whereby we may serve God acceptably are these—"Let brotherly love continue."

To love our brother is to worship the Consuming Fire.

PARTIAL REVELATION

The symbol of *the consuming fire* would seem to have been suggested to the writer of Hebrews by the fire that burned on the mountain of the old law. That fire was part of the revelation of God there made to the Israelites. Nor was it the first instance of such a revelation.

The symbol of God's presence, before which Moses had to take off his shoes and to which it was not safe for him to draw near, was a fire that *did not consume the bush in which it burned.* Both revelations were of terror. But the same symbol employed by a writer of the New Testament should mean more, not than it meant before, but more than it was previously employed to express. For it could not have been employed to express more than it was possible for them to perceive. What else than terror could a nation of slaves, into whose very souls the rust of their chains had eaten, in whose memory lingered the smoke of the flesh-pots of Egypt, who, rather than not eat of the food they liked best, would have gone back to the house of their bondage—what else could such a nation see in that fire than terror and destruction?

How could they possibly think of *purification* by fire? They had yet no such condition of mind as could generate such a thought. And if they had had the thought, the notion of the suffering involved would soon have overwhelmed the notion of purification. Such a nation would not have listened to any teaching that was not supported by terror. Fear was that for which they were fit. They had no worship for any being of whom they had not to be afraid.

Was then this show upon Mount Sinai a device to move obedience such as bad nurses employ with children—a mere hint of vague and false horror? Was it not a true revelation of God?

If it was not a true revelation, it was none at all. In that case, the story is either false, or else the whole display was a political trick of Moses. Those who can read the mind of Moses will not easily believe the latter. Those who understand the scope of the pretended revelation will see no reason to suppose the former. That which would be politic, if it were a deception, is not therefore excluded from the possibility of another source. Some people believe so little in a cosmos or ordered world, that the very argument of fitness is a reason for unbelief.

In any event, if God showed them these things, he showed them what was true. It was a revelation of himself. He will not put on a mask. He puts on a face. He will not speak out of flaming fire if that flaming fire is alien to him, if there is nothing in him for that flaming fire to reveal. Be his children ever so brutish, he will not terrify them with a lie.

It was a revelation, but a partial one. It was a true symbol, but not a final vision.

No revelation can be other than partial. If for true revelation a man must be told all the truth, then farewell to revelation—yea, farewell to the sonship. For what revelation, other than a partial, can the highest spiritual condition receive of the infinite God?

But a revelation is not therefore untrue because it is partial. Relative to a lower condition of the receiver, a more partial revelation might be truer than one which constituted a fuller revelation to one in a higher condition. The former might reveal much to him, the latter might reveal nothing. But whatever it might reveal, if its nature were such as to preclude development and growth, thus chaining the man to its incompleteness, it would have the effect of a false revelation fighting against all the divine laws of human existence.

All true revelation rouses the desire to know more by the truth of its incompleteness.

Here was a nation at its lowest. Could it receive anything but a partial revelation, a revelation of fear? How should the Hebrews be other than terrified at that which was opposed to all they knew of themselves, beings judging it good to honour a golden calf? Such as they were, they did well to be afraid. They were in a better condition, acknowledging if only a terror above them, flaming on that unknown mountain height, than stooping to worship the idol below them.

Fear is nobler than sensuality. Fear is better than no God, better than a god made with hands. In that fear lay deep hidden the sense of the infinite.

The worship of fear is true, although very low. Fear is not acceptable to God in itself, for only the worship of spirit and of truth is acceptable to him. Yet even in his sight it is precious. For he regards men not as they are merely, but as they shall be, not as they shall be merely, but as they are now growing, or capable of growing, towards that image after which he made them that they might grow to it.

Therefore a thousand stages, each in itself all but valueless, are of inestimable worth as the necessary and connected gradations of an infinite progress. A condition which of declension would indicate a devil, may of growth indicate a saint. So far then the revelation—not being final any more than complete, and calling forth the best of which they were now capable, so making future and higher revelation possible—may have been a true one.

SAINT AND SINNER ALIKE

But we shall find that this very revelation of fire is itself, in a higher sense, as true to the mind of the rejoicing saint as to the mind of the trembling sinner. For the former sees farther into the meaning of the fire, and knows better what it will do to him. It is a symbol which needed not to be superseded, only unfolded.

While men take part *with* their sins, while they feel as if, separated from their sins, they would be no longer themselves, how can they understand that the lightning word is a Saviour? How can they possibly understand a fire which pierces to the dividing between the man and the evil, which will slay the sin and give life to the sinner?

Can it be any comfort to them to be told that God loves them so that he will burn them clean? Can the cleansing of the fire appear to them anything beyond what it must always, more or less, be—a process of torture?

They do not want to be clean, and they cannot bear to be tortured. Can they then do other, or can we desire that they should do other, than fear God, even with the fear of the wicked, until they learn to love him with the love of the holy? To them Mount Sinai is crowned with the signs of vengeance.

And is not God ready to do unto them even as they fear, though with another feeling and a different end from any which they are capable of supposing? He is against sin. In so far as, and while, they and sin are one, he is against them—against their desires, their aims, their fears, and their hopes. Thus he is altogether and always *for them.* That thunder and lightning and tempest, that blackness torn with the sound of a trumpet, that visible horror billowed with the voice of words, was all but a faint image to the senses of the slaves of what God thinks and feels against vileness and selfishness, of the unrest of unassuageable repulsion with which he regards such conditions. He spoke in such a manner so that the stupid people, fearing somewhat to do as they would, might leave a little room for that grace to grow in them which would at length make them see that evil, and not fire, is the fearful thing. He spoke to leave room for that grace which would transform them that they would gladly rush up into the trumpet-blast of Sinai to escape the flutes around the golden calf. Could they have understood this, they would have needed no Mount Sinai.

It was a true, and of necessity a partial, revelation—partial in order to be true.

Even Moses, the man of God, was not ready to receive the revelation in store—not ready, although from love to his people he prayed that God would even blot him out of his book of life. If this means that he offered to give himself as a sacrifice *instead of* them, it would show reason enough why he could not be glorified with the vision of the Redeemer. For so he would think to appease God, not seeing that God was as tender as himself, not seeing that God is the Reconciler, the Redeemer, not seeing that the sacrifice of the heart is the atonement for which alone he cares. He would be blotted out, that their names might be kept in. Certainly when God told him that he that had sinned should suffer for it, Moses could not see that this was the kindest thing that God could do.

But I doubt if that was what Moses meant. It seems rather the utterance of a divine despair. He would not survive the children of his people. He did not care for a love that would save him alone, and send to the dust those thousands of calf-worshipping brothers and sisters.

But in either case, how much could Moses have understood, if he had seen the face instead of the back of that form that passed the clift of the rock amidst the thunderous vapours of Sinai? It was the face of him who was more man than any man. It was the face through which the divine emotion would, in the ages to come, manifest itself to the eyes of men, bowed, it might well be, at such a moment, in anticipation of the crown with which the children of the people for whom Moses pleaded with his life, would one day crown him. It was the face of him who was bearing and was yet to bear their griefs and carry their sorrows, who is now bearing our griefs and carrying our sorrows. It was the face of the Son of God, who, instead of accepting the sacrifice of one of his creatures to satisfy his justice or support his dignity, gave himself utterly unto them, and therein to the Father by doing his lovely will. It was the face of him who suffered unto the death, not that men might not suffer, but that their suffering might be like his, and lead them up to his perfection. Had that face turned and looked upon Moses, would Moses have lived? Would he not have died, not of splendour, not of sorrow, (terror was not there,) but of the actual sight of the incomprehensible?

If infinite mystery had not slain him, would he not have gone about dazed, doing nothing, having no more any business that he could do in the world, seeing God was to him altogether unknown? For thus a full revelation would not only be no revelation, but the destruction of all revelation.

May it not then hurt to say that God is Love, all love, and nothing other than love? It is not enough to answer that such is the truth, even granted that it is. Upon your own showing, too much revelation may hurt by dazzling and blinding.

OF THE UNDERSTANDING OF MYSTERIES

There is a great difference between a mystery of God that no man understands, and a mystery of God laid hold of, even if by only one single man. The latter is already a revelation. Passing through that man's mind, it will be so presented, perhaps *feebly*, that it will not hurt his fellows. Let God conceal as he will. The light which any man has received is not to be put under a bushel. It is for him and his fellows. (I believe, however, that God is ever destroying concealment, ever giving all that he can, all that men can receive at his hands. I believe that he does not want to conceal anything, but to reveal everything,)

In sowing the seed he will not withhold his hand because there are thorns and stony places and waysides. He will think that in some cases even a bird of the air may carry the matter, that the good seed may be too much for the thorns, that that which withers away upon the stony place may yet leave there, by its own decay, a deeper soil for the next seed to root itself in. Besides, only those who have ears to hear can receive the truth. If the selfish man could believe it, he would misinterpret it. But he cannot believe it. It is not possible that he should. But the loving soul, oppressed by wrong teaching, or partial truth claiming to be the whole, will hear, understand, rejoice.

When we say that God is Love, do we teach men that their fear of him is groundless?

No. For as much as they fear will come upon them, possibly far more. But there is something beyond their fear—a divine fate which they cannot withstand. The love of God works along with the human individuality which the divine individuality has created in all men. The wrath of God will consume what they *call* themselves. Then the selves God made shall appear, coming out with tenfold consciousness of being. That true self shall bring with it all that made the blessedness of the life they tried to lead without God. They will know that for the first time they are now fully themselves. The avaricious, weary, selfish, suspicious old man shall have passed away. The young, ever young self, will remain. That which they *thought* themselves shall have vanished. That which they *felt* themselves, though they misjudged their own feelings, shall remain—remain glorified in repentant hope. For that which cannot be shaken shall remain. That which is immortal in God shall remain in man. The death that is in them shall be consumed.

It is the law of Nature—that is, the law of God—that all that is destructible shall be destroyed. When that part of man which is immortal buries itself in the destructible, it cannot, though immortal, know its own immortality. As long as it receives its life-messages through the surrounding outer region of decadence, and not from the eternal doors within, its immortality is not yet alive. The destructible must be burned out of it, or begin to be burned out of it, before it can *partake* of eternal life. When that is all burnt away and gone, then it has eternal life. Or rather, when the fire of eternal life has possessed a man, then the destructible is gone utterly, and he is pure.

Many a man's work must be burned, that by that very burning he may be saved—so as by fire.

Away in smoke go the lordships, the Rabbihoods of the world. The man who acquiesces in the burning is saved by the fire—for it has destroyed the destructible, which is the vantage point of the deathly, which would destroy both body and soul in hell. If still he cling to that which can be burned, the burning goes on deeper and deeper into his bosom, till it reaches the roots of the falsehood that enslaves him— possibly by looking like the truth.

The man who loves God, and is not yet pure, courts the burning of God. Nor is it always torture. The fire shows itself sometimes only as light. Yet even then it will still be fire of purifying. The consuming fire is just the original, the active form of Purity. It is that which makes pure, that which is indeed Love. It is nothing less than the creative energy of God. Without Purity, as there can be no creation so there can be no persistence. That which is not pure is corruptible, and corruption cannot inherit incorruption.

FIRE WITHOUT LIGHT

The man whose deeds are evil, fears the burning. But the burning will not come the less that he fears it or denies it. Escape is hopeless. For Love is inexorable. Our God is a consuming fire. He shall not come out till he has paid the uttermost farthing.

If a man or woman resists the burning of God, the consuming fire of Love, a terrible doom awaits him, and its day will come. He who hates the fire of God shall be cast into the outer darkness. What sick dismay shall then seize upon him! For let a man think and care ever so little about God, he does not therefore exist without God. God is here with him, upholding, warming, delighting, teaching him—making life a good thing to him. God gives him himself, though he knows it not. But when God withdraws from a man as far as that can be without the man's ceasing to be, then indeed the fire turns black. When the man feels himself abandoned, hanging in a ceaseless vertigo of existence upon the verge of the gulf of his being, without support, without refuge, without aim, without end—for the soul has no weapons wherewith to destroy herself—with no inbreathing of joy, with nothing to make life good:—then at last will he listen in agony for the faintest sound of life from the closed door. If the moan of suffering humanity ever reaches the ear of the outcast of darkness, then he will be ready to rush into the very heart of the Consuming Fire to know life once more, to change this terror of sick negation, of unspeakable death, for that region of painful hope.

Imagination cannot mislead us into too much horror of being without God—that one living death. Is not this

> *to be worse than worst*
> *Of those that lawless and in certain thoughts*
> *Imagine howling?*

But with this divine difference: that the outer darkness is but the most dreadful form of the consuming fire—the fire without light—the darkness visible, the black flame. God hath withdrawn himself, but not lost his hold. His face is turned away, but his hand is laid upon him still. His heart has ceased to beat into the man's heart, but he keeps him alive by his fire. And that fire will go searching and burning on in him, as in the highest saint who is not yet pure as he is pure.

But at length, O God, wilt thou not cast Death and Hell into the lake of fire—even into thine own consuming self? Death shall then die everlastingly,

> *And Hell itself will pass away,*
> *And leave her dolorous mansions to the peering day.*

Then indeed wilt thou be all in all. For then our poor brothers and sisters, every one—O God, we trust in thee, the Consuming Fire—shall have been burnt clean and brought home.

For if their moans, myriads of ages away, would turn heaven into hell for *us*…shall a man be more merciful than *God*?

Shall, of all his glories, his mercy alone not be infinite? Shall a brother love a brother more than The Father loves a son?—more than The Brother Christ loves his brother? Would he not die yet again to save one brother more?

As for us, now will we come to thee, our Consuming Fire. And thou wilt not burn us more than we can bear. But thou wilt burn us. And although thou seem to slay us, yet will we trust in thee even for that which thou hast not spoken, if by any means at length we may attain unto the blessedness of those who have not seen and yet have believed.

Eight

Fundamentalism's Dirty Little Secret

Scriptural Ambiguity About Hell

by
Michael Phillips

A dirty little secret lies at the heart of fundamentalist Christian orthodoxy.

It is easily enough stated: The widely accepted doctrine of an unending, punitive hell where unbelieving sinners are tormented forever, is not categorically taught by the Bible.

We have all been *told* that the doctrine of everlasting punishment is taught in Scripture as plain as day. It has been drilled into us from our spiritual infancies that alternate viewpoints are suspect, dangerous, and unscriptural.

But these contentions are untrue.

To be sure, everlasting torment is *hinted* at, and to all appearances proved by certain translations of a few key passages. But this seeming evidence is scantier and shakier than most of its proponents realize. And on the other side of it, the eternal victory of Love is also hinted at, with scriptures that enforce a very different view.

Both sides in this debate can point to scriptural evidence in support of their perspectives. We cannot ignore hell because it is unpleasant. But neither can we ignore what must be a patently obvious fact—God's love and forgiveness have no end, and *must*, by the very nature of God's being, conquer hell and sin and the devil in the final reckoning of eternity.

Therefore, we have to figure out what hell *means*. How do unending Love and hell coexist? How do they work together to accomplish God's eternal purposes?

The dichotomy between these seemingly opposite positions drives us to an inescapable conclusion: —

The Bible is completely and unashamedly ambiguous about the duration and purpose of hell.

It is impossible to emphasize this imperative point strongly enough but by repeating it: *The Bible is completely and unashamedly ambiguous about the duration and purpose of hell.*

This must be the basis for our discussion. This is the entire foundation of everything involved in the so-called "hell debate." This is the framework for study, research, and interpretation.

If you take nothing else away from this book, remember this: *The Bible is ambiguous about hell.*

This eye-opening revelation is the necessary first-step toward understanding the deep purposes of God. Recognizing that we cannot KNOW sets our steps on the path toward *beginning to know.*

With this necessary foundation in place, we can proceed to inquire into this state of affairs, why it exists, how this "dirty little secret" is still able to exercise such a stranglehold on evangelical doctrine...and what ought to be our response.

HUSHING UP THE EVIDENCE

The reason a great hell debate is swirling at this late hour in the church's history strikes to the heart of this ambiguity. A debate exists because scriptural evidence exists on *both* sides of the fence. If the Bible's teaching were plain, there would be no debate.

This is the dirty little secret. Most of us have never been told about the scriptural evidence *supporting* the possibility that everyone may ultimately repent and be embraced into the loving arms of their Creator-Father? That half of the scriptural evidence has been hushed up, all evidence of it swept under the carpet. The orthodoxy of eternal punitive hell is preserved and no one questions it.

Imagine a curious new Christian reading in his or her New Testament and innocently wondering, "Hmm...this is curious—Jesus says he will draw *all* men to himself. [31] Paul says that *every* knee will bow and *every* tongue confess that Jesus is Lord. [32] I've been told to take the Bible literally. These passages make it sound as though everyone will eventually come to Christ."

Immediately an innocent response like this would be met with alarm, and with arguments why in this case we must *not* take the Bible literally. A list of contorted explanations and countering passages from Scripture would follow. Doctrinally minded mentors would studiously explain why, in these particular instances, we must ignore what Jesus and Paul actually said. Don't pay attention to the literal words, the young Christian is told. Jesus and Paul meant something else.

The orthodoxy *must* be preserved at all costs.

It is time for thinking, serious-minded, objective students of the Bible to lay this dirty little secret bare. The Bible plainly teaches that hell exists. The Bible just as plainly does *not* tell us how long it will last, or how God may have in mind to use it to accomplish his reconciliatory purposes.

THE FIX IS IN…AND BIBLE TRANSLATORS SEEM TO BE IN ON IT!

It gets worse!

Because the doctrine of eternal punitive hell has been a solidly entrenched pillar of fundamentalist orthodoxy for so long, Bible translators skew their word choices to substantiate it. This factor must be taken into account when employing most translations, where subtleties of usage, tense, and actual word meanings from the original languages disappear from sight.

This is an equally disturbing component of the dirty little secret—the very Bibles you read are not objective. The men and women who have produced those translations, and the commentators who supply the marginal notes instructing you in the doctrinally correct interpretations…they are all in on it.

The fix is in!

It is not for me to judge the motives of those who have taken upon themselves the hold task of rendering God's Word to his people. But it *seems* that many of these translators view their job, not necessarily always to give you an accurate rendition of the Greek originals…*but to keep the orthodoxy intact.* Not only do they slant their word choices, sometimes they blatantly introduce *erroneous* translations of the Greek…to make sure no doubt arises about the orthodoxy. As we investigate these things more thoroughly, you will have to judge for yourself, but so it strikes me.

We will encounter several examples of such translational liberties as we progress. Matthew 25:46 provides one of the most blatant examples of this attempt to keep the doctrine of eternal punishment alive by fuzzy, if not outright incorrect, translation. No hint is given, either in translation or marginal notes, of the deeper meanings to which the original Greek words point. When you discover what the words in this passage *really* mean, you will be stunned. We will consider Matthew 25:46 in detail in Chapter 22.

Mark 3:29 provides another unbelievable example where *incorrect* translation of the Greek has given an appallingly inaccurate twist to Jesus' words about blaspheming the work of the Holy Spirit. Most translations of the verse, by implication, demean God's forgiveness, and thus degrade the nature of God himself. This verse, too, will be explored later. [33]

Where the Greek constructions are too straightforward to be explained away (such as in Philippians 2:10-11—that *every* knee might bow...and *every* tongue confess) commentators circuitously work their own opinions into their interpretations.

The distorted translations and biased marginal notes that result from all this are a constant difficulty which the perceptive Bible student must take into account when examining the scriptural record.

THE GREAT HELL COVER UP

Both heaven and hell remained vague in the years before Jesus' birth. The Old Testament spoke primarily of fire, destruction, and restoration— all of which intermingled ambiguously in the minds of Old Testament Jews. This confusion is evidenced by James' and John's question to the Lord in Luke 9:54 about invoking fire to come down from heaven. [34]

The primary word used specifically to refer to the afterlife in the Old Testament is *Sheol*, rendered *Hades* in Greek, which simply means *unseen* or *invisible*. The fire of destruction and the unseen place of the dead, however, were not fused into the single destination called hell until New Testament times.

None of the biblical words associated with hell (*sheol, abyssos, hades, gehenna, katoteros*—lower) convey by internal meaning or historical etymology, a place of eternal punishment. Hades, in fact, was universally seen as a *temporary* home for the dead. In Scripture Sheol and Hades (both of which are often rendered *Hell*) merely denoted the unseen. The "lake of fire" of Revelation is a different term altogether.

Adlai Loudy explains the etymology of the word *hell*: "It is astonishing to note the various ideas attached to the word *hell* in the English language...It is of Saxon origin, and is derived from the verb *helan*, and was spelled *hele, helle, hell, heile,* and *helan.* In this original state, the word had a very mild and harmless significance. It meant simply to *cover up, conceal,* or *hide.* The word in its primitive form is still retained, especially in the western counties of England, and means something concealed, covered, the grave. To *hele* over a thing, meant to *cover* it. Dr. Clarke says, that tiling or slating of a house is called in Cornwall, *heling,* to this day; and in Lancashire the *covers* of books are so called. Doubtless the first translators of our English Bible used the word hell in the sense of a covered or *unseen* place, the grave, or perhaps the state of death." [35]

The doctrine of hell as we know it today largely emerges out of Jewish apocalyptic literature and post-first-century creedology largely based on the grievous mistranslation of Matthew 25:46 and the final chapters of Revelation.

84

This clarifies an extremely significant point—the fundamental orthodoxy concerning the doctrine of hell is one with roots in *tradition* and *interpretation*, not in irrefutable scriptural fact.

The New Testament Scriptures are as confusing as those from the Old. Jesus expanded on the earlier themes of afterlife "fire" and "punishment," applying it to *religious* hypocrites more frequently than to those commonly called "sinners". His definitive statement, of course, came in Matthew 25:46. Whether or not Jesus was articulating what later developed into the dogma of everlasting hell remains open to conjecture. Paul developed the doctrine of the afterlife still further, followed by John's final apocalyptic vision of the end times.

The concept of "hell" as a prison of eternal torment for the wicked from which there is no escape is probably a late-first century or second-century notion. From there it sent down and expanded its roots in the following centuries, amplified by theologians like Augustine and bolstered by grotesque imagery culminating in Dante's *Inferno* and Michelangelo's "Last Judgment" wall in the Sistine Chapel. The Bible's portrayal of the wonderful victory of the cross, by which it was God's plan to redeem his entire creation was squelched, silenced, and hidden from view. The massive concealing of this high truth is truly the cover-up of the ages.

God's glorious revelation of his reconciliatory purpose was thus stamped out and expunged from the biblical record. It was never expunged from the Greek originals. But once the Bible began to appear in English, its first translators set the cover-up into hardened cement.

As historically breathtaking as is their achievement, we have the translators of the King James Version to thank (or blame) for the mistranslation of Matthew 25:46 that reads, *and these shall go away into everlasting punishment,*[36] and for the horrifying blunder they introduced into Mark 3:29 that has struck terror into so many through the years *hath never forgiveness, but is in danger of eternal damnation.* [37]

The cover-up has been so pervasively influential throughout Christendom that most Christians believe that Jesus actually spoke those words.

God forbid that Jesus would say that there are certain sins that will *never* be forgiven, or that his Father would even be capable of *never* forgiving.

That single word *never* does not exist in the Greek of Mark 3:29. The King James translators inserted it because it supported the doctrine of an unforgiving God who would eternally damn sinners to everlasting punishment. They had mistranslated Matthew 25:46. It was easy enough now to "add to Scripture" when dealing with Mark 3:29.

Most subsequent translators gave in to the lie against God's character and perpetuated the mistranslations of these two pivotal verses. These will be investigated in more detail in Chapter 21.

The cover up was complete.

ANOTHER PERSPECTIVE—GOD'S COMPLETE VICTORY

Leaving the cover-up behind, there exists an alternate perspective of hell, a beautiful picture of God's purposes that is energetically supported by Scripture. It is precisely this alternate perspective that George MacDonald illuminated in his writings.

The Spirit by which the biblical writers were inspired intended for the Old and New Testament models to be harmonized into a single unity. In such, the nature of fire (refinement and purification), and the disciplinary progression so evident throughout the Word of God (*destruction* and *correction* leading to *restoration*), paves the way for a triumphant and complete portrait of God's ultimate victory.

The books of *Malachi* and *Revelation* hold equal importance. Both Testaments climax with a prophetic view of evil not merely being punished, but being *destroyed* by the fire of purification. Malachi calls it "the day of the Lord's coming."

The vision of John in *Revelation*, therefore, to be understood accurately, must be seen as the New Testament fulfillment of its Old Testament counterpart. The *hell* which New Testament writers attempted to explain was none other than the *furnace of fire* prophesied by Malachi—a furnace of cleansing and purification.

A FREQUENTLY USED OLD TESTAMENT PROGRESSION

The following progression is offered to illuminate a progressive prophetic unfolding of God's purpose. Out of it ultimately emerges the perfect and complete worship of God by all his creation, forever.

> *I have decided to assemble the nations, to gather the kingdoms...The whole world will be consumed by the fire...(Zephaniah 3:8)*
>
> *Then death and Hades were thrown into the lake of fire. The lake of fire is the second death. If anyone's name was not found written in the book of life, he was thrown into the lake of fire. (Revelation 20:14)*
>
> *Who can endure the day of the Lord's coming? Who can stand when he appears? He will be like a refiner's fire. He will sit as a refiner and purifier of*

silver; he will purify the Levites and refine them like gold and silver. *(Malachi 3:2-3)*

Then will I purify the lips of the peoples, that all of them may call on the name of the Lord. *(Zephaniah 3:9)*

Then the Lord will have men who will bring offerings in righteousness, and the offerings of Judah and Jerusalem will be acceptable to the Lord, as in days gone by, as in former years... "Test me in this," says the Lord Almighty, "and see if I will not throw open the floodgates of heaven and pour out so much blessing that you will not have room enough for it." *(Malachi 3:3, 10)*

Then I saw a new heaven and a new earth, for the first heaven and the first earth had passed away...And I heard a loud voice from the throne saying, "Now the dwelling of God is with men, and he will live with them. They will be his people, and God himself will be with them and be their God. He will wipe every tear from their eyes. There will be no more death or mourning or crying or pain, for the old order of things has passed away. *(Revelation 21:1, 3-4)*

For you who revere my name, the sun of righteousness will rise with healing in its wings. *(Malachi 4:2)*

He said to me: "It is done. I am the Alpha and the Omega, the Beginning and the End...On each side of the river stood the tree of life...And the leaves of the tree are for the healing of the nations. No longer will there be any curse. *(Revelation 21:6, 22:2-3)*

At the name of Jesus every knee should bow...and every tongue confess that Jesus Christ is Lord, to the glory of God the Father. *(Philippians 2:10-11)*

...his name will be on their foreheads. There will be no more night. They will not need the light of a lamp or the light of the sun, for the Lord God will give them light. And they will reign for ever and ever. *(Revelation 22:4-5)*

PART 2

IS ANYBODY HOME IN THE UNIVERSE?

God's Redemptive Purpose For Mankind

NINE

HOW WELL DO YOU KNOW YOUR FATHER?

The Ancient Truth of Universal Fatherhood

by
Michael Phillips

As we turn our attention to several foundational elements within evangelical theology that require rethinking, it will be good to remind ourselves of Jesus' method for differentiating between the false and the true. He used this pattern throughout the Sermon on the Mount, most notably in Matthew 5 and 6.

Jesus contrasted the two with the words, "You have heard that it was said...but I say to you..."

That last phrase fully encapsulates his teaching: *But I say to you...*

It was another way of expressing, "This is the *old* way of thinking...but I want you to see everything differently, through a *new* lens of truth."

This contrast between the old and the new permeates the Lord's teaching on every page—the old and new wineskins, old garments and new cloth, old legalisms vs. a new righteousness, old Jewish exclusivity vs. love for all men. The contrast is summed up by Paul in 2 Corinthians 5:17, "All things have become new."

A subtle twist on this old-new contrast, however, throws a monkey wrench into our attempt to penetrate the gospel message. Many Christians assume that the "old" is the old covenant of Judaism, and that the "new" is the new covenant in Christ, with the entire evangelically-orthodox theological package that comes with it.

Unfortunately, it may not be quite so simple.

In fact, Christianity's orthodoxy of this so-called "new" is so riddled with old-covenantal thinking that it is not *new* at all. It is a mere extension of the old. It's a new packaging of an old doctrine. The seemingly "new" terms and theories of the atonement are *not* new. They are attempts to do what Jesus said we could not do—sew a new piece of cloth (the new Christian orthodoxy) onto an old garment (the old legalism of Judaism.) Scarce wonder that much of Evangelical and Reformed orthodoxy is fraying at the seams.

When we use the terms *old* and *new*, therefore, we must be very attentive to what we mean. We are not speaking of Judaism vs. Christianity. We are speaking of "Christian" orthodoxies that have allowed *old*-covenantal perspectives to infect them like a cancer. We are speaking of the *old* of ancient Catholicism, the *old* of Calvinism, even the *old* of modern evangelicalism. All these "olds" have combined to produce a thoroughly Jewish *old*-covenantal legalistic orthodoxy that masquerades as being "Christian," but which is completely *unlike* the actual good "news" that Jesus brought to the world.

By "old," we mean the orthodoxy of old-covenantal legalism no matter how dressed up that legalism may be in "Christian" clothes.

By "new," we mean the true gospel of Jesus Christ—a gospel of eternal Fatherhood and obedient childship.

THE ULTIMATE NEW—THE UNIVERSALITY OF FATHERHOOD

Anyone who takes a position outside the mainstream, especially on an issue with thorny and controversial edges, will be subject to criticism from those of the majority or "orthodox" view. As a writer, especially as my work has been so closely affiliated with George MacDonald—himself a lightning rod for controversy in the church for a century and a half—I expect it.

One of the most persistent criticisms to come my way from readers, however, has caught me utterly by surprise. I receive regular correspondence taking me to task for failing to endorse the exclusivism which many Christians seem to take pleasure in, and for implying by something I have written that God is the Father of *all* mankind. I always reply with the same question—"Who *else's* children could anyone possibly be? God created us, didn't he?"

Somehow the obvious simplicity of God's Fatherhood is too much for many to take in.

Of course we are aware that most of mankind neither acknowledges nor lives in the reality of God's Fatherhood. But does that fact alter the fundamental order of God's universe?

As we embark on this reevaluation of certain key aspects of evangelical theology, the imperative foundation we must lay between old thinking and new may be simply stated. It concisely summarizes the good news of Jesus' teaching:

You have heard that it was said that man is totally depraved, lost in his sin, and condemned to eternal death by a tyrannically holy God of judgment. *But I say to you*...man bears the image of goodness in his soul, because God is your Father.

FOUNDATIONS—GOING BACK TO THE BEGINNING

The following four sections were originally included in a lengthy letter to a reader which was later reprinted in the magazine *Leben*.[38] Because these themes strike to the heart of much unscriptural foolishness that has infiltrated evangelical theology about who man is, and who God is (the "old" wineskins dressed up to look new), it strikes me that it may be helpful to reproduce a portion of it here.

That response is as follows:

"This second important question raised by your letter concerns the goodness/badness of humanity. You have put your finger exactly on the nub of something that genuinely plagues most thinking Christians. It probes to the core of what we believe about God and about ourselves. Most Christians never bother to ask these important questions. Thus their beliefs drift into dogma and a rote recitation of precepts they have been taught. They *think* they understand the intricacies of these doctrines, but really don't. Meanwhile, the far-reaching implications of the character of God never come within a mile of their vision throughout the whole of their churchy, religious lives. I honor you for having the courage to probe and ask how big God might really be.

"Having grown up in evangelicalism, I recognize in your questions my own struggles with much I had been taught. One of the most grievous wrongs that evangelical theology has done, in my opinion, is to ingrain the foolishness in us that man is bad, all bad, depraved, wicked, utterly sinful, with a desperately wicked heart, whose righteousness is as filthy rags...you are well familiar with the dogma. You have articulated it in your letter.

"I struggled with this doctrine for years. Then I made a remarkable discovery that liberated me to explore the infinity of God's goodness. I discovered that the evangelical theology of humanity—that man is *all* bad, a *complete* sinner through and through, and that *nothing* good dwells in his fallen heart—was unscriptural. Simply put, that doctrine is false. I don't know how to state it any more plainly than that.

"I will try to summarize the conclusions of my twenty year scriptural search.

"I believe in foundations. Foundations are the key to understanding all truth. For any spiritual question you can think to pose, if you go back to foundations to discover what God *intended* from the beginning, truth will emerge. If one is satisfied with partial truth, he can begin anywhere and can arrive at almost any conclusion he wants. But *full* truth requires investigating foundational beginnings.

GOD'S FOUNDATION—THE *VERY*-GOODNESS OF CREATION

"In my search for foundations, I often return to the book of Genesis. And there, at the very beginning of all foundations, I discovered a remarkable truth. Not only is it in the book of Genesis, it is in the very first chapter!

"What is God's purpose in the universe? If you want a partial and incomplete answer, a theology rooted in sin, hell, and God's judgment will do just fine. Indeed, many evangelicals major on the judgment required by God's so-called 'holiness.' Yet the foundational beginnings of the universe tell a far different story.

"Are sin, judgment, and hell anywhere in Genesis 1 or 2?

"No. They aren't there. God did not *intend* for them to be there. His *intent* was perfection. I believe such a foundation leads to the inescapable conclusion that perfection will again reign throughout the universe, and that sin will be triumphantly defeated. How else will God's original intent be ultimately accomplished? Some will draw a different conclusion. However, I cannot envision a final summation of all things in which God's originating purpose is thwarted for all time. In this sense, Genesis 1 may hold the key to understanding eternity. For that is where God's originating *intent* and *purpose* for the universe is revealed.

"What, then, is this originating principle that represents *the* Foundation of all foundations, the undergirding Truth upon which the entire creation was established? It is there in black and white for all to see.

"GOODNESS!

"Everything that God created was *good.*

"After decades being steeped in the *righteousness-as-filthy-rags, heart-is-deceitful-and-wicked* doctrine, I could hardly believe that so foundational a truth could have escaped me.

"The Word of God simply says:

"God saw that it was good.

"And then it continues to reaffirm it:

"God saw that it was good.

"God saw that it was good.

"God saw that it was good.

"God saw that it was good.

"God saw that it was good.

"It is repeated six times for each of the six days. And then, the resounding, conclusion on the seventh day, the seven of perfection, when the creation was complete—a creation that *included* man…

"God saw that it was good…very good…*VERY good!*

"What a triumphant foundation upon which to establish a world—*goodness*, the very goodness of God himself! Every time I think of it, my heart overflows with quiet praise. What a wonderful…what a *good* God we have!

"Yet for many years—immersed in bad teaching and holiness doctrines and *God-cannot-coexist-with-sin* theologies that *separate* God's Fatherhood from man's childness—I was oblivious to this elemental truth of the universe.

"Oh, God, may these wonderful scriptural facts sink into our beings! They will open our hearts to your character in a thousand ways.

"You and I have goodness within us that bears the imprint of the nature of God himself! It is too wonderful for words! This stupendous fact is the door-opener into a whole new realm of understanding God's being.

"After that foundational fact has been assimilated into our consciousness, only *then* are we in a position to put into perspective what happened next.

MAN'S INTRINSIC NATURE

"Of course, sin entered the world. But it came *later*. It was not *intrinsic* to creation, it infected creation like a virus. Sin is not the foundation of creation, nor is sin the foundation of the heart of man. *Goodness* is the foundation—God's word says it with unmistakable clarity. Sin is merely the corrupting virus that has infiltrated that goodness.

"The foundation (Genesis 1) was goodness. Sin (Genesis 3) was an after-virus.

"The universe began with goodness. It was founded and established in goodness. God is good. His creation was good. Mankind was created with goodness in his nature.

"So if you are asking about humanity, and the nature of humanity, as your letter does, you have to go back to the foundation and investigate what humanity was when God created it. You cannot get to the basic meaning of anything—marriage, God's plan for eternity, how far his forgiveness will extend, or the nature of humanity—without inquiring into its foundational nature.

"What do we know of *man's* foundational nature?

"We know two facts—that man was created *in God's image*, and that man, as part of the Genesis 1 creation, was *good*. God saw *all* that he had made…and it was *very* good.

"Man was not excluded from that goodness. So foundationally we know that in the beginning man was good. But we also know that God's goodness was corrupted by sin.

"And there we are presented with the dichotomy that is mankind. That dichotomy explains the human condition, the rest of the biblical story, why Jesus had to come, and why the universe is a great battleground between good and evil.

"The created *foundation* remains goodness. Only by grasping that truth can we understand the redemption story correctly. Of course there is a contorted theology based on man's 'sin nature.' This anti-goodness theology is so prevalent that for a time I wondered if 'goodness' itself was actually a *bad* thing. That's how backwards the misshapen orthodoxies of man can become. They twist common sense up in knots. How many times have I heard skepticism voiced when talking about so-called 'good' people—as if that very goodness implied that they were actually bad and on their way to hell because they were 'trusting in their own merits without Christ.' It is true that goodness alone does not imply full childship obedience. It is true that unredeemed man can, and often does, give himself over to hideous sinfulness. But that does not mean that goodness isn't 'good.'

"Goodness is a good thing! It comes from God himself. We ought to look at people and say, "Goodness in humanity is *good*, not bad. That individual bears the reflection of God. His goodness is a delight to his Creator. If only that man or woman knew where his goodness originated, and could thus enter into a relationship of obedient childness with God his Father…how much *better* it would be! Then his goodness would be fulfilled. I shall have to pray for an opportunity to tell him about his loving Father."

"The problem with traditional evangelical theology is simple: It is not deeply rooted enough. It is rooted in Genesis 3. I prefer to establish my beliefs in the bedrock of Genesis 1, all the way at the foundation—what C.S. Lewis calls the 'deeper magic from *before* the dawn of time.'

"The goodness in our hearts lies deeper than the sin. Goodness is of our intrinsic nature, sin is not. Sin has come from the outside but is not an intrinsic part of man's *in-God's-imageness*. But now that we *are* sinners, we need a Savior. All the theological explanations of God's provision for sin remains. We are fallen men. Our hearts are indeed deceitful precisely because the sin-virus has so thoroughly infected us. History since the garden is the gradual story of how God is slowly putting that wrongness right.

"Sin is a virus. It is not *us*. These are post-foundational 'facts,' not foundational *truths*. They are temporary bumps in the road, not eternal truths. They do not lie so deep in the heart of God as his foundational goodness. We are still created in God's image. We yet bear the imprint of that being in our spirits. The foundation of creation remains goodness.

"Genesis 1 is rooted in eternity, in the character of God himself. [39]

WHO ARE GOD'S CHILDREN?

"We are all aware that Jesus called the Pharisees the children of the devil. But he was merely making a point about truth and from whom we get what we call truth.

"The fact is, all men and women are God's children. It is so obvious, it is astounding that it is a debated point within Christendom. God is the Father and creator of all living things. God is the Father of the universe and everything in it. That makes all living things his children. They do not necessarily acknowledge the relationship. But all humanity is nonetheless of his family.

"Within God's universal family, there are *obedient* children and there are *wayward* children. Such is the human condition. But the family of God's creation, the family God has fathered, is a *universal* family of humanity.

"Judy and I have three grown sons. A number of years ago, two of them estranged themselves from us and left home. Thankfully they are now once more in relationship with us. The third remained with us all along. Is this not a picture of God's up and down, constantly shifting relationship with humanity? People move in and out of closeness with him, and in and out of obedience to him. One of my sons even disavowed me as his father.

"But was he any less my son? Of course not. My blood flowed in his veins throughout all the years of his estrangement. Our son who never left was not any *more* my son, he simply walked in greater acknowledgment of my fatherhood.

"God's spirit flows in the spirit-veins of *every* man and woman ever created. That's what it means to be made in his image. We each determine how we will respond to that fact of our nature—walk with our Father in obedience, or allow the self-motive of sin to be our life's ruling dictum? Will we be *obedient children*, or *children of rebellion?*"

THE FOUNDATION OF GOD'S CHARACTER—LOVE OR WRATH?

Let us now turn to inquire how George MacDonald faced this same doctrinal dilemma that I have described facing early in my own walk with

God, and see how he, as I did, rediscovered the ancient truth of God's universal Fatherhood.

In George MacDonald's words, we know that from an early age he began to recoil with disgust from the Calvinist view of election and predestination in which he was steeped as a boy. The strict delineation of humanity into two camps—the saved and the unsaved, God's elect and the lost, those on their way to heaven and those doomed to hell—became repugnant to him.

Of his own youthful questions, MacDonald wrote, "To myself, in the morning of childhood, the evil doctrine was a mist through which the light came struggling, a cloud-phantom of repellent mien—requiring maturer thought and truer knowledge to dissipate it." [40] And, "One of my earliest recollections is of beginning to be at strife with the false system...Such paganism I scorn as heartily in the name of Christ, as I scorn it in the name of righteousness." [41]

Though subtleties have softened the nature of the Calvinist doctrine of "election"—that certain individuals are destined ahead of time for salvation and others to perdition, and that eternal torment in hell is inevitable for the latter—its influence remains darkly pervasive throughout much of Christian theology, both Catholic and Protestant. This ugliness at the heart of Christianity—subtle though may be its shades as it lingers in the church—surely accounts for much of the world's rejection of Christianity through the centuries.

The Shorter Catechism, that staple of instruction for all Scottish boys and girls of MacDonald's time, in Questions and Answers 19-21, outlines the doctrine that God's exclusivist redemption is not intended for all. The italics, added to highlight the contemptible notion that Jesus is not the Savior of all men, are mine.

"All mankind by their fall lost communion with God, are under his wrath and curse, and so made liable to all miseries in this life, to death itself, and to the pains of hell for ever. God having, out of his mere good pleasure, from all eternity, elected *some* to everlasting life, did enter into a covenant of grace, to deliver them out of the estate of sin and misery, and to bring them into an estate of salvation by a Redeemer. The only Redeemer *of God's elect* is the Lord Jesus Christ." [42]

To the boy George MacDonald, the implication was a simple one: God loved some people, and chose to withhold his love from others. *The Shorter Catechism*, derived primarily for the purpose of teaching young people the correct doctrine from the complete 1646 *Westminster Confession of Faith* mentions God's "love" nowhere in its depiction of God. Man is commanded to love God, but toward man God displays not love but his "wrath and curse." Such is the definition of God that young Calvinist children are still being taught to this day that it is their duty to love—a God whose character is defined by wrath not love, and whose curse is upon mankind.

Read it for yourself. It is shocking to see the extent to which *love* has been stricken from the divine character.

The gloomy perspective of *The Shorter Catechism* can be seen in that in its entire contents, the word *love* is found a total of four times, only once in relation to God. The word *sin* is used more than twenty times, culminating in the question—"What doth every sin deserve?" The answer ("Every sin deserveth God's wrath and curse, both in this life, and that which is to come,") is given a humorous twist through the mouth of Annie Anderson in *Alec Forbes of Howglen*. Not knowing the right answer, Annie blurts out the best guess she is capable of: *A lickin'*. [43]

Obviously, if God intends to send certain individuals to hell, there to torment them forever without hope of reprieve, what conclusion can be drawn but that God never loved them at all. The inconsistency of the entire doctrinal system is not merely confusing, it is blasphemous against the character of God.

MACDONALD'S EARLY QUESTIONS

The boy George MacDonald reached a point early in his life when he concluded that he did not want God to love him if he did not love everyone. The words, inserted as an aside in his novel *Weighed and Wanting*, give a clear picture of the incubation in MacDonald's young soul of a larger vision of God's universal Fatherhood. "I well remember feeling as a child," he writes, "that I did not care for God to love me if he did not love everybody: the kind of love I needed was love essential to my nature—the love therefore that all men needed, the love that belonged to their nature as the children of the Father, a love he could not give me except he gave it to all men." [44]

George MacDonald's grandmother, who half-raised him after the death of his mother, was a stern Calvinist woman of the old school. To what extent she resembled the fictional Grandmother Falconer we can only speculate. But though the details of the story no doubt differ much from actual occurrences in MacDonald's own life, I take the portraiture as a substantially true one. This being so, I read the passage from Chapter 55 of *Robert Falconer* (quoted at the end of Chapter 11) as spiritually autobiographical. In it we find succinctly stated, the basic elements of that Calvinist creed MacDonald so abhorred. The passage highlights and adds detail to the heretical notion much earlier in the story from the boy Robert's mouth. I believe the question gives us a window into the early age at which young George MacDonald himself was questioning within himself about the universality of salvation: "Shargar, what think ye..." he writes. "Gin a de'il war to repent, wad God forgie him?" (*If a devil were to repent, would God forgive him?*) [45]

Out of MacDonald's gradual rejection of these pillars of Calvinist theology eventually emerged an alternate perspective of God's nature that would undergird all his future work—that God was the universal Father of *all* mankind. In MacDonald's new outlook, God's love rises triumphantly above his wrath. God's Fatherhood is universal, not partial. His love is complete not subjective nor arbitrary.

Upon this new (and to Calvinist theology revolutionary) image of God as the universal Father of mankind, a wonderfully inclusive perspective of God's purpose and plan in the universe could be built. God's character was not defined by an almighty "holiness" which *must*, by virtue of that holiness, punish all sin—indeed, punish it forever. God's true character, rather, could now be defined by tender Fatherhood.

God is a loving Father pursuing his wayward children—to hell and beyond if need be—with the relentless outpouring of his love. God's purpose in the universe is to bring his children home, back to the source of their origins, the home of his heart.

EXCERPTS FROM THE WRITINGS OF GEORGE MACDONALD
ON UNIVERSAL FATHERHOOD

The homily...that evening, bore upon the same subject nominally as the chapter that preceded it—that of election; a doctrine which in the Bible asserts the fact of God's choosing certain persons for the specific purpose of receiving first, and so communicating the gifts of his grace to the whole world; but which, in the homily referred to, was taken to mean the choice of certain persons for ultimate salvation, to the exclusion of the rest. They were sitting in silence after the close, when Harry started up suddenly, saying: "I don't want God to love me, if he does not love everybody;" and, bursting into tears, hurried out of the room...Euphra, hastened after him; but he would not return, and went supperless to bed. Euphra, however, carried him some supper. He sat up in bed and ate it with the tears in his eyes. She kissed him, and bade him good night; when, just as she was leaving the room, he broke out with:

"But only think, Euphra, if it should be true! I would rather not have been made."

"It is not true," said Euphra, in whom a faint glimmer of faith in God awoke for the sake of the boy whom she loved—

awoke to comfort him, when it would not open its eyes for herself. "No, Harry dear, if there is a God at all, he is not like that."

"No, he can't be," said Harry, vehemently, and with the brightness of a sudden thought; "for if he were like that, he wouldn't be a God worth being; and that couldn't be, you know." [46]

There is another kind of forsaking that may fall to the lot of some, and which they may find very difficult—the forsaking of such notions of God and his Christ as they were taught in their youth. These are ideas they held, and could hardly help holding, during the years when they first began to believe, but concerning which they now have begun to doubt the truth. And yet to cast them away seems like parting with every assurance of safety.

There are so-called doctrines long accepted of good people, which how any man can love God and hold, except indeed by tightly shutting his spiritual eyes, I find it hard to understand...

But for him who is in earnest about the will of God, it is of endless consequence that he should think rightly of God. He cannot come close to him, cannot truly know his will, while his notion of him is in any point that of a false god. The thing shows itself absurd...

Many good souls will one day be horrified at the things they now believe of God. If they have not thought about them, but given themselves to obedience, they may not have done themselves much harm as yet. But they can make little progress in the knowledge of God, while, even if but passively, holding evil things true of him. If, on the other hand, they do think about them, and find in them no obstruction, they must indeed be far from anything to be called a true knowledge of God. [47]

God is represented in Jesus, for God is *like* Jesus. In the same way, Jesus is represented in the child, for Jesus is *like* the child. Therefore, God is represented in the child, for he too is *like* the child.

God is child-like...he was, is, and ever shall be *divinely childlike.*

Childhood belongs to the divine nature...

We are careful, in our unbelief, over the divine dignity, of which he is too grand to think. Better pleasing to God, it needs little daring to say, is the audacity of Job, who, rushing into his presence, and flinging the door of his presence-chamber to the wall, like a troubled, it may be angry, but yet faithful child, calls aloud in the ear of him whose perfect Fatherhood he has yet to learn: "Am I a sea or a whale, that thou settest a watch over me?"...

For when is the child the ideal child in our eyes and to our hearts? Is it not when with gentle hand he takes his father by the beard, and turns that father's face up to his brothers and sisters to kiss?...

In this, then, is God like the child: He is simply and altogether our friend, our father—our more than friend, father, and mother—our infinite love-perfect God.

Grand and strong beyond all that human imagination can conceive of poet-thinking and kingly action, he is delicate beyond all that human tenderness can conceive of husband or wife, homely beyond all that human heart can conceive of father or mother. He does not have two opposing thoughts about us. With him all is simplicity of purpose and meaning and effort and end—namely, that we should be as he is, think the same thoughts, mean the same things, possess the same blessedness.

It is so plain that anyone may see it, every one ought to see it, everyone shall see it. It must be so. He is utterly true and good to us, not shall anything withstand his will. [48]

How terribly, then, have the theologians misrepresented God in the measure of the low and showy, not the lofty and simple humanities! Nearly all of them represent him as a great King on a grand throne, thinking how grand he is, and making it the business of his being and the end of his universe to keep up his glory, wielding the bolts of a Jupiter against them that take his name in vain.

They would not admit such a statement, but follow out what they say, and it amounts to this. [49]

The root of every heresy popular in the church draws its nourishment merely and only from the soil of unbelief. The idea that God would be God all the same, as glorious as he needed to be, had he not taken upon himself the divine toil of bringing home his wandered children, had he done nothing to seek and save the lost, is false as hell...As if the idea of God admitted of his being less than he is, less than perfect, less than all-in-all, less than Jesus Christ! less than Love absolute, less than entire unselfishness...So it might be, if he were not our father. But to think of the living God not as our father, but as one who has condescended greatly, being nowise, in his own willed grandeur of righteous nature, bound to do as he has done, is killing to all but a slavish devotion. It is to think of him as nothing like the God we see in Jesus Christ. [50]

"Have you really been reading my books, and at this time ask me what have I lost of the old faith? Much have I rejected of the new, but I have never rejected anything I could keep.... With the faith itself to be found in the old Scottish manse I trust I have a true sympathy. With many of the forms gathered around that faith, I have none. At a very early age I had begun to cast them from me; but all the time my faith in Jesus as the Son of the Father of men and the Savior of us all, has been growing. If it were not for the fear of its sounding unkind, I would say that if you had been a disciple of his instead of mine, you would not have mistaken me so much. Do not suppose that I believe in Jesus because it is said so-and-so in a book. I believe in him because he is himself. The vision of him in that book, and, I trust, his own living power in me, have enabled me to understand him, to look him in the face, as it were, and accept him as my Master and Savior, in following whom I shall come to the rest of the Father's peace. The Bible is to me the most precious thing in the world, because it tells me his story; and what good men thought about him who know him and accepted him.

"But those who hold to the common theory of the inspiration of the words, instead of the breathing of God's truth into the hearts and souls of those who wrote it...are in danger of worshipping the letter instead of living in the Spirit, of being idolators of the Bible instead of disciples of Jesus...It is *Jesus* who is the Revelation of God.... Jesus alone is The Word of God.

"With all sorts of doubt I am familiar, and the result of them is, has been, and will be, a widening of my heart and soul and mind to greater glories of the truth—the truth that is in Jesus—and not in Calvin or Luther or St. Paul or St. John, save as they got it from Him, from whom every simple heart may have it, and can alone get it. You cannot have such proof of the existence of God or the truth of the Gospel story as you can have of a...chemical experiment. But the man who will order his way by the word of the Master shall partake of his peace, and shall have in himself a growing conviction that in him are hid all the treasures of wisdom and knowledge...

"From your letter it seems that to be assured of my faith would be a help to you. I cannot say I never doubt, nor until I hold the very heart of good as my very own in Him, can I wish not to doubt. For doubt is the hammer that breaks the windows clouded with human fancies, and lets in the pure light. But I do say that all my hope, all my joy, all my strength are in the Lord

Christ and his Father; that all my theories of life and growth are rooted in him; that his truth is gradually clearing up the mysteries of this world....To Him I belong heart and soul and body, and he may do with me as he will—nay, nay—I pray him to do with me as he wills: for that is my only well-being and freedom." [51]

TEN

ABBA, FATHER!

by
George MacDonald

From *Unspoken Sermons, Second Series*
as reprinted in *Your Life in Christ* [52]

Edited by Michael Phillips

"—the spirit of adoption, whereby we cry, Abba, Father."
—Romans viii 15

The hardest, gladdest thing in all the world is, to cry *Father!* from a full heart. I would help whom I may to call thus upon the Father.

LOVE AND COURAGE TO QUESTION PHANTOM DOCTRINES

There are many things in all forms of the systematic teaching of Christianity to block such an outgoing of the heart as this most elemental human cry. With some they render it simply impossible. The more delicate the affections, the less easy to satisfy, the readier are they to be dampened and discouraged, yea quite blown aside. Even the suspicion of a cold reception is enough to paralyze them.

Such a cold wind blowing at the very gate of heaven—thank God, blowing *outside* the gate!—is the so-called doctrine of *Adoption*.

When a heart hears—and believes, or half believes—that he or she is not the child of God by origin, from the first of its being, but may possibly be "adopted" into his family, the love of such a one sinks at once in a cold faint. Where is that heart's own father? And who is this almighty one, as they call him, who would adopt it?

To myself, in the morning of my childhood, the evil doctrine was a mist through which the light came struggling, a cloud-phantom of repellent appearance—requiring the maturer thought and truer knowledge of later years to dissipate it. But in truth it requires neither much knowledge nor much insight to stand up against its hideousness. It needs but *love* that will not be denied, and *courage* to question the phantom.

A devout and honest skepticism on God's side, not to be put down by anything called authority, is absolutely necessary to him who would know the liberty wherewith Christ maketh free. Whatever any company of good men thinks or believes is to be approached with respect. But nothing claimed or taught—be the claimers or the teachers who they may—must come between the soul and the spirit of the father. For he himself is the teacher of his children. Nay, to accept authority may be to refuse the very thing the "authority" would teach. It may remain altogether misunderstood precisely for lack of that natural process of doubt and inquiry, which we were intended to go through by him who would have us understand.

WHO IS MY FATHER!

As no scripture is of private interpretation, so is there no feeling in human heart which exists in that heart alone, which is not, in some form or degree, in every heart. Thence I conclude that many must have groaned like myself under the supposed authority of this doctrine. The refusal to look up to God as our Father is the one central wrong in the whole human affair. The inability to do so is our one central misery. Whatever helps to clear away any difficulty from our recognition of the Father, will more or less eliminate every difficulty in life.

"Is God then not my Father," cries the heart of the child. "Do I need to be adopted by him? Adoption! That can never satisfy me. Who is my true father? Am I not his to begin with? Is God not my very own Father? Is he my Father in word only—by a sort of legal contrivance? Truly, much love may lie in adoption, but if I accept it from anyone, that makes me in reality the actual offspring of another! The adoption of God would indeed be a blessed thing if another than he had given me being! But if he gave me being, then it means no reception, but a repudiation.—*O Father, am I not your child?"*

"No," they say, "but he will adopt you. He will not acknowledge you as his child, but he will *call* you his child, and be a father to you."

"Alas!" cries the child, "if he is not my father, he cannot *become* my father. A father is a father from the beginning. A primary relation cannot be superinduced. The consequence might be small where earthly fatherhood is concerned, but the very origin of my being—alas, if he be only a maker and not a father! Then am I only a machine, and not a child—not a man! If what you say is so, then it is false to say I was created in his image!

"It does not help if you tell me that we lost our birthright by the fall. I do not care to argue that I *personally* did not fall when Adam fell, for I have fallen many a time, and there is a shadow on my soul which I or another may call a curse. I cannot get rid of a something that always intrudes between my heart and the blue of every sky. But it avails nothing, either for my heart or their argument, to say I have fallen and been cast out. Can any repudiation, even that of God, undo the facts of an existent origin? Nor is it merely that he *made* me. By whose power do I *go on* living? When he cast me out, as you say, did I then begin to draw my being from myself—or from the devil? In *whom* do I live and move and have my being? It cannot be that I am not the creature of God."

"But *creation* is not *fatherhood*," they argue yet further.

"Perhaps," I say. "But creation in the image of God, *is*. And if I am not in the image of God, how can the word of God be of any meaning to me? 'He called them gods to whom the word of God came,' says the Master himself. To be fit to receive his word implies being of his kind. No matter how his image may have been defaced in me, the thing defaced remains his image. It remains his defaced image—an image that can yet hear his word. What makes me evil and miserable is that the thing spoiled in me is the image of the Perfect. Nothing can be evil but in virtue of a good underlying substance. No, no! Nothing can convince me that I am not the child of God. If one say, 'Look at the animals—God made them but you do not call them the children of God!' I answer, 'But I am to blame. They are not to blame! Indeed, I cling fast to my blame, for it is the seal of my childhood.' I have no argument to make on the basis of the animals, for I do not understand them. Two things only I am sure of with regard to them—that God is to them a faithful creator, and that the sooner I put in force my claim to be child of God, the better for them. For they too are fallen, though without blame."

"But you are evil," comes the argument of the doctrine further. "How can you be a child of the Good?"

"Just as many an evil son is the child of a good parent."

"But in him you call a good parent, there yet lay evil, and that accounts for the child being evil."

"I cannot explain. God let me be born through evil channels. But in whatever manner I may have become an unworthy child, I cannot thereby have ceased to be a child of God—his child in the way that a child must always be the child of the man of whom he comes. Is it not proof—this complaint of my heart at the word *Adoption*? Is it not the spirit of the child, crying out, 'Abba, Father?'"

"Yes, but that is the spirit of adoption. The text says so."

"Away with your adoption! I could not even be adopted if I were not such as the adoption could reach—that is, of the nature of God. Much as he may love him, can a man adopt a dog? I must be of a nature for the word of God to come to. Indeed, I must be of the divine nature, of the image of God! Heartily do I grant that, had I been left to myself, had God dropped me, held no communication with me, I could never have thus cried, never have cared when they told me I was not a child of God. But he has *never* repudiated me, and does not now desire to adopt me. Why should it grieve me to be told I am not a child of God if I am not a child of God? If you say—Because you have learned to love him, I answer— Adoption would satisfy the love of one who was not but wants to be a child. For me, I cannot do without a father, nor can any adoption give me one."

"But what is the good of all you say, if the child is such that the father cannot take him to his heart?"

"Ah, indeed, I grant you, nothing! So long as the child does not desire to be taken to the father's heart. But the moment he does, then it is everything to the child's heart that he should be indeed the child of him after whom his soul is thirsting. However bad I may be, I am the child of God. And therein lies my blame. Ah, I would not lose my blame! In my blame lies my hope. It is the pledge of what I am, and what I am not. It is the pledge of what I am meant to be, and what I shall one day be,—the child of God in spirit and in truth."

"Then do you dare to say the apostle is wrong in what he so plainly teaches?"

"By no means," I answer. "What I do say is, that our English presentation of his teaching is very misleading. It is not for me to judge the learned and good men who have revised the translation of the New Testament—with so much gain to every one whose love of truth is greater than his loving prejudice for accustomed form. I can only say that I wonder what may have been their reasons for retaining this word *adoption*."

AN INACCURATE RENDITION

In the New Testament the word is used only by the apostle Paul. Liddell and Scott give the meaning as, "Adoption as a son," which is a mere submission to popular theology. They give no reference except to the New Testament.

The relation of the word *huiōthesía* (υιοθεσια) to the form *thetòs* (θετος,) which means "taken," or rather, "*placed* as one's child," is, I presume, the sole ground for the translating of it so. Usage plentiful and invariable, however, could not justify that translation here, in the face of what St. Paul elsewhere shows he means by the word.

The Greek word *might* be variously interpreted—though I can find no use of it earlier than St. Paul. But the English can mean only one thing, and that is *not* what St. Paul means. "The spirit of adoption" Luther translates "the spirit of a child." Adoption he translates *kindschaft*, or *childship*.

Of two things I am sure. First, that by υιοθεσια St. Paul did not intend *adoption*. And second, that if the Revisers had gone through what I have gone through because of the word, if they had felt it come between God and their hearts as I have felt it, they could not have allowed it to remain in their version.

Once more I say, the word used by St. Paul does not imply that God adopts children that are *not* his own, but rather that a second time he *fathers* his own. A second time they are born—this time from above. He will make himself tenfold, yea, infinitely their father. He will have them return into the very bosom whence they came…and left that they might learn they could live nowhere else. He will have them one with himself. It was for the sake of this that, in his Son, he died for them.

A SPIRITUAL COMING OF AGE

Let us look at the passage where Paul reveals his use of the word. It is in another of his epistles—that to the Galatians, in 4:1-7:

But I say that so long as the heir is a child, he differeth nothing from a bondservant, though he is lord of all; but is under guardians and stewards until the term appointed of the father. So we also, when we were children, were held in bondage under the rudiments of the world: but when the fulness of the time came, God sent forth his Son, born of a woman, born under the law, that he might redeem them which were under the law, that we might receive the adoption of sons. And because ye are sons, God sent forth the Spirit of his Son into our hearts, crying, Abba, Father. So that thou art no longer a bondservant, but a son; and if a son, then an heir through God.

How could the Revisers choose this last reading, "an heir through God," and keep the word *adoption*? From the passage it is as plain as St. Paul could make it, that, by the word translated *adoption*, he means the raising of a father's own child from the condition of tutelage and subjection to others—a state which he says is no better than that of a slave—to the position and rights of a son. None but a *child* could become a *son*. The idea is a spiritual coming of age. *Only when the child is a man is he really and fully a son.*

This meaning is held up in its earthly parallel. How many children of good parents—good children in the main too—never know those parents, never feel towards them as children might, until, grown up, they have left the house—until, perhaps, they are parents themselves, or are parted from them by death!

To be a child is not necessarily to be a son or daughter. The childship is the lower condition of the upward process towards the sonship. It is the soil out of which the true sonship shall grow. It is the former without which the latter would be impossible.

SONS AND DAUGHTERS OF GOD'S SPIRIT

No more than an earthly parent, God cannot be content to have only children. He must have sons and daughters—children of his soul, of his spirit, of his love—not merely in the sense that he loves them, or even that they love him, but in the sense that they love *like* him, love as he loves. For this he does not adopt them. He dies to give them himself, thereby to raise his own to his heart. He gives them a birth from above. They are born again out of himself and into himself—for he is the one and the all.

His children are not his real, true sons and daughters until they think like him, feel with him, judge as he judges, until they are at home with him, and without fear before him because he and they mean the same thing, love the same things, seek the same ends.

For this are we created. It is the one end of our being, and includes all other ends whatever.

It can come only of unbelief and not faith, to make men believe that God has cast them off, repudiated them, said they are not and never were, his children. Yet even in the midst of such unbelief, he has been all the time spending himself to make us the children he designed and foreordained us to be—children who would take him for their Father!

He is our father all the time, for he is true. But until we respond with the truth of children, he cannot let all the father out to us. There is no place for the dove of his tenderness to alight. He is our father, but we are not his children. Because we are his children, we must become his sons and daughters. Nothing will satisfy him, or do for us, but that we be one with our father! What else could serve! How else should life ever be a good!

Because we are the sons of God, we must become the sons of God.

BETTER THAN ANY POSSIBLE EARTHLY MEANING

There may be among my readers—alas for such!—to whom the word *Father* brings no cheer, no dawn, in whose heart it rouses no tremble of even a vanished emotion. It is hardly likely to be their fault. For as children we seldom love up to the mark of reason. We often offend. And the conduct of some children is inexplicable to the parent who loves them. Yet, if the parent has been but ordinarily kind, even the son who has grown up a worthless man, will now and then feel, in his better moments, some dim reflex of childship, some faintly pleasant, some slightly sorrowful remembrance of the father around whose neck his arms had sometimes clung.

In my own childhood and boyhood my father was the refuge from all the ills of life, even sharp pain itself. Therefore I say to son or daughter who has no pleasure in the name *Father*, "You must interpret the word by all that you have missed in life. Every time a man might have been to you a refuge from the wind, a covert from the tempest, the shadow of a great rock in a weary land, that was a time when a father might have been a father indeed. Happy you are yet, if you have found man or woman such a refuge. So far have you known a shadow of the perfect, seen the back of the only man, the perfect Son of the perfect Father. All that human tenderness can give or desire in the nearness and readiness of love, all and infinitely more must be true of the perfect Father—of the maker of fatherhood, the Father of all the fathers of the earth, specially the Father of those who have specially shown a father-heart."

This Father would make to himself sons and daughters indeed. He would make such sons and daughters as shall be his sons and daughters not merely by having *come* from his heart, but by having *returned* thither—children in virtue of being such as whence they came, such as choose to be what he is.

He will have them share in his being and nature—strong wherein he cares for strength. He will have them tender and gracious as he is tender and gracious. He will have them angry where and as he is angry. Even in the small matter of power, he will have them able to do whatever his Son Jesus could on the earth, whose was the life of the perfect man, whose works were those of perfected humanity.

Everything must at length be subject to man, as it was to The Man. When God can do what he will with a man, the man may do what he will with the world. He may walk on the sea like his Lord. The deadliest thing will not he able to hurt him:—"He that believeth on me, the works that I do shall he do also; and greater than these shall he do."

God, whose pleasure brought
Man into being, stands away
As it were, an handbreath off, to give
Room for the newly-made to live.

GOD WILL NOT MAKE US SONS, WE MUST CHOOSE TO BE SONS

God has made us, but we have to be.

All things were made *through* the Word, but that which was made *in* the Word was life, and that life is the light of men. They who live by this light, that is, live as Jesus lived—namely, by obedience to the Father— have a share in their own making. The light becomes life in them. They are, in their lower way, alive with the life that was first born in Jesus and has now, through him, also been born in them. By obedience they become one with the godhead.

"As many as received him, to them gave he power to become the sons of God." He does not *make* them the sons of God, but he gives them power to *become* the sons of God. In choosing and obeying the truth, man becomes the true son of the Father of lights.

OTHER NEW TESTAMENT INDICATORS

It is enough to read with understanding the passage I have quoted from his epistle to the Galatians, to see that the word *adoption* does not in the least fit St. Paul's idea, or suit the things he says. While we but obey the law God has laid upon us, without knowing the heart of the Father whence comes the law, we are but slaves—not necessarily ignoble slaves, yet slaves nonetheless. But when we come to think *with* him, when the mind of the son is as the mind of the Father, when the action of the son is the same as that of the Father, then is that son *of* the Father indeed. Then is he a true son of God.

And in both passages—this from Galatians and that from St. Paul's epistle to the Romans which I have placed at the beginning of this sermon—we find the same phrase, *Abba, Father.* This shows, if proof is needed, that he uses the word υιοθεσια in the same sense in both. Nothing can be plainer than what that sense is.

Let us glance at the other passages in which St. Paul uses the same word. As he is the only writer of the New Testament who does use it, for all I know, he may have made it for himself. One of these uses is in the same eighth chapter of the epistle to the Romans. That one, however, I will keep to the last.

Another is in the following chapter, the fourth verse. There he speaks of the υιοθεσια, literally the *son-placing* (that is, the placing of sons in the true place of sons), as belonging to the Jews. On this I have but to remark that "whose is the υιοθεσια" cannot mean either that they had already received it, or that it belonged to the Jews more than to the Gentiles. It can only mean that, as the elder brother-nation, they had a foremost claim to it. They would naturally be the first to receive it, and, in their best men, had always been nearest to it. It must be brought to fruition first in those who had received the preparation necessary to receive it. Such were the Jews. And of the Jews, such was the Son, who brought the υιοθεσια, the sonship, to all.

Therefore to the Jew belonged the υιοθεσια, just as theirs was the gospel. It was to the Jew first, then to the Gentile—though many a Gentile would have it before many a Jew. Those and only those who out of a true heart cry "*Abba Father,*" be they of what paltry little so-called church, other than the body of Christ, they may, or of no other at all, are the sons and daughters of God.

St. Paul uses the word also in his epistle to the Ephesians, the first chapter, the fifth verse. "Having predestinated us unto the adoption of children by Jesus Christ to himself," says the authorized version; "Having foreordained us unto adoption as sons through Jesus Christ unto himself," says the revised. I see little difference between them—neither gives the meaning of St. Paul. If there is anything gained by the addition of the words *of children* in the one case, and *as sons* in the other, to translate the word for which "adoption" alone is made to serve in the other passages, the advantage is only to the minus-side, to that of the *wrong* interpretation.

Children we were. True sons we could never be, except through The Son. He brothers us. He takes us to the knees of the Father, beholding whose face we grow sons indeed. Never could we have known the heart of the Father, never felt it possible to love him as sons, except for him who cast himself into the gulf that yawned between us.

In and through him we were foreordained to the sonship. Even had we never sinned, we could never reach sonship without him. We should have been little children loving the Father indeed, but children far from the sonhood that understands and adores.

"For as many as are led by the spirit of God, these are sons of God."

"If any man hath not the spirit of Christ, he is none of his."

Indeed, if we have not each other's spirits, we do not belong to each other. There is no unity but having the same spirit. There is but one spirit, that of truth.

ST. PAUL'S LARGE MEANING

It remains to note yet one more passage.

Never in anything he wrote was it St. Paul's intention to contribute towards a system of theology. This is easy enough to show. One sign of the fact is that he does not hesitate to use this word he has perhaps himself made up, in different, and apparently opposing though by no means contradictory, senses.

St. Paul's meanings always enliven one another. His ideas are so large that they tax his utterance and make him strain the use of words. But there is no danger to the honest heart, which alone he regards, of misunderstanding them, though "the ignorant and unstedfast wrest them" yet. At one time he speaks of the sonship as being the possession of the Israelite, at another as his who has learned to cry *Abba, Father. A*nd here, in the passage I have now last to consider, that from the 18th to the 25th verse of this same eighth chapter of his epistle to the Romans, he speaks of the υιοθεσια as yet to come—and as if it had to do, not with our *spiritual*, but our *bodily* condition. This use of the word, however, though not the same use as we find anywhere else, is nevertheless entirely consistent with his other uses of it.

The 23rd verse says, "And not only so, but ourselves also, which have the first fruits of the spirit, even we ourselves groan within ourselves, waiting for adoption, the redemption of our body."

It is not difficult to discern that the ideas in this and his main use are necessarily associated and more than consistent. The putting of a son into his true, his foreordained place, has outward relations as well as inward reality. The outward depends on the inward. It arises from it and reveals it. When the child whose condition under former tutors has passed away, takes his position as a son, he naturally changes his dress and modes of life. When God's children cease to be slaves doing right from law and duty, and become his sons doing right from the essential love of God and their neighbour, they too must change the garments of their slavery for the robes of liberty. They will then lay aside the body of this death, and appear in bodies like that of Christ, with whom they inherit of the Father.

But many children who have learned to cry *Abba, Father*, are yet far from the liberty of the sons of God. Sons they are and no longer children, yet they groan as being still in bondage!

Plainly the apostle has no thought of working out a theologic doctrine. With burning heart he is writing a letter. Nevertheless, he gives lines plentifully sufficient for us to work out his idea. And this is how it takes clear shape:—

We are the sons of God the moment we lift up our hearts, seeking to be sons—the moment we begin to cry *Father*. But as the world must be redeemed in a few men to begin with, so the soul is redeemed in a few of its thoughts and wants and ways, to begin with. It takes a long time to finish the new creation of this redemption. Shall it have taken millions of years to bring the world up to the point where a few of its inhabitants shall desire God, and then shall the creature of this new birth be perfected in a day? The divine process may indeed now go on with tenfold rapidity, for the new factor of man's fellow-working, for the sake of which the whole previous array of means and forces existed, is now developed. But its end is yet far below the horizon of man's vision:—

The apostle speaks at one time of the thing as to come, at another time as finished—when because of our ways of thought it is but begun. A man's heart may leap for joy the moment when, amidst the sea-waves, a strong hand has laid hold of the hair of his head. He may cry aloud, "I am saved." And indeed, he may be safe. But he is not yet saved. This is far from a sufficient salvation. So are we sons even when we begin to cry *Father*. But we are far from perfected sons. So long as there is in us the least taint of distrust, the least lingering of hate or fear, we have not fully received the sonship. We do not yet have such life in us as raised the body of Jesus. We have not yet attained to the resurrection of the dead—by which word, in his epistle to the Philippians (3:2), St. Paul means, I think, the same thing as here he means by the sonship which he puts in apposition with the redemption of the body:—

Until our outward condition is that of full royal and divine sons, so long as the garments of our souls, these mortal bodies, are mean and torn and dragged and stained, so long as we groan under sickness and weakness and weariness and old age and forgetfulness and all things heavy to bear...so long we have not yet received the sonship in full. So long as all these conditions remain in us, we are but getting ready one day to creep from our chrysalids, and spread the great heaven-storming wings of the psyches of God.

We groan being burdened. We groan as we wait for the sonship—which is the redemption of the body, the uplifting of the body to be a fit house and revelation of the indwelling spirit, and even more, to be like that of Christ, a fit temple and revelation of *the deeper indwelling God.*

For we shall always need bodies to manifest and reveal us to each other—bodies, then, that fit the soul with absolute truth of presentment and revelation. Hence the revealing of the sons of God, spoken of in the 19th verse, is the same thing as the redemption of the body. The body is redeemed when it is made fit for the sons of God. Then it becomes a revelation of them—the thing it was meant for and always, more or less imperfectly, was. Such it shall be when truth is strong enough in the sons of God to make it such—for it is the soul that makes the body. When we are the sons of God in heart and soul, then shall we be the sons of God in body too: "We shall be like him, for we shall see him as he is."

I care little to speculate on the nature of this redeemed body. I will say only two things as necessary to be believed about it. First, it will be a body that will reveal the same self as before. But, second, it will be a body to reveal the being *truly*—without the defects and imperfections of the former bodily revelation. Even through their corporeal presence we shall then know our own infinitely better, and find in them endlessly more delight, than before. These things we must believe, or else distrust the Father of our spirits. Till this redemption of the body arrives, the υιοθεσια is not fully accomplished, it is only upon the way. Nor can it come but by our working out the salvation he is working in us.

This redemption of the body—its deliverance from all that is amiss, awry, unfinished, weak, worn out, all that prevents the revelation of the sons of God, is called by the apostle, not certainly the "adoption," but the υιοθεσια, *the sonship in full manifestation.* It is the slave yet left in the sons and daughters of God that has betrayed them into even permitting the word *adoption* to mislead them!

To see how the whole utterance hangs together, read from the 18th verse to the 25th, especially noticing the 19th: "For the earnest expectation of the creation waiteth for the revealing" *(the outshining)* "of the sons of God." When the sons of God show as they are, taking, with the character, the appearance and the place that belong to their sonship, when the sons of God sit with *the* Son of God on the throne of their Father, then shall they be in potency of fact the lords of the lower creation, the bestowers of liberty and peace upon it. Then shall the creation, subjected to vanity for their sakes, find its freedom in their freedom, its gladness in their sonship. The animals will glory to serve them, will joy to come to them for help.

Let the heartless scoff, the unjust despise! The heart that cries *Abba, Father,* cries to the God of the sparrow and the oxen. Nor can hope go too far in hoping what that God will do for the creation that now groans and travails in pain because our higher birth is delayed. Shall not the judge of all the earth do right? Shall my heart be more compassionate than his?

If to any reader my interpretation be unsatisfactory, I pray him not to spend his strength in disputing my faith, but in making sure of his own progress on the way to freedom and sonship.

Only to the child of God is true judgment possible. Were it otherwise, what would it avail to prove this one or that right or wrong? Right opinion on questions the most momentous will deliver no man. Cure for any ill in me or about me there is none, but to become the son of God I was born to be. Until such I am, until Christ is born in me, until I am revealed a son of God, pain and trouble will endure—and God grant they may!

Call this presumption, and I can only widen my assertion—until you yourself are the son of God you were born to be, you will never find life a good thing. If I presume for myself, I presume for you also.

But I do not presume. Thus have both Jesus Christ and his love-slave Paul represented God—as a Father perfect in love, grand in self-forgetfulness, supreme in righteousness, devoted to the lives he has uttered. I will not believe less of the Father than I can conceive of glory after the lines he has given me, after the radiation of his glory in the face of his Son. He is the express image of the Father, by which we, his imperfect images, are to read and understand him. Imperfect, we have yet perfection enough to spell towards the perfect.

WHAT GLORY SHALL BE WHEN ALL CREATION KNOWS ITS FATHER

It comes to this then, after the grand theory of the apostle:—

The world exists for our education. It is the nursery of God's children served by troubled slaves, troubled because the children are themselves slaves—children but not good children. Beyond its own will or knowledge, the whole creation works for the development of the children of God into the sons of God.

When at last the children have arisen and gone to their Father, when they are clothed in the best robe with a ring on their hands and shoes on their feet, when they are shining out at length in their natural and predestined sonship, then shall the mountains and the hills break forth before them into singing. Then shall all the trees of the field clap their hands. Then shall the wolf dwell with the lamb, and the leopard lie down with the kid and the calf, and the young lion and the fatling together, and a little child shall lead them. Then shall the fables of a golden age which faith invented and unbelief threw into the past, unfold their essential reality, and the tale of paradise prove itself a truth by becoming a fact.

Then shall every ideal reveal itself a necessity, all aspiration although satisfied put forth yet longer wings, and the hunger after righteousness know itself blessed, because truth is at last revealed in its fullness, not as the opinion of any man, but as the Truth that is God himself.

Eleven

The Sword and the Shield

The Ancient Truth of Salvation

by
Michael Phillips

What, then, does the rediscovery of Universal Fatherhood imply about salvation?

Does it lessen the need for salvation? Does it change how we view salvation? Where do sin and the fall now fit into the equation?

One thing is certain: The truth of universal Fatherhood changes the *context* and *purpose* of salvation—its need, how it functions, and what it is intended to accomplish.

This new perspective—which is not *new* at all, but which represents the rediscovery of an ancient scriptural truth—neither ignores the fall nor makes the sin of mankind less serious. Sin, however, is now placed in its proper perspective—as a curse from which we must be *freed*, a virus from which we must be *healed*, a stumbling-block to childness which we must be *empowered to conquer*...not a capital crime for which we must be eternally *punished*.

Neither does this rediscovery of salvation's true nature ignore the differences that exist in humanity. Within God's family there are wayward children and obedient children. Some of the former are wildly rebellious and evil. Some of the latter are hypocritical and self-righteous. God has different purposes to accomplish within the hearts of each.

Childness is his eternal objective. Salvation is the means to accomplish that goal. But the journey toward that childness is uniquely individual, and will be an eternal pilgrimage for all.

BUT I SAY TO YOU—FATHERHOOD!

Jesus' "all things new" can be gloriously stated:
The Christian message is not one of *vengeance and doom*—God will punish sin forever. That is *old* covenant thinking. The *new* is a gospel of *love and hope*.
*But I say to you...*God is your Father!
He will help free and rescue you from your waywardness. He will empower you to put sin to death within yourselves, so that you can become his children.
He will heal you from the virus by saving you from all that is working the death of selfishness within you, redeeming you to become good and happy children. He brings salvation indeed.
From this recovered foundation of scriptural truth, salvation can be perceived in a wonderful new light—not based on a man-devised line of demarcation through the center of humanity separating the saved and the lost. Salvation, rather, is the glorious means by which a loving Father is reconciling his universal family back into oneness with himself and with one another.
His Fathering purpose is to save his children from every influence that prevents them living in the home of his Fatherhood. His salvation leads them toward what he created them to be—his perfect sons and daughters.

FROM-SALVATION

We can view salvation from two divergent perspectives.
Two opposite-pointing prepositions highlight this distinction. Are we being saved *from*...or saved *to*?
Are we fleeing *away*...or running *toward*?
Are we attempting to escape *out of*...or enter *into*?
From...or *to*?
Upon this imperative distinction hangs the essential core of the Christian faith. What *is* Christianity? Our answer to that question is determined by which of these two prepositions we define our relationship to God's Fatherhood.
Sad to say, the majority of Christians are believers in *From*-salvation. Because of their sin, they believe that they deserve eternal damnation. They are, with every other human being, on death row. The image of "God" represented by this theology is an Old Testament Sinai tyrant—an Almighty Holiness wielding a great sword of justice by which he is bound

to carry out that death sentence. They stand as a criminal under capital indictment, guilty as charged and deserving death.

If they turn to him, however, Jesus steps in front of the great Sword of God and holds up the Shield of Salvation. "Wait," he says. "Your Sword cannot touch the prisoner. He is protected by my Shield. If you must exact a death sentence, let the blade of your Sword fall on me. I lay the Shield down on my own behalf and place it in front of the sinner instead. You must honor its protection of him."

By claiming the advantage of a legal loophole in the spiritual law God has established, salvation is thus a mechanism, an escape hatch, a pardon and reprieve to "save" those who believe in Christ's Shield *from* hell and the death sentence of sin. If one knows how to appropriate the protection of the Shield, the sentence is commuted.

Knowing the mechanics of the legal loophole is the key. One must apply the formula of belief so that the Shield will avert the wrath of the Sword. Pardon from death row is instantly granted.

From-salvation saves the sinner *from* God, *from* the Sword of death, and *from* an eternity in hell.

TO-SALVATION

The rediscovery of the ancient truth of scripturally *true* salvation, on the other hand, builds upon an entirely different foundation.

There are no old-covenantal legal contrivances. Salvation grows out of Fatherhood and childship. As God's children we deserve *life*—indeed, perfect life. We are not on death row, we are children who have wandered from our Father.

Salvation is the roadmap back to our origin. Jesus is our elder brother. He knows the way to our Father. He offers us no *shield* to protect us from God, he offers his *hand.* He desires to lead us home.

We are saved so that we can run *to* our Father and leap into the embrace of his open arms.

Once begun on that journey, the salvationary roadmap is our instruction manual—with our hand in the hand of Jesus as he guides, teaches, and leads along the way—in learning to put to death the impulses that prevent living the life we were created to enjoy, and which caused us to stray in the first place.

To-salvation offers return into life within the Father's family. It offers freedom from the selfish independence that blocks childness. No docrinal mechanism of *belief* defines salvation but a restored relationship with our Creator.

Out of this new relationship flows a practical lifestyle of childlike obedient *faith* (defined and exampled by Jesus.) It becomes our joy to live in obedience as sons and daughters. We know that we dwell, as MacDonald phrases it, "in the air of an eternal fatherhood." [53]

The preposition "from" remains powerfully alive at the center of this revolutionary salvationary paradigm. But the "from" of old-covenantalism is turned upside-down. The salvation God offers is a salvation *from* sin...*into* Fatherhood!

CHILDSHIP WITHIN THE DIVINE FATHERHOOD

George MacDonald goes yet farther. Salvation, he maintains, offers the opportunity to be eternally delivered, not from the *consequences* of sin, but, far more importantly, from the *desire* to sin, and ultimately even from the *capacity* to sin. We are saved from that within ourselves which causes sin.

"God is determined..." MacDonald writes, "to have his children clean, clear, pure as very snow...that not only shall they with his help make up for whatever wrong they have done, but at length be incapable, by eternal choice of good, under any temptation, of doing...the thing God would not do." [54]

This new paradigm of salvation requires an entirely overhauled perspective of sin—what it is, its cause, and wherein lies our deliverance from its control.

Sin is *whatever* prevents us being fully God's children. Sin is selfishness of motive, attitude, and action. Sin is disobeying and disregarding God as the Father of life. Sin is living unto ourselves without regard for our Father-God.

Paul truly says that the wages of sin are death. This death, however, is not the death of eternal damnation. The death produced by sin is the death of a child's heart. The wages of sin is the death of childship. We must be saved from this death and made alive to childship.

Jesus came as the perfect and obedient Son to redeem and deliver us, not from death at the Sword of Justice, but from the death of childship. The obedient childship of Jesus is our eternal destiny.

He examples to us the childship.

He awakens within us childship

He leads us into childship.

The new birth, therefore, saves us *to* become children again! We are saved into childship within the divine Fatherhood. Our salvation births the potentiality of putting to death within ourselves the motives of independence that prevent us being pure and obedient sons and daughters of God, as Jesus himself was *the* pure and perfect Son of God.

To-salvation takes us *to* our Father, *to* life in his family, and *to* a contented walk through the rest of our days in the humility of childness.

Problems will not disappear. Blessings will not automatically flow in. Sickness and heartache will not be eliminated. We will not be happy every moment. In some ways life does not change at all. At the same time, *everything* changes. Walking in childness in the air of an eternal Fatherhood, defining life by his will not our own, modifies our outlook and perspective in the midst of everything life throws at us. We have a good Father, not who removes life's troubles, but who is watching out for us and taking care of us in the midst of them. It is those very troubles he uses to fashion us into his own likeness. They are a necessary part of salvation's ultimate purpose.

A LIFETIME OF GROWTH INTO CHILDSHIP

The practical and theological result of all this reveals a simple truth: Salvation is a *process* not an *event*. Salvation does not take place in a moment, it deepens over a lifetime. We are not "saved," we are in the process of *becoming* saved.

Being saved from the capacity and desire to sin takes a lifetime of self-denial and relinquishment of self-motive. It requires years of reorientation away from the values of the world toward God's ways. This overhaul of perspective necessitates an equally revamped focus toward much in the Christian "world" steeped in belief-legalisms rather than the self-denying faith of childness.

Wrongly taught that salvation is a life-event rather than a lifetime of childship, the vast majority of believers never begin such growth in this life. They are no more "saved" into the childship of Christlikeness than most non-Christians. The sin-deathing process of self-denying salvation is scarcely begun in them.

For all these reasons, MacDonald loathed so-called "plans of salvation," which were just as prevalent in his day as they are in ours. He loathed them because, purporting to tell people how to be saved, they actually teach people *falsely* about what God desires to accomplish in their lives.

WHAT ABOUT FEAR?

A common argument against universal reconciliation stems from the concern that it removes fear from the salvationary equation. Human beings are motivated by fear. Fear of getting in trouble makes us mind our parents. Fear of failure makes us study. Fear of getting fired makes us work hard. And for some, fear of hell lurking in the background makes them obey the Bible and go to church and live upright lives.

It would make an interesting study to know, in the history of

123

Christianity, what percentage of "sinner's prayers" and "altar confessions" have been prompted in some measure by fear of hell. The urgent pleas of many of history's renown evangelists have clearly been based on fear of God's wrath. This emphasis, however, is not observed in "hellfire and brimstone" preachers alone. In how many subtle ways do the usual offers of "eternal life" presented within Christendom rely on the unscriptural salvationary paradigm of being saved *from* God's Sword of Punishment, rather being saved to *become* children of a good and loving and open-armed forgiving Father.

Remove fear, say opponents of a message of hope, and the basis for evangelism is gone.

Such objections highlight the truth that universal reconciliation assuredly changes the salvation message. Yet do we cling to a falsehood to preserve an imaginary threat to hold over people's heads? What a perverted basis by which to introduce a new believer into a life of faith. If such is the basis for our evangelism, we might as well eat, drink, and make merry for tomorrow we die. If we cannot introduce the world to the claims of Jesus and the Fatherhood of God by *truth*, we have little to offer at all.

We must preach *true* salvation. If there are fewer responses to impassioned altar calls, those who do respond to the gospel message will be responding to *truth*. They will thus have the means to respond to Fatherhood, not to an imaginary "Christian" Molech of a god.

WHERE DOES HELL FIT INTO THE NEW EQUATION OF SALVATION?

All this, however, begs a deeper point: Universal reconciliation does *not* remove the basis for fear of hell.

The fear-objection is raised by those who have no understanding of what is actually involved in the profound teaching of universal reconciliation. That "deeper magic from before the dawn of time" points toward a *more* stringent level of personal accountability for sin than the "cheap grace" of traditional orthodoxy.

An afterlife vision with God's continued work of redemption as an active force to root sin out of the universe gives *more* urgency to our need of salvation, properly understood, not less. Accountability is *heightened*. In truth, it is the "cheap grace" of Calvinistic theology that offers the easy way out. Those who object to universal reconciliation on the basis of a too-easy salvation have their argument exactly upside down.

With power and precision, George MacDonald clarifies this new salvationary paradigm of fear in his sermon "The Consuming Fire." His words from Chapter 7 bear repeating: "When we say that *God is Love*, do we teach men that their fear of him is groundless? No. For as much as they fear will come upon them, possibly far more…Can it be any comfort to them to be told that God loves them so that he will burn them clean? Can the cleansing of the fire appear to them anything beyond what it must always, more or less, be—a process of torture?" [55]

The message of universal reconciliation, therefore, is no casual theology that blithely asserts that everyone will eventually be saved, adding the unspoken corollary that nothing in this life really matters. This simplistic construction completely misses the imperative foundation. The glorious truth woven through MacDonald's writings as a crystalline, subtly-conveyed vision never obscures the truth of *how* God's final redemption will be achieved—through Malachi's purifying furnace of fire.

The *full* message of this wonderful truth must be seen. The Lord's "all things new" salvation is no peaches-and-cream escape hatch. It is salvation unto sonship. It is salvation from ourselves. It is salvation *into* childship!

God *will* make us into sons and daughters. We must *choose* to be his sons and daughters. The longer we delay, the more painful will be that choosing and the self-deathing process that childship requires. Delaying *too* long may render inevitable that our salvation has no means of consummation other than through the consuming fire of the great purifying Furnace.

All half truth leads ultimately to error. The truth that God may redeem the whole universe is but *half* the truth. Misunderstood, this half of the equation leads to error as surely as its opposite. All mankind *may* be saved. But all mankind will *also* be held accountable. That accountability is founded not on fear of God's wrath but in the penetrating, forgiving, childship-producing love of his Fatherhood.

What else does the pure heart want but to be held accountable? We have a Father who will hold us accountable because he desires that we become like him…and who, in the purity of his love for us, is waiting for us to run into his arms.

This is gospel indeed!

A CHILDSHIP OF *BECOMING*

The truth needs repeating: Salvation does not occur in a moment of time. This truth requires continual emphasis because the "salvation moment" mentality is so deeply ingrained in Christendom. It is a false notion that must be utterly swept away before we can apprehend God's high eternal purposes.

Salvation *cannot* be achieved by a public profession of faith, by a moment of repentance, in the act of joining a church, through baptism, by a sinner's prayer, by confirmation, nor by any other act or event. All these may open doors *toward* salvation, but they do not *produce* salvation. Neither is salvation characterized by the assent to a particular set of ideas or doctrines. Nor is it marked by the faithful adherence to those beliefs, whether Catholic, Protestant, Orthodox, or any other set of doctrinal formulas.

Salvation is neither experiential nor intellectual, neither doctrinal nor theological, nor identified primarily by *belief.* All these, MacDonald says, may make one a good "churchman." They will not make one a Christian. [56]

Salvation can *only* be defined as *living lifestyle* of childship-faith within the family of God's Fatherhood, energized by God's Spirit, and characterized by *obedience* to the commands, instructions, and example of Jesus Christ as they come to us in the four gospels.

The question, "When were you saved?" exposes an entirely false premise. Though they may (or may not) *begin* at an instant of time, all the complex components of what the Bible means by "salvation" are progressive. Such *beginnings* constitute the genesis of a lifelong *process* of salvation.

Salvation has no past tense. Salvation is an ongoing, moment-by-moment eternal *Now* of becoming.

EXCERPTS FROM THE WRITINGS OF GEORGE MACDONALD
ON SALVATION

At the moment he says *Follow me,* he is following the Father. His face is set homeward. He would have us follow him because he is bent on the will of the Blessed. It is nothing even thus to think of him, except thus we *believe* in him—that is, so *do.*

To believe in him is to do as he does, to follow him where he goes.

We must believe in him *practically*—altogether practically, as he believed in his Father. Our belief is not in one concerning whom we have to hold something, but as one whom we have to follow out of the body of this death into life eternal. To follow him is not to take him in any way theoretically, to hold this or that theory about why he died, or wherein lay his atonement. Such things can be revealed only to those who follow him in his active being and the principle of his life—who *do as he did* and *live as he lived.*

There is no other following. He is all for the Father. We must be all for the Father too, otherwise are we not following him. To follow him is to be learning of him, to think his thoughts, to use his judgments, to see things as he saw them, to feel things as he felt them, to be hearted, souled, minded, as he was—that so also we may be of the same mind with his Father.

This it is to deny self and go after him. Nothing less, even if it be working miracles and casting out devils, is to be his disciple. Busy from morning to night doing great things for him on any other road, we will but earn the reception, "I never knew you.". [57]

"God's not like a proud man to take offense, Grannie. There's nothing that pleases him like the truth, and there's nothing that displeases him like lying, particularly when it's pretended praise. He wants no false praising. Now, *you* say things about him sometimes that sound fearsome to me."

"What kind o' things, laddie?" asked the old lady, with offense glooming in the background.

"Like when you speak of him as if he was a poor, proud man, full of his own importance and ready to be down on anybody that didn't call him by the name of his office—always thinking about his own glory, instead of the quiet, mighty, grand, self-forgetting, all-creating, loving being that he is. Eh, Grannie! Think of the face of that man of sorrows, that never said a hard word to a sinful woman or a despised publican. Was he thinking about his own glory, do you think? And whatever isn't like Christ isn't like God."

"But laddie, he came t' satisfy God's justice by sufferin' the punishment due t' oor sins, t' turn aside his wrath an' curse. So Jesus couldn't be *altogether* God."

"Oh, but he is, Grannie. He came to satisfy God's justice by giving him back his children, by making them see that God was just, by sending them back home to fall at his feet. He came to lift the weight of the sins off the shoulders of them that did them by making them turn against the sin and before God. And there isn't a word of reconciling God to us in the Testament, for there was no need of that; it was *us* that needed to be reconciled to him. And so he bore our sins and carried our sorrows, for those sins caused him no end of grief of mind and pain in his body. It wasn't his own sins or God's wrath that caused him suffering, but our own sins. And he took them away. He took our sins upon him, for he came into the middle of them and took them up—by no sleight of hand, by no quibbling of the preachers about imputing his righteousness to us and such like. But he took them and took them away, and here am I, Grannie, growing out of my sins in consequence, and there are you, growing out of yours in consequences, too." [58]

Twelve

Salvation From Sin

by
George MacDonald

From *The Hope of the Gospel* [59]

Edited by Michael Phillips

—and thou shalt call his name Jesus; for he shall save his people from their sins.
—Matthew 1:21

Everything in the world is more or less misunderstood at first. We have to learn what it is, and come at length to see that it must be so, that it could not be otherwise. Then we will know it. And we never *really* know a truth until we know it in this way.

In this light, I would help some understand what Jesus came from the home of our Father to be to us, and do for us.

THE TRUE SOURCE OF LIFE'S DISCOMFORTS

There is no doubt scarcely a person alive who, if he or she spoke openly, would not confess to things that plague him from which he would like to be free and that make it impossible for him to regard life as an altogether good thing. Most imagine that, free of such and such antagonistic influences, life would be much happier, and that this happiness could be prolonged indefinitely.

The causes of these discomforts are of all kinds. They extend from simple uneasiness to such severe suffering as makes death itself seem welcome. Perhaps the greater part of this world's energy is consumed in some way with the effort to rid ourselves of discomfort.

To escape it, some attempt to leave their natural surroundings behind them. With strong and continuous effort to rise in the social scale, they discover at every new ascent fresh trouble, as they think, awaiting them. In truth they have brought the trouble with them.

Others, striving to be rich, are slow to find out that the poverty of their souls, none the less that their bank accounts are growing, will yet keep them unhappy.

Some seek endless change, never realizing that the only change that will set them free is the change that must come within their own hearts.

Others expand their souls with knowledge, only to find that contentment will not dwell in the great house they have built.

To number the varieties of such human endeavour to escape discomfort would be to list all the kinds of such life as does not know how to live. All such people seek to eliminate what they perceive as the *cause* of their misery, but which is only the changeable *expression* of it—the cause of the shape it takes, not of the misery itself. For when one apparent cause is removed, another at once rises to take its place. The real cause of the trouble is something whose existence such persons do not yet even recognize. In any case, they are not yet acquainted with its true nature.

However absurd the statement may appear to one who has not yet discovered the fact for himself, the cause of every man's discomfort is evil, moral evil.

This evil appears first of all in himself. It is his own sin, his own wrongness, his own unrightness. Then secondly, it appears in those he loves. I will not now deal with this latter, for the only way to get rid of it is for the man to get rid of his own sin.

No special sin may be recognizable as causing this or that special physical discomfort. Such may indeed have originated with some ancestor. But sin in ourselves is the cause of its continuance. Our own sin is also the source of its necessity, and is the very thing that prevents that patience which would soon take the discomfort from it, or at least blunt its sting.

The evil is *essentially* unnecessary. It passes as soon as pure will in man is attained, which is the only reason it is permitted. The suffering also is essentially unnecessary. But while the evil lasts, the suffering, whether resulting from or merely accompanying it, is absolutely necessary.

MAN'S FIRST BUSINESS

Foolish is the man, and there are many such men, who would rid himself or his fellows of discomfort by setting the world right, by waging war on the evils around him, while he neglects that integral part of the world where lies his business, his first business—namely, his own character and conduct. Even if it were possible—an absurd supposition—that the world could thus be righted from the outside, it would yet be impossible for the man who had contributed to the work, remaining what he was, to enjoy the perfection of the result. He would still himself not be in tune with the organ he had tuned. It would still sound to him a confused, jarring instrument.

The philanthropist who regards the wrong as in the race, forgetting that the race is made up of conscious and wrongly tuned individuals, forgets also that wrong is always generated in and done by an individual. Those who attempt to do good by overlooking the wrongness in the individual, ignore the root cause of sin by attributing wrong merely to a *tendency* in the race.

But no evil can be cured in the race, except by its being cured in its individuals. The tendency toward sin is not absolute evil. The tendency is there that it may be resisted, not yielded to. There is no way of making three men right but by making right each one of the three. But a cure in one man who repents and turns is a beginning of the cure of the whole human race.

Even if a man's suffering did not originate with his own sin, and even if this life would not be long enough by faith and obedience to cure it, faith and obedience will yet render it endurable, and will overflow in help to his fellow-sufferers. The groaning body, wrapped in the garment of hope, will, with outstretched neck, look for its redemption, and endure.

THE ONLY CURE

The one cure for any organism is to be set right—to have all its parts brought into harmony with each other. The one comfort is to know that this cure is in process.

Rightness alone is cure. The return of the organism to its true self is its only possible ease. To free a man from suffering, he must be set right, put in health.

The health at the root of man's being, his rightness, is to be free from wrongness. In other words, from sin. A man is right when there is no wrong in him. The wrong, the evil, is *in* him. He must be set free from it.

I do not mean set free from the sins he has done: that will follow. I mean set free from the sins he is *doing*, or is capable of doing. I mean set free from the sins in his being which spoil his nature—the wrongness in him. I mean set free from the evil he consents to.

In short, a man must be set free from the sin he *is*, which makes him do the sin he *does*.

To save a man from his sins is to say to him in a perfect and eternal sense, "Rise up and walk. Be at liberty in your essential being. Be free as the son of God is free."

To do this for us, Jesus was born, and remains born to all the ages.

When misery drives a man to call out to the source of his life—and I take the increasing outcry in our day against existence as a sign of the growth of the race toward a sense of the need of regeneration—the answer, I think, will come in a quickening of his conscience. This will probably not be what the man desires, for no man wants an uneasy conscience. He wants only to be rid of his suffering. But that he cannot have except in being delivered from its essential root, a thing infinitely worse than any suffering it can produce. If he will not accept that deliverance, he must endure his suffering. And often it is only through the chastisement of further suffering that he at last comes to accept the only way that leads into the freedom of being.

There can be no deliverance but to come out of his evil dream into the glory of God.

It is true that Jesus came, in delivering us from our sins, to deliver us also from the painful consequences of those sins. But these consequences exist by one law of the universe, the true will of the perfect God. When that law is broken and disobeyed by the creature, suffering is inevitable. It is the natural consequence of an unnatural relation. And in the perfection of God's creation, the result tends toward the cure of the cause. The pain works toward the healing of the breach.

The Lord never came to deliver men from the consequences of their sins while yet those sins remained. That would be to cast out of the window the medicine of cure while yet the man lay sick. It goes directly against the very laws of being. Yet men, loving their sins, and feeling nothing of their dread hatefulness, have, consistent with their low condition, constantly taken this word concerning the Lord to mean that he came to save them from the punishment of their sins.

HE DID NOT COME TO SAVE US FROM HELL

This idea—which I would rather call a miserable fancy—has terribly corrupted the preaching of the gospel. The message of the good news has not been truly delivered. Unable to believe in the forgiveness of their Father in heaven, imagining him not at liberty to forgive, or incapable of forgiving freely, not really believing him God our Saviour but rather a God bound, either in his own nature or by a law above him and compulsory upon him, to exact some recompense or satisfaction for sin, a multitude of teaching men have taught their fellows that Jesus came to bear our punishment and save us from hell. They have represented a *result* as the *object* of his mission. And this result is one that would not even be desired by true men unless it produced fulfillment of the Lord's higher objective.

The mission of Jesus came from the same source and had the same objective as the punishment of our sins. He came to work *along with* our punishment. He came to side with it, and thus set us free from our sins.

No man is safe from hell until he is free from his sins. But a man to whom the evil in him is a burden, while he may indeed sometimes feel as if he were in hell, will soon forget that ever he had any other hell to think of than that of his sinful condition. To him his sins are hell enough. He would gladly go to the other hell to be free of them. Free of them, hell itself would be endurable.

For hell is God's and not the devil's. Hell is on the side of God and man, to free the child of God from the corruption of death. Not one soul will ever be redeemed from hell but by being saved from his sins, from the evil in him. If hell be needful to save him, hell will blaze, and the worm will writhe and bite, until he takes refuge in the will of the Father. "Salvation from hell" is salvation as conceived by such to whom hell and not evil is the terror. But if even for dread of hell a poor soul seek the Father, he will be heard by him in his terror, and taught by him to seek the immeasurably greater gift. And thus in the greater will he also receive the less.

JESUS SAVES FROM ONGOING LIVE SIN

There is another important misapprehension of the words of the messengers of the good tidings—that they threaten us with punishment because of the sins we have committed, whereas their true message is of *forgiveness* not *vengeance*, of deliverance not punishment to come. Not for anything he has committed does the gospel threaten a man with the outer darkness. A man shall not be condemned for any or all of his sins that are past. Not for the worst of them needs he dread remaining unforgiven. The sin he dwells in, the sin he will not come out of, is the sole ruin of a man.

Our present *live* sins—those pervading our thoughts and ruling our conduct, the sins we keep doing, and will not give up, the sins we are called to abandon yet cling to, the same sins which are the cause of our misery though we may not know it—these are they for which we are even now condemned. It is true that the memory of the wrongs we have done may become very bitter. But we are not condemned for those. And if that in our character which made them possible is abolished, remorse will lose its worst bitterness in the hope of future amends. "This is the condemnation, that light is come into the world, and men loved darkness rather than light, because their deeds were evil."

It is the indwelling badness, ready to produce bad actions, that we need to be delivered from. If a man will not fight against this badness, he is left to sin and reap the consequences. To be saved from these consequences would be no deliverance. It would be an immediate and ever deepening damnation.

He came to deliver us from the evil in our being—no essential part of it, thank God! He came to free us from the miserable fact that as children of God we do not care for our father and will not obey him, causing us to *desire* wrongly, *act* wrongly, or, even when we try not to act wrongly, yet still *feeling* wrongly. He came to deliver us, not from the things we have done, but the possibility of doing such things anymore.

With the departure of this possibility, and with the hope of confession hereafter to those we have wronged, will depart also the power over us of the evil things we have done. And so we shall be saved from them also.

The bad that lives in us, our evil judgments, our unjust desires, our hate and pride and envy and greed and self-satisfaction—these are the souls of our sins. These live sins are more terrible than the bodies of our sins, namely the deeds we do. For our live sin not only produces these loathsome things, but makes us as loathsome as they. Our wrong deeds are but dead works. Our evil thoughts are live sins. These sins that dwell and work in us are the essential opposites of faith and love and are the sins from which Jesus came to deliver us. When we turn against them and refuse to obey them, they rise in fierce insistence. But the same moment they begin to die. We are then on the Lord's side, as he has always been on ours, and he begins to deliver us from them.

EVEN TINY SINS MUST GO

Anything in you, which, in your own child, would make you feel him not so pleasant as you would have him, is something wrong. This may mean much to one, little or nothing to another. Things in a child which to one parent would not seem worth minding, would fill another with horror. Concerning his moral development, where the one parent would smile, the other would look aghast, perceiving both the present evil and the serpent-brood to follow.

But as the love of him who is love transcends ours as the heavens are higher than the earth, so must he desire in his child infinitely more than the most vigilant love of the best mother can desire in hers. He would have each of us rid of all discontent, all fear, all grudging, all bitterness in word or thought, all gauging and measuring of our own with a different standard from what we apply to others. He will have no curling of the lip, no indifference in us to the one whose service in any form comes to us, no desire to excel another, no contentment at gaining by someone else's loss. He will not have us receive the smallest kindness without gratitude, would not hear from us so much as a tone of voice to jar the heart of another, nor word to make it ache, be the ache ever so fleeting.

Jesus was born to deliver us from all such and other sin—not, primarily from the punishment of any of them. When all are gone, the holy punishment will have departed also.

He came to make us good, and therein blessed children.

THE HIGHEST IN MAN—THE WILL

One master-sin is at the root of all the rest. It is no individual action, or anything that comes of mood or feeling. It is the non-recognition by man, and consequent inactivity in him, of the highest of all relations, that relation which is the root and first essential condition of every other true relation in the human soul. It is the absence in man of harmony with the Being whose thought is man's existence, whose word is man's power of thought.

It is true that, being thus his offspring, as St. Paul affirms, God cannot ever be far from any one of us. If we were not in closest contact to the creating and creative love, we could not exist at all. We have within ourselves no power to live nor to continue living. But there is a closer contact still that is absolutely necessary to our well-being and highest existence.

For the highest creation of God in man is his will. And until the highest in man meets the highest in God, their true relation is not yet a spiritual fact. The flower lies in the root, but the root is not the flower. The relation exists, but while one of the parties neither knows, loves, nor acts upon it, the relation is yet unborn.

The highest in man is neither his intellect nor his imagination nor his reason. All are inferior to his will, and indeed, in a grand way, dependent upon it. Man's will must meet God's—a will *distinct* from God's, otherwise no *harmony* is possible between them. Not the less, therefore, but the more, is all God's. For God creates in man the power to will His will. It may cost God a suffering man can never know to bring individual men and women to the point at which they will His will. But when we are brought to that point, and commit ourselves to the doing of the will of God, we become one with God, and the end of God in man, and the end for which Jesus was born and died, is gained. The man is saved from his sins, and the universe flowers yet again in his redemption.

THE ONLY WAY—TO BE LIKE HIM

I would not be supposed, from what I have said, to imagine the Lord without sympathy for the sorrows and pains which reveal what sin is, and by means of which he would make men sick of sin. He sympathizes with everything human. But evil is not human. It is the defect and opposite of the human. The suffering that follows it, however, is human. It belongs of necessity to the human that has sinned. While it is at root caused by sin, suffering acts for the *benefit* of the sinner, helping toward his deliverance from his sin.

Jesus is in himself aware of every human pain. He feels it also. In him too it is pain. With the energy of tenderest love he wills his brothers and sisters free, that he may fill them to overflowing with essential joy. For that they were indeed created.

But from the moment of their existence, truth becomes a yet higher thing than happiness. And he must first of all make them true. If it were possible, however, for pain to continue after evil was gone, he would never rest while one ache yet remained in the world. Perfect in sympathy, he feels in himself the tortured presence of every nerve that lacks its true rest. The man may recognize the wrongness in him only as pain. He may know little and care nothing about his sins. Yet nonetheless is the Lord sorry for his pain.

He cries aloud, "Come unto me, all ye that labour and are heavy laden, and I will give you rest." He does not say, "Come unto me, all ye that feel the burden of your sins." He opens his arms to all who are weary enough to come to him in the poorest hope of rest. Right gladly would he free them from their misery. But he knows only one way: He will teach them to be like himself, meek and lowly, bearing with gladness the yoke of his father's will.

THE CURE FOR ALL—THE WILL OF THE FATHER

This is the one, the only right, the only possible way of freeing mankind from the sins which are the cause of their unrest. With man the weariness, discomfort, and suffering come first. With him the sins are first. There is but one cure for both—the will of the Father. That which is his joy will be our deliverance!

The disobedient and selfish would prefer to keep hell in their hearts and yet possess the liberty and gladness that belong to purity and love. But they cannot have them. They are weary and heavy-laden, both with what they are, and because of what they were made for but are not. The

Lord knows what they need. They know only what they want. They want ease. He knows they need purity.

But for his resolve to purify them, their very existence would be an evil of which their maker must rid his universe. That which is not growing must at length die out of creation. How can he keep in his sight a foul presence? Will the creator send forth his virtue to keep alive a thing that is determined to remain evil—a thing that ought not to exist and has no claim but to cease? The Lord himself would not live except with an existence absolutely good.

IN OBEDIENCE IS OUR ONLY DELIVERANCE

It may be my reader will desire me to say *how* the Lord will deliver us from our sins. That is like the lawyer's "Who is my neighbour?" The spirit of such a mode of receiving the offer of the Lord's deliverance is the root of all the horrors of a corrupt theology, so acceptable to those who love weak and beggarly hornbooks of religion. Such questions spring from the passion for the fruit of the tree of knowledge not the fruit of the tree of life.

Men would understand: they do not care to *obey*—understand where it is impossible they should understand except by obeying. They would search into the work of the Lord instead of doing their part in it—thus making it impossible both for the Lord to go on with his work, and for themselves to become capable of seeing and understanding what he does. Instead of immediately obeying the Lord of life, the one condition upon which he can help them, and in itself the beginning their deliverance, they set themselves to question their unenlightened intellects as to his plans for their deliverance—and not merely how he means to effect it, but how he can be able to effect it.

They would bind their Samson until they have scanned his limbs and muscles. Incapable of understanding the first motions of freedom in themselves, they proceed to interpret the riches of God's divine soul in terms of their own beggarly notions— paraphrasing his glorious verse into their own paltry commercial prose. And then, in the growing presumption of imagined success, they insist upon their neighbours' acceptance of their distorted shadows of "the plan of salvation" as the truth of him in whom is no darkness, and the one condition of their acceptance with him.

They delay setting their foot on the stair which alone can lead them to the house of wisdom, until they shall have determined the material and mode of its construction. For the sake of knowing, they postpone that which alone can enable them to know. They substitute for the true understanding which lies beyond, a false persuasion that they already understand. They will not accept, that is, act upon, their highest privilege, that of obeying the Son of God.

It is on them that do his will, that the day dawns. To them the day-star arises in their hearts. Obedience is the soul of knowledge.

By obedience, I intend no kind of obedience to man, or submission to authority claimed by man or community of men. I mean obedience to the will of the Father, however revealed in our conscience.

God forbid I should seem to despise understanding. The New Testament is full of urgings to understand. Our whole life, to be life at all, must be a growth in understanding. What I cry out upon is the misunderstanding that comes of man's endeavour to understand while not obeying. Upon obedience our energy must be spent. Understanding will follow.

Not anxious to know our duty, or knowing it and not doing it, how shall we understand that which only a true heart and a clean soul can ever understand? The power in us that would understand if it were free, lies in the bonds of imperfection and impurity. It is therefore incapable of judging the divine. It cannot see the truth. If it could see it, it would not know it and would not have it. Until a man begins to obey, the light that is in him is darkness.

WHEN WE SET OURSELVES TO OBEY THE LORD HELPS US

Any honest soul may understand this much, however—for it is a thing we may of ourselves judge to be right—that the Lord cannot save anyone from his sins while that man or woman yet holds to his sins.

It is a notion too absurd for mockery that an omnipotent God could do and not do the same thing at the same moment. An omnipotence that could at once make a man free, and at the same time leave him a self-degraded slave, is equally absurd. That God could make him the very likeness of himself, and yet good only because he could not help being good, is an idea of the same character and equally self-contradictory.

But the Lord is not unreasonable. He requires no high motives where such could not yet exist. He does not say, "You must be sorry for your sins, or you need not come to me." To be sorry for his sins a man must love God and man, and love is the very thing that has to be developed in him. It is but common sense that a man, longing to be freed from suffering, or made able to bear it, should take himself to the Power who created him and gives him life. Equally is it common sense that, if a man would be delivered from the sin within him, he must himself begin to cast it out. He must himself begin to disobey the urge to sin, and work toward righteousness within himself. Furthermore, it is common sense that a man should look for and expect the help of his Father in the endeavour. Alone, he might labour to all eternity and not succeed. He who has not made himself, cannot set himself right without him who made him. But his maker is in him, and is his strength.

The man, however, who, instead of doing what he is told, broods speculating on the metaphysics of him who calls him to his work, stands leaning his back against the door by which the Lord would enter to help him. The moment he sets about putting straight the thing that is crooked— I mean doing right where he has been doing wrong—he withdraws from the entrance, and makes room for the Master to come in.

We cannot make ourselves pure, but we can leave that which is impure. We can spread out the "defiled, discoloured web" of our lives before the bleaching sun of righteousness. We cannot save ourselves, but we can let the Lord save us. The struggle of our weakness is as essential to the coming victory as the strength of Him who resisted unto death, striving against sin.

The sum of the whole matter is this:—The Son has come from the Father to set the children free from their sins. The children must hear and obey him, that he may send forth judgment unto victory.

Son of our Father, help us to do what thou sayest, and so with thee die unto sin, that we may rise to the sonship for which we were created. Help us to repent even to the sending away of our sins.

THIRTEEN

GOD GONE WRONG

How old covenant legalism infiltrated the new wineskins:
A revised perspective of wrath and predestination

by
Michael Phillips

M any may wonder, if the perspectives of the prevalent orthodoxy of
Christianity are in error, why multitudes of Christians believe them
so readily?

How could falsehoods take such deep and extensive root throughout
Christendom? Does not their widespread acceptance actually argue in
favor of their veracity? Surely the vast majority of Christians and their
leaders, teachers, pastors, theologians, and priests cannot be so unseeing
of truth.

How could Christian theology have gone so wrong?

CHRISTIAN TEACHERS HAVE MISREPRESENTED GOD

George MacDonald puzzled over this very perplexity. His conclusion
was that God has gone wrong in the belief systems of Christians because
of a passion for *knowledge*, in the form of *intellectual legalism*, rather
than a passion for truth.

Men love doctrine, men love the intellect, men love *head-knowledge*
more than they love *heart-obedience*. Not obeying, therefore, their
theories of Christianity become darkness. According to MacDonald,
unbelieving legalism is at root of all the evils that grew out of the gospel
to explain rather than to *do* it.

"The greatest obscuration of the words of the Lord..." he wrote
"comes from those who give themselves to interpret rather than do them.

Theologians have done more to hide the gospel of Christ than any of its adversaries. It was not for our understandings, but our will, that Christ came. He who does that which he sees, shall understand; he who is set upon understanding rather than doing, shall go on stumbling and mistaking and speaking foolishness." [60]

He continues with strong words for the theologians and teachers who perpetuate these ideas. "How terribly...have the theologians misrepresented God...Nearly all of them represent him as a great King on a grand throne, thinking how grand he is, and making it the business of his being and the end of his universe to keep up his glory, wielding the bolts of a Jupiter against them that take his name in vain. They would not allow this, but follow out what they say, and it comes much to this." [61]

"Such miserable theologians...so cut and pare the words of the Lord as to take the very life from them, quenching all their glory and colour in their own inability to believe, and still would have the dead letter of them accepted as the comfort of a creator to the sore hearts he made in his own image!" [62]

MacDonald's conclusion is as hard-hitting as it is doctrinally incorrect. He assails the very heart of Jewish and Christian theology—the nature of the sacrifice itself.

"How did it come ever to be imagined?" he asks of such a belief system. "It sprang from the trustless dread that cannot believe in the forgiveness of the Father...cannot trust him without a legal arrangement to bind him...It sprang from the pride that will understand what it cannot, before it will obey what it sees. He that will understand first will believe a lie—a lie from which obedience alone will at length deliver him...It is the merest, poorest, most shameless fiction, invented without the perception that it was an invention—fit to satisfy the intellect...

"If it be asked how, if it be false, the doctrine...can have been permitted to remain so long an article of faith to so many, I answer, On the same principle on which God took up and made use of the sacrifices men had, in their lack of faith, invented as a way of pleasing him...God accepted men's sacrifices until he could get them to see—and with how many has he yet not succeeded, in the church and out of it!—that he does not care for such things.

"'But,' again it may well be asked, 'whence then has sprung the undeniable potency of that teaching?'

"I answer, From its having in it a notion of God and his Christ...but, by the very poverty and untruth in its presentation, fitted to the weakness and unbelief of men, seeing it was by men invented to meet and ease the demand made upon their own weakness and unbelief. Thus the leaven spreads. The truth is there. It is Christ the glory of God. But the ideas that poor slavish souls breed concerning this glory the moment the darkness begins to disperse, is quite another thing. Truth is indeed too good for men to believe; they must dilute it before they can take it; they must dilute it before they dare give it. They must make it less true before they can believe it enough to get any good of it. Unable to believe in the love of the Lord Jesus Christ...unable to believe in the forgivingness of their father in heaven, they invented a way to be forgiven that should not demand of him so much...which should save them from having to believe downright in the tenderness of his father-heart, for that they found impossible....they could not believe in clear forgiveness...so they invented...a satisfaction for sin which was an insult to God. He sought no satisfaction, but an obedient return to the Father." [63]

MacDonald's powerful conclusion, though we read it in the previous chapter, bears repeating almost in full. It strikes to the heart of MacDonald's perspective of all spirituality, as well as pinpointing precisely why much of Christendom's theology has "gone wrong."

"The spirit of such a mode of receiving the offer of the Lord's deliverance, is the root of all the horrors of a corrupt theology....the passion for the fruit of the tree of knowledge, not the fruit of the tree of life. Men would understand: they do not care to obey;—understand where it is impossible they should understand save by obeying. They would search into the work of the Lord instead of doing their part in it... Instead of immediately obeying the Lord of life...they set themselves to question their unenlightened intellects as to his plans for their deliverance... Incapable of understanding...they proceed to interpret the riches of his divine soul in terms of their own beggarly notions...and then...to insist upon their neighbours' acceptance of their distorted shadows of 'the plan of salvation' as the truth of him in whom is no darkness...They will not accept, that is, act upon, their highest privilege, that of obeying the Son of God. It is on them that do his will, that the day dawns; to them the day-star arises in their hearts. Obedience is the soul of knowledge." [64]

If MacDonald is right, that much in the orthodox belief system is based on a series of misunderstandings, if not outright falsehoods, surely a great renaissance of reevaluation in the church is not far away.

Let us look further at how the God and Father of Jesus Christ could have gone so wrong in the eyes of the very men and women who believe that they have given their lives to him. To do so, we need to turn to the writings and teachings of Paul. In his towering letter to the Romans, two doctrines stand as gigantic twin stumbling-blocks to an accurate reception of the true message of the gospel. Every Christian, every *non*-Christian in western culture, is familiar with these doctrines. Recoiling at our first encounter with them, we have only two choices—either to accept them blindly, or to repudiate them.

Ignoring the dilemma posed by these doctrines introduces a schizophrenia into the Christian message that has, as much as any single element of our creed, caused millions to reject the claims of Christ altogether.

If we would discover how our God has gone so wrong in the eyes of the world, this is where we need to begin.

The two troublesome doctrines are the *wrath of God* and the doctrine of a *predestined elect.*

TWO KINDS OF STUMBLING BLOCKS

No man can dictate what another ought to believe. It should not be the priority of this or any book to tell people *what* they should believe, but to help readers learn how to think, how to read Scripture, and thus *how* to believe. We must each then go to the Spirit of Truth and pray for insight and wisdom. If we are thinking boldly, imaginatively, creatively, open-mindedly, humbly, intelligently, submissively, fearlessly, non-doctrinally, and personally, then it matters not so much whether any two people agree on some point of scriptural interpretation. When we are learning to think properly about God and his work, then we can be confident that the Holy Spirit will reveal truth in the end. It is clear that enormous theological conundrums are raised by *Romans*—in many regions of inquiry. The narrow and occasional twisting of Paul's words in regions of scriptural ambiguity has caused doctrinal havoc within the church.

So whereas *Romans* gives us some of the richest treasure troves of Paul's thought, it has also become the scriptural foundation for many doctrinal errors that have arisen from a *mis*reading of Paul's intended meanings. The two scriptural riddles we will now look at pose significant stumbling blocks in the unbelieving world to an accurate reception of the gospel. "If God is a God who is like *that*," many say, "I want nothing to do with him."

How ought a serious Christian respond?

Though they would not perhaps phrase it quite so bluntly, Many Christians respond essentially, "That's their tough luck. They've been warned."

The underlying problem with this response is that deep down such individuals believe that God *is* like what the world thinks of him—that he is intent on punishing the unbelieving to the utmost of his power. That fact may be of more import than the world's unbelief.

If stumbling blocks exist to an accurate reception of the gospel message, that ought to concern us. It is not that we need to change the gospel to make it more palatable. We do need to be certain, however, that we are presenting an *accurate* gospel. Honest and truth loving people flocked to Jesus. That they are not flocking to the gospel in our day may not only reveal the condition of today's world, it may also reveal that we are not sharing the same gospel that Jesus did.

It is true that Paul says the cross will be a stumbling block to the world. The cross is assuredly a stumbling block to pride, independence, and motives of self. The message of the cross is self-denial, relinquishment, and death to all that self represents. Our world is so in love with the rebellious, independent, self-motivated, self-satisfied, narcissistic, pleasure-seeking, prideful SELF that the message of the cross is perhaps a greater stumbling block than at any other time in history.

But there are *false* stumbling blocks too. These are stumbling blocks that *we* put in the way, that we erect in front of the cross, barring the world from perceiving its message accurately. It may be, when the time of judgment comes, that God the Father will not turn to the unbelievers who have crossed our path in life with a message of condemnation, but rather to *us* with a stern rebuke. "You prevented these who might have believed in me from an accurate understanding of who I am. You were so in love with your doctrines that you never knew me truly. It was *you* who erected the stumbling blocks that kept them from knowing me as their loving and forgiving Father."

The most serious stumbling block that Christians put in front of the true message of the gospel and the true meaning of the cross is the stumbling block of a distorted image of God's nature and character.

The church has forgotten the universal Fatherhood.

THE ENIGMA OF GOD'S WRATH

It may be that wrath represents *the* single most troublesome doctrine that prevents many from embracing the truths of Christianity. The reason people recoil is simple—*wrathfulness*, by its very nature and wrongly understood, carries hideous implications about the character of God.

Paul establishes the principle of God's wrath in Romans 1:18: "For the wrath of God is revealed from heaven against all ungodliness and wickedness of men who by their wickedness suppress the truth." From this beginning, he goes on throughout the letter to amplify the theme. God's wrath is mentioned more times in *Romans* than in any other New Testament book except *Revelation*.

Clearly, the wrath of God is troublesome for thinking Christians. Every one of us has wondered about the God portrayed in the Old Testament. We have all asked, "How could a loving God order the killing of innocents?" We are mostly able to look beyond it with, "That was in ancient times. Once Jesus came everything was different."

But the unbelieving world is *not* able to look beyond it. This is the greatest of all stumbling blocks. Is God really a vengeful tyrant intent on punishing his enemies?

A series of penetrating and difficult questions lies at the heart of this inquiry:

Has our image of God really changed? Have we listened to what Jesus told us? Or are we still really Old Testament Jews at heart?

Deep down many Christians still maintain an image that is essentially the same as it was for the ancient Hebrews 3,000 years ago. Their worship is directed to a God whose hatred of sin is so fierce and his wrath so hot that he will punish unrepentant sinners in hell forever. Though manifested differently now through the person of Jesus, the harshness mitigated somewhat, a little kinder and gentler around the edges perhaps, wearing more respectable clothes...lurking in the shadows behind the Son whom they revere, the being they call "God" remains the Sinai-god of smoke, fire, thunderbolts, and retribution.

George MacDonald speaks of his personal abhorrence to this "softened" but essentially identical image:

"I desire to wake no dispute, will myself dispute with no man," he writes, "but for the sake of those whom certain believers trouble, I have spoken my mind. I love the one God seen in the face of Jesus Christ. From all copies of Jonathan Edwards's portrait of God, however faded by time, however softened by the use of less glaring pigments, I turn with loathing. Not such a God is he concerning whom was the message John heard from Jesus, that he is light, and in him is no darkness at all." [65]

Yet in *Romans* Paul seems to give scriptural validity to exactly this perspective that MacDonald says he turns from with loathing. What do we do with the seeming tyrant of wrath given to the world from Paul's pen?

The question reduces to this: Is the image of God of vengeance and wrath against sin that has come to us through the Old Testament a true picture of the Father of Jesus Christ? Do Paul's many references in *Romans* to the *wrath of God* support this image...or have we misunderstood Paul's message and intent?

WHAT DO OUR HEARTS SAY—PERSONAL INSIGHT TO A DEEP RIDDLE

It would be possible to engage in a major theological study at this point. We could devote an entire book to the Old Testament image of God, and to the subject of God's wrath. We would still not scratch the surface. Thousands of books *have* been written. One wonders if Christendom is any better off for whatever enlightenment they have produced.

There are times when a more personal approach is needed to understand the deep things of God. Jesus did not come to teach studies about God...he came to *show* us the Father. It was a *personal* revelation.

Most readers will be familiar with C.S. Lewis's classic *Mere Christianity.* One of the secrets to the book's power is the simplicity of its personal approach to the existence of God. Lewis makes a startlingly obvious yet unbelievably profound case. All the evidence we need for the existence for God, he says, is found within our own humanity. He calls this "inside information." [66] Lewis engages in no deep theology. He simply says, "We know this about ourselves. What does this tell us about the universe...and ultimately about God?"

Perhaps we can take Lewis's method a step further. Let us employ the same common sense reasoning to help us understand the nature and character of God. It is not only possible, it is altogether *likely*, that we can say exactly the same thing here: "We know this about ourselves. What does this tell us about God?"

Lewis's point is that God created us. He put certain movements inside us. Those traits of our humanity bear the fingerprint of our Creator. They speak truth about him.

Perhaps we should frame a hugely important corollary to Lewis's argument. It may be that the traits of our humanity not only tell us that God exists, but also tell us what kind of God he is.

To probe the heart of God requires that we understand him as a *Father*. He is not only the Father of Jesus. He is the creating Father of every one of us. If we would understand his nature and character, we must begin with his Fatherhood. That is also where we must begin if we would understand his wrath. What wrath does a Father feel? What does it mean? What is its purpose? What is its result?

I find it necessary here to speak very personally. There is no way to explore God's Fatherhood in the abstract. What good are abstractions when it comes to the life and death question of who God is and what he is like? Theological abstractions do no one any good.

To understand the intimate *reality* of Fatherhood, I have to look inside *myself*, deep inside my own father's heart. It is there that I discover, exactly as Lewis says, clues about *God's* Father heart. That is where we uncover the "inside information" God gave us about himself. I must take what pulses inside *my* father heart, even in the midst of a sinful nature, as a precious and holy living picture of what pulses in God's heart too. Of course there are many who have not attempted to attune themselves to such divine motions. But I am ME. I have to use the "inside information" God has given *me*—no one else—to try to get to the bottom of his nature. This will necessarily be an individual quest for every man and woman on the planet.

What a stupendous thing—God allows me to feel fragmentary stirrings and emotions of what he himself feels!

What an incredible gift. God has given us himself!

WHAT DOES *MY* FATHER HEART TELL ME
ABOUT *GOD'S* FATHER HEART?

Every parent will recognize what I am talking about. I use the word "father" because I am a man and I happen to be the father of three sons. Mothers will feel the same stirrings that equally reflect the parental Fatherhood of God. Like God, all mothers and fathers have given life to children that bear our image, look like us, sound like us, remind us of ourselves, and that share many of our traits.

I recognize that I am a sinful, weak, frail, struggling man who made more mistakes as a father than I can count. In spite of that weakness and those mistakes, however, I love my sons. I love them beyond their capacity to grasp a thousandth how much I love them. I would do *anything* for them that I perceive to be for their ultimate good and their ultimate sonship in God. I would give my life for any one of them if that's what it took for Christlikeness to be achieved in them. Most mothers and fathers would say the same. Fathers and mothers *love*. That's what they do. They do not merely "love," they love sacrificially and selflessly. They do not love perfectly by any means, or even well in many cases. Yet those stirrings of sacrifice and selflessness are inbred into their parental DNA as miniscule reflections of God's infinitely loving Fatherhood.

I recognize mine as an incomplete love. My love *reflects* God's love, but weakly, faintly, sporadically, even to some degree selfishly. In my selfless motives toward my sons, I remain a selfish human being. In my weak humanity, I have hurt them. There have been times when they have hurt me. It's part of the human predicament. Sometimes they hurt me in ways they never knew, as I am aware that I never knew many of the hurts I inflicted upon them.

What intrigues me about their violations against my fatherhood is *my* response. How have I reacted? Was I filled with wrath toward their offense? Was my fatherhood so offended that I "could not coexist" with their sin? Did I say, "Until you repent, I can have nothing more to do with you?"

Such responses are attributed to God in light of mankind's sin. Are they consistent with the inside information I possess from within *myself* about a father's response to a wayward son or daughter?

In fact, they are just the opposite of what I find in my own heart.

Far from anger, I want to take my sons in my arms and simply *love* them. This is not to say that anger did not occasionally rise within me, nor that occasions did not arise when I grieved to see divergence from the path that would grow righteousness and wisdom. But my anger has always been informed by the higher objective that love might triumph in the end. Forgiveness was in my heart even without repentance. Forgiveness was ever and always co-existent with my father's love.

What does all this tell me?

If Lewis is right, then this inside information tells me that the same stirrings and motives must also exist in God's heart...with one difference. With God, the good, the love, the patience, and the forgiveness must be infinitely *greater*.

Where I would love my sons, God loves *more*.

Where I would forgive my sons, God forgives *more*.

Where I would never cast out my sons, God would far *less* cast out one of his children.

Where my anger is a reflection of my love, God's anger is far *more* a reflection of his love.

Where my anger leads to the triumph of love, God's anger must far *more* lead to forgiveness and the ultimate triumph of his love.

Many Christians may find such reasoning presumptuous. "God's ways are higher than your ways," they would say. "You cannot compare yourself with him."

They are right, insofar as it goes. But God must be *more and higher* than me in every way, not less.

Can my heart contain more love and higher forgiveness than the *perfect* love and forgiveness of God's Father heart? Of course not. Yet this is the implication of their objection—that I in my sin am *willing* to forgive, where God in his perfection is *unwilling* to forgive?

It is an absurd argument. It is exactly upside-down. Can the created rise higher than the Creator in any of his attributes? "More is required of the maker, by his own act of creation, than can be required of men," writes MacDonald. "More and higher justice and righteousness is required of him by himself, the Truth;—greater nobleness, more penetrating sympathy; and nothing but what, if an honest man understood it, he would say was right." [67]

The equation of earthly parenthood and earthly childship, gazing in both generational directions, was designed to reveal to us the nature and character of God, and then point us from the incomplete earthly fatherhood to seek the perfect heavenly Fatherhood. The fact that in many cases those earthly images and reflections are broken and shattered, sometimes grievously, does not remove the imperative upon all of us to discover the universal Fatherhood according to the earthly relational path set before each of us to follow.

UNWILLINGNESS TO LAY DOWN STUMBLING BLOCKS OF ILLOGIC

Christians by the millions have been eager to embrace Lewis's "inside information" progression about the *existence* of God. But Christendom as a whole has been unwilling to use the same logical information to help it understand the character of God's Fatherhood more accurately. It appears that for some, the more difficult they can make the gospel message the better they like it. They almost seem to relish in the fact that unbelievers stumble over their doctrines of illogic, rather than doing everything possible to remove those stumbling blocks.

All creation reflects its Creator. If *my* father-heart has been born in *God's* Father-heart, how was a theology devised to explain God's wrathful response toward the sin of *his* children that is completely *opposite* to what I as a father—made in the image of God—feel toward my own sons?

Perhaps the reason may be found in the fact that many do *not* feel such stirrings as I am describing, but rather feel that unforgiveness is not only justified but right. Perhaps many *do* view fatherhood from the vantage point of judgment. By the same logic, they assume that God must respond with judgment to the transgressions of mankind. Using the same reasoning I have, they arrive at an opposite conclusion. I cannot speak for them. This is not a conundrum I can resolve for any reader. I would only say, if judgment is a root in one's perspective of God, then they must seek to discover in that image the *best* possible "judgment" imaginable, all the best of earthly fatherhood, and far more besides. We must each seek the truth this principle has to reveal by gazing deep into the mirrors of our *own* souls.

What I am left to conclude is that *my* limited human fatherhood is born in *God's* infinite Fatherhood. I am able to love a little because he loves much. I am a poor reflection, but I am nevertheless a reflection of him. Therefore, my love for my sons mirrors to an infinitesimal degree God's vast love for his children. That my response to the sin of my sons is forgiveness must indicate something far higher about God's *infinite* forgiveness.

"You are thinking with the carnal mind," comes the objection. "Man cannot understand God's ways. They are higher than man's. Scripture says that the ways of God are foolishness to man. It is only because you are finite and sinful that you love your sons without the wrath of God. It is because God is perfect in love that he is also perfect in holiness and thus also perfect in wrath. You don't really love with God's love. God's holiness is so pure that it hates sin with a pure hate. His holiness cannot coexist with sin. You don't truly hate sin because you are sinful. Holy wrath is God's only possible response to sin. Because you are sinful, you are willing to forgive where God cannot forgive. Your sin makes you unable to hate sin *enough*. Because God is holy, perfect, and pure he must punish sin. God's ways aren't *supposed* to make sense to the carnal mind. That they *don't* make sense to the mind of man that proves them true."

Can there be a greater perversion of logic than this, that the *illogic* of the doctrine proves it true?

PERFECT HOLY WRATH—THE ULTIMATE CONTRADICTION

How did a devious doctrine arise that holiness cannot coexist with sin, and that wrath is an expression of *perfect* holiness? It is an abhorrent idea, a blasphemy against the character of God's Fatherhood.

In God's economy, holiness and sin coexist all the time. Nothing in the nature of the universe *prohibits* clean and unclean, perfect and imperfect, existing side by side. Paul calls Jesus the perfect image of God. We observe him coexisting with sin on every page of the gospels, and speaking no word of wrath against that sin. His wrath was reserved for religious hypocrites, not the sin of so-called sinners.

When they were young, what my heart wanted to do in the presence of the sin of my sons is run straight to them, embrace them, and love the selfishness out of them. Such an open-armed embrace is not always possible. Sin usually prevents the return to right relationship for a season. But the moment an opening came, perhaps after an offense, I rushed toward it. My forgiveness was not conditional. In my heart was love, all love, nothing but love, ready, waiting, anxious to flow in the instant a crack of light presented itself. George MacDonald writes: "For the spirit of God lies all about the spirit of man like a mighty sea, ready to rush in at the smallest chink in the walls that shut him out from his own." [68]

What an image of Fatherhood!

Yet the holiness doctrine maintains that God is *prevented* such feelings toward his creatures, or, if he feels them, is prevented from acting upon them. God loves, says the doctrine, but the purity of his holiness *prevents* his pouring that love out upon sinners. Could ever a more ridiculous doctrine be imagined?

WHAT IS GOD'S WRATH?

What, then, is the "wrath" of God?

Without being overly simplistic, we can with confidence remind ourselves of the great truth in the saying, "God hates the sin but loves the sinner." Is this not precisely what my own fathers heart tells me? It is so simple and obvious we should have seen it all along. All we have to do is take a closer look at Romans 1:18. God's wrath is not revealed against the *men*, but against the *ungodliness and wickedness* of those men. His wrath is all against the sin, not the sinner.

If God's wrath manifests itself against the *sin*, is it not intuitively obvious that sinners *themselves* will somehow be rescued from the death-working power of that sin? How, then, did a doctrine arise which has at its foundation God's ultimate wrath against *sinners* as well as their sin?

We sinful human mothers and fathers often allow our anger to blur the distinction. In our weakness, we wrongly lash out at both sin and sinner. We forget that the basis of our punishment must be to root out the sin that the sinner may be healed, forgiven, and restored.

But God's Fatherhood is perfect. His punishment is *always* against the sin, that the sinner may turn to his Father in repentance and be healed, forgiven, and restored.

God *is* holy and pure. There *is* a wrath of God. Indeed, he *hates* sin. There *will* be an accounting. There *will* be a chastising and purifying. The wrath of God will surely achieve its appointed eternal purpose.

But we must discover how the attributes of God's nature will accomplish his Abba-purposes for the redemption of his universe.

Let us seek to discover what Paul *really* meant. Let us hold God's character up to the mirror of our own hearts and ask whether it is possible for God to be *less* loving and *less* eternally forgiving than we. Let us look to the dawn, where the glorious sunlight of restoration, healing, forgiveness, and redemption will rise over the horizon of eternity.

THE CONUNDRUM OF A PREDESTINED ELECT

In Romans 8:29-30, Paul writes, "For those God *foreknew* he also *predestined* to be conformed to the likeness of his Son, that he might be the firstborn among many brothers. And those he *predestined,* he also called; those he called he also justified; those he justified, he also glorified. "(NIV)

"Predestine," as a translation of the Greek, is found in but one other instance in the New Testament (Ephesians 1:5.). Thus *Romans* serves as the foundation not only for the doctrine of God's wrath, but also for the doctrine of predestination upon which, in large measure, Calvinist theology is based.

Many will be familiar with Calvinism's well known acrostic T-U-L-I-P which outlines what are called the "five points of Calvinism."

"Predestination" as such does not appear in the creed, but a brief review of the second two of the five elements (the U and the L) shows that an exclusionary system of theocratic hierarchy (justified under the guise of God's "sovereignty") undergirds the whole system. It gives rise to what Francis Schaeffer called the "two exclusive humanities" view of the world—one lost, one saved. [69] Two of the pillars of that belief system are as follows:

Unconditional Election. God has chosen certain individuals for salvation (the "elect") before the foundation of the world. His choice is based solely on his own purpose and desire. The word "predestination" is used to describe this election of some for salvation. God's predestining of some to be saved and others to be lost is influenced by nothing in man—not by goodness or disposition to believe nor even upon God's foreknowledge that one individual will come to believe and another will not. It is based solely upon his good pleasure.

Limited Atonement. The death of Jesus Christ was intended from the beginning to make possible the salvation of the predestined elect, and *only* that elect. Jesus died for the elect alone. Also called "particular redemption," this doctrine stands in opposition to the Arminian view that salvation is possible for all, but that the particular redemption of no one is certain. Arminianism holds that "free will" in responding to Christ's atoning death is the sole determining factor in who will and who will not be saved, and that all men have equal opportunity to participate in that salvation. In strict Calvinism, all men do not have such equal opportunity.

A CENTURIES LONG DEBATE

The great difficulty with the doctrine of predestination is not with the first highlighted word in the above passage from Romans 8. Few have a problem with God's *foreknowledge*. The next two highlighted words, however, seem to remove free will from salvation altogether.

A more accurate translation of the Greek than "predestine" is *foreordained*. The two concepts are obviously intertwined. Does God merely *know* in advance, or does he *determine* and *ordain* each human being's eternal salvationary outcome in advance? The King James translated this "foreordained" as *predestinate*, the Revised Standard followed with *predestined*, and thus the word *predestination*, though found nowhere in the Bible, has come down to us as one of the most controversial theories in all Christian theology.

If predestination as commonly understood is true, then in a sense *everything* about Christianity changes. If one's eternal destiny (pre-*destine*) is "foreordained," determined, marked out in advance by an all-powerful God, then the personal imperative of individual choice, even salvation itself, if not entirely vanishes, certainly loses much of its potency in the gospel message.

This is the doctrine of "election"—that some are elected for salvation, and some are not, simply on the basis of God's sovereign "good pleasure." No merit, choice, good life, bad life, or human worthiness comes into it.

So much has been written in the last four centuries, since John Calvin popularized the doctrine, about the long-standing debate between Calvinism and Arminianism (vastly simplified—predestination vs. free will) that it would be futile and redundant to attempt a summary of that scriptural tussle here. The Dutch theologian Jacobus Arminius (1560-1609) was largely reacting against much that Frenchman John Calvin (1509-1564) had written in his *Institutes of the Christian Religion.* The disagreement has been contentious and divisive ever since. Even setting down the debate as "predestination vs. free will" enormously oversimplifies the complex scriptural issues involved. For our purposes, however, that simplification will do well enough. We are not trying to set out two-sided talking points for an intellectual polemic, but to understand who our God is and what he purposes for his creation.

SEEK HIGHER GROUND!

In order to prevent miring ourselves in the details of analysis, we need to seek a higher vantage point from which to discover helpful conclusions. In the face of any scriptural conundrum, when we lose sight of the path, when our direction becomes uncertain, when the surrounding terrain is unfamiliar, the only sure rule is—*Seek higher ground!* If we can reach the lofty vista of the mountaintop, we will be able to see about us in every direction. Then we will know where we are and where we are bound.

Many of the ideas of Christianity are conflicting, confusing, and tangled. Everyone disagrees. Argumentation is more common in the body of Christ than unity. How can one know what is true and what is not?

The only solution is—*Seek higher ground!* Get out of the valleys of doctrine to the mountaintop where vision is clear.

And what do we find when we escape the valley fogs? We find God himself! The point is so imperative that we return to it over and over—The *character of God* must be the defining and governing Truth upon which we base our attempt to understand every doctrine of the Christian faith.

The character of God is the high mountain vista from which, through which, and in relation to which we must view all truth.

We cannot begin with doctrines *about* God...we must start with God himself.

We cannot begin with the *omnipotence* of God...we must start with the *character* of God.

We cannot begin with the *sovereignty* of God...we must start with the *character* of God.

We cannot begin with the almighty *holiness* of God...we must start with the *character* of God.

The principle remains the foundation of every inquiry: *Undergirding every other characteristic in the divine nature, we know that God is a loving Father. This is his essence. Any theology of truth must begin with that Fatherhood. It is the fundamental truth of the universe. All foundations must be laid in God's Fatherhood or eventually they will drift and diverge from truth.*

CAN PREDESTINATION BE TRUE?

The truth about predestination, then, must also originate in God's Fatherhood.

With that foundation, all the myriad points and counterpoints by which Calvinists and Arminianists bolster their arguments, the hundreds of scriptural proof texts, the indisputable logic and analysis...everything dissolves in the radiant mountain sunlight of the divine Fatherhood.

God the Creator-Father of the universe *loves*!

He loves all the children of his creation. *Every* one—good, bad, and in-between. He loves the totally depraved (as the Calvinists would have it) and the partially depraved (as the Arminianists have it.) He loves the saved and the unsaved, the repentant and the unrepentant, the elect and the non-elect, saints and sinners, men and women, Jews and Gentiles, young and old.

God *loves*. He cannot *not* love. He *is* love.

He is a loving Father. Perfect "Fatherhood" is outflowing, infinitely giving, infinitely forgiving. His love can be nothing else but life-producing, life-sustaining, *goodness*.

Imperfect fatherhood may be less, may do less, may require less of itself than infinite goodness. But *perfect* Fatherhood can be and do nothing less.

A loving Father would not, *could* not by the nature of his essence pre-determine, foreordain, or doom in advance one of his created children to an eternity apart from him. Whether some may choose to spend eternity apart from him is an entirely different question. But a Father would never *determine* the inevitability of such a separation between himself and a child whom he loves. An infinite "Sovereign" might do so. A Father could *not* do so.

Like so many of the ideas to which Christians grow accustomed, it is easy to become anesthetized to the horrid implications of predestination. It is a monstrous doctrine. The very thought of it should make any thinking

Christian shudder. That so many through the years have not only embraced it, but done so eagerly, says more about them than it does about the doctrine.

The thing is so self-evidently false there are no words strong enough to refute it. Yet those who *want* to believe it, that their pride in their imagined status as of the elect may be preserved, *will* believe it. Each will follow the inclinations of his or her own heart, and will believe of God what they want to believe of him.

Only one argument can sustain predestination. It begins by removing Fatherhood from the divine character. That done, the entire teaching of Jesus immediately crumbles. The stubborn doctrinalist who adheres rigidly to the dogma is left with the lifeless shell of an Old Testament Sinai Sovereign, not the Father whom Jesus spoke to as *Abba*.

The conclusion is so simple and self-evident it is astonishing that so much energy is expended debating the point:

The predestination of sinners, unbelievers, and the non-elect to destruction, by the definition of God's Fatherhood, *cannot* be a true doctrine. It needs no arguments nor proof texts to reveal its falsehood. It is *a priori* rendered false by the existence and character of God himself.

Fatherhood proves the predestination of the non-elect to perdition false. The very idea is a blasphemy against the Father of Jesus Christ.

Though the boldness and unequivocation of this statement may cause unrepentant Calvinists to retreat behind the barricades of their proof-texts, there is little need to carry the debate further. Let those who can content themselves with a god who would doom half his creation to an eternity in hell from no fault of their own be so satisfied, until the day they meet their Maker face to face and he says to them with tears in his eyes, "How could you believe such things of me when my Son told you so clearly what kind of Father I was?"

THE FRUIT OF THE DOCTRINE

Perhaps the most offensive aspect of the doctrine of limited atonement is the preposterous notion that foreordaining some to an eternity in hell originates in God's "good pleasure." To quote George MacDonald: *Very God forbid!*

The Calvinistic theologic system as a whole is deviously clever. Under the umbrella of God's infinite *Sovereignty* over the universe, over mankind, and over every individual, it masquerades as being rooted in God's greatness and man's fallen nature. It *seems* to have God and man perfectly positioned in relationship. God is sovereign, man is utterly dependent upon him. Perfectly true…every word.

This is what makes the system so appealing—it *seems* to originate from the sunlight of truth. But its doctrines lurk in the shadows cast by that sun, not in the light itself. Thus Calvinism apprehends the light through truth's dark opposite.

This Reformed system as a whole thrives in the soil of spiritual self-righteousness. Calvinism, its followers are convinced, possesses *full* truth. Calvinism possesses the only complete revelation of the life of Christ. Only Reformed doctrine understands the Bible accurately.

Calvinists have no questions to ask. Their faith harbors no uncertainties. Ask anything. The answer and scriptural proof-texts will be forthcoming. Calvinism knows all.

By its absolute assurance at *every* point of doctrine, Calvinism breeds spiritual vanity and conceit with lethal effectiveness. Paying doctrinal heed to man's humility toward God, *personal* humility is the last of its virtues. Possessing so much of the truth, the Reformed system is thus also the chief repository of spiritual pride in the church.

The fruit that predestination has grown over the years proceeds out of the soil in which the tree grows. It is the fruit of self-righteousness.

TWO QUESTIONS

But we still have a problem.

Recognizing that the doctrine of limited atonement is by definition false, and that its fruit in the Reformed theology that birthed it is the spoiled fruit of self-righteousness, we remain face to face with a scriptural conundrum. We still have Romans 8:29-30 and Ephesians 1:5 staring us in the eyeballs. We cannot ignore these difficult passages.

Two questions come into focus that will place the debating points into perspective and help us resolve the dilemma.

One—Has Paul's apparent meaning in Romans 8:29-30 and Ephesians 1:5 been *misunderstood*? Did he *not* actually intend to imply that God specifically decides ahead of time who will be saved and who will not?

Two—If Paul DID intend to say that God predetermines some for salvation and others for damnation...was Paul *wrong*?

The conundrum thus reduces to: *Have we misunderstood Paul's meaning, or was Paul simply wrong?*

In subjecting these passages to the same standard to which we continually return, we need to ask whether Paul's apparent meaning lines up with the character of God, with what Jesus told us about his Father, and with the rest of Paul's teaching.

When we hold the doctrine up to the measuring rod of the rest of Paul's writings, we uncover an astonishing truth. Usually Paul teaches exactly the *opposite* of limited atonement. Indeed, throughout his letters he contradicts the notion of predestination *many* times.

It would be contrary to the spirit of this study to bring forward a list of proof-texts to support this point. The hungry reader will be well capable of discovering numerous instances that flow from Paul's pen that conspicuously nullify predestination and everything it conveys about a partial atonement. Paul's repeated use of such words as *all* and *every* indicate a more comprehensive salvation than predestination implies. Those interested in the pursuit of this inquiry should keep their eyes open for the use of such terms. The simple conclusion is that Paul himself often argues *against* predestination with equal vigor as Romans 8:29-30 seems to argue for it.

We will note but one passage and leave it at that. This is found in Ephesians 1:9-10. The proximity to verse 5 is striking. Within a mere six verses, Paul states that God "predestines" those who will be his sons through Jesus Christ (verse 5), and then states that the mystery of God's will and purpose is to "unite all things in him, things in heaven and things on earth" (verse 10.) The *uniting of all things* is clearly inconsistent with a predetermined and foreordained eternal division between the elect and non-elect. In the same passage Paul seems to be arguing for *and* against predestination!

THERE IS NO SCRIPTURAL NON-ELECT

The conclusion seems apparent that Paul meant something much different than what is commonly called "predestination."

In the two predestination passages, *Paul speaks only of the elect,* those predestined to be God's sons (and daughters) in Jesus Christ. He says nothing about the non-elect. The fate that lies in store for the unsaved is an aspect of the doctrine incorporated into Calvinist theology without a word of support from either Romans 8:29-30 or Ephesians 1:5.

The *non*-elect do not enter the discussion! The term exists nowhere in Scripture. *No one* is predestined for damnation. Calvinism made the whole concept up.

Calvinism has fabricated a doctrine about the grisly fate of the non-elect in hell out of thin air.

IS PREDESTINATION—PROPERLY UNDERSTOOD—TRUE AFTER ALL!

Putting all this together, we see that Paul speaks of a predestined elect, then adds that it is God's purpose and will to unite *all* things in Christ. What can this mean other than that God purposes and foreordains *all* creation to be drawn up into that grand unity? He does not speak of the non-elect because there is no non-elect!

How else can we read this passage but that God predestines and foreordains ALL his created children to become his sons and daughters in Jesus Christ.

Perhaps predestination is true...which is the predestination of *everyone*.

Paul understood the great unity toward which the predestination of the elect (*all* the elect, *all* creation) will lead in the end.

What else does our sovereign and holy Father-God foreordain than the final unity of *all* things in heaven and on earth!

FOURTEEN

THE VOODOO CROSS

The Ancient Truth of the Atonement

by
Michael Phillips

T he cross.
It stands as the center and focal point of Christianity. The death and resurrection of Jesus Christ IS Christianity. The atonement, therefore, is the preeminent doctrine of the Christian faith—what the cross accomplished, how Jesus redeemed us, and how atonement for sin is made.

Nowhere in our beliefs is it so vital to discover the contrast inherent in the Lord's, "You have heard that it was said...but I say to you."

Though George MacDonald energetically repudiates the doctrine of vicarious sacrifice, he yet falls short of articulating with precision how he views the atonement to function in the life of the believer. It is therefore difficult to assess exactly what he believed on this most central of doctrines. As a result, controversy arising out of his nebulous perspectives followed him all his life. Indeed, during their courtship his future wife Louisa, from a doctrinally correct fundamentalist family, was slow to accept young George until he had answered himself satisfactorily on the atonement. [70]

The atonement is an extremely complex doctrine, with roots extending deep into the Old Testament. The blood sacrifice is ancient beyond reckoning, originating in the pagan mists of pre-history, and incorporated by the Hebrews into Mosaic Law. MacDonald argues that God cared nothing for the ancient sacrifice, but only made use of it because it was all the Hebrews, at that state in their human development, immersed in the paganism of the time, were capable of understanding. [71]

If he is right, then it seems that the highest priority of Christian theologians through the years, from Paul down to those of our own time, would have been to find out what was really in God's heart to accomplish. If sin was not to be eradicated according to the Old Testament paradigm of an innocent being sacrificed to atone for the sins of the guilty, what then *was* God's intended provision for dealing with sin?

Unfortunately, Christian theologians have *not* made this the highest focus of their scriptural inquiries. Instead, they have devised systems to perpetuate the Old Testament paradigm, twisting the Christian message and the gospel of Christ into a series of legalistic knots held together by the old-covenantal doctrine of sacrifice.

Can we discover how Christianity was turned from a vibrant gospel where "all things were made new," into a reflective fading remnant of ancient Judaism.

To answer such questions, we return to Paul.

THE ATONEMENT: COURT OF LAW OR FAMILY RECONCILIATION

Paul's background made inevitable that he would view Christianity through the lens of his own training and temperament. We each respond to the principles and imperatives of God's truths *individually*. Our responses depend on how we have come to the point in our individual journeys when the truths of the gospel become a way of life.

The lens through which Paul viewed Christianity was the lens of legalism. Rome was a nation of law. Israel was a nation based on the Old Testament law. Paul was steeped in both traditions, an expert in deductive reasoning, well familiar with legal terminology. Paul's entire life as a Roman of Tarsus and a Pharisee educated under the revered rabbi Gamaliel was founded in a tradition of law.

In Christianity's early leadership, Paul was a latecomer. He did not have the benefit of those three years walking side-by-side with Jesus. It was not only the twelve disciples who had enjoyed such a wonderful level of intimacy. So too had Barnabas and the seventy. The church was full of men and women who had known Jesus personally. Their perspectives of everything about their Christian faith, everything Christianity *meant*, from its theology to its practice, were grounded in having gazed personally into Jesus' eyes and listened to his voice as he spoke of his Father and his Father's purposes among men.

Their "theology" of Christian discipleship needed little more than to remember those eyes, to hear again that tender voice, and to recall Jesus speaking of his Father's love. The very way Jesus addressed his disciples on the night before his crucifixion rooted the theology of that death in the

Father's love for his own. "Little children," he said to them, "yet a little while I am with you."

For Jesus, as for those who knew him, the redemption of mankind was about a Father seeking to bring his children back to the home of his heart. Jesus came as the firstborn and elder brother to take his younger brethren and "little children" by the hand and lead them back to the Father. Jesus was first and foremost a *Son*.

The redemption of mankind, for those who had heard Jesus, was a story of family reconciliation.

PAUL'S PERSPECTIVE: LAW

Paul had never looked into those eyes.

He had not heard that voice in the flesh. He had not listened for hours as Jesus spoke of the Father and his children.

But Paul was an intelligent and educated man—perhaps an intellectual genius. He desired with all his heart to understand what had happened to him, and to make comprehensive sense of this new faith to which he had given his life. Yet he did not have those three years as a foundation upon which to build. Therefore, he fell back on his own background and training to try to explain this wonderful new life-changing reality that was embodied in the person of Jesus Christ.

The foundation by which Paul sought to explain Christianity's truths originated in his upbringing as a Roman and a Pharisee. He was not a fisherman from Galilee. Paul was a cosmopolitan intellectual. The world of the Roman and the Pharisee was all Paul knew. For him to view Christianity through a prism of law was a completely natural response.

We have no idea what Paul's earthly father was like. All we know is that Paul did not fall back on *fatherhood* to explain what had happened to him on the Damascus road. Fatherhood was not so close to Paul's heart as *law*.

So law, not fatherhood, suffused Paul's explanations of his Christian experience.

Another factor lay heavy on Paul's heart as he sought a theological framework for the new Christian faith. That was the burning reality of his own sin. Paul knew what he had been. He had persecuted his very brothers. He had watched Stephen die.

Suddenly all his pharisaic righteousness became ugly and detestable in his eyes. He was the lowest man on earth, a sinner, a hypocrite, perhaps even a murderer. He stood condemned by his own sin. By any standard of law, he was guilty. He deserved nothing but death. When Paul wrote, "The wages of sin is death," he was speaking of himself. He never forgot what he had been.

And yet...God had *forgiven* him! How could he satisfactorily explain the mighty fact of forgiveness toward one who did not deserve it?

To make sense of the stupendous miracle of forgiveness, Paul called upon the Levitical law in which he had been schooled from his boyhood, and specifically the blood sacrifice. In Old Testament times, the shedding of sacrificial blood provided absolution for sin.

Paul was a sinner. He deserved death. Yet Jesus had shed his blood and had forgiven him. His own life brought into clear focus the fulfillment of what Paul had been taught the sacrifice had always been intended to mean. This purpose Paul now saw as culminating in Jesus' sacrificial death and the forgiveness of man's sin—which for Paul would always mean *his* sin.

Paul brought in his Roman background to further clarify and focus exactly what had taken place in his life, and which by extension would explain God's provision for sin for all mankind. To do so he invented a courtroom metaphor. Three characters play prominent roles in Paul's drama—Judge, prisoner, Defense Attorney. The prisoner is found guilty. The judge renders the sentence. The sentence is death. The prisoner sits in the dock condemned.

Paul is creating a picture of his own life. He knows that *he* is that condemned prisoner. He is condemned by what he himself has done.

At the last minute, however, the Defense Attorney steps forward with a plan that will both satisfy the requirement of the law and at the same time allow the prisoner to go free. "I'll take the prisoner's place," he says to the judge. "You can lay his punishment on me and let the guilty go."

The judge agrees because the law of death-for-sin will still be satisfied. He sentences the Defense Attorney to death instead, and sets the prisoner free. The penalty for his sin is thus paid in full.

Paul's courtroom image is useful as far as it goes. But theologians through the years have developed it into a contorted theological monstrosity far beyond what we can legitimately assume Paul intended. This doctrinal behemoth reached its zenith in the Reformed view of the atonement of the 17th century as outlined in the *Westminster Confession of Faith* of 1646. According to that influential document, the atonement represents the pardoning legal loophole, supposedly devised by God so that he could allow the predestined elect out from under the eternal curse of sin. The theology maintains that the sacrifice was devised from the beginning by God as the provision for sin. Jesus represents the ultimate substitutionary sacrifice. Christ "atones" for our sin. He suffers the penalty that should, by the demand of the law, fall on us. His blood "purchases" our freedom.

Such a perspective turns the blood of Christ into a sort of "divine pixie dust" sprinkled on the believer to absolve him of the consequences of sin. Whatever image or analogy one uses, the effect is the same. The pixie dust makes the sin disappear. The Shield of Christ protects the sinner from God's Sword of Wrath. The legal loophole of the courtroom lets him off from his death sentence. Many other such metaphors and analogies have been devised through the years—one of the favorites envisioning the cross as a great bridge over the chasm of hell.

All these images convey the same—that Jesus protects the elect from God's wrath and from the judgment and curse of sin. In the Old Testament, the blood causes God to "pass over" the sin. Sin is not eliminated, it is passed over. The new covenant arrangement is substantially the same. Man's sinful nature remains, but grace covers the sin. His faith is imputed to him as righteousness. There is no *true* righteousness that results from the atonement...only "imputed" righteousness.

The whole thing is accomplished by a divine sleight of hand. It's a voodoo cross of old-covenental pagan magic. There is no significant difference between the old Jewish blood sacrifice and the sacrifice Christ made on the cross. The sinner remains a sinner whom God treats *as if* he is clean. It's all pretend. Christ is pure, therefore God will *pretend* that we are too.

TWO FOUNDATIONAL SUPPOSITIONS:
THE DEATH SENTENCE, THE INNOCENT SUBSTITUTE

Christians have been so indoctrinated into this 17th century Calvinist perspective that they scarcely pause to consider how completely it fails to deal with sin.

In MacDonald's view, a substitutionary blood-sacrifice was *never* God's intended remedy for sin. He expresses his outrage with the whole arrangement, and his disbelief that Christians so gullibly assent to it.

"This is the best device, according to the prevailing theology, that the God of truth—the God of mercy, whose glory is that he is just to men by forgiving their sins—could devise to save his creatures!

"The device is an absurdity—a grotesquely deformed absurdity. To represent the living God as a party to such a style of action, is to veil with a mask of cruelty...the face whose glory can be seen only in the face of Jesus." [72]

Let us return to the courtroom for a moment and analyze Paul's image in more detail.

The verses of Romans 3:23 and 6:23 stand as twin pillars in the courtroom orthodoxy of salvation: Everyone is pronounced guilty of sin (*3:23: All have sinned and fall short of the glory of God.*) The sentence for sin is death (*6:23: For the wages of sin is death, but the free gift of God is eternal life in Jesus Christ our Lord.*)

The common plan of salvation is built upon this foundation: Man stands condemned...God must punish all sin...man needs a savior to rescue him from the death sentence...Jesus takes the sentence on himself in man's stead.

This progression gives an appearance of being logical. It makes pretense of consistency with Scripture. But this salvation formula is based on two enormous presuppositions that may not be accurate at all.

Supposition 1: God is a judge who is *required* to pass a death sentence on sin.

Supposition 2: The law allows for an *innocent* to take the place of the guilty in satisfaction of the death sentence.

The most obvious question is a simple one that children ask all the time when something doesn't make sense:

Who says?

It may be as profound as it is simple. Who says that God is *required* to pass a death sentence on sin, especially on *all* sin? Where did such an idea come from?

And who says that it is possible for an innocent to satisfy the legal requirement against one convicted of a capital crime?

Such notions would make a mockery of any human court of law. How did such ideas come to occupy the core of Christian orthodoxy?

WHAT JESUS—AS BROTHER NOT DEFENSE ATTORNEY—*ACTUALLY* SAYS

It is not hard to see that Paul's courtroom image of the atonement is breaking down. The actual scenario should be played out something like this: The judge looks down on the prisoner and says: —

"Yes, my son, you *are* guilty. Your sin deserves death because it is working deeper death in you every day. You are in the process of dying, over and over. You are dying daily to all that is good. But you are my son. I do not condemn you—I love you. And my firstborn Son, your Attorney and Elder Brother...he and I can help you. If you allow us, we will turn that sin within you into *life*. If you let him, my Son will show you how to die as you are supposed to die—to the sin within you. If you die with him, as he died to his own will, and take my will as your own, just as he did, my Spirit and his Spirit will come and live within you. *Together*—you and

I and my Son Jesus—we will conquer sin and defeat the evil that is working death in you. Your sin will be forgiven and you will be raised to new life, just as He was raised from the dead to show you the way into that life. If you let us, we will work a supernatural miracle of grace and forgiveness in your heart. You will take your part with us every day in conquering sin and growing eternal life within you."

This is surely the perspective God intended man to apprehend from Jesus' death. This is what the cross means! The atonement is about *family reconciliation.*

PAUL'S METAPHOR PERVERTED INTO INJUSTICE—
A WEAK JUDGE AND UNJUST GOD

It may surprise many to know that the words *the wrath of God* or *God's wrath* never fell from Jesus' lips. Not once. You can search the red letters of your Bibles and you simply will not find them. Yet Paul's writings, and especially his letter to the Romans, are full of these phrases.

The Reformed theology of the atonement based on God's wrath takes the courtroom imagery to a hideous conclusion. The prisoner sits in the docket condemned. The judge stands ready to carry out the sentence. The judge HAS to carry it out. The law requiring death for sin is inviolate. That Law is greater than the judge. Even the judge has to abide by the law. Sin MUST result in death. The judge has no means, no right, no authority to ameliorate that sentence. The judge is weak, unyielding, ineffective. He has no power to do *right*. He is at the mercy of the law.

Against all conventions of *true* justice, therefore, against everything known of righteousness and truth, the judge agrees to a completely inverted scheme of direct *injustice*, lays the sentence on the willing substitute, and allows the prisoner to walk.

The whole notion is a perversion of true justice. The only way it can be read as anything but nonsensical is through a lens of hyper-legalism where the strict letter of an imaginary law trumps justice itself.

In other words, a penalty for the offence *must* be paid. It doesn't matter on whom it falls, as long as the guilt penalty is satisfied. Even if it falls on an *innocent*—the most perverse inversion of justice imaginable— that does not matter. If the penalty is paid, the law is satisfied, even if the mechanism of the whole process is *unjust*.

The spirit of the law matters nothing, the letter of the law matters everything.

Obviously any rational and thinking individual would conclude that a judge who would countenance such a contrivance is no judge of justice, but of an absurdly illogical legalism, a judge willing to cheat true justice with a judicial perversion.

Sad to say, a large segment of Christendom actually takes pride in the illogic of this arrangement by quoting Paul's words, "For the word of the cross is folly to whose who are perishing...For the foolishness of God is wiser than men." (1 Corinthians 1:18, 25)

The sonship of Jesus is so familiar to us that we mustn't miss its significance. Jesus was a *Son*, not a defense attorney. He came not to defend them in a court of law against a judge of condemnation, but to bring his brethren home to his Father's heart.

The doctrine took a wrong road centuries ago. We've got to go back to the fork in the road...and get it right.

The atonement is founded not in a courtroom, not in a predestined elect, not in a judge of wrath...but in a family.

The entire story of redemption, the entire theology of the atonement, must be viewed in this context—as an elder brother in search of his younger prodigals, with a loving and forgiving Father waiting with open arms to welcome those prodigals home.

GOD'S ESSENTIAL NATURE—FATHER NOT JUDGE

In the final analysis, most theological conundrums reduce to the character of God. When we truly know who God is, everything we think to wonder about falls into place.

What, then, do we know about God? What does Jesus tell us?

Undergirding every other characteristic in the divine nature, we know that God is a loving *Father*. This is his essence. Any theology of truth must begin with that Fatherhood and the Son's devoted love to that Fatherhood.

"The bond of the universe," MacDonald writes, "the chain that holds it together, the one active unity, the harmony of things...is the devotion of the Son to the Father. It is the life of the universe." [73]

All foundations must be laid in God's Fatherhood or eventually they will diverge from truth. Families will drift from truth. Churches will drift from truth. Philosophies will drift from truth. Religions will drift from truth. Scriptural interpretations will drift from truth. Theology will drift from truth. Doctrine will drift from truth. *Everything* that is not founded in the Fatherhood of God will eventually drift from truth.

God *does* judge. He *will* judge. But his judgment is righteous and true because he is a Father. His essential nature is not of a judge, but of a Father. As a Father he is not *required* to pass a death sentence on sin. That is what a *judge* might do. But it is not what a *Father*, by his essential nature is required to do.

FATHERHOOD MUST DESTROY SIN NOT PUNISH SIN

A father is required by the essence of his fatherhood to nourish goodness within his children. His heart's desire is to raise them to become sons and daughters that reflect kindness, goodness, selflessness, and love. He may find it necessary occasionally to punish in order to work toward that objective. But punishment, in and of itself, is not his objective.

Think of the repellant and gruesome implications were a father to punish every sin of his child to the utmost. Such a man would be a monster.

God cannot be *less* loving than a good-hearted human father. He must be *more* loving and forgiving than the best human father we could imagine. He is thus not required to *punish* all sin. He is required by his nature to *undo* sin, to *conquer* sin, to *overcome* sin, to *unmake* the effects of sin, to make sin forever impossible in his creation. In short, he is required by his nature to *destroy* sin.

The only way he can accomplish such a high purpose is by empowering the sinner, with his divine help, to destroy sin within himself. It is this single and eternal objective that imbues Gethsemane and Calvary with their deepest meaning and explains the sin-destroying power of the atonement.

The last thing a loving father would do is impose a *death* sentence on one of his children. The idea is appalling to contemplate. Even if punishment is needed along the way, the goal of a true father's heart is to find means to enable his children to conquer their selfishness so that they might become his wise and mature sons and daughters.

The *requirement* that God punish all sin, that a death sentence upon sin is a *mandatory* consequence of God's holiness, is an invention of small-minded theologians whose foundations have drifted. They have forgotten the universal Fatherhood. Leaving the anchoring truth of God's essential character, error has infected their theologies like a cancer.

In the radiant light of God's Fatherhood, Supposition 1 falls apart. *God is not required to pass a death sentence on sin.* The idea is a theological fiction invented by men.

SUBSTITUTION—PAGANISM SMUGGLED INTO JUDAISM AND THEN INTO CHRISTIANITY

Supposition 2 above becomes almost absurd when placed alongside *Fatherhood* rather than *judgment*. What Father would punish an innocent in place of the guilty?

How such an idea smuggled its way into Christian orthodoxy on the basis of the primitive pagan sacrifice is not only a mystery, it is an abomination. One would assume that Christian thinkers and theologians through the years would have inquired more deeply into the thing rather than allowing themselves to perpetuate such a grotesque misreading of the Old Testament blood sacrifice.

Imagine a father questioning his two children. There has been a serious transgression—intentional, malicious, and with far-reaching consequences. Jerry has been found guilty and is ready to face the music. He knows he must be punished. At his side, however, Chris says to his father, "Punish me instead and let Jerry off."

What justice-loving father would agree?

How would imposing the required discipline on Chris help *Jerry* face the consequences of his actions? The very idea represents the *antithesis* of justice.

A sadistic judge who loved neither Jerry nor Chris might agree. But a *father* would never agree. Their father knows that he needs to help Jerry learn to conquer the tendencies within him that led to the sin. His heart's desire is for Jerry to become good and selfless. Punishing Chris in Jerry's place won't help either of them become true sons.

In the radiant light of common sense and loving fatherhood, Supposition 2 also falls apart. *The substitution of an innocent for the guilty provides no remedy for sin.*

THE WAGES OF SIN: PENAL SENTENCE OR INEVITABLE OUTCOME

These two erroneous suppositions originate out of a fundamental misunderstanding of "the wages of sin." To get to the bottom of this confusion, we need to find out just what are the *wages* that result from sin.

The courtroom analogy forces us to the assumption that these wages are a "sentence" imposed. Sin *earns* or *deserves* death. Therefore, God as judge passes a *sentence* of death. This interpretation of the wages of sin proceeds directly from the fallacy that a *requirement* exists on the judge to impose a sentence of death—that the wages of sin are an *imposed* and *mandatory* penalty...that the Law of the universe *requires* it. Not even God can countermand the universal Law.

This requirement that theologians have laid upon God, however, is imaginary. No such scriptural mandate or universal Law exists. There *are* requirements demanded by God's Fatherhood to be sure—love, forgiveness, and infinite patience working unto repentance. But a sentence of death upon his created children is not one of them.

If the "wages" of sin are not mandated, imposed, or sentenced *externally*, then, where shall we look to discover what these wages are?

To find an answer, we again probe that region where we uncover solutions to many spiritual riddles—deep within ourselves.

At this point, Paul's marvelous wisdom unlocks a huge truth. Recall the inner war so graphically portrayed in Romans 7 between the flesh and the spirit. In the thirteenth verse Paul uses an extraordinary phrase to describe the effect of sin—*working death*. "It was sin working death in me..." He uses the ongoing, continual form of the verb to describe what sin does.

The wages of sin are *internal* not external.

Paul tells us precisely what those wages are. *The wages of sin are the working of death.* Paul's progression is clear: The *wages of sin* is death (6:23)...it is *sin working death* in me (7:13).

Paul's hugely significant insight into this inner battle, and the personal effects of sin upon human character, changes the entire salvationary equation.

Sin is continually *working* death. This death is not a *sentence imposed*, it is the inevitable result of *what sin does*. It is not imposed from the *outside*, it is the *internal* effect upon the men and women you and I are in the process of becoming.

The wages of sin are simply the net result of what effect sin has upon the human heart and character. The wages are not a sentence *against* sin, but the harvest *of* sin.

Sin *produces* death. Its wages are not the *pay* we receive but the *harvest* from what we plant.

SIN PRODUCES DEATH TO CHARACTER

The death that sin works is the ongoing daily death of goodness. The core soul of our being that was created in the image of God is slowly dying. The death is self-inflicted. We are dying to the *life* of God within us by a million cuts of sin. We are deathing *ourselves*. We are planting seeds whose harvest-wages are death.

Deep within our souls, life and death are thus engaged in the continual war of Romans 7. Jesus' prayer in Gethsemane examples the door out of that self-deathing prison. By doing as Jesus did, by following his *Not my will* example, and by allowing the miracle of his spirit-life to transform our inner nature, the downward decline of sin-working death is reversed.

In Gethsemane, we are able to lay claim to the *life* Jesus came to give and step out of the despair of Romans 7 into the power and reality of Romans 8.

UNLOCKING THE SALVATIONARY MESSAGE OF THE GOSPEL

The difference between "wages" *externally* imposed and "wages" *internally* self-grown is in one sense semantic. Sin *produces* death. We also *deserve* death. But it matters very much what foundation we lay in seeking to understand the mechanics of salvation.

What does Jesus save us from? At the point of this question, the two perspectives of wages diverge starkly.

Wages externally imposed: Do I need to be saved from a death sentence imposed by a condemning judge? Am I seeking to hide from God's Sword of Judgment behind Christ's Giant Shield of the Atonement?

Wages internally self-grown: Or do I need to be saved from the power of sin to destroy my manhood and prevent me growing into the man God created me to become?

These two contrasting scenarios are separated by an enormous theological divide. Which image most accurately reflects the work of the cross in my life? The two views produce opposite perspectives of God's work in the universe.

What do we need to be saved from?

Upon our response is based our outlook of what Christianity is about, who God is, and what the life of Jesus means. Our entire understanding of faith proceeds from the answer.

Do I need to be saved from *God*...or from *sin*?

From *God's sentence of death*...or from *sin's harvest within ME*?

Am I sitting in the dock of a courtroom listening to a judge handing down a death sentence against me? Or am I a child who needs the help of my Father and my elder Brother to become a good and obedient son?

Is the atonement a *Court of Law* or an eternal plan of *Family Reconciliation*?

Escaping the shackles of long-held retribution orthodoxies, at last we are freed to understand the atonement in a wonderful new light. We now perceive what both Father and Son contribute to mankind's salvation. The Son does not save us *from* the Father. The Son and the Father *together* help defeat the sin that is working death in us.

Erasing` from our theologies the imagery of a biblical penal system, the overarching message of family reconciliation explodes off the pages of Scripture wherever you look.

This is the salvationary power of the gospel.

The Father sent Jesus to bring his children home!

EXCERPTS FROM THE WRITINGS OF GEORGE MACDONALD
ON ATONEMENT

He made himself what he is by deathing himself into the will of the eternal Father, through which will he was the eternal Son—thus plunging into the fountain of his own life, the everlasting Fatherhood, and taking the Godhead of the Son.

This is the *life* that was made in Jesus: "That which was made in him was life."

This life, self-willed in Jesus, is the one thing that makes such life—the eternal life, the true life—possible, imperative, essential, to every man, woman, and child. The Father has sent us all into this outer world that we may go back into the inner world of his own heart. As the self-existent life of the Father has given us *being*, so the willed devotion of Jesus is his power to give us *eternal life* like his own—to enable us to do the same…

Because we are come out of the divine nature, which chooses to be divine, we also must *choose* to be divine. We must choose to be of God, to be one with God. We must choose to love and live as he loves and lives. We must choose to be partakers of the divine nature or we perish.

Man cannot originate this life. It must be shown him, and he must choose it. God is the father of Jesus and of us—of every possibility of our being. But while God is the father of his children, Jesus is the father of their childship. For in him is made the life which is sonship to the Father—namely the recognition, in fact and life, that the Father has his claim upon his sons and daughters.

We are not and cannot become true sons without our will willing his will. Our doing follows his making. It was the will of Jesus to be the thing God willed and meant him, that made him the true son of God. He was not the son of God because he could not help it, but because he willed to be in himself the son that he was in the divine idea.

So with us: We must *be* the sons and daughters we are. We are not made to be what we cannot help being. True sons and daughters do not exist after such fashion! We are sons and daughters in God's claim. Then we must *be* sons and daughters in our will. [74]

We can live in no way but that in which Jesus lived, in which life was made in him.

That way is to give up our life. This is the one supreme action of life possible to us for the making of life in ourselves. Christ did it of himself, and so became light to us that we might be able to do it in ourselves, after him, and through his originating act.

I repeat: We must do it ourselves. The help that he has given and gives, the light and the spirit-working of the Lord, the spirit, in our hearts, is all in order that we may, as we must, do it ourselves. Till then we are not alive. Life is not made in us. [75]

Very different are the good news Jesus brings us from certain prevalent representations of the gospel, founded on the pagan notion that suffering is an offset for sin, and culminating in the vile assertion that the suffering of an innocent man, just because he is innocent, yea perfect, is a satisfaction to the holy Father for the evil deeds of his children. As a theory concerning the atonement nothing could be worse, either intellectually, morally, or spiritually; announced as the gospel itself, as the good news of the kingdom of heaven, the idea is monstrous as any Chinese dragon. Such a so-called gospel is no gospel, however accepted as God sent by good men of a certain development...Doubtless some elements of the gospel are mixed up with it on most occasions of its announcement; none the more is it the message received from him. It can be good news only to such as are prudently willing to be delivered from a God they fear, but unable to accept the gospel of a perfect God, in whom to trust perfectly. [76]

Man finds it hard to get what he wants, because he does not want the best; God finds it hard to give, because he would give the best, and man will not take it. What Jesus did, was what the Father is always doing; the suffering he endured was that of the Father from the foundation of the world, reaching its climax in the person of his Son. God provides the sacrifice; the sacrifice is himself. He is always, and has ever been, sacrificing himself to and for his creatures...The worst heresy, next to that of dividing religion and righteousness, is to divide the Father from the Son...to represent the Son as doing that which the Father does not himself do. Jesus did nothing but what the Father did and does. If Jesus suffered for men, it was because his Father suffers for men...He is God our Saviour: it is because God is our Saviour that Jesus is our Saviour. [77]

In his second epistle to the Corinthians Paul says, "He hath made him to be sin for us who knew no sin, that we might be made the righteousness of God in him." (verse 5:21) This is read by some as: "He gave him to be treated like a sinner...that we might in him be made righteous like God...that Jesus was treated by God as if he were a sinner, our sins being imputed to him, in order that we might be treated as if we were righteous, his righteousness being imputed to us."

In other words, by a sort of legal fiction, Jesus was treated as what *he was not*, in order that we might be treated as what *we are not*. This is the best device, according to the prevailing theology, that the God of truth—the God of mercy, whose glory is that he is just to men by forgiving their sins—could devise to save his creatures!

I had thought that this most contemptible of false doctrines would have by now ceased to be presented, though I knew it would be long before it ceased to exercise its baneful influence. But to my astonishment I came upon it recently in quite a modern commentary which I happened to look into in a friend's house...

It seems to me, seeing how much duplicity exists in the body of Christ, that every honest member of it should protest against any word tending to imply the existence of falsehood in the indwelling spirit of that body.

Therefore, I now offer my protest against this so-called *doctrine*. I count it the rightful prey of the foolishest wind in the limbo of vanities, whither I would gladly do my best to send it. It is a mean, nauseous invention, false, and productive of falsehood.

If you say it is only a "picture" of truth, I will answer that it is not only a false one but an embodiment of untruth. If you say that it expresses a reality, I say it teaches the worst of lies. If you say that there is a shadow of truth in it, I answer it may be so, but there is no truth touched in it that could not be taught infinitely better without it.

It is the meagre misshapen offspring of the legalism of a poverty-stricken mechanical fancy, unlighted by a gleam of divine imagination. No one who knows his New Testament will dare to say that the figure is once used in it.

I have dealt already with the source from which the doctrine comes. They say first that God must punish the sinner, for justice requires it. Then they say that he does *not* punish the sinner, but punishes a perfectly righteous man instead—attributing that man's righteousness to the sinner—and by such a means God's justice is not compromised.

Was there ever such a confusion, such an inversion of right and wrong!

Justice *could not* treat a righteous man as an unrighteous. Neither, if justice required the punishment of sin, *could* justice let the sinner go unpunished. Justice is plainly compromised—and on both sides of the argument.

To lay the pain upon the righteous in the name of justice

is simply monstrous. No wonder unbelief is rampant. Believe in Moloch if you will, but call him Moloch, not Justice.

Be sure that the thing that God gives—the righteousness that is of God—is a real thing, and not a contemptible legalism. Pray God I have no righteousness imputed to me. Let me be regarded as the sinner I am, for nothing will serve my need but to be made a *truly* righteous man, one that will sin no more. [78]

This then, or something like this, for words are poor to tell the best things, is the righteousness which is of God by faith. It is so far from being a thing built of the rubbish heap of legal fiction called *vicarious sacrifice*, or its shadow called *imputed righteousness,* that only the child with a child-heart, so far ahead of and so different from those who think themselves wise and prudent, can understand it. [79]

"I believe in the Father of Jesus Christ, and do not tremble."

"You ought to tremble before an unreconciled God!"...

"Mother, I would gladly perish forever to save God from being the kind of God you would have me believe him..."

"We will not dispute about words! The question is, do you place your faith for salvation in the sufferings of Christ for you?"

"I do not, Mother. My faith is in Jesus himself, not in his sufferings."

"Then the anger of God is not turned away from you."...

"Mother, to say that the justice of God is satisfied with suffering is a piece of the darkness of hell. God is willing to suffer, and ready to inflict suffering to save from sin, but no suffering is satisfaction to him or his justice."

"What do you mean by his justice, then?"

"That he gives you and me and everybody fair play."

The ordinary sound of the phrase offended the moral ear of the mother...

"Then you do not believe that the justice of God demands the satisfaction of the sinner's endless punishment?"

"I do not...The justice of God is the love of what is right, and the doing of what is right. Eternal misery in the name of justice could satisfy none but a demon whose bad laws had been broken."

"But it is the Holy One who suffers for our sins."

"Oh, Mother! Can justice do wrong to satisfy itself? Did Jesus *deserve* punishment? If not, then to punish him was to wrong him."

"But he was willing; he consented."

"He yielded to injustice—but the injustice was man's, not God's. If justice insisted on punishment, it would at least insist on the guilty being punished, not the innocent…It satisfied *love* to suffer for another, but it does not satisfy *justice* that the innocent should be punished for the guilty. The whole idea of the atonement in that light is the merest figment of the paltry human intellect to reconcile difficulties of its own invention…"

"But why, then, should Christ have suffered?"

"It is the one fact that explains everything else," said Ian. "But I see no reason to talk about that now. So long as your theory satisfies you, Mother, why should I show you mine? When it no longer satisfies you, when it troubles you as it has troubled me, and as I pray God it may trouble you, then I will share my very soul with you."

"I do not see what other meaning you can put upon the statement that he was a sacrifice for our sins."

"Had we not sinned he would never have died; and he died to deliver us from our sins. He against whom was the sin became the sacrifice for it; the Father suffered in the Son, for they are one…"

"How can you say you believe in Christ when you do not believe in the atonement!"

"It is not so, Mother. I do not believe what you mean by the atonement. What God means by it, I do believe…"

"What do you call believing in him, then?"

"Obeying him, Mother—to say it as briefly as I can. I try to obey him in the smallest things he says…I strive to be what he would have me. A man may trust in Christ's atonement to his absolute assurance, but if he does not do the things he tells him—he does not yet believe in him. He may be a good man, but if he does not obey—well, you know what Jesus said would become of those who called him, Lord, Lord, but did not do what he said." [80]

"And is not God kinder than your father?"

"He canna weel be that, sir. And there's the Scripter!"

"But he sent his only Son to die for us."

"Ay—for the eleck, sir," returned the little theologian.

Now this was more than Mr. Cowie was well prepared to meet, for certainly this terrible doctrine was perfectly developed in the creed of the Scotch Church; the assembly of divines having sat upon the Scripture egg till they had hatched it in their own likeness. [81]

FIFTEEN

JUSTICE

by
George MacDonald

From *Unspoken Sermons, Third Series* [82]

Edited by Michael Phillips

Also unto thee, O Lord, belongeth mercy;
for thou renderest to every man according to his work—
Psalm lxii.12

S ome of the translators make it kindness and goodness. But I presume
there is no real difference among them as to the character of the word
which in Psalm 62:12 in the English Bible is translated *mercy*.

The religious mind, however, educated in the doctrines prevailing in
the so-called religious world, must here recognize a departure from what
they have been taught. To make the psalm speak according to prevalent
theology, the verse would have to be changed to read instead:—

"To thee, O Lord, belongeth *justice*, for thou renderest to every man
according to his work."

Let the reason of my choosing this passage, so remarkable in itself,
for a text to the sermon which follows, remain for the present
unexplained. I need hardly say that I mean to found no logical argument
upon it.

JUSTICE AS A LEGAL IDEAL

Let us endeavour to see plainly what we mean when we use the word
"justice," and whether we mean what we ought to mean when we use it—

especially with reference to God. Let us come nearer to knowing what we ought to understand by justice, that is, the justice of God. For his justice is the live, active justice, giving existence to the idea of justice in our minds and hearts. Because he *is* just, we are capable of knowing justice. It is because he is just, that we have the idea of justice so deeply imbedded in us.

What do we oftenest mean by justice? Is it not the carrying out of the law, the infliction of penalty assigned to offence? By a just judge we mean a man who administers the law without prejudice, without favour or dislike. And where guilt is plain, he punishes as much as, and no more than, the law has in the case laid down. It may not be that justice has therefore been done. The law itself may be unjust, and the judge may be mistaken. Or, which is more likely, the working of the law may be foiled by the parasites of law for their own gain. But even if the law be good, and thoroughly administered, it does not necessarily follow that justice is done.

Suppose my watch has been taken from my pocket. I lay hold of the thief. He is dragged before the magistrate, proved guilty, and sentenced to a just imprisonment. Will I then walk home satisfied with the result? Have I had justice done me?

The thief may have had justice done him—but where is my watch? It is gone, and I remain a man wronged.

Who has done me the wrong? The thief. Who can set right the wrong? The thief, and only the thief—nobody but the man that did the wrong.

God may be able to move the man to right the wrong, but God himself cannot right it without the man.

Suppose my watch is found and restored, is the account settled between me and the thief? I may forgive him, but is the wrong removed? By no means.

But suppose the thief think himself to repent. He has, we shall say, put it out of his power to return the watch, but he comes to me and says he is sorry he stole it and begs me to accept for the present what little he is able to bring, as a beginning of atonement. How should I then regard the matter? Should I not feel that he had gone far to make atonement—done more to make up for the injury he had inflicted upon me than the mere restoration of the watch, even by himself, could reach to?

Would there not lie, in the thief's confession and submission and initial restoration, an appeal to the divinest in me—to the eternal brotherhood? Would it not indeed amount to a sufficing atonement as between man and man?

If he offered to bear what I chose to lay upon him, should I feel it necessary, for the sake of justice, to inflict additional suffering upon him as demanded by righteousness? I should still have a claim upon him for my watch, but should I not be apt to forget it? He who commits the offence can make up for it—and he alone.

One thing must surely be plain—that the *punishment* of the wrong-doer makes no *atonement* for the wrong done. How could it make up to me for the stealing of my watch that the man was punished? The wrong would be there all the same.

I am not saying the man ought not to be punished—far from it. I am only saying that the punishment nowise makes up to the man wronged. Suppose the man, with the watch in his pocket, were to inflict the severest flagellation on himself. Would that lessen my sense of injury? Would it set anything right? Would it anyway atone? Would it give him a right to the watch? Punishment may do good to the man who does the wrong, but that is a thing as different as important.

Another thing, too, is plain, that, even without the material rectification of the wrong where that is impossible, repentance removes the offence which no suffering could. I at least should feel that I had no more quarrel with the man. I should even feel that the gift he had made me, giving into my heart a repentant brother, was infinitely beyond the restitution of what he had taken from me. True, he owed me both himself and the watch, but such a greater does more than include such a less.

If it be objected, "You may forgive, but the man has sinned against God!"—I return with the question: Is it not a part of the divine to be merciful? And then: Is it possible for a man to be more merciful than his maker! Is it possible for a man to do that which would be *too* merciful in God! If so, then mercy is not a divine attribute, for it may exceed and be too much; it must not be infinite, therefore cannot be God's own.

Perhaps it will be objected further: "Mercy may be against justice."

I answer, Never—if you mean by justice what I mean by justice. If anything be against justice, it cannot be called mercy, for it is cruelty. *"To thee, O Lord, belongeth mercy, for thou renderest to every man according to his work."*

There is no opposition, no strife whatever, between mercy and justice. Those who say justice means the *punishing of sin*, and mercy the *not* punishing of sin, and attribute both to God, would make a schism in the very idea of God.

And this brings me to the question, What is meant by *divine* justice?

DIVINE JUSTICE AS DISTINCT FROM HUMAN JUSTICE

Human justice may be a poor distortion of justice, a mere shadow of it. But the justice of God must be perfect. We cannot frustrate it in its working—we must be just to it in our idea of it.

If you ask any ordinary Sunday congregation in England, what is meant by the justice of God, would not nineteen out of twenty answer, that it means his punishing of sin? Think for a moment what degree of justice it would indicate in a man—that he punished every wrong. A Roman emperor, a Turkish cadi, might do that, and be the most unjust both of men and judges. Ahab might be just on the throne of punishment, and in his garden the murderer of Naboth.

In God shall we imagine a distinction of office and character? God is one. And the depth of foolishness is reached by that theology which talks of God as if he held different offices, and differed in each. It sets a contradiction in the very nature of God himself. It represents him, for instance, as having to do that as a magistrate which as a father he would not do! Is it possible that the love of the father would make him desire to be unjust as a magistrate!

Oh the folly of any mind that would explain God before obeying him! that would map out the character of God, instead of crying, *Lord, what wouldst thou have me to do?*

God is no magistrate. But if he were it would be a position to which his fatherhood alone gave him the right. His rights as a father cover every right he can be analytically supposed to possess.

The justice of God is this, that—to use a boyish phrase, the best the language will now afford me because of misuse—he gives every man, woman, child, and beast, everything that has being, *fair play.* He renders to every man according to his work. And therein lies his perfect mercy. For nothing else could be merciful to the man, and nothing but mercy could be fair to him.

God does nothing of which any just man, the thing set fairly and fully before him so that he understood, would not say, "That is fair."

Who would, I repeat, say a man was a just man because he insisted on prosecuting every offender? A scoundrel might do that. Yet the justice of God, forsooth, is imagined to consist of his punishment of sin!

A just man is one who cares, and tries, and always tries, to give fair play to everyone in every thing. When we speak of the justice of God, let us see that we do mean justice! Punishment of the guilty may be involved in justice, but it does not constitute the justice of God one atom more than it would constitute the justice of a man.

RIGHT AND WRONG BELIEF ABOUT GOD

"But no one ever doubts that God gives fair play!"

"That may be—but does not go for much, if you say that God does this or that which is not fair."

"If he does it, you may be sure it is fair."

"Doubtless, or he could not be God—except to devils. But you say he does so and so, and is just. I say, he does *not* do so and so, and is just. You say he does, for the Bible says so. I say, if the Bible said so, the Bible would lie, but the Bible does not say so.

The lord of life complains of men for not judging right. To say on the authority of the Bible that God does a thing no honourable man would do, is to lie against God. To say that it is therefore right, is to lie against the very spirit of God. To uphold a lie for God's sake is to be against God, not for him.

God cannot be lied for. He is the truth. The truth alone is on his side. While his child could not see the rectitude of a thing, he would infinitely rather, even if the thing were right, have him say, *God could not do that thing,* than have him believe that he did it. If the man were sure God did it, the thing he ought to say would be, "Then there must be something about it I do not know, which if I did know, I should see the thing quite differently."

But where an evil thing is invented to explain and account for a good thing, and a lover of God is called upon to believe the invention or be cast out, he needs not mind being cast out, for it is into the company of Jesus. Where there is no ground to believe that God does a thing except that men who would explain God have believed and taught it, he is not a true man who accepts men against his own conscience of God.

I acknowledge no authority calling upon me to believe a thing of God, which I could not be a man and believe right in my fellow-man. I will accept no explanation of any way of God which explanation involves what I should scorn as false and unfair in a man.

If you say, That may be right of God to do which it would not be right of man to do, I answer, Yes, because the relation of the maker to his creatures is very different from the relation of one of those creatures to another, and he has therefore duties toward his creatures requiring of him what no man would have the right to do to his fellow-man. But he can have no duty that is not both just *and* merciful.

More is required of the maker, by his own act of creation, than can be required of men. *More* and *higher* justice and righteousness is required of him by himself, the Truth— *greater* nobleness, *more* penetrating sympathy, and *nothing* but what, if an honest man understood it, he would say was right. If it be a thing man cannot understand, then man can say nothing as to whether it is right or wrong. He cannot even know that God does it, when the *it* is unintelligible to him. It may be but the smallest facet of a composite action. His part is silence.

If it be said by any that God does a thing, and the thing seems to me unjust, then either I do not know what the thing is, or God does not do it. The saying cannot mean what it seems to mean, or the saying is not true.

If, for instance, it be said that God visits the sins of the fathers on the children, a man who takes *visits upon* to mean *punishes*, and *the children* to mean *the innocent children,* ought to say, "Either I do not understand the statement, or the thing is not true, whoever says it."

God *may* do what seems to a man not right, but it must so seem to him because God works on *higher*, on divine, on *perfect* principles, *too* right for a selfish, unfair, or unloving man to understand. But least of all must we accept some low notion of justice in a man, and argue that God is just in acting in that low manner.

WHY IS PUNISHMENT NECESSARY?

The common idea, then, is, that the justice of God consists in punishing sin. It is in the hope of giving a larger idea to the justice of God in punishing sin that I ask, *"Why is God bound to punish sin?"*

It may be replied: "How could he be a just God and not punish sin?"

"Mercy is a good and right thing," I answer, "and but for sin there could be no mercy. We are enjoined to forgive, to be merciful, to be as our father in heaven. Two rights cannot possibly be opposed to each other. If God punish sin, it must be merciful to punish sin. And if God forgive sin, it must be just to forgive sin.

"*We* are required to forgive, with the argument that our father forgives. It must, I say, be right to forgive.

"Every attribute of God must be infinite as himself. He cannot be sometimes merciful, and not always merciful. He cannot be just, and not always just. Mercy belongs to him, and needs no contrivance of theologic chicanery to justify it."

"Then you mean that it is wrong to punish sin, therefore God does not punish sin?"

"By no means. God does punish sin, but there is no opposition between punishment and forgiveness. The one may be essential to the possibility of the other. *Why*, I repeat, does God punish sin? That is my point."

"Because in itself sin deserves punishment."

"Then how can he tell us to forgive it?"

"He punishes, and having punished he forgives?"

"That will hardly do. If sin demands punishment, and the righteous punishment is given, then the man is free. Why should he be forgiven?"

"He needs forgiveness because no amount of punishment will be as much as he deserves."

I avoid for the present, as anyone may perceive, the probable expansion of this reply.

"Then why not forgive him at once if the punishment is not essential—if part can be pretermitted?" And I ask again, Can that be required which, according to what you have said, is not adequate?

You will perhaps answer, "God may please to take what little he can have."

And this brings me to the fault in the whole idea.

Punishment is *nowise* an *offset* to sin. Foolish people sometimes, in a tone of self-gratulatory pity, will say, "If I have sinned I have suffered."

Yes, to be sure, but what of that? What merit is there in it? Even had you laid the suffering upon yourself, what did that do to make up for the wrong? That you may have been bettered by your suffering is well for you, but what atonement is there in the suffering?

The notion is a false one altogether. Punishment, deserved suffering, is no equipoise to sin. It is no use laying it in the other scale. It will not move it a hair's breadth. Suffering weighs nothing at all against sin. It is not of the same kind, not under the same laws, any more than mind and matter.

We say a man deserves punishment. But when we forgive and do not punish him, we do not *always* feel that we have done wrong. Neither when we do punish him do we feel that any amend has been made for his wrongdoing. If it were an offset to wrong, then God would be bound to punish for the sake of the punishment. But he cannot be, for he forgives.

Then it is not for the sake of the punishment, as a thing that in itself ought to be done, but for the sake of something *else*, as a *means to an end,* that God punishes. It is not directly for justice, else how could he show mercy, for that would involve injustice?

DESTRUCTION NOT PUNISHMENT

Primarily, God is not bound to *punish* sin; he is bound to *destroy* sin. If he were not the Maker, he might not be bound to destroy sin—I do not know. But seeing he has created creatures who have sinned, and therefore sin has, by the creating act of God, come into the world, God is, in his own righteousness, bound to destroy sin.

"But that is to have no mercy."

You mistake. God does destroy sin. He is always destroying sin. In him I trust that he is destroying sin in me. He is always saving the sinner from his sins, and that is destroying sin. But vengeance on the sinner, the law of a tooth for a tooth, is not in the heart of God, neither in his hand.

If the sinner and the sin in him, are the concrete object of the divine wrath, then indeed there can be no mercy. Then indeed there will be an end put to sin by the destruction of the sin and the sinner together.

But thus would no atonement be wrought—nothing be done to make up for the wrong God has allowed to come into being by creating man. There must be an atonement, a making-up, a bringing together—an atonement which, I say, cannot be made except by the man who has sinned.

Punishment, I repeat, is not the thing required of God, but the absolute destruction of sin. What better is the world, what better is the sinner, what better is God, what better is the truth, that the sinner should suffer—continue suffering to all eternity? Would there be less sin in the universe? Would there be any making-up for sin? Would it show God justified in doing what he knew would bring sin into the world, justified in making creatures who he knew would sin? What setting-right would come of the sinner's suffering? If justice demand it, if suffering be the equivalent for sin, then the sinner must suffer, then God is bound to exact his suffering, and not pardon. If this be so, the making of man was a tyrannical deed, a creative cruelty.

But grant that the sinner has deserved to suffer, no amount of suffering is any atonement for his sin. To suffer to all eternity could not make up for one unjust word. Does that mean, then, that for an unjust word I deserve to suffer to all eternity? The unjust word is an eternally evil thing. Nothing but God in my heart can cleanse me from the evil that uttered it. But does it follow that I saw the evil of what I did so perfectly, that eternal punishment for it would be just? Sorrow and confession and self-abasing love will make up for the evil word. Suffering will not.

For evil in the abstract, nothing can be done. It is eternally evil. But I may be saved from it by learning to loathe it, to hate it, to shrink from it with an eternal avoidance.

The only vengeance worth having on sin is to make the sinner himself its executioner.

Sin and punishment are in no antagonism to each other in man, any more than pardon and punishment are in God. They can perfectly co-exist. The one naturally follows the other, punishment being born of sin, because evil exists only by the life of good and has no life of its own, being in itself death. Sin and suffering are not natural opposites. The opposite of evil is good, not suffering. The opposite of sin is not suffering, but righteousness. The path across the gulf that divides right from wrong is not the fire, but repentance.

If my friend has wronged me, will it console me to see him punished? Will that be a rendering to me of my due? Will his agony be a balm to my deep wound? Should I be fit for any friendship if that were possible even in regard to my enemy? But would not the shadow of repentant grief, the light of reviving love on his countenance, heal it at once however deep?

Take any of those wicked people in Dante's hell, and ask wherein is justice served by their punishment. Mind, I am not saying it is not right to punish them. I am saying that justice is not, never can be, satisfied by suffering—nay, cannot have any satisfaction in or from suffering. Human resentment, human revenge, human hate may. Such justice as Dante's keeps wickedness alive in its most terrible forms. It sees the life of God as going forth to inform, or at least give a home to victorious evil. Is he not defeated every time that one of those lost souls defies him? All hell cannot make Vanni Fucci say "I was wrong."

God is triumphantly defeated, I say, throughout the hell of such a vengeance. Although against evil, it is but the vain and wasted cruelty of a tyrant. There is no destruction of evil thereby, but an enhancing of its horrible power in the midst of the most agonizing and disgusting tortures a divine imagination can invent.

If sin must be kept alive, then hell must be kept alive. But while I regard the smallest sin as infinitely loathsome, I do not believe that any being, never good enough to see the essential ugliness of sin, could sin so as to *deserve* such punishment.

I am not now, however, dealing with the question of the *duration* of punishment, but with the *idea* of punishment itself. I would only say in passing, that the notion that a creature born imperfect, nay, born with impulses to evil not of his own generating, and which he could not help having, a creature to whom the true face of God was never presented, and by whom it never could have been seen, should be thus condemned, is as loathsome a lie against God as could find place in heart too undeveloped to understand what justice is, and too low to look up into the face of Jesus. It never in truth found place in any heart, though in many a pettifogging brain.

There is but one thing lower than deliberately to believe such a lie, and that is to worship the God of whom it is believed.

The one deepest, highest, truest, fittest, most wholesome suffering must be generated in the wicked by a vision, a true sight, more or less adequate, of the hideousness of their lives, of the horror of the wrongs they have done. Physical suffering may be a factor in rousing this mental pain. But "I would I had never been born!" must be the cry of Judas, not because of the hell-fire around him, but because he loathes the man that betrayed his friend, the world's friend.

When a man loathes himself, he has begun to be saved. Punishment tends to this result. Not for its own sake, not as a make-up for sin, not for divine revenge—horrible word. Not for any satisfaction to justice, can punishment exist.

PUNISHMENT EXISTS TO PRODUCE REPENTANCE

Punishment is for the sake of amendment and atonement. God is bound by his love to punish sin *in order to deliver his creature.* He is bound by his justice to destroy sin in his creation. Love is justice—is the fulfilling of the law, for God as well as for his children.

This is the reason of punishment. This is why justice requires that the wicked shall not go unpunished—that they, through the eye-opening power of pain, may come to see and do justice, may be brought to desire and make all possible amends, and so become just. Such punishment concerns justice in the deepest degree.

For Justice, that is God, is bound in himself to see justice done by his children—not in the mere outward act, but in their very being.

He is bound in himself to make up for wrong done by his children, and he can do nothing to make up for wrong done but by bringing about the repentance of the wrong-doer.

When the man says, "I did wrong. I hate myself and my deed. I cannot endure to think that I did it!" then, I say, is atonement begun. Without that, all that the Lord did would be lost. He would have made no atonement. Repentance, restitution, confession, prayer for forgiveness, righteous dealing thereafter, is the sole possible, the only true make-up for sin. For nothing less than this did Christ die.

When a man acknowledges the right he denied before, when he says to the wrong, "I abjure, I loathe you, I see now what you are, I could not see it before because I would not. God forgive me. Make me clean, or let me die!" then justice, that is God, has conquered—and not till then.

"What atonement is there in that?" you ask.

Every atonement that God cares for. And the work of Jesus Christ on earth was the creative atonement, because it works atonement in every heart. He brings and is bringing God and man, and man and man, into perfect unity: "I in them and thou in me, that they may be made perfect in one."

"That is a dangerous doctrine!" many will object.

More dangerous than they think to many things—to every evil, to every lie, and among the rest to every false trust in what Christ did, instead of in Christ himself. Paul glories in the cross of Christ, but he does not *trust* in the cross. He trusts in the living Christ and his living father.

SIN MUST BE PUT AN END TO

Justice then requires that sin should be put an end to. And not that only, but that it should be atoned for.

Where punishment can do anything to this end, where it can help the sinner to know what he has been guilty of, where it can soften his heart to see his pride and wrong and cruelty, justice requires that punishment shall not be spared.

The more we believe in God, the surer we shall be that he will spare nothing that suffering can do to deliver his child from death. If suffering cannot serve this end, we need look for no more hell, but for the destruction of sin by the destruction of the sinner. That, however, would, it appears to me, be for God to suffer defeat, blameless indeed, but defeat.

If God be defeated, he must destroy—that is, he must withdraw life. How can he go on sending forth his life into irreclaimable souls, to keep sin alive in them throughout the ages of eternity? But then, I say, no atonement would be made for the wrongs they have done. God remains defeated, for he has created that which sinned, and which would not repent and make up for its sin.

But those who believe that God will thus be defeated by many souls, must surely be of those who do not believe he cares enough to do his very best for them.

He is their Father. He had power to make them out of himself, separate from himself, and capable of being one with him. Surely he will somehow save and keep them! Not the power of sin itself can close *all* the channels between creating and created.

FALSE NOTIONS OF SUFFERING

The notion of suffering as an offset for sin, the foolish idea that a man by suffering borne may get out from under the hostile claim to which his wrong-doing has subjected him, comes first of all, I think, from the satisfaction we feel when wrong comes to grief.

Why do we feel this satisfaction? Because we hate wrong, but, not being righteous ourselves, we more or less hate the wronger as well as his wrong. Hence, we are not only righteously pleased to behold the law's disapproval proclaimed in his punishment, but unrighteously pleased with his suffering, because of the impact upon us of his wrong. In this way the inborn justice of our nature passes over to evil.

It is no pleasure to God, as it so often is to us, to see the wicked suffer. To regard any suffering with satisfaction, except it be sympathetically with its curative quality, comes of evil, is inhuman because undivine, is a thing God is incapable of.

His nature is always to forgive, and just because he forgives, he punishes. Because God is so altogether alien to wrong, because it is to him a heart-pain and trouble that one of his little ones should do the evil thing, there is, I believe, no extreme of suffering to which, for the sake of destroying the evil thing in them, he would not subject them. A man might flatter, or bribe, or coax a tyrant. But there is no refuge from the love of God. That love will, for very love, insist upon the uttermost farthing.

"That is not the sort of love I care about!"

No—how should you? I well believe it! You cannot care for it until you begin to know it. But the eternal love will not be moved to yield you to the selfishness that is killing you. What lover would yield his lady to her passion for morphia? You may sneer at such love, but the Son of God who took the weight of that love, and bore it through the world, is content with it, and so is everyone who knows it.

The love of the Father is a radiant perfection. Love and not self-love is lord of the universe.

Justice demands your punishment, because justice demands, and will have, the destruction of sin. Justice demands your punishment because it demands that your father should do his best for you. God, being the God of justice, that is of fair-play, and having made us what we are, apt to fall and capable of being raised again, is in himself bound to punish in order to deliver us—otherwise is his relation to us poor beside that of an earthly father. "To thee, O Lord, belongeth mercy, for thou renderest to every man according to his work." A man's work is his character, and God in his mercy is not indifferent, but treats him according to his work.

FALSE NOTIONS OF SALVATION

The notion that the salvation of Jesus is a salvation from the consequences of our sins, is a false, mean, low notion.

The salvation of Christ is salvation from the smallest tendency or leaning to sin. It is a deliverance into the pure air of God's ways of thinking and feeling. It is a salvation that makes the heart pure, with the will and choice of the heart to be pure.

To such a heart, sin is disgusting. It sees a thing as it is—that is, as God sees it. For God sees everything as it is. The soul thus saved would rather sink into the flames of hell than steal into heaven and skulk there under the shadow of an imputed righteousness. No soul is saved that would not prefer hell to sin.

Jesus did not die to save us from punishment. He was called Jesus because he should save his people from their sins.

If punishment in and of itself be no atonement for sin, how does the fact bear on the popular theology accepted by every one of the opposers of what they call Christianity, as representing its doc-trines? Most of us have been more or less trained in that theology, and not a few of us have thereby, thank God, learned what it is—an evil thing, to be cast out of intellect and heart. Many imagine such theology dead and gone, but in reality it lies at the root (the intellectual root only, thank God) of much the greater part of the teaching of Christianity in the country. It is believed in—so far as the false *can* be believed in—by many who think they have left it behind, when they have merely omitted the truest, most offensive modes of expressing its doctrines. It is humiliating to find how many comparatively honest people think they get rid of a falsehood by softening the statement of it, by giving it the shape and placing it in the light in which it will least assert itself. In so doing they are able to pass both with such as hold it thoroughly, and such as might revolt against it more plainly spoken.

NOT TO PERSUADE BUT TO LIFT FALSE BURDENS

Once for all I will ease my soul regarding the horrid phantasm. I have passed through no change of opinion concerning it since first I began to write or speak. But I have written little and spoken less about it, because I would preach no mere negation. My work was not to destroy the false, except as it came in the way of building the true. Therefore I sought to speak but what I believed, saying little concerning what I did not believe, trusting, as now I trust, in the true to cast out the false, and shunning dispute. Neither will I now enter any theological lists to be the champion for or against mere doctrine.

I have no desire to change the opinion of man or woman. Let everyone for me hold what he pleases. But I would do my utmost to disable such as think correct opinion essential to salvation from laying any other burden on the shoulders of true men and women than the yoke of their Master. And such burden, if already oppressing any, I would gladly lift.

Let the Lord himself teach them, I say. A man who has not the mind of Christ—and no man has the mind of Christ except him who makes it his business to obey him—cannot have correct opinions concerning him. Neither, if he could, would they be of any value to him: he would be nothing the better, he would be the worse for having them. Our business is not to think correctly, but to live truly. Then first will there be a possibility of our thinking correctly.

One chief cause of the amount of unbelief in the world is, that those who have seen something of the glory of Christ, set themselves to theorize concerning him rather than to obey him. In teaching men, they have not taught them Christ, but taught them about Christ. More eager after credible theory than after doing the truth, they have speculated in a condition of heart in which it was impossible they should understand. They have presumed to explain a Christ whom years and years of obedience could alone have made them able to comprehend. Their teaching of him, therefore, has been repugnant to the common sense of many who had not half their privileges, but in whom, as in Nathanael, there was no guile. Such, naturally, press their theories, in general derived from them of old time, upon others, insisting on their thinking about

Christ as they think, instead of urging them to go to Christ to be taught by him whatever he chooses to teach them. They do their unintentional worst to stop all growth, all life.

From such and their false teaching I would gladly help to deliver the true-hearted. Let the dead bury their dead, but I would do what I may to keep them from burying the living.

GOD'S JUSTICE CANNOT BE SATISFIED WITH DIRECT INJUSTICE

If there be no satisfaction to justice in the mere punishment of the wrong-doer, what shall we say of the notion of satisfying justice by causing one to suffer who is *not* the wrong-doer? And what, moreover, shall we say to the notion that, just because he is not the person who deserves to be punished, but is absolutely innocent, his suffering gives perfect satisfaction to the perfect justice?

That the injustice be done with the consent of the person maltreated makes no difference: It makes it even worse, seeing, as they say, that justice requires the punishment of the sinner, and here is one far more than *innocent*.

They have shifted their ground. It is no more *punishment*, but mere *suffering* the law requires!

The thing gets worse and worse. I declare my utter and absolute repudiation of the idea in any form whatever. Rather than believe in a justice—that is, a God—to whose righteousness, abstract or concrete, it could be any satisfaction for the wrong-doing of a man that a man who did no wrong should suffer, I would be driven from among men, and dwell with the wild beasts that have not reason enough to be unreasonable.

What! God, the father of Jesus Christ, like that! His justice contented with direst injustice! The anger of him who will nowise clear the guilty, appeased by the suffering of the innocent!

Very God forbid!

Observe: The evil fancy actually substitutes for punishment not mere suffering, but that suffering which is farthest from punishment.

And this when, as I have shown, punishment, the severest, can be no satisfaction to justice!

TO BELIEVE A LIE OF GOD IS ITS OWN REWARD...AND PUNISHMENT

How did it come ever to be imagined? It sprang from the trustless dread that cannot believe in the forgiveness of the Father, cannot believe that even God will do anything for nothing, cannot trust him without a legal arrangement to bind him. How many, failing to trust God, fall back on *a text*, as they call it! It sprang from the pride that will understand what it cannot, before it will obey what it sees.

He that will understand *first* will believe a lie—a lie from which obedience alone will at length deliver him.

If anyone say, "But I believe what you despise," I answer, To believe it is your punishment for being able to believe it; you may call it your reward, if you will. You ought not to be able to believe it. It is the merest, poorest, most shameless fiction, invented without the perception that it was an invention—fit to satisfy the intellect, doubtless, of the inventor, else he could not have invented it. It has seemed to satisfy also many a humble soul, content to take what was given, and not think, content that another should think for him, and tell him what was the mind of his Father in heaven.

Again I say, let the person who can be so satisfied be so satisfied. I have not to trouble myself with him. That he can be content with it, argues him unready to receive better. So long as he can believe false things concerning God, he is such as is capable of believing them—with how much or how little of blame, God knows.

Opinion, right or wrong, will do nothing to save him. I would that he thought no more about this or any other opinion, but set himself to do the work of the Master. With his opinions, true or false, I have nothing to do. It is because such as he force evil things upon their fellows—utter or imply them from the seat of authority or influence—to their agony, their paralysation, their unbelief, their indignation, their stumbling, that I have any right to speak. I would save my fellows from having what notion of God is possible to them blotted out by a lie.

WHY HAS SUBSTITUTION REMAINED AN ACCEPTED DOCTRINE SO LONG?

If it be asked how, if it be false, the doctrine of substitution can have been permitted to remain so long an article of faith to so many, I answer, On the same principle on which God took up and made use of the sacrifices men had, in their lack of faith, invented as a way of pleasing him.

Some children will tell lies to please the parents that hate lying. They will even confess to having done a wrong they have not done, thinking their parents would like them to say they had done it, because they teach them to confess. God accepted men's sacrifices until he could get them to see—and with how many has he yet not succeeded, in the church and out of it!—that he does not care for such things.

"But," again it may well be asked, "whence then has sprung the undeniable potency of that teaching?"

I answer, From its having in it a notion of God and his Christ, poor indeed and faint, but, by the very poverty and untruth in its presentation, fitted to the weakness and unbelief of men, seeing it was by men invented to meet and ease the demand made upon their own weakness and unbelief.

Thus the leaven spreads. The truth is there. It is Christ the glory of God. But the ideas that poor slavish souls breed concerning this glory the moment the darkness begins to disperse, is quite another thing.

Truth is indeed too good for men to believe. They must dilute it before they can take it. They must dilute it before they dare give it. They must make it *less* true before they can believe it enough to get any good of it.

Unable to believe in the love of the Lord Jesus Christ, they invented a mediator in his mother, and so were able to approach a little where else they had stood away. Unable to believe in the forgivingness of their father in heaven, they invented a way to be forgiven that should not demand of him so much, which might make it right for him to forgive, but which at the same time should save them from having to believe downright in the tenderness of his father-heart, for that they found impossible.

They thought him bound to punish for the sake of punishing, as an offset to their sin; they could not believe in clear forgiveness. That did not seem divine. It needed itself to be justified, so they invented for its justification a horrible injustice, involving all that was bad in sacrifice, even human sacrifice.

They invented a satisfaction for sin which was an insult to God. He sought no satisfaction, but an obedient return to the Father. What satisfaction was needed he made himself in what he did to cause them to turn from evil and go back to him.

The thing was too simple for complicated unbelief and the arguing spirit.

Gladly would I help their followers to loathe such thoughts of God. But for that, they themselves must grow to become better men and women. While they are capable of being satisfied with such ideas, there would be no advantage in their becoming intellectually convinced that they were wrong. I would not speak a word to persuade them of it. Success would be worthless. They would but remain what they were— children capable of thinking meanly of their father.

When the heart recoils, discovering how horrible it would be to have such an unreality for God, it will begin to search about and see whether it must indeed accept such statements concerning God. It will search after a real God by whom to hold fast, a real God to deliver them from the terrible idol.

It is for those thus moved that I write, not at all for the sake of disputing with those who love the lie they may not be to blame for holding. The latter are like the Jews of old who would cast out of their synagogue the man who doubts the genuineness of their moral caricature of God. They would now cast out he who doubts the travesty they make of the grandest truth in the universe, the atonement of Jesus Christ. Of such a man they will unhesitatingly report that he does not believe in the atonement. But a lie for God is against God, and carries the sentence of death in itself.

Instead of giving their energy to do the will of God, men of power have given it to the construction of a system by which to explain why Christ must die, what were the necessities and designs of God in permitting his death. And men of power of our own day, while casting from them not a little of the good in the teaching of the Roman Church, have clung to the morally and spiritually vulgar idea of justice and satisfaction held by pagan Rome, buttressed by the Jewish notion of sacrifice, and in its very home, alas, with the mother of all the western churches! Better the reformers had kept their belief in a purgatory, and parted with what is called vicarious sacrifice!

THE DOCTRINE OF VICARIOUS SACRIFICE

Their system is briefly this: God is bound to punish sin, and to punish it to the uttermost. His justice requires that sin be punished. But he loves man, and does not want to punish him if he can help it. Jesus Christ says, "I will take his punishment upon me." God accepts his offer, and lets man go unpunished—upon a condition. His justice is more than satisfied by the punishment of an infinite being instead of a world of worthless creatures. The suffering of Jesus is of greater value than that of all the generations, through endless ages, because he is infinite, pure, perfect in love and truth, being God's own everlasting son. God's condition with man is, that he believe in Christ's atonement thus explained. A man must say, "I have sinned, and deserve to be tortured to all eternity. But Christ has paid my debts, by being punished instead of me. Therefore he is my Saviour. I am now bound by gratitude to him to turn away from evil."

Some would doubtless insist on his saying a good deal more, but this is enough for my purpose.

As to the justice of God requiring the punishment of the sinner, I have said enough. That the mere suffering of the sinner can be no satisfaction to justice, I have also tried to show. If the suffering of the sinner be indeed required by the justice of God, let it be administered.

But what is it possible to say adequate to confront the base representation that it is not punishment, not the suffering of the sinner that is required, but suffering!—nay, as if this were not depth enough of baseness to crown all heathenish representation of the ways of God—that the suffering of the innocent is unspeakably preferable in his eyes to that of the wicked, as a make-up for wrong done! nay, again, "in the lowest deep a lower deep," that the suffering of the holy, the suffering of the loving, the suffering of the eternally and perfectly good, is supremely satisfactory to the pure justice of the Father of spirits!

Not all the suffering that could be heaped upon the wicked could buy them a moment's respite, so little is their suffering a counterpoise to their wrong. In the working of this law of equivalents, this *lex talionis*, the suffering of millions of years could not equal the sin of a moment. No amount of suffering could pay off one farthing of the deep debt. But so much more valuable, precious, and dear, is the suffering of the innocent, so much *more* of a satisfaction—observe—to the *justice* of God, that in return for that suffering *another* wrong is done: The sinners who deserve and ought to be punished are set free.

I know the root of all that can be said on the subject. The notion is imbedded in the gray matter of my Scotch brains. And if I reject it, I know what I reject. For the love of God my heart rose early against the low invention.

Strange that in a Christian land it should need to be said, that to punish the innocent and let the guilty go free is unjust! It wrongs the innocent, the guilty, and God himself. It would be the worst of all wrongs to the guilty to treat them as innocent. The whole device is a piece of spiritual charlatanry—fit only for a fraudulent jail-delivery. If the wicked ought to be punished, it is the worst possible perversion of justice to take a righteous being, however strong, and punish him instead of the sinner, however weak.

To the poorest idea of justice in punishment, it is essential that the sinner, and no other than the sinner, should receive the punishment. The strong being that was willing to bear such punishment might well be regarded as worshipful, but what of the God whose so-called justice he thus defeats?

If you say it is justice, not God that demands the suffering, I say justice cannot demand that which is unjust. Indeed, the whole thing is unjust.

God is absolutely just, and there is no deliverance from his justice, which is one with his mercy.

The device is an absurdity—a grotesquely deformed absurdity. To represent the living God as a party to such a style of action, is to veil with a mask of cruelty and hypocrisy the face whose glory can be seen only in the face of Jesus. It is to put a tirade of vulgar Roman legality into the mouth of the Lord God merciful and gracious, who will by no means clear the guilty.

I HAVE SEEN HIS FACE IN THE FACE OF JESUS

Rather than believe such ugly folly of him whose very name is enough to make those that know him heave the breath of the hart panting for the waterbrooks, rather than think of him what in a man would make me avoid him at the risk of my life, I would say, "There is no God. Let us neither eat nor drink, that we may die! For lo, this is not our God! This is not he for whom we have waited!"

But I have seen his face and heard his voice in the face and the voice of Jesus Christ. And I say this is our God, the very one whose being the Creator makes it an infinite gladness to be the created. I will not have the God of the scribes and the pharisees whether Jewish or Christian, protestant, Roman, or Greek, but thy father, O Christ! He is my God.

If you say, "That is our God, not yours!" I answer, "Your portrait of your God is an evil caricature of the face of Christ."

To believe in a vicarious sacrifice, is to think to take refuge with the Son from the righteousness of the Father, to take refuge with his work instead of with the Son himself, to take refuge with a theory of that work instead of the work itself. It is to shelter behind a false quirk of law instead of nestling in the eternal heart of the unchangeable and righteous Father, who is merciful in that he renders to every man according to his work. He compels their obedience, but will not admit judicial quibble or subterfuge.

God will never let a man off with any fault. He must have him clean. He will excuse him to the very uttermost of truth, but not a hair's-breadth beyond it. He is his true father, and will have his child true as his son Jesus Christ is true.

He will impute to him nothing that he has not, will lose sight of no smallest good that he has. He will quench no smoking flax, break no bruised reed, but send forth judgment unto victory.

He is God beyond all that heart hungriest for love and righteousness could to eternity desire.

SOME NEVER LOOK THEIR IDEAS IN THE FACE

If you say the best of men have held the opinions I stigmatize, I answer, "Some of the best of men have indeed held these theories, and of men who have held them I have loved and honoured some heartily and humbly—but because of what they *were*, not because of what they *thought*.

They were what they were because of their obedient faith, not because of their opinion. They were not better men because of holding these theories. In virtue of knowing God by obeying his son, they rose above the theories they had never looked in the face, and so had never recognized as evil. Many have arrived, in the natural progress of their sacred growth, at the point where they must abandon them.

The man of whom I knew the most good gave them up gladly. Good to worshipfulness may be the man that holds them, and I hate them the more therefore. They are lies that, working under cover of the truth mingled with them, burrow as near the heart of the good man as they can go.

Whoever, from whatever reason of blindness, may be the holder of a lie, the thing is still a lie, and no falsehood must mingle with the justice we mete out to it.

There is nothing for any lie but the pit of hell. Yet until the man sees the thing to be a lie, how shall he but hold it! Are there not mingled with it shadows of the best truth in the universe? So long as a man is able to love a lie, he is incapable of seeing it is a lie.

He who is true, out and out, will know at once an untruth. And to that vision we must all come.

I do not write for the sake of those who either make or heartily accept any lie. When they see the glory of God, they will see the eternal difference between the false and the true, and not till then.

I write for those whom such teaching as theirs has folded in a cloud through which they cannot see the stars of heaven, so that some of them even doubt if there be any stars of heaven. For the holy ones who believed and taught these things in days gone by, all is well. Many of the holiest of them cast the lies from them long before the present teachers of them were born. Many who would never have invented them for themselves, yet receiving them with the seals affixed of so many good men, took them in their humility as recognized truths, instead of inventions of men. Oppressed by authority, the authority of men far inferior to themselves, they did not dare dispute them, but proceeded to order their lives by what truths they found in their company, and so had their reward, the reward of obedience. By that obedience they were brought to know God, and that knowledge broke for them the net of a presumptuous self-styled orthodoxy.

Every man who tries to obey the Master is my brother, whether he counts me such or not, and I revere him. But dare I give quarter to what I see to be a lie, because my brother believes it? The lie is not of God, whoever may hold it.

WHAT THEN IS MY DOCTRINE?

"Well, then," one may say, "If you thus unceremoniously cast to the winds the doctrine of vicarious sacrifice, what theory do you propose to substitute in its stead?"

"In the name of the truth," I answer, *None*. I will send out no theory of mine to rouse afresh little whirlwinds of dialogistic dust mixed with dirt and straws and holy words, hiding the Master in talk about him. If I have any such, I will not cast it on the road as I walk, but present it on a fair patine to him to whom I may think it well to show it.

Only eyes opened by the sun of righteousness, and made single by obedience, can judge even the poor moony pearl of formulated thought. Say if you will that I fear to show my opinion. Is the man a coward who will not fling his child to the wolves? What faith in this kind I have, I will have to myself before God, till I see better reason for uttering it than I do now.

"Will you then take from me my faith, and help me to no other?"

Your faith! God forbid. Your theory is not your faith, nor anything like it. Your faith is your obedience, your theory I know not what.

Yes, I will gladly leave you without any of what you *call* faith. Trust in God. Obey the word—every word of the Master. That is faith. So believing, your opinion will grow out of your true life, and be worthy of it.

Peter says the Lord gives the spirit to them that obey him: The spirit of the Master, and that alone, can guide you to any theory that it will be of use to you to hold. A theory arrived at any other way is not worth the time spent on it.

Jesus is the creating and saving lord of our intellects as well as of our more precious hearts. Nothing that he does not think is worth thinking. No man can think as he thinks, except he be pure like him. No man can be pure like him, except he go with him, and learn from him.

To put off obeying him till we find a credible theory concerning him, is to set aside the potion we know it our duty to drink, for the study of the various schools of therapy. You know what Christ requires of you is right—much of it at least you believe to be right, and your duty to do, whether he said it or not: *Do it.* If you do not do what you know of the truth, I do not wonder that you seek it intellectually, for that kind of search may well be, as Milton represents it, a solace even to the fallen angels. But do not call anything that may be so gained, *The Truth*.

How can you, not caring to *be* true, judge concerning him whose life was to do for very love the things you confess your duty, yet do them not?

Obey the truth, I say, and let theory wait. Theory may spring from life, but never life from theory.

I BELIEVE

I will not then tell you what I think, but I will tell any man who cares to hear it what I believe. I will do it now. Of course what I say must partake thus much of the character of theory that I cannot prove it. I can only endeavour to order my life by it.

I believe in Jesus Christ, the eternal Son of God, my elder brother, my lord and master. I believe that he has a right to my absolute obedience whereinsoever I know or shall come to know his will, that to obey him is to ascend the pinnacle of my being, that not to obey him would be to deny him. I believe that he died that I might die like him—die to any ruling power in me but the will of God—and thus live ready to be nailed to the cross as he was, if God will it. I believe that he is my Saviour from myself, and from all that has come of loving myself, from all that God does not love, and would not have me love—all that is not worth loving. I believe that he died that the justice, the mercy of God, might have its way with me, making me just as God is just, merciful as he is merciful, perfect as my father in heaven is perfect. I believe and pray that he will give me what punishment I need to set me right, or keep me from going wrong. I believe that he died to deliver me from all meanness, all pretence, all falseness, all unfairness, all poverty of spirit, all cowardice, all fear, all anxiety, all forms of self-love, all trust or hope in possession. I believe that he died to make me merry as a child, the child of our father in heaven, loving nothing but what is lovely, desiring nothing I should be ashamed to let the universe of God see me desire. I believe that God is just like Jesus, only greater yet, for Jesus said so. I believe that God is absolutely, grandly beautiful, even as the highest soul of man counts beauty, but infinitely beyond that soul's highest idea—with the beauty that creates beauty, not merely shows it, or itself exists beautiful. I believe that God has always done, is always doing his best for every man. I believe that no man is miserable because God is forgetting him. I believe that he is not a God to crouch before, but our father, to whom the child-heart cries exultant, "Do with me as thou wilt."

I believe that there is nothing good for me or for any man but God, and more and more of God, and that alone through knowing Christ can we come nigh to him.

I believe that no man is ever condemned for any sin except one—that he will not leave his sins and come out of them, and be the child of him who is his father.

I believe that justice and mercy are simply one and the same thing. Without justice to the full there can be no mercy, and without mercy to the full there can be no justice. Such is the mercy of God that he will hold his children in the consuming fire of his distance until they pay the uttermost farthing, until they drop the purse of selfishness with all the dross that is in it, and rush home to the Father and the Son, and the many brethren— rush inside the centre of the life-giving fire whose outer circles burn. I believe that no hell will be lacking which would help the just mercy of God to redeem his children.

I believe that to him who obeys, and thus opens the doors of his heart to receive the eternal gift, God gives the spirit of his son, the spirit of himself, to be in him, and lead him to the understanding of all truth. I believe that the true disciple shall thus always know what he ought to do, though not necessarily what another ought to do. I believe that the spirit of the father and the son enlightens by teaching righteousness. I believe that no teacher should strive to make men think as he thinks, but to lead them to the living Truth, to the Master himself, of whom alone they can learn anything, who will make them in themselves know what is true by the very seeing of it. I believe that the inspiration of the Almighty alone gives understanding. I believe that to be the disciple of Christ is the end of being, and that to persuade men to be his disciples is the end of teaching.

HE MADE ATONEMENT!

"The sum of all this," will be the complaint of some against me, "is that you do not believe in the atonement?"

I believe in Jesus Christ. Nowhere am I requested to believe *in* any thing, or *in* any statement, but everywhere to believe in God and in Jesus Christ.

In what you call *the atonement*, in what you mean by the word, what I have already written must make it plain enough I do not believe. God forbid I should, for it would be to believe a lie, and a lie which is to blame for much non-acceptance of the gospel in this and other lands. But, as the word was used by the best English writers at the time when the translation of the Bible was made—with all my heart, and soul, and strength, and mind, I believe in the atonement, call it the *a-tone-ment,* or the *at-one-ment,* as you please.

I believe that Jesus Christ is our atonement, that through him we are reconciled to, made one with God.

There is not one word in the New Testament about reconciling God to us. It is we that have to be reconciled to God. I am not writing, neither desire to write, a treatise on the atonement, my business being to persuade men to be atoned to God. But I will go so far to meet my questioner as to say—without the slightest expectation of satisfying him, or the least care whether I do so or not, for his opinion is of no value to me, though his truth is of endless value to me and to the universe—that, even in the sense

of the atonement being a making-up for the evil done by men toward God,
I believe in the atonement. Did not the Lord cast himself into the eternal
gulf of evil yawning between the children and the Father? Did he not
bring the Father to us, let us look on our eternal Sire in the face of his true
son, that we might have that in our hearts which alone could make us love
him—a true sight of him?

Did he not insist on the one truth of the universe, the one saving truth,
that God was just what he was? Did he not hold to that assertion to the
last, in the face of contradiction and death? Did he not thus lay down his
life persuading us to lay down ours at the feet of the Father? Has not his
very life by which he died passed into those who have received him, and
re-created theirs, so that now they live with the life which alone is life?
Did he not foil and slay evil by letting all the waves and billows of its
horrid sea break upon him, go over him, and die without rebound—spend
their rage, fall defeated, and cease?

Verily, he made atonement!

We sacrifice to God!—it is God who has sacrificed his own son to us.
There was no way else of getting the gift of himself into our hearts.

Jesus sacrificed himself to his father and the children to bring them
together—all the love on the side of the Father and the Son, all the
selfishness on the side of the children. If the joy that alone makes life
worth living, the joy that God is such as Christ, be a true thing in my
heart, how can I but believe in the atonement of Jesus Christ? I believe it
heartily, as God means it.

HE MAKES US MAKE ATONEMENT

Then again, as the power that brings about a making-up for any
wrong done by man to man, I believe in the atonement. Who that believes
in Jesus does not long to atone to his brother for the injury he has done
him? What repentant child, feeling he has wronged his father, does not
desire to make atonement?

Who is the mover, the causer, the persuader, the creator of the
repentance, of the passion that restores fourfold?—Jesus, our propitiation,
our atonement.

He is the head and leader, the prince of the atonement. He could not
do it without us, but he leads us up to the Father's knee: He makes us
make atonement.

Learning Christ, we are not only sorry for what we have done wrong,
we not only turn from it and hate it, but we become able to serve both God
and man with an infinitely high and true service, a soul-service. We are
able to offer our whole being to God to whom by deepest right it belongs.

Have I injured anyone? With him to aid my justice, new risen with him from the dead, shall I not make good amends? Have I failed in love to my neighbour? Shall I not now love him with an infinitely better love than was possible to me before? That I will and can make atonement, thanks be to him who is my atonement, making me at one with God and my fellows! He is my life, my joy, my lord, my owner, the perfecter of my being by the perfection of his own.

I dare not say with Paul that I am the slave of Christ. But my highest aspiration and desire is to be the slave of Christ.

"But you do not believe that the sufferings of Christ, as sufferings, justified the supreme ruler in doing anything which he would not have been at liberty to do but for those sufferings?"

I do not.

I believe the notion as unworthy of man's belief, as it is dishonouring to God. It has its origin doubtless in a salutary sense of sin. But sense of sin is not inspiration, though it may lie not far from the temple-door. It is indeed an opener of the eyes, but upon home-defilement, not upon heavenly truth. It is not the revealer of secrets.

Also there is another factor in the theory, and that is unbelief—incapacity to accept the freedom of God's forgiveness, the incapacity to believe that it is God's chosen nature to forgive, that he is bound in his own divinely willed nature to forgive.

No atonement is necessary to him but that men should leave their sins and come back to his heart.

But men cannot believe in the forgiveness of God. Therefore they need, therefore he has given them a mediator. And yet they will not know him. They think of the father of souls as if he had abdicated his fatherhood for their sins, and assumed the role of judge. If he put off his fatherhood, which he cannot do, for it is an eternal fact, he puts off with it all relation to us. He cannot repudiate the essential and keep the resultant.

Men cannot, or will not, or dare not see that nothing but his being our father gives him any right over us—that nothing but that could give him a perfect right. They regard the father of their spirits as their governor! They yield the idea of the Ancient of Days, "the glad creator," and put in its stead a miserable, puritanical martinet of a God, caring not for righteousness, but for his rights, caring not for the eternal purities, but the goody proprieties.

The prophets of such a God take all the glow, all the hope, all the colour, all the worth, out of life on earth, and offer you instead what they call eternal bliss—a pale, tearless hell.

Of all things, turn from a mean, poverty stricken faith. But, if you are straitened in your own mammon-worshipping soul, how shall you believe in a God any greater than can stand up in that prison-chamber?

I desire to wake no dispute. I will myself dispute with no man. But for the sake of those whom certain *believers* trouble, I have spoken my mind.

I love the one God seen in the face of Jesus Christ. From all copies of Jonathan Edwards's portrait of God, however faded by time, however softened by the use of less glaring pigments, I turn with loathing.

Not such a God is he concerning whom was the message John heard from Jesus, that he is light, and in him is no darkness at all.

SIXTEEN

WHO IS HOLDING THE SCISSORS?

The Ancient Truth of Sanctification [83]

by
Michael Phillips

The flip side, or perhaps we should call it the "continuation side," of the atonement is represented by the doctrine of sanctification—the transformation of character that takes place in the life of a believer as a result of the atonement.

The operative questions are: Who is the author of that transformation, and what are the mechanics of how it happens?

How does a Christian grow into Christlikeness? Does being a Christian *insure* growth toward Christlikeness? Is sanctification automatic?

Questions such as these were not essential elements of Old Testament Jewish spirituality. Bound by legalism, personal righteousness was not a focus of Judaism's creed. In this case, therefore, Jesus' *You have heard that it was said* applies to old-covenant thinking that has infected what passes as new-covenant Christian theology, but is in fact still mired in ancient legalisms. Such legalisms Jesus sweeps away with his, *But I say to you.*

The image indicated by the title of this chapter may help us visualize the doctrine practically. We each have sin within us—a "sin nature" that predisposes us toward sin. It makes us do wrong, think wrong thoughts, make bad choices, put ourselves first. It rouses anger, resentments, bitternesses, and selfish responses.

How do we put those sinful tendencies to death so that we slowly grow more like Christ?

If the operation is a process of spiritual surgery—cutting out the cancerous sin of Self so that the Christ-nature of new life flourishes and grows and bears fruit in our lives—who does the cutting and how? How do the "scissors of sanctification" snip sin out of our lives?

Or is such a thing even necessary? Does Jesus' death on the cross take care of it for us? Is the pixie dust blood sprinkled over our heads and into our hearts so that sanctification is accomplished of itself? By believing in Christ, are we sanctified already? Is this what is meant by Christ's "finished work?"

PASSIVE VS. ACTIVE SANCTIFICATION

We previously noted George MacDonald's conviction that the atonement is entirely *active* from man's side. There is no magic trick. He emphasizes that man must take his own willing, choosing, ongoing share in making "atonement" for sin. Without Christ we cannot do it. But with Christ, *we* must do it. We are not mere observers. We are not automatically *made* into God's obedient children. We *become* sons and daughters of the Father by one means only, through obedience. MacDonald would say that the scissors work by obedience. When we obey, sin's power is lessened, cut away bit by bit. The work of the cross may be "finished" in theory. But it is not finished in us. That work continues daily.

Many will object on the basis of the old boogieman of "works." Such is a common response to the suggestion that we must take accountability on our own shoulders for spiritual growth. But "works" is an imaginary phantasm.

To the ears of the prevailing orthodoxy of fundamentalism, the idea of "taking a share in our own making" is radical indeed. The phrase, "we must do it ourselves" is nothing short of heresy to those who believe such an idea demeans the work of Christ on the cross. They want to cling to the doctrinal mirage that they don't have to *do* anything except believe.

This error comes straight from 17th century Reformed thinking. The Westminster Shorter Catechism terms sanctification "the work of God's free grace, whereby we are renewed in the whole man after the image of God, and are enabled more and more to die unto sin, and live unto righteousness." [84]

Every verb construction is passive. We don't have to *do* any renewing, we don't have to *die* to sin, we *are renewed* and *are enabled*. It's all done for us.

J.I. Packer adds: "The concept is...of a divinely wrought character change freeing us from sinful habits and forming in us Christlike affections, dispositions, and virtues. Sanctification ...engenders real righteousness within the frame of relational holiness. Relational sanctification, the state of being permanently set apart for God, flows from the cross, where God through Christ purchased and claimed us for himself." [85]

It's all in God's hands. We just stand back passively and let the Holy Spirit change us. It happens automatically. Discipleship on the easy-does-it-plan.

But is this scriptural?

When Peter blew it, Jesus didn't put his arm on his shoulder and say, "Hey, no problem, Pete. The Holy Spirit will engender real righteousness with a frame of relational holiness within you after a while. Just wait a few years and you will experience a divinely wrought character change that will free you from your sinful habits."

No. He spun around and said, "Get behind me, Satan! You don't have in mind the things of God, but the things of men."

The obedience Jesus commanded was no passive obedience. When he finished the parable of the good Samaritan, he didn't look at his listeners and say, "Okay now, folks, study this principle and memorize this story. I hope you were taking notes and learning the principles, because over time a divinely wrought character change will engender righteousness within you."

He said, "Go and do the same."

The word is unambiguous—DO the same.

A DUAL PARTNERSHIP ATONEMENT

The doctrine of imputed righteousness is central to this passive Reformed sanctification, in which man is *made* righteous by legal mechanisms rather than *becoming* righteous by DOING what Jesus said.

MacDonald saw the atonement, and the resultant sanctification that is God's purpose to work into us, as a miraculous partnership between Christ and man. Jesus shows us how atonement is to be made by putting motives of self-will to death. *Not my will but your will be done*, is not only a prayer, it is the entire moment-by-moment life-focus of obedient self-relinquishment into the will of the Father. It is the heart's cry that enlivens the reality of the atonement within us.

With the Lord's help, we must do as he did.

We put self motive to death in the same way he did—by dying into the will of the Father through the exercise of free will, by *choosing* obedience.

Such atonement, like salvation, is an ongoing lifelong *process*. The atonement and sanctification shine the same light onto the steps of our daily path through different facets of the Fatherhood prism.

"Our Satan must go," MacDonald wrote, "every hair and feather! Neither shalt thou think to be delivered from the necessity of *being* good by being made good." [86]

Responsibility for the development of childness thus rests on *our* shoulders. Jesus cannot do it *for* us. We must put to death our own sin by *choosing* not to sin, by *choosing* unselfishness, by *choosing* forgiveness, by *choosing* to put others ahead of ourselves, by *choosing* self-denial, by *choosing* to endure our personal crosses with humility and gratitude, by *choosing* kindness, by *choosing* the gracious response, by *choosing* the smile and kind word, by *choosing* cheerfulness, by *choosing* a quiet spirit, by *choosing* to pray *Not my will.*

This ongoing moment-by-moment "choosing" represents the scissors of sanctification. In such choosing is sin sliced away—a thousand times, ten thousand times...choices, tiny daily choices to die to self as Jesus died to self, that the Father's life might flow out of us as it flowed out of him.

Jesus originates the possibility of *our* choosing in *his* choosing.

SELF-WILL—THE TRUE NEW COVENANT SACRIFICE

Risking the objection of another evangelical boogieman, we now add the word *example* to the discussion as an alternative to "substitution," and suggest that atonement is accomplished by an interfusing within the life of the believer of *miracle* and *example.* Obedience is the means by which we bring the Lord's example into the moment-by-moment choices that every day throws at us. As we thus obey, a transforming miracle infuses that obedience with power.

True atonement for sin must exist on a higher and different plane than the Old Testament sacrifice, even than the *fulfillment* of that sacrifice. It must not merely be a new *interpretation* of the old blood sacrifice. It must be a new *type* of sacrifice.

The sacrifice Christ made to atone for sin was the self-denying relinquishment of his will into the Father's will. He consented to the cross *so that we would see what the atoning sacrifice truly was.*

That sacrifice was not *blood* but *self-will.* Its purpose was to empower us to do as he had done, putting our *own* sin to death on our own daily crosses of self-denying choices.

"The only vengeance worth having on sin," MacDonald writes, "is to make the sinner himself its executioner." [87]

Christ's sacrifice of self-will cannot substitute for *our* making the same sacrifice. He made the sacrifice so that we too would know *how* to make it. He sacrificed *his* self-will that we might be empowered to sacrifice *our* self will.

Then his Spirit helps us to do it.

The Old Testament sacrifice was indeed "substitutionary," but not as many suppose. It foreshadowed what was to come. It demonstrated that *something* must be killed on the altar to make atonement for sin. That "something," however, was no human sacrifice, but self-will. The power does not exist in the blood. The power exists in chosen relinquishment of self-will.

Self-will is the new-covenant sacrifice. Its altar exists in the depths of our hearts.

This is the road home. This is the path to oneness, the means by which, using MacDonald's word, *at-one-ment* with our Father is restored.

THE MYSTERIOUS INTERPENETRATION OF MIRACLE *AND* EXAMPLE

The interworking of miracle and example in Christ's death is a great spiritual wonder whose power to change human life and draw humanity up into God's heart, and make weak mortals into his sons and daughters, is a mystery we cannot entirely penetrate.

By calling it a pattern we must follow, it is yet something we cannot achieve alone. It is not *mere* example. It is God-infused miraculous example. Christ made the sacrifice so that we would likewise be enabled to make it. But it is a sacrifice *we* must make, in a sense, on our own.

Miracle does not substitute for example. Neither does example substitute for miracle. Miracle opens the door. Obedience takes us through it.

We are now in a position to answer the question posed by the title of this chapter. Who is holding the scissors of sanctification? As C.S. Lewis says, this is like asking which blade of the scissors does the most work. [88]

Sanctification as we grow into Christlikeness is a joint process, a spiritual *partnership* where miracle and example fuse as one.

The Holy Spirit is holding one blade, we hold the other. The two blades work together, or they don't work at all.

SUMMARY OF GOD'S REDEMPTIVE PURPOSE FOR MANKIND

When the ancient truths of universal Fatherhood, salvation, atonement, and sanctification are rediscovered and brought into harmony, a picture emerges of a salvationary atoning work far more encompassing than that represented by the orthodox paradigm popularized and hardened into cement by Reformed theology.

Man becomes more personally accountable for his own fate and eternal destiny. Far from diminishing Christ's role in redemption, strengthening man's role actually enlarges, practicalizes, and further glorifies Christ's eternal work.

Once this larger picture begins to unfold, the clouds of many troublesome remnants of Calvinist doctrine break apart, and the sun of God's true nature shines through with greatly renewed clarity and radiance.

EXCERPTS FROM THE WRITINGS OF GEORGE MACDONALD
ON SANCTIFICATION

He made himself what he is by deathing himself into the will of the eternal Father, through which will he was the eternal Son—thus plunging into the fountain of his own life, the everlasting Fatherhood, and taking the Godhead of the Son.

This is the *life* that was made in Jesus: "That which was made in him was life."

This life, self-willed in Jesus, is the one thing that makes such life—the eternal life, the true life—possible, imperative, essential, to every man, woman, and child. The Father has sent us all into this outer world that we may go back into the inner world of his own heart. As the self-existent life of the Father has given us *being*, so the willed devotion of Jesus is his power to give us *eternal life* like his own—to enable us to do the same...

Because we are come out of the divine nature, which chooses to be divine, we also must *choose* to be divine. We must choose to be of God, to be one with God. We must choose to love and live as he loves and lives. We must choose to be partakers of the divine nature or we perish.

Man cannot originate this life. It must be shown him, and he must choose it. God is the father of Jesus and of us—of every possibility of our being. But while God is the father of his children, Jesus is the father of their childship. For in him is made the life which is sonship to the Father—namely the recognition, in fact and life, that the Father has his claim upon his sons and daughters.

We are not and cannot become true sons without our will willing his will. Our doing follows his making. It was the will of Jesus to be the thing God willed and meant him, that made him the true son of God. He was not the son of God because he could not help it, but because he willed to be in himself the son that he was in the divine idea.

So with us: We must *be* the sons and daughters we are. We are not made to be what we cannot help being. True sons and daughters do not exist after such fashion! We are sons and daughters in God's claim. Then we must *be* sons and daughters in our will. [89]

We can live in no way but that in which Jesus lived, in which life was made in him.

That way is to give up our life. This is the one supreme action of life possible to us for the making of life in ourselves. Christ did it of himself, and so became light to us that we might be able to do it in ourselves, after him, and through his originating act.

I repeat: We must do it ourselves. The help that he has given and gives, the light and the spirit-working of the Lord, the spirit, in our hearts, is all in order that we may, as we must, do it ourselves. Till then we are not alive. Life is not made in us. [90]

We live by the will of the self-existent God. The links of unity with him already exist within us. All they need is to be brought together. In order to find the link in our being with which to close the circle of immortal oneness with the Father, we must of course search the deepest of man's nature. There only can it be found.

And there we do find it. For the *will* is the deepest, the strongest, the divinest thing in man. So, I presume, is it in God, for such we find it in Jesus Christ. Here, and here only, in the relation of the two wills, God's and his own, can a man come into vital contact with the All-in-all. And it is no one-sided unity of complete dependence, but is the eternal idea of willed harmony of dual oneness. When a man can and does entirely say, *Not my will, but thine be done*—when he so wills the will of God as to do it, then is he one with God—one, as a true son with a true father.

God's life within him is the causing and bearing of his life. It is therefore absolutely and only of its kind, one with it more and deeper than words or figures can say. It is the life which is itself, only more of itself, and more than that, which *causes* itself. When a man wills that his being be conformed to that being of his origin, which is the life in his life, when a man thus accepts his own causing life, *and sets himself to live the will of that causing life,* humbly eager after the privileges of his origin, he thus receives God's life into himself. He becomes, in the act, a partaker of the divine nature, a true son of the living God, and an heir of all he possesses. By the obedience of a son, he receives into himself the very life of the Father.

Obedience is the joining of the links of the eternal round. Obedience is but the other side of the creative will. Will is God's will, obedience is man's will. The two make one. The root-life, knowing well the thousand troubles it would bring upon him, has created, and goes on creating other lives, that, though incapable of self-being, they may, by willed obedience, share in the bliss of his essential self-ordained being.

If we do the will of God, eternal life is ours. It is no mere continuity of existence, for that in itself is worthless as hell. Rather it is a being that is one with God's essential Life, and so able to fill us with the abundant and endless outgoings of his life. Our souls shall thus become vessels ever growing. And ever as they grow shall they be filled with more and more life proceeding from the Father and the Son, from God the ordaining, and God the obedient. [91]

PART 3

JONATHAN EDWARDS REDUX— SINNERS IN THE HANDS OF AN ANGRY GOD

Unlocking the Truth About Hell

Seventeen

The Tree Lies Where it Falls

An Ancient Truth About Death

by
Michael Phillips

With rediscovered foundations in place of universal Fatherhood, salvation, atonement, and sanctification, we are in a position to probe higher into God's plan for man and the universe as they reach toward eternity.

Examining God's redemptive purpose thus far, we have focused chiefly on the Christian life—how we are to relate to God, what salvation in *this* life means, how the atonement and sanctification function in a daily and ongoing way to produce Christlikeness in the character of the Christian.

Eventually death comes. Everything changes. What then?

What if the job God intended to accomplish isn't finished? What if the believer *hasn't* learned to death his self on the altar of sacrifice? What if the scissors of sanctification *haven't* cut away sin? What if correct beliefs notwithstanding, selfishness, pride, hypocrisy, and mammon still rule?

Or will such things even matter then? Is "belief" the sole entry qualification for heaven? At the moment of death, will any distinction exist between those Christians who have spent their lives growing more to reflect the image of God's Son, and those who haven't?

More importantly, what about those who have not begun the homeward journey toward reconciliation at all, those who have professed no belief in Jesus, and outright sinners who are evil through and through? Are all these doomed to an eternity in hell?

As we turn our focus from this life to the next, the question looms large on the theologic horizon: How will God work to accomplish his eternal purposes in whatever forms life's journey takes *after* death?

This odyssey we are on together will often cause three major charges to be brought against those who are bold to search the Scriptures for its deeper truths. There will be dozens of minor unorthodoxies. But three in particular represent Heresies with a capital H.

One we have already considered—an atonement of *mutuality*, which reveals the hidden, mysterious, yet surely obvious truth that we are responsible for taking our *own* daily share in Christ's work of the cross.

The other two are post-death heresies. We come to one of those now. That is the possibility that death does not close the door to the operation of God's redemptive work.

You will know by now that the word "heresy" is used facetiously. These are not heresies at all. They are phantom boogiemen that many are afraid of in the dark. But no monster is there. As "works" is an imaginary boogieman, so are these so-called "heresies."

DOES DEATH FOREVER CLOSE THE DOOR
BETWEEN CREATOR AND UNREPENTANT CREATED?

An expansive vision of God's reconciliatory purpose explodes out of the fog with the shocking, stunning, breathtaking, wonderful recognition that spiritual growth and response may not cease at death. This incredible idea blows the doors off our customary images of heaven and hell. It may not be so simple as that after death everyone walks through one door or the other. There may yet be more growth required before those final determinations are made

This turns the entire universe of our salvationary preconceptions on its head!

Do you mean...but the idea is too huge...can it possibly be...are you saying...that God is able to *continue* wooing and drawing, redeeming and saving, forgiving and healing...in the *next* life as well as this!

The orthodoxy stiffens in anger.

No! it shouts *Death is the end. The tree lies where it falls. The sheep and the goats. There are no second chances!*

One can only wonder in amazement *why* traditionalists become angry with the suggestion that death is not a final closed door. Why do not Christians everywhere rejoice at such a glorious prospect?

It was the idea of "post death opportunity" that first landed George MacDonald in controversy. His expressed belief, as the deacons of his church described it, in "a future state of probation" for the heathen, was the primary reason given for his dismissal in 1853 from the first and only pulpit he held. [92]

Once we get beyond what we have been taught, however, the truth emerges as obvious: God's *spiritually* redemptive work cannot suddenly stop because *physical* life ceases. How can we say that God's work will *cease*...forever? The very idea is a contradiction in God's character.

MAY AND CAN

The difference between *may* and *can* is illuminating. Their distinction raises intriguing questions about repentance in the afterlife.

Will people be *capable* of repenting after death, but God won't *permit* it? Or will they be *incapable* of it and so the question of God's permitting it won't come up?

Imagine after death, perhaps even in hell, that a man or woman gains an audience with God, or prays to him—who hasn't wondered if prayer in hell is possible? His prayer goes like this:

"God, I see my sin for what it is. I repent of it."

What would be God's response?

"Too late, you are not *permitted* to repent now...repentance is no longer allowed. You *may* not repent."

Or would he say, "You only imagine yourself repentant. Now that your earthly life is past, however, you are no longer *capable* of true repentance. You *can* not repent."

In other words, does the commonly held theology prohibiting post-death repentance fall under the purview of *can* not or *may* not?

Or perhaps the man prays, "God, I am truly sorry for my sin. Please forgive me."

Would God reply, "I am unable to forgive you now. I am *prevented* from doing so. I neither can *nor* may forgive you. A law higher even than my own omnipotence constrains me and makes forgiveness now impossible."

In other words—is God constrained by laws of *may* and *can* higher than himself, higher than his own being?

The very idea seems ludicrous. Yet traditional orthodoxy is built upon precisely this foundation—that God is *powerless* to do certain things.

He wants to, but he just can't. He *wants* to save his whole creation, but he has no means to do so without violating certain spiritual legalities incumbent upon him by the laws of the universe. Thus, he is *impotent* from carrying out the work that is natural to his being (love, forgiveness, redemption, healing, reconciliation) beyond the moment of death.

He is *prevented* from doing so.

WHAT IS INFINITY?

Consider what *infinite* love and *infinite* forgiveness must mean.

Is it possible that they will cease, that a time will come when God the Almighty will no longer be able to love and forgive certain of his created beings?

We say that God's love is unceasing, unending, infinite. At what point, then, does his forgiveness, or his *capacity* to forgive, or his *willingness* to forgive, come to an end? Is *love* infinite, but *forgiveness* finite?

Some would say that God continues to love and continues to forgive even those souls lost in the torments of hell, yet in spite of this love it will nevertheless give him pleasure and serve his purpose to punish them for their sin forever. Thus, his love is indeed infinite, yet so is his wrath against sin. Such nonsensical arguments amount to talking in circles. We might as well say that white is black and black is white. God's love is infinite...or it is not. We can't have it both ways.

The very definition of "infinite" is limitless, unending, going on forever...in *all* directions, not just some directions. We find ourselves butting up against a very simple yet profound question:

Is the God we worship infinite in *all* his attributes...or only *some* of them? Do aspects of the divine character exist where God is actually *finite* and limited?

On the other hand, if God's love and forgiveness are truly infinite, they must, by definition, remain active in the universe *forever!*

In the face of these high conundrums, George MacDonald and many others through the years drew an obvious though controversial conclusion. It can be stated thus: As long as a sinner is *capable* of repenting, or a sin capable of being repented *of*—throughout all the aeons of eternity—such sinners will be given that opportunity. Those of this view differ about what will be the final result of this opportunity, whether all will eventually repent, or whether some will remain separate from God forever. But they agree that God will never turn his back on one who desires to repent.

All we can therefore say about repentance after death is that the *opportunity* will exist. What will be the means and end result of that opportunity will remain a point of conjecture and debate.

As to the potential mechanism of such repentance we can only guess. While we are yet in the flesh, repentance is intimately connected to that fleshly nature. Introspection, emotion, self-awareness, sorrow, remorse, shame, guilt...all these human responses are intrinsic to the process.

What might be a very different range of personal and inward characteristics "repentance" takes when the fleshly nature no longer exists we can scarcely imagine. I explored some of these in *Hell and Beyond.* Those responses will surely be much different from the thoughts and emotions we associate with the word "repentance" here. The nature of the obedience required on the other side is utterly unimaginable.

One of the most unexpected ideas explored in *Hell and Beyond* is that the desire to repent in the next life may be so intense that it will lead to the *choosing* of the fires of purification. Many readers are so staggered by that possibility they don't know what to make of it. How incongruous this is with the common image we have grown up with of a wrathful judge consigning the unrepentant sinner to the fires of torment as a sentence of eternal doom. That one would, of his own free will, *choose* the flames in order to be made pure and whole—it is an idea that sends our brains spinning with wonder.

These are admittedly deep theological waters.

WILL SANCTIFICATION AS WELL AS REDEMPTION CONTINUE AFTER DEATH?

Our eyes are opening to see how simplistic is the notion that the afterlife will merely involve the distribution of rewards and punishment and that is the end of it—eternal bliss or eternal misery.

Suddenly more enormous questions rear their heads.

What about sanctification?

If it is a *process* of growth into Christlikeness, what about the *uncompleted* work at death?

What happens to the believer who has *resisted* God's work of sanctification—those mentioned before who *haven't* been obedient as Christians and who died just as carnal, full of self, and self-righteous as any prideful non-Christian?

This is an age-old conundrum for which many responses spring to mind. Yet most of these are unsatisfactory. Thus it remains an important query that plunges us to the heart of our belief system. Do all "believers" simply skip ahead to the finish line and waltz into heaven with identical crowns of righteousness though they died at different stages of life's eternal race? Is sanctification *completed* at death in the twinkling of an eye, everyone made perfect and whole together?

These questions carry enormous implications. If growth continues after death for non-Christians, might the ongoing work of sanctification also continue the needful surgery in the hearts of those who *believed* but who never submitted to the transformation of God's scalpel?

If true, the greatest shock would therefore likely come to those spiritually complacent Christians who never made obedience a priority, who all along imagined that their *beliefs* alone were sufficient to get them into heaven. What a bitterly painful awakening may await them, to realize that their beliefs were mere wood, hay, and stubble alongside the pride and self-righteousness that obedience alone would have allowed God to purge out of their hearts.

The parameters of God's ongoing work will obviously change on the other side of death's door. Certainly his surgical operations will address different needs in the heart of believer and non-believer. But unredeemed and unsanctified pockets of Self will remain within us all. How will God deal with them?

"Think what it must be for a man counting himself religious," MacDonald writes, "to perceive suddenly that there was no religion in him, only love of self...What a discovery—that he was simply a hypocrite." [93]

C.S. Lewis illustrates the perspective of progressive post-death growth toward Christlikeness in *The Great Divorce*. He enforces this idea with several comments in *Mere Christianity*. [94]

MacDonald insists that we *must* be made pure. After death, God will of necessity employ increasingly more stringent means to accomplish this end, compelling us by what he calls the eye-opening power of pain to do what in this life we had the opportunity to do by free choice.

God desires that we yield to the atoning, redemptive, sanctifying work of the Holy Spirit in *this* life. But he will not give up on that purpose simply because we refuse to fall in with it. Indeed, he will step up his efforts by more persistent means.

Post-death growth into Christlikeness is God's "Plan B." It may involve consequences excruciating and painful—urging repentance and obedience *there* more vigorously than the Spirit's quiet whispers *here*.

EXCERPTS FROM THE WRITINGS OF GEORGE MACDONALD
ON DEATH

Thus death may give a new opportunity—with some hope for the multitude counting themselves Christians...who stand well in their church... [95]

We dare not say that this or that man would not have come to the light had he seen it. We do not know that he will not come to the light the moment he does see it.

God gives every man time. [96]

There is no excuse for this refusal. If we were punished for every fault, there would be no end, no respite—we should have no quiet wherein to repent. But God passes by all he can.

He passes by and forgets a thousand sins, yea, tens of thousands, forgiving them all—only we must begin to be good, begin to do evil no more.

He who refuses must be punished and punished—punished through all the ages—punished until he gives way, yields, and comes to the light, that his deeds may be seen by himself to be what they are, and be by himself reproved, and the Father at last have his child again. For the man who in this world resists to the full, there may be, perhaps, a whole age or era in the history of the universe during which his sin shall not be forgiven. But *never* can it be forgiven until he repents. How can they who will not repent be forgiven, except in the sense that God does and will do all he can to make them repent. Who knows but such sin may need for its cure the continuous punishment of an eon? [97]

Must we believe that Judas, who repented even to agony, who repented so that his high-prized life, self, soul, became worthless in his eyes and met with no mercy at his own hand,—must we believe that he could find no mercy in such a God? I think, when Judas fled from his hanged and fallen body, he fled to the tender help of Jesus, and found it—I say not how. He was in a more hopeful condition now than during any moment of his past life, for he had never repented before. [98]

If God sees that heart corroded with the rust of cares, riddled into caverns and films by the worms of ambition and greed, then your heart is as God sees it, for God sees things as they are. And one day you will be compelled to see, nay, to *feel* your heart as God sees it; and to know that the cankered thing which you have within you, a prey to the vilest of diseases, is indeed the centre of your being, your very heart. [99]

A Christian who looks gloomy at the mention of death, still more, one who talks of his friends as if he had lost them, turns the bushel of his little-faith over the lamp of the Lord's light. Death is but our visible horizon, and our look ought always to be focused beyond it. We should never talk as if death were the end of anything. [100]

EIGHTEEN

BURN, SINNER, BURN!

The Ancient Truth of Fire

by
Michael Phillips

Naturally as one looks beyond death, immediately a specter looms...the flames of hell.

In this freshly rediscovered paradigm of God's eternal plan, the purpose of hell and the nature of God's fire shift dramatically. Truly has the *old* way of seeing passed away in light of the *new*.

We must always search to discover God's ultimate *intent*, not satisfy ourselves with intermediate and superficial causes and effects along the way. To understand the full imagery and purpose of fire, therefore, we must look at the entire scope of Scripture.

Man's reconciliation with God necessarily involves a two-step process—a negative and a positive, a tearing down and a building up. We are all intimately familiar with this process in our individual lives as Christians. Old habits must die so that new habits can form. Selfish responses must be overcome so that Godly responses can emerge. The old man must be put to death so that the fruits of the Spirit of the new man can grow in our characters. As sinners, we must repent and turn from sin...*so that* we can grow into Christlikeness.

However, we have been slow to apprehend that God uses, and is using, this same progression in his eternal plan to bring his creation back into harmony.

Sin must be eliminated before unity in the universe can be restored.

Sin must be destroyed in the world and in us, *so that* we and the creation can become again what God created it to be.

The question is—what are God's means for purging sin from his creation? Obviously the cross of Christ stands at the focal center of that work. Jesus is the chief cornerstone of God's work of redemption. But what other ways and means does God have at his disposal through which the cross achieves its complete and final victory?

That question brings us face to face with the fire. *Why* the fire?

THE PURPOSE OF FIRE IN SCRIPTURE

It is commonly assumed that fire in Scripture is exclusively a symbol of destruction and judgment. But like so many misunderstood aspects of old paradigm thinking—this is wrong.

Fire throughout Scripture is primarily an image of purification. Indeed, fire is one of God's chosen tools in carrying out the post-death work of redemption.

Destruction precedes restoration. Fire is God's means of achieving this twofold purpose. Fire both destroys and it purifies. Destruction is but an intermediate step along the way. Purification is the *ultimate* purpose. We see this obvious progression in the use of fire to burn impurities out of gold and silver so that nothing is left but pure alloy. Yes there must be destruction. But it always leads to the final objective, which is purity.

Two aspects always exist in redemption, restoration, healing, and reconciliation. Fire provides an image of both. God's judgment indeed falls on sin. Judgment comes, however, *so that* God's creation may be brought into the eternal unity for which it was created. The fire of judgment burns away dross, *so that* the fire of purification can produce gold.

We mustn't content ourselves with only half of God's equations. To repeat yet again—we must always look to *ultimate* purposes.

The rationale of God's fire, therefore, is not primarily vengeful or punitive, nor is it born in his wrath against sinners. Fire is an expression of God's wrath *against sin.* Its high objective is purposeful. The fire chastens, cleanses, and purifies the heart of the sinner until the radiant alloy of a Christlike character shines forth.

When at last the dross, the impurities, the parasites of sin are burned away, only pure radiant childness will remain!

In its simplest terms, fire destroys sin as it purifies the sinner.

The source of the fire, therefore, is Love. All its lesser functions subserve and reinforce the ultimate high outcome of that eternal Love.

God's fire burns from the heart of his purifying Love.

FIRE IN THE MINOR PROPHETS—*FOREVER* VS. *UNTIL*

We find the clearest scriptural perspective of fire in the Old Testament Prophets. This image rises to a climax in the great book of

Malachi. There we observe the high truth that fire is a means of purification. We note further that it is not a purification reserved for sinners alone. The fire is also used for the purification of God's people and their priests. [101]

The implication of this truth will knock many Christians out of their smugness about the afterlife. The fire purifies believers also!

We are not necessarily speaking of hell at this point. We are only recognizing that the work of purification will continue after death, and that fire will be one of the agents of that purifying work...in *all* hearts, unbelievers *and* believers, Christians *and* non-Christians, atheists, agnostics, saints, sinners...everyone.

The Old Testament Prophets understood this purpose more clearly than have most Christians.

"I will thoroughly purge away your dross and remove all your impurities. I have refined you...I have tested you in the furnace of affliction. (Isaiah 1:25; 48:10)

"This third I will bring into the fire; I will refine them like silver and test them like gold." (Zechariah 13:9)

"For he is like a refiner's fire and like fuller's soap; he will sit as a refiner and purifier of silver, and he will purify the sons of Levi and refine them like gold and silver, till they present right offerings to the Lord...For behold, the day comes, burning like an oven...the day that comes shall burn ...But for you who fear my name the sun of righteousness shall rise, with healing in its wings." (Malachi 3:2-3; 4:1-2)

Misunderstanding this principle, as did the Children of Israel at the foot of Sinai, much Christian theology has mistakenly interpreted the fire of Scripture as exclusively a vehicle of judgment. But this is a short-sighted and incomplete view. God's purpose is not to punish sin, but to *eradicate* sin from his creation. The judgment of fire is all *against the sin*, while its purification is all *for the sinner*.

THE FIRE BURNS ONLY UNTIL ITS PURPOSE IS ACHIEVED

Judgment and punishment are required in the purification process.

There must be a judgment between the impure and the pure. The fire probes to the essence of distinction, dividing bone from marrow, and judges it rightly and swiftly.

Then the fire punishes all that is impure, ultimately destroying it completely.

Judgment and punishment thus do their work. They are not in themselves the objective nor final result. Their purpose achieved, purity remains. It is for purity that judgment was made and punishment rendered.

The fire does not burn forever. Malachi's purifying fire burns *until* the sons of Levi present right offerings to the Lord…after which the sun of righteousness shall rise with healing in its wings. [102]

The crucial word *till* or *until* in Malachi 3:3 is pivotal in our attempt to grapple with the mystery of the afterlife: "He will purify the sons of Levi, and refine them like gold and silver, till (*so that*—KJV) they present right offerings to the Lord." In Scripture healing *always* follows the fire of judgment and punishment.

The Minor Prophets hold the key to understanding the prophetic restoration that lies ahead. To grasp their message one must read their words on several levels, and perceive multiple frames of reference.

In the prophetic writings, the word "forever" is often followed by a description of what will happen *after* that forever. Statements such as, "I will punish my people Israel forever…*until* they repent of their sin and I restore them in the land I gave their fathers," can be found on nearly every page.

This is how the Prophets wrote. Duration of time may carry a different meaning than is obvious at first glance. Healing *always* follows judgment. When the Prophets speak of judgment, "forever" doesn't always literally mean *forever*. Purification and restoration are *always* the objective. The Prophets' true "forevers" are reserved for the endless eternity *after* healing and reconciliation have been restored.

THE SHIFT FROM JUDGMENT TO HEALING

In Malachi 3, after asking "who can endure the day of the Lord's coming," the prophet goes on, with that oft-used word that signals the shift from judgment and punishment to restoration, "*Then* the Lord will have men who will bring offerings in righteousness."

In Zephaniah 3, we observe first judgment: "I have decided to assemble the nations…to pour out my wrath upon them—all my fierce anger. The whole world will be consumed by the fire of my jealous anger." [103]

But everything is *not* consumed. For the punishment is followed by healing: "*Then* I will purify the lips of the peoples that all of them may call on the name of the Lord." [104] Here we have one more example of this "forever…until" progression.

And again, from Amos 9:8: "I will destroy it from the surface of the ground; except that I will not utterly destroy the house of Jacob."

The biblical record is interwoven from beginning to end with this progression. It is imperative and foundational to all scriptural interpretation. To omit this healing cycle from small theologies of the afterlife can only lead to a misunderstanding of God's true intent.

God's way, God's method, God's purpose is clear: *I will bring judgment...THEN I will bring healing.*

Examples of this progression in the Prophets are literally legion. We could cite dozens exactly like these. By now the point will be obvious. Once you see it, the reconciliatory purposes of God jump off the page everywhere you look.

The ninth and final chapter of Amos is wonderfully illustrative. For ten verses Amos prophesies the destruction of Israel. Suddenly in chapter 10 he shifts to healing and restoration: "In that day I will restore...I will repair...and build...I will bring back my exiled people Israel...never again to be uprooted from the land I have given them." [105]

Those who interpret such passages in the context of physical, temporal Israel, and the "land" as physical, temporal Palestine, have not yet recognized the true high theme of prophecy in Scripture.

God is speaking through the Prophets of the restoration not of temporal Israel alone, but of his entire creation!

THE FINAL PURIFICATION OF FIRE—THE GOLD OF MALACHI'S FURNACE

Once the fire has done its work, the season for healing has come.

From the failure to recognize this imperative progression, along with a subtle but damaging mistranslation of Matthew 25:46 (which we will detail in Chapter 21), a completely erroneous doctrine of hell has emerged. This grievously unfortunate perspective has miscolored the entire Christian message. It has caused most of Christ's Church to adopt a garbled and distorted picture of the purposes of God in the universe and in the heart of mankind.

How astonishing it is that Christians do not read the New Testament prophecies through the lens of this scriptural progression,[106] nor ask what wonderful healing and reconciliation will take place in Malachi's purifying furnace between Revelation 20:15 and 22:3. What comes *after* the lake of fire and the second death—God's *defeat*, or God's *triumph* in the hearts of the billions of souls of his creation?

This may be one of the most important regions of inquiry in all prophetic studies: How will God move from Revelation 20:15 to the fulfillment of Revelation 22:3? This was a question I attempted to explore in *Hell and Beyond.*

God's eternal purpose is to bring his children home. Nothing will satisfy and fulfill his love but to see them pure and perfect as he is pure and perfect. We must therefore ask how Malachi's furnace of purification actually works. What does the fire *do* to accomplish its cleansing?

The fire of God's purification does not burn *us*, our essential being created in his image. It burns away the parasites of sin that cling so close they suffocate our true selves. The fire burns out the impurities that are *not* gold but that are embedded into the gold...so that only the gold remains. That's why we *need* God's purifying fire.

I need it as much as any so-called sinner who ever lived. Sin parasites cling to me too! Impurities are mixed in with the true me that God created in his image. I want those impurities gone! I need them burned away! The fire contributes to the work of sanctification unto Christlikeness!

Though many misunderstand me when I say it, it is for this reason that I long for God's fire.

DISTINCT JUDGMENTS, SAME ULTIMATE PURPOSE

The purpose of fire in the economy of God is thus to purify the heart of saint and sinner alike—by different means, and enforced by distinctive judgments and punishments to be sure, but with the *same* purpose as the final objective—purity.

The fire is not the enemy. It is the *agent* of God's work. The child of God who desires to be pure and clean will thus welcome God's fire. When that day arrives—and foreshadowings of it come every day—I pray that I will have the courage to lay my Self on God's altar, and then beseech him with all the desperate hunger of a will that desires to be pure, "Come, fire of God, and burn me clean!"

Nor is the fire merely intended for the burning out of sin. It is also the fire of light, the fire of God's love, the fire of comfort, the light of purity—what George MacDonald calls "the fire-core of the universe." [107]

MacDonald amplifies his thoughts on the purifying nature of God's fire throughout his writings, most notably in the sermons entitled, "The Consuming Fire" and "The Fear of God." The first we have already considered. We will read the second in the next chapter. The essential theme of these sermons bears repeating.

"The fire of God," MacDonald writes, "which is his essential being, his love, his creative power, is a fire unlike its earthly symbol in this, that it is only at a distance it burns—that the farther from him, it burns the worse, and that when we...approach him, the burning begins to change to comfort." [108]

EXCERPTS FROM THE WRITINGS OF GEORGE MACDONALD
ON FIRE

Who shall set bounds to the consuming of the fire of our God, and the purifying that dwells therein? [109]

It was not often that Falconer went to church; but he seemed to have some design in going oftener than usual at present. The Sunday after the one last mentioned, he went...and calling for Hugh took him with him...

"I seldom go to church," said Falconer; "but when I do, I come here: and always feel that I am in the presence of one of the holy servants of God's great temple not made with hands. I heartily trust that man. He is what he seems to be."

"They say he is awfully heterodox."

"They do."

"How then can he remain in the church, if he is as honest as you say?"

"In this way, as I humbly venture to think," Falconer answered. "He looks upon the formulæ of the church as utterances of living truth...I had a vision of him this morning as I sat and listened to his voice, which always seems to me to come immediately from his heart...Shall I tell you my vision?—

"I saw a crowd—priests and laymen—speeding, hurrying, darting away, up a steep, crumbling height...Every one for himself, with hands and feet they scramble and flee, to save their souls from the fires of hell which come rolling in along the hollow below...But beneath, right in the course of the fire, stands one man upon a little rock which goes down to the centre of the great world, and faces the approaching flames. He stands bareheaded, his eyes bright with faith in God, and the mighty mouth that utters his truth, fixed in holy defiance. His denial comes from no fear, or weak dislike to that which is painful. On neither side will he tell lies for peace. He is ready to be lost for his fellow-men. In the name of God he rebukes the flames of hell. The fugitives pause on the top, look back, call him lying prophet, and shout evil opprobrious names at the man who counts not his own life dear to him, who has forgotten his own soul in his sacred devotion to men...Be sure that, come what may of the rest, let the flames of hell ebb or flow, that man is safe, for he is delivered already from the only devil that can make hell itself a torture, the devil of selfishness—the only one that can possess a man and make himself his own living hell. He is out of all that region of things, and already dwelling in the secret place of the Almighty."

"Go on, go on."

"He trusts in God so absolutely, that he leaves his salvation to him—utterly, fearlessly; and, forgetting it, as being no concern of his, sets himself to do the work that God has given him to do, even as his Lord did before him...Let God's will be done, and all is well. If God's will be done, he cannot fare ill. To him, God is all in all. If it be possible to separate such things, it is the glory of God, even more than the salvation of men, that he seeks. He will not have it that his Father in heaven is not perfect. He believes entirely that God loves, yea, is love; and, therefore, that hell itself must be subservient to that love, and but an embodiment of it; that the grand work of Justice is to make way for a Love which will give to every man that which is right and ten times more, even if it should be by means of awful suffering—a suffering which the Love of the Father will not shun, either for himself or his children, but will eagerly meet for their sakes, that he may give them all that is in his heart."

"Surely you speak your own opinions in describing thus warmly the faith of the preacher."

"I do. He is accountable for nothing I say..."

"How is it that so many good people call him heterodox?"

"I do not mind that... To these, theology must be like a map—with plenty of lines in it. They cannot trust their house on the high table-land of his theology, because they cannot see the outlines bounding the said table-land. It is not small enough for them. They cannot take it in. Such can hardly be satisfied with the creation, one would think, seeing there is no line of division anywhere in it..."

"Does God draw no lines, then?"

"When he does, they are pure lines, without breadth, and consequently invisible to mortal eyes; not...walls of separation, such as these definers would construct...

"But can those theories in religion be correct which are so hard to see?"

"They are only hard to certain natures."

"But those natures are above the average. You have granted them heart."

"Not much; but what there is, good."

"That is allowing a great deal, though. Is it not hard then to say that such cannot understand him?"

"Why? They will get to heaven, which is all they want. And they will understand him one day, which is more than they pray for. Till they have done being anxious about their own salvation, we must forgive them that they can contemplate with calmness the damnation of a universe, and believe that God is yet more indifferent than they."

"But do they not bring the charges likewise against you, of being unable to understand them?"

"Yes. And so it must remain, till the Spirit of God decide the matter, which I presume must take place by slow degrees...Till then, the Right must be content to be called the Wrong, and—which is far harder—to seem the Wrong. There is no spiritual victory gained by a verbal conquest." [110]

NINETEEN

THE FEAR OF GOD

by
George MacDonald

From *Unspoken Sermons, Second Series* [111]

Edited by Michael Phillips

"And when I saw him, I fell at his feet as one dead. And he
laid his right hand upon me, saying, Fear not; I am the first
and the last and the Living one."
—Rev. i. 17, 18

It is not only the first beginnings of religion that are full of fear. So long
as love is imperfect, there is room for torment. That love only which
fills the heart—and nothing but love can fill any heart—is able to cast out
fear, leaving no room for its presence. What we find in the beginnings of
religion will hold in varying degree, until the religion, that is the love, be
perfected.

FEAR IS NECESSARY WHERE TRUTH IS IMPERFECT

The thing that is unknown, yet known to exist around us, will always
be more or less formidable. When it is known as immeasurably greater
than we, and as having claims and making demands upon us, the more
vaguely these are apprehended, the more room is there for anxiety. When
the conscience is not clear, this anxiety may well mount to terror.

According to the nature of the idea of the Supreme occupied by the
mind, whether regarded as maker or ruler, will be the kind and degree of

231

the terror. To this terror need belong no exalted ideas of God. Those fear him most who most imagine him like their own evil selves, only beyond them in power, easily able to work his arbitrary will with them. That they hold him but a little higher than themselves does not tend to produce unity with him.

Who are so far apart as those who actually exist on the same level of hate and distrust? Power without love, dependence where is no righteousness, wake a worship without devotion, a loathliness of servile flattery. Neither, where the notion of God is perhaps better, but the conscience is troubled, will his goodness do much to cast out apprehension and fear.

The same consciousness of evil and of offence which gave rise to the bloody sacrifice, is still at work in the minds of most who call themselves Christians. Naturally the first emotion of man towards the being he calls God, but of whom he knows so little, is fear.

Where it is possible that fear should exist, it is well it should exist, and cause continual uneasiness, and be cast out by nothing less than love. In him who does not know God, and must be anything but satisfied with himself, fear towards God is as reasonable as it is natural. Such fear serves powerfully towards the development of his true humanity.

Neither the savage, nor the self-sufficient sage, is rightly human. It matters nothing whether we regard the one or the other as degenerate or as undeveloped—neither I say is fully human. The humanity is there, but has to be born in each. For this birth everything natural must contribute its part. Fear is natural, and has a role to perform that nothing but itself could perform in the birth of the true humanity.

Until love, which is the truth towards God, is able to cast out fear, it is well that fear should hold. It is a bond, however poor, between that which is and that which creates—a bond that must be broken, but a bond that can be broken only by the tightening of an infinitely closer bond.

Verily, God must be terrible to those that are far from him, for they fear he will do, yea, he is doing with them what they do not, cannot desire, and can ill endure. Such as many men are, such as all without God would become, they must prefer a devil, because of his supreme selfishness, to a God who will die for his creatures—a God who insists upon giving himself to them, insists upon their being unselfish and blessed like himself.

That which is the power and worth of life they must be, or die, and the vague consciousness of this imperative becoming makes them afraid. They love their poor existence as it is. God loves it as it must be—and they fear him.

GOD HELPS MEN OUTGROW FEAR BY THE TRUTH

The false notions of men of low, undeveloped nature both with regard to what is good and what the Power requires of them, are such that they cannot but fear, and devotion is lost in the sacrifices of ingratiation. However, God takes them where they are, accepts whatever they honestly offer, and so helps them to outgrow themselves, preparing them to offer the true offering, and to know him whom they ignorantly worship. He will not abolish their fear except with the truth of his own being. Till they apprehend that, and in order that they may come to apprehend it, he receives their sacrifices of blood, the invention of their sore need, only influencing for the time the modes of them.

He will destroy the lie that is not all a lie only by the truth which is all true. Although he loves them utterly, he does not tell them there is nothing in him to make them afraid. That would be to drive them from him for ever. While they are such as they are, there is much in him that cannot but affright them. They ought, they do well to fear him. That fear, while they remain what they are, is the only true relation between them. To remove such fear from their hearts, except by letting them know his love with its purifying fire, a love which for ages, it may be, they cannot know, would be to give them up utterly to the power of evil.

Persuade men that fear is a vile thing, that it is an insult to God, that he will none of it—while yet they are in love with their own will, and slaves to every movement of passionate impulse, and what will the consequence be? That they will insult God as a discarded idol, a superstition, a falsehood, as a thing under whose evil influence they have too long groaned, a thing to be cast out and spit upon. After that how much will they learn of him?

Nor would it be long before the old fear would return—with this difference, perhaps, that instead of trembling before a live energy, they would tremble before powers which formerly they regarded as inanimate, and have now endowed with souls after the imagination of their fears. Then would spiritual chaos with all its monsters come again.

God being what he is, a God who loves righteousness, a God who, rather than do an unfair thing, would lay down his Godhead and assert himself in ceasing to be, may well look fearful from afar to the creature who recognizes in himself no imperative good. A God who, that his creature might not die of ignorance, died as much as a God could die—and that is divinely more than man can die—to give him himself, will always be fearful to one who fears only suffering, and who has no aspiration but wretched ambition!

But in proportion as such a creature comes nearer, grows towards him in and for whose likeness he was created...in proportion as the eternal right begins to disclose itself to him...in proportion as he becomes capable of the idea that man belongs to God as he could never belong to himself—then at last he is on his way toward being able to see the truth. As such a one approaches the capacity of seeing and understanding that his individuality can be perfected only in the love of his neighbour, and that his being can find its end only in oneness with the source from which it came...in proportion, I do not say, as he sees these things, but as he nears the *possibility* of seeing them, will his terror at the God of his life begin to lessen.

Though he still remains far indeed from surmising the bliss that awaits him, he has begun to draw more nigh to the goal of his nature, the central secret joy of sonship to a God who loves righteousness and hates iniquity, a God who does nothing he would not permit in his creature, demands nothing of his creature he would not do himself.

THE FIRE OF GOD

The fire of God, which is his essential being, his love, his creative power, is a fire unlike its earthly symbol in this, that it is only at a distance it burns—that the farther from him, it burns the worse. When we turn and begin to approach him, the burning begins to change to comfort. This comfort will grow to such bliss that the heart at length cries out with a gladness no other gladness can reach, "Whom have I in heaven but thee? and there is none upon earth that I desire besides thee!"

The glory of being, the essence of life and its joy, shining upon the corrupt and deathly, must, like the sun, consume the dead and send corruption down to the dust. That which it burns in the soul is not of the soul, yea, is at utter variance with it. Yet so close to the soul is the foul fungous growth sprung from and subsisting upon it, that the burning of it is felt through every spiritual nerve. When the evil parasites are consumed away, that is when the man yields his self and all that self's low world, and returns to his lord and God, then that which he was before aware of only as burning he will now feel as love, comfort, strength—an eternal, ever-growing life in him. For now he lives. Life cannot hurt life, it can only hurt death, which needs and ought to be destroyed.

SALVATION—RUSHING INTO THE FATHER'S ARMS!

God is life essential and eternal. Death cannot live in his sight, for death is corruption. It has no existence in itself. It lives only in the decay of the things of life.

If then any child of the father finds that he is afraid before him, finds that the thought of God is a discomfort to him, or even a terror, let him make haste. Let him not linger to put on any garment. Let him rush at once in his nakedness, a true child, to find shelter from his own evil and God's terror in the salvation of the Father's arms. There is the home whence he was sent that he might learn that it was home.

What father being evil would it not win to see the child with whom he was vexed running to his embrace? How much more will not the Father of our spirits, who seeks nothing but his children themselves, receive him with open arms!

Self, accepted as the law of self, is the one demon-enemy of life. God is the only Saviour from it, and from all that is not God.

For God is life, and all that is not God is death. Life is the destruction of death, of all that kills, of all that is of death's kind.

JOHN'S VISION—THE FIRE-CORE OF THE UNIVERSE

When John saw the glory of the Son of Man, he fell at his feet as one dead. In what way John saw him, whether in what we vaguely call a vision, or in as human a way as when he leaned back on his bosom and looked up in his face, I do not now care to ask. It would take all the glorious shapes of humanity to reveal Jesus, and he knew the right way to show himself to John. It seems to me that such words as were spoken can have come from the mouth of no mere vision, can have been allowed to enter no merely tranced ear, that the mouth of the very Lord himself spoke them, and that none but the living present Jesus could have spoken or may be supposed to speak them. Plainly John received and felt them as a message he had to give again. There are also, strangely as the whole may affect us, various points in his description of the Lord's appearance which commend themselves even to our ignorance by their grandeur and fitness.

Why then was John overcome with terror? We recall the fact that something akin to terror overwhelmed the minds of the three disciples who saw his glory on the mount. But since then John had leaned on the bosom of his Lord, He had followed him to the judgment seat and had not denied his name. He had borne witness to his resurrection and suffered for his sake. He was now "in the isle that is called Patmos, for the word of God and the testimony of Jesus."

Why, I say, was he, why should he be afraid? No glory even of God *should* breed terror. When a child of God is afraid, it is a sign that the word *Father* is not yet freely fashioned by the child's spiritual mouth. The glory can breed terror only in him who is capable of being terrified by it. While he is such, it is well the terror should be bred and maintained, until the man seek refuge from it in the only place where it is not—in the bosom of the glory.

There is one point not distinguishable in the Greek: whether is meant, "one like unto *the* Son of Man," or, "one like unto *a* son of Man." The authorized version has the former, the revised prefers the latter. I incline to the former, and think that John saw him like the man he had known so well, and that it was the too much glory, dimming his vision, that made him unsure, not any perceived unlikeness mingling with the likeness. Nothing blinds so much as light, and their very glory might well render him unable to distinguish plainly the familiar features of *The* Son of Man.

But the appearance of The Son of Man was not intended to breed terror in the son of man to whom he came. Why then was John afraid? Why did the servant of the Lord fall at his feet as one dead? Joy to us that he did, for the words that follow—surely no phantasmic outcome of uncertain vision or blinding terror! They bear the best sign of their source. However given to his ears, they must be from the heart of our great Brother, the one Man, Christ Jesus, divinely human!

It was still and only the imperfection of the disciple, unfinished in faith, so unfinished in everything a man needs, that was the cause of his terror. This is surely implied in the words the Lord said to John when he fell! The thing that made John afraid, he speaks of as the thing that ought to have taken from him all fear.

What glory John saw!—the head and hair pouring from it such a radiance of light that they were white as white wool, snow-white, as were his garments on mount Hermon. In the midst of this radiance his eyes pierced like a flame of fire. His countenance shone as the sun shineth in his strength. The darker glow of the feet—yet as of fine brass burning in a furnace, as if they, in memory of the twilight of his humiliation and now touching the earth again—took a humbler glory than his head high in the empyrean of undisturbed perfection. The girdle under his breast reflected a golden hue between the snow and the brass.

What were these all but the effulgence of his glory who was himself the effulgence of the Father's, the poor expression of the unutterable verity which was itself the reason why John ought *not* to be afraid?—"He laid his right hand upon me, saying unto me, Fear not; I am the first and the last, and the living one."

Endless must be our terror, until we come heart to heart with the fire-core of the universe, the first and the last and the living one!

THE ONLY SAFETY IN THE UNIVERSE IS NEARNESS TO THE FATHER

But oh, the joy to be told, by Power himself, the first and the last, the living one—told what we can indeed then see *must* be true, but which we are so slow to believe—that the cure for trembling is the presence of Power, that fear cannot stand before Strength, that the visible God is the destruction of death, that the one and only safety in the universe, is the perfect nearness of the Living One!

God is being. Death is nowhere! What a thing to be taught by the very mouth of him who knows!

He told his servant Paul that strength is made perfect in weakness. Here he instructs his servant John that the thing to be afraid of is weakness, not strength. All appearances of strength, such as might rightly move terror, are but false appearances. The true Strong is the *One*, even as the true Good is the *One*. The Living One has the power of life. The Evil One but the power of death—whose very nature is a self-necessity for being destroyed.

But the glory of the mildest show of the Living One is such that even the dearest of his apostles, the best of the children of men, is cowed at the sight. He has not yet learned that glory itself is a part of his inheritance, yea is of the natural condition of his being. He has not yet learned that there is nothing in the man made in the image of God alien from the most glorious of heavenly shows. He has not learned this yet, and falls as dead before it—when lo, the voice of him that was and is and is for evermore, is telling him not to be afraid—for the very reason, the one only reason, that he is the first and the last, the living one!

For what shall be the joy, the peace, the completion of him that lives but closest contact with his Life?—a contact close as before he was created out of that Life, only in infinitely higher kind, inasmuch as it is now willed on *both* sides.

THE ENDLESS ENDING OF BEING

He who has had a beginning, needs the indwelling power of that beginning to make his being complete—not merely complete to his consciousness, but complete in itself—justified, rounded, ended where it began—with an "endless ending."

Then will his being be complete even as God's is complete, for it will be one with the self-existent, blossoming in the air of that world wherein it is rooted, wherein it lives and grows. Far indeed from trembling because he on whose bosom he had leaned when the light of his love was all but shut in now stands with the glory of that love streaming forth, John Boanerges ought to have felt the more joyful and safe as the strength of the living one was more manifested.

It was never because Jesus was clothed in the weakness of the flesh that he was fit to be trusted, but because he was strong with a strength able to take the weakness of the flesh for the garment wherein it could best work its work. That strength was now shining out with its own light, so lately pent within the revealing veil. Had John been as close in spirit to the Son of Man as he had been in bodily presence, he would have indeed fallen at his feet, but not as one dead—as one too full of joy to stand before the life that was feeding his. He would have fallen, but not to lie there senseless with awe in the presence of the most holy. He would have fallen to embrace and kiss the feet of him who had now a second time, as with a resurrection from above, arisen before him, in yet heavenlier plenitude of glory.

It is the man of evil, the man of self-seeking design, not he who would fain do right—not he who, even in his worst time, would at once submit to the word of the Master—who is reasonably afraid of power.

When God is no longer the ruler of the world, and there is a stronger than he, when there is might inherent in evil, and making-energy in that whose nature is destruction, then will be the time to stand in dread of power. But even then the bad man would have no security against the chance of crossing some scheme of the lawless moment, where disintegration is the sole unity of plan, and being ground up and destroyed for some no-idea of the Power of darkness.

And then would be the time for the good—no, not to tremble, but to resolve with the Lord of light to endure all, to let every billow of evil dash and break upon him, nor do the smallest ill, tell the whitest lie for God— knowing that any territory so gained could belong to no kingdom of heaven but could be but a province of the kingdom of darkness.

If there were two powers, the one of evil, the other of good, as men have not unnaturally in ignorance imagined, his sense of duty would reveal the being born of the good power, while he born of the evil could have no choice but be evil.

But only Good can create. If Evil were ever so much the stronger, the duty of men would remain the same—to hold by the Living One, and defy Evil to its worst—like Prometheus on his rock, defying Jove, and for ever dying—thus for ever foiling the Evil. For Evil can destroy only itself and its own. It could destroy no enemy—could at worst but cause a succession of deaths, from each of which the defiant soul would rise to loftier defiance, to more victorious endurance— until at length it laughed Evil in the face, and the demon-god shrunk withered before it. In those then who believe that good is the one power, and that evil exists only because for a time it subserves, cannot help subserving the good, what place can there be for fear?

THE CHILDREN CAN DO WITH NOTHING LESS THAN THE FATHER

The strong and the good are one. If our hope coincides with that of God, if it is rooted in his will, what should we do but rejoice in the effulgent glory of the First and the Last?

The First and the Last is the inclosing defence of the castle of our being. The Master is before and behind. He began, he will see that it be endless. He garrisons the place. He is the living, the live-making one.

The reason then for not fearing before God is, that he is all-glorious, all-perfect. Our being needs the all-glorious, all-perfect God. The children can do with nothing less than the Father. They need the infinite one. Beyond all wherein the poor intellect can descry order, beyond all that the rich imagination can devise, beyond all that hungriest heart could long, fullest heart thank for—beyond all these, as the heavens are higher than the earth, rise the thought, the creation, the love of the God who is in Christ, his God and our God, his Father and our Father.

Ages before the birth of Jesus, while, or at least where yet even Moses and his law were unknown, the suffering heart of humanity saw and was persuaded that nowhere else lay its peace than with the first, the last, the living one.

TWENTY

DUNGEON OR WORKSHOP?

The Ancient Truth of Hell

by
Michael Phillips

We come to the climax.

At last we arrive upon the threshold of the great scriptural conundrum which for many represents the reason they picked up this book in the first place—the title theme of our adventure together.

Hell.

The words on the cover were not merely chosen as a clever reminder of a former best-selling volume on prophecy. A serious hope underlies that choice of phrase—that indeed the great debate about hell is reaching its final death throes...and that future generations of Christians will look back and wonder what all the fuss was about for so long. It will by then indeed have become a "late" debate—passed, gone, and deceased, a relic from former times when Christians were still clinging to abhorrent doctrines about their Father passed down from medieval mists, doctrines which were freshly imbued with contorted old covenantal legalisms by 16th and 17th centuries reformers who did not reform those aspects of medieval theology which most needed reforming.

Will new enlightenment truly come in a comprehensive way to Christ's church about his Father's eternal reconciliatory purposes?

Will the great debate about hell eventually become a *late* debate?

As I say, we can only *hope*. George MacDonald has been a voice crying in the wilderness about these themes for 150 years. I have been writing about them for forty years, as have scores of others. There are certainly signs of expanding awareness of Scripture's high themes in these early years of the third millennium. George MacDonald's name is far more widely known than it was a generation ago. We must also admit, however, that the great debate continues heated and contentious. The adherents of the Reformed orthodoxy will not allow the doctrine to go quietly into the night. The stranglehold that exclusivist theology holds on the hearts and minds of so many is as bewildering as it is heartbreaking. Therefore, what the harvest of this new season of awakening will be...only time will tell.

We who wrestle with the most effective means of uncovering and communicating these long hidden truths to an occasionally fearful, often skeptical new generation of open-minded Christians are part of the awakening ourselves. We too have had to grow *out* of old orthodoxies and *into* a new paradigm. I have faced the same struggles as those of you who read my words. This is no antiseptic spiritual quest. This is a *very* difficult struggle. These are *hard* things to understand. Future generations may look back on my halting attempt to bring light into the dark corners of these fading orthodoxies and exclaim, "You scarcely grasped how great the purposes of God truly are. Your efforts to penetrate the high things of God were but the fumbling words of a second grader trying to tell a first grader what he sees. In reality, you saw but through a glass darkly yourself."

I recognize, therefore, that a book like this, and those others of our time that strive to expand our perceptions, are all incomplete...vague and shadowy efforts to understand what may yet lie light years beyond us.

Still, however, the quest must go on. Light brings more light. We all continue to grow toward truth together.

The conundrum at its most basic reduces to this: What are we to make of hell, and the imagery that has grown up around the imaginative world associated with this most controversial yet uncertain doctrine of Christianity?

IN WHOSE DOMAIN DOES HELL LIE—GOD'S OR THE DEVIL'S?

Because the fire of God has been so sorely misconstrued by Christian theologians, an afterlife theology has grown up through the centuries which may not represent the intent of the New Testament writers at all, nor even of Jesus himself.

The prevailing doctrine perceives hell as entirely the devil's domain.

Though God *sends* people to hell, and *uses* hell...the orthodoxy would say that the devil *owns* hell. The devil, not God, is hell's C.E.O., President, and Chairman of the Board.

Interestingly, however, the theology maintains that God makes use of this place of the devil's for his own purposes. God employs hell to exact his retribution against sin. In hell, says the doctrine, God will punish sin and sinner alike, tormenting them forever.

Hell is therefore God's *tool*, but the devil's *domain*.

It's something like one man (God) asking his neighbor (Satan) to borrow a tool (hell) for something he needs to use it for (to punish sinners.)

This dichotomy places an intriguing contradiction at the heart of the doctrine. If true, then is the devil truly the C.E.O. of the place? If God *uses* it as a tool, then does he subserve himself, insofar as hell is concerned, to the devil's supreme authority?

As I say, this is an intriguing contradiction. How could God submit to the devil's authority *anywhere*?

On the other hand, if this perspective of the doctrine is backwards, and it is actually God's tool, invented by him for *his* purposes, then we have a bigger problem!

If *God* is C.E.O. of hell, and everlasting torment proceeds from *his* hand, what ghastly cruelty this implies. The contradictions become more and more hideous.

So who owns hell anyway...and for what purpose was it invented?

THE DISPARITY BETWEEN REVELATION 21:8 AND 22:3

The problems and inconsistencies with the theology of hell don't stop there. That theology also wreaks havoc with Scripture. To sustain itself, the doctrine of everlasting, punitive, retributive hell requires us to cut the last two pages out of our Bibles. Insofar as sin and sinners are concerned, the orthodoxy forces the biblical record to end at Revelation 21:8.

The prevailing doctrine allows for no *final* making right. Though the writer of *Revelation* warns against taking away from the words of the prophecy, the orthodoxy of hell effectively removes half of Revelation 21 and nearly all of Revelation 22 from the biblical record.

"There shall no more be *anything* accursed." The words are unambiguous. Where does the orthodoxy of hell place this verse in its lexicon of afterlife doctrine?

It has no place for it. Therefore, it obliterates Revelation 22:3 from Scripture.

At some point Christians must inquire more deeply into the doctrine of everlasting torment than they have been willing to till now. Paul did not teach it. We may legitimately conclude that Jesus did not believe such a doctrine. He taught just the *opposite* concerning his Father's work.

If the notion is *not* true that hell is punitive and that God will pour out his Wrath to all eternity, while his love retreats into the shadows as a lesser attribute of his character, when will Christendom awaken to that reality?

If it is *not* a doctrine supported by the Bible except by turning the eternal truths of God's character upside down, what can it be but the historical invention of men who did not understand either God or his purposes?

Again we are forced to ask...when will Christendom awaken to this reality?

As MacDonald says of this view, "God is triumphantly defeated." [112]

Can there be a more degrading, demeaning blasphemy against the love of God than to believe that he would *intentionally* devise such a cruel system? MacDonald's passions reached their height against Christians who willingly, even eagerly, believe such about the Father of Jesus Christ:

"Was there ever such a confusion, such an inversion of right and wrong...There is but one thing lower than deliberately to believe such a lie, and that is to worship the God of whom it is believed." [113]

In the words of Robert Falconer, he adds:

"We must forgive them that they can contemplate with calmness the damnation of a universe, and believe that God is yet more indifferent than they." [114]

HELL'S PURPOSE

MacDonald poses a shocking alternative to the traditional perspective—that *God* is C.E.O. of hell, not the devil. Furthermore, his purpose is to use it for good.

"For hell is God's and not the devil's," he insists. "Hell is on the side of God and man, to free the child of God from the corruption of death." [115]

In other words, hell is God's final workplace to accomplish what this life could not, his Malachi's furnace for the purging out of sin and for the refining and purifying of his children to become his sons and daughters.

MacDonald's words drive us deeper, always deeper, to the source and foundation of our inquiry:

What is the *purpose* of hell?

Two possibilities present themselves: That hell is *punitive*, or that hell is *corrective*.

In the first view, hell accomplishes nothing. It represents but an eternal life sentence of endless punishment.

In the latter view, hell serves a larger end, a higher purpose. It leads toward corrective, chastening, redemptive change, betterment, growth, and the final restoration of unity and reconciliation throughout the universe of God's creation.

The debate between these two possibilities is long-standing. Many Bible scholars and theologians are convinced that Scripture clearly and unequivocally supports the idea of hell's redemptive purpose. They would say that such is the *only* possible interpretation consistent with the character of God.

Obviously all do not agree. Many others remain solidly convinced of hell's punitive, penal nature as the final expression of God's retribution against sin.

How long this debate will continue, who can say? In the end, we each have to determine within our own hearts what we believe about the God we worship.

THE LAST FARTHING

George MacDonald occasionally refers to hell as God's "prison" where payment must be made and out of which those who resist him will not come until they have paid the uttermost farthing of what is due. His perspective is reminiscent of the penal courtroom analogy used earlier, with the difference resting on the Lord's use of the significant word *out*. They will not come out...*until* the last farthing of needful penitence is paid. There may indeed be a sentence, but it is not an everlasting life sentence. There always remains an "out." The door of that *out* is repentance.

MacDonald's thinking can be understood as follows:

We "owe" certain debts. These are not debts against God's holiness. It is not the debt of damnation. It is not the debt of retribution handed down by an indignant, wrathful, judge.

Rather, these are debts we have incurred throughout life against childness, against others, against ourselves. These must be paid. We must forgive and ask forgiveness. To pay the debt is to become a child.

This is no mere Law-ish "debt of sin" that Jesus pays *for* us. *We* are responsible, like Zacchaeus, to make right, to make ourselves right with God, others, and ourselves. Zacchaeus is the model of what hell means!

We make *at-one-ment* by repenting, taking account, and paying our due.

To pay the last farthing is to give up the final vestige of self, emptying our hands in unashamed nakedness before our Creator, and abandon ourselves to utter childness.

THE FINAL COMPULSION OF LOVE

One of MacDonald's repeated themes to explain how God will effect this last-farthing repentance in the hearts of the most stubborn is by *compelling* repentance.

"Do not drive Justice to extremities," he says. "Duty is imperative; it must be done. It is useless to think to escape the eternal law of things; yield of yourself, nor compel God to compel you...Putting off is of no use. You must. The thing has to be done; there are means of compelling you." [116]

The argument brought against the idea of post death repentance under the force of compulsion is that it renders free will meaningless. God must, says the argument, honor the choice of free will that man makes in *this* life. There are no second chances. Your choices *here* determine your final destiny *there*.

MacDonald counters that in the flesh men are incapable of recognizing the true stakes of their choices. To make man eternally accountable for weak fleshly choices is unfair. God will never base eternity on an unjust foundation.

MacDonald continues by insisting that God's compulsion exists beyond what we can envision. It is not "coercion" but the infinite compulsion of a Father's love. It will not *override* free will. Indeed, God's compulsion will *use* the will.

It is the will itself that shall be compelled.

Our finite intellects perceive an either-or exclusivity between compulsion and free will. In our world, the two cannot mutually coexist. In God's post-death economy, however, *both* God's compulsion and man's will will be operative. We may get closer to the idea of it with the word "pressure." God will *pressure* the will such that it will want to choose rightly.

God's eternal purposes lie in the realm of infinity, where parallel lines meet, where Love and wrath point toward a single objective...and where compulsion and free will contribute toward the same final making right of God's creation.

We perceive impossibilities. *You will choose to choose what you must choose in the end.* We say, "Such cannot be."

God perceives not only eternal possibilities, but eternal necessities, imperatives of being, inescapable mandates of his Fatherhood and our childness.

"'Another has made you," MacDonald writes in *Lilith*, "and can compel you to see what you have made yourself...Compulsion [against free will] would be without value. But there is a light that goes deeper than the will, a light that lights up the darkness behind it: that light can change your will, can make it truly yours and not another's...Into the created can pour itself the creating will, and so redeem it!" [117]

It is "compulsion" without *coersion*, and without the weakening or mitigation of will.

To those who ask how a sinner, lost in utter blackness and aloneness of his sin, could repent in the outer darkness of hell, MacDonald offers a graphic image. It is found in the last and final of MacDonald's sermons that we will consider in Chapter 23, not surprisingly entitled, "The Last Farthing." The following brief quote provides a fitting close to this chapter's discussion.

"So might I imagine a thousand steps up from the darkness," MacDonald writes, "each a little less dark, a little nearer the light...Repentance once begun, however, may grow more and more rapid! If God once get a willing hold, if with but one finger he touch the man's self, swift as possibility will he draw him from the darkness into the light. For that for which the forlorn, self-ruined wretch was made, was to be a child of God.... Out of the abyss into which he cast himself...he must rise and be raised. To the heart of God, the one and only goal of the human race—the refuge and home of all and each, he must set out and go." [118]

EXCERPTS FROM THE WRITINGS OF GEORGE MACDONALD
ON HELL

He taught that hell itself is yet within
The confines of thy kingdom; and its fires
The endless conflict of thy love with sin,
That even by horror works its pure desires. [119]

For now arose within him, not without ultimate good, the evil phantasms of a theology which would explain all God's doings by low conceptions...In such a system, hell is invariably the deepest truth, and the love of God is not so deep as hell. Hence, as foundations must be laid in the deepest, the system is founded in hell, and the first article in the creed that Robert Falconer learned was, "I believe in hell." Practically, I mean, it was so; else how should it be that as often as a thought of religious duty arose in his mind, it appeared in the form of escaping hell, of fleeing from the wrath to come? For his very nature was hell, being not born in sin and brought forth in iniquity, but born sin and brought forth iniquity. And yet God made him. He must believe that. And he must believe, too, that God was just, awfully just, punishing with fearful pains those who did not go through a certain process of mind which it was utterly impossible they should go through without a help which he would give to some, and withhold from others, the reason of the difference not being such, to say the least of it, as to come within the reach of the persons concerned. And this God they said was love. It was logically absurd, of course, yet, thank God, they did say that God was love; and many of them succeeded in believing it, too…

Robert consequently began to take fits of soul-saving, a most rational exercise, worldly wise and prudent—right too on the principles he had received, but not in the least Christian in its nature, or even God-fearing. His imagination began to busy itself in representing the dire consequences of not entering into the one refuge of faith. He made many frantic efforts to believe that he believed; took to keeping the Sabbath very carefully— that is, by going to church three times, and to Sunday-school as well; by never walking a step save to or from church; by never saying a word upon any subject unconnected with religion, chiefly theoretical; by never reading any but religious books; by never whistling; by never thinking of his lost fiddle, and so on—all the time feeling that God was ready to pounce upon him if he failed once; till again and again the intensity of his efforts utterly defeated their object by destroying for the time the desire to prosecute them with the power to will them. [120]

Nor will God force any door to enter in. He may send a tempest about the house; the wind of his admonishment may burst doors and windows, yea, shake the house to its foundations; but not then, not so, will he enter. The door must be opened by the willing hand, ere the foot of Love will cross the threshold. He watches to see the door move from within. Every tempest is but an assault in the siege of love. The terror of God is but the other side of his love; it is love outside the house, that would be inside. [121]

No prayer for any revenge that would gratify the selfishness of our nature, a thing to be burned out of us by the fire of God, needs think to be heard…"Vengeance is mine," he says: with a right understanding of it, we might as well pray for God's vengeance as for his forgiveness; that vengeance is, to destroy the sin—to make the sinner abjure and hate it; nor is there any satisfaction in a vengeance that seeks or effects less. The man himself must turn against himself, and so be for himself. If nothing else will do, then hell-fire; if less will do, whatever brings repentance and self-repudiation, is God's repayment. [122]

The...supremely terrible revelation is that of a man to himself. What a horror will it not be to a vile man...that knew himself such as men of ordinary morals would turn from with disgust, but who has hitherto had no insight into what he is—what a horror will it not be to him when his eyes are opened to see himself as the pure see him, as God sees him! Imagine such a man waking all at once, not only to see the eyes of the universe fixed upon him with loathing astonishment, but to see himself at the same moment as those eyes see him! What a waking!—into the full blaze of fact and consciousness, of truth and violation!...

Or think what it must be for a man counting himself religious...to perceive suddenly that there was no religion in him, only love of self...What a discovery—that he was simply a hypocrite. [123]

A man may sink by such slow degrees that, long after he is a devil, he may go on being a good churchman...and thinking himself a good Christian. Continuously repeated sin against the poorest consciousness of evil must have a dread rousing. There are men who never wake to know how wicked they are, till, lo, the gaze of the multitude is upon them! [124]

Therefore, while a satisfied justice is an unavoidable eternal event, a satisfied revenge is an eternal impossibility. For the moment that the sole adequate punishment, a vision of himself, begins to take true effect upon the sinner, that moment the sinner has begun to grow a righteous man...Behold the meeting of the divine extremes—the extreme of punishment, the embrace of heaven! They run together; "the wheel is come full circle." For, I venture to think, there can be no such agony for created soul, as to see itself vile—vile by its own action and choice. Also I venture to think there can be no delight for created soul—short, that is, of being one with the Father—so deep as that of seeing the heaven of forgiveness open, and disclose the shining stair that leads to its own natural home, where the eternal father has been all the time awaiting this return of his child. [125]

TWENTY-ONE

IT'S ALL GREEK TO ME

Some Crucial Words Illuminated

by
Michael Phillips

A fter our discussion of the specific aspects of this sweeping new vision of the afterlife, it is time for us to focus on the Scriptures themselves. Several passages of particular import rise up before us demanding a response. We have said that "proof" as such is not to be had. What we will discover in this chapter, however, may come as close to *proving* the case for universal reconciliation as is possible.

Three passages we need to scrutinize are Matthew 25:46, Mark 3:29, and Philippians 2:10-11.

We will look closely at several words in these verses:

OUK ECHEI—translated "never" in Mark 3:29: "...whoever blasphemes against the Holy Spirit *ouk echei/never* has forgiveness, but is guilty of an eternal sin."

EIS TON AIONA—which translates from the Greek as *unto the age.*

KOLASIN—translated "punishment" in Matthew 25:46: "And they will go away into eternal *kolasin/punishment...*"

AIONION—translated "everlasting" or "eternal" in Matthew 25:46: "And they will go away into *aionion/eternal* punishment..."; and Mark 3:29: "...never forgiveness, but is guilty of an *aionion/eternal* sin."

KAMPTO—translated "bow" in Philippians 2:10: "...that at the name of Jesus every knee should *kampto/bow...*"

EXOMOLOGEO—translated "confess" in Philippians 2:11: "...every knee should bow...and every tongue *exomologeo/confess* that Jesus Christ is Lord."

By the time you reach the end of this chapter, these words *won't* be all just Greek to you. They may be words that will change your entire spiritual outlook!

PROBLEM PASSAGE 1—MARK 3:29:

THE DREADED UNFORGIVABLE SIN: AN ERRONEOUS FOUNDATION FOR UNFORGIVENESS

Though the so-called "unforgivable sin" does not address the doctrine of hell directly, the subtle connection is unmistakable. For here we have the definitive pronouncement that there are some sins that God will *never* forgive. Jesus' words point not merely to blasphemy against the Holy Spirit. They carry enormous implications about the nature of forgiveness itself. They imply that God's forgiveness is *not* infinite. Especially grievous sins will remain unforgiven *forever*.

Mark 3:29 thus indirectly establishes the fact of eternal punishment of sin. With that principle in place, the doctrine of eternal hell, where retribution will be meted out upon those who commit such "unforgivable" sins, is not far behind.

Mingling two translations, the verse reads:

"But whoever blasphemes against the Holy Spirit will never be forgiven [NIV], but is in danger of eternal damnation [KJV]."

The statement we have presented us here as coming from Jesus' mouth has surely caused as much fear, condemnation, and confusion as any single verse in the Bible. It is especially worthy of serious examination for what it suggests about the character of God, and the foundation it sets in place for the doctrine of unforgiveness.

WHAT KIND OF GOD IS OUR GOD?

Not all doctrines are created equal. Some have more widespread consequences for our belief systems than others. Those that wrongly teach concerning the nature and purposes of God, and thus that misrepresent God *himself*, are those we should be most diligent to examine with a scrutinizing eye.

What is commonly referred to as "blasphemy against the Holy Spirit" represents one of these pivotal studies in which the character of God is at stake. The irrevocable judgment of this passage has weighed heavily on the hearts of multitudes through the years, producing a totally erroneous view of God, and probably keeping many out of the kingdom. The words jump out as a scriptural "I dare you," a sort of spiritual Russian roulette

252

with eternal consequences. *I dare you*, the brain taunts—*curse the Holy Spirit!* Haunted by ominous words they cannot dislodge from their minds and which lay in the memory as a sentence of doom, many feel that there is no hope for them. Guilt may be at root. But a far deeper problem exists here than that—the corrosive effect it has on our portrayal of God's nature.

All this misunderstanding is based on an *incomplete* translation of this passage.

INTERPRETIVE TRANSLATIONS

A serious difficulty facing us is the fact that Bible translation is not as objective as we might wish. Again, attempting not to disparage motive, which we are bound to trust as admirable and true, the fact cannot be ignored that most translations reflect the opinions of those who compile them. Bible translators tilt their word choices in ways that corroborate their doctrinal preferences. Subtleties of usage, tense, and actual word meanings from the original languages often disappear from sight to be replaced by doctrinally-biased word selection.

As we alluded to earlier, no matter what translation we use, we are not reading a perfect reconstruction of the original Greek or Hebrew, but an *interpretive* rendition as seen through the eyes of its translators. To some degree this cannot be helped. Where ambiguity exists, one *has* to fall back on his or her own perspectives to determine what a particular portion of Scripture means. The serious student must therefore ask questions and read between the lines.

As we do, we often find ourselves forced to look beyond the traditional reproduction of certain passages. The NIV of Mark 3:29 has it, "Whoever blasphemes against the Holy Spirit will never be forgiven; he is guilty of an eternal sin."

The King James is even more hideous: "But he that shall blaspheme against the Holy Ghost hath never forgiveness, but is in danger of eternal damnation." No wonder people labor under terrible guilt from this horrifying pronouncement.

WILL VS. SHALL

Four troublesome words occur in Mark 3:29 where the NIV, and most other translations, badly err: *will, never, guilty,* and *eternal*:

"Whoever blasphemes against the Holy Spirit <u>will</u> <u>never</u> be forgiven; he is <u>guilty</u> of an <u>eternal</u> sin."

The translation as given implies exactly what people fear—that the blasphemer has been pronounced guilty, that God himself renders the

253

verdict, and that the judgment is irrevocable. All four of these words, however, have been either *mis*translated or *incompletely* translated. We are left with a completely wrong account of what Jesus said.

Let us investigate the time sequence of the verse.

The phrase "will never be forgiven" implies two factors of timing—it implies a *future* judgment, and that this judgment is *permanent.*

Additionally, the word *will* makes the judgment passed *upon* the blasphemer from the outside. It is not a neutral judgment, it is a condemnatory sentence—a *life*-sentence. The judge is God, who chooses to "will" permanent and eternal judgment.

To "will" requires volition by *somebody.* Someone is the causative force behind the verb. "Will" is not a verb of impersonal passivity but of decision and volition. It requires a personal *will-er. Someone* has to choose to exercise that active "will." Obviously that someone is God.

The word "will" can also be used to indicate the future tense. But there are two ways to express the future—*will* and *shall,* one personal and implying the chosen *act of willing,* the other an *impersonal* statement concerning the future.

"Will" carries with it motive. "Shall" does not. *Shall* indicates the neutral future. *Will* indicates a willed and chosen future.

Noted grammarian William Strunk clarifies the distinction by saying that "*will* expresses...determination or... consent. A swimmer in distress cries, 'I shall drown; no one will save me!' A suicide puts it the other way: 'I will drown; no one shall save me.'" [126]

In the case of Mark 3:29, the translators have not written "*shall* never be forgiven," but "*will* never be forgiven." This implies a chosen "will" exerting itself which results in the future and permanent condition of judgment by God.

If *shall* had been used, it would merely indicate a neutral future state in which forgiveness did not exist. Consider what a difference would be conveyed if the words read "cannot" be forgiven. Yet neither *shall* nor *cannot* is used, but "*will* never be forgiven," a purposeful, willed judgment by God.

But it is all wrong. The word *will* does not appear in the Greek at all! It is simply not there. The translators *added* it. In so doing they completely altered the meaning of the Greek text. It is an "interpretive" addition.

Neither does *shall* appear in Greek. The original gives no sign of the *future* whatever. Not only have they inaccurately rendered the words, they have changed the timing. The tense indicated in the Greek of this verse is the *present.* Yet the translators have changed the *present* of the original into a *future* of judgment.

The conclusion is inescapable: The translators *mistranslated* Jesus' words to bolster the orthodoxy of permanent future unforgiveness.

NEVER

The translated word *never* is yet more troublesome. It likewise does not exist in the Greek. The original employs the word *not* rather than "never."

The passage literally reads, "has not forgiveness."

It is a state of *present* "condition," not *future* "judgment."

What a damaging liberty the translators took by changing *has not forgiveness* to *will never be forgiven.* Not only did they change the original from present to future, they turned a present condition into a *permanent* judgment.

The entire force of the passage is altered.

Jesus is speaking of no future condemnation but of a present state of affairs that exists—*has not forgiveness.* In the text as Mark wrote it, God nowhere occupies the role of a judge passing sentence.

In this particular phrase, the KJV is closer with its "hath never forgiveness," though still substitutes *never* for *not* and implies a permanency not found in the Greek text. One of the few translations to get it right is Young's Literal Translation: *hath not forgiveness.* [127]

The amazing conclusion is unmistakable exactly as we saw a moment ago: The translators added the word "never," which Jesus did *not* say, to bolster the orthodoxy of permanent future unforgiveness.

εις τον αιωνα—UNTO THE AGE...STRICKEN FROM THE TEXT!

Following the word "forgiveness" in the text appear the above three words—εις τον αιωνα.

I place them here in their original Greek for a simple reason. I want us to *look* at these three words, whether we can "read" them or not, and ponder them. Maybe it will simply give new meaning to the expression, "It's all Greek to me!" Yet it is important for us to realize that each of these Greek characters, funny squiggles and all, actually flowed from the ink in Mark's quill.

Mark *wrote* these words εις τον αιωνα. He knew what they meant, even if we don't. He *wrote* them down on a papyrus roll as a direct quote from the Lord's mouth.

And yet when it comes to our English translations, these three words simply *vanish.*

ειζ τον αιωνα...EIS TON AIONA— when translated, mean *unto the age*. When you read this passage in your Bible, however, you will *not* see these three words.

They are *gone!*

Open your Bible to Mark 3:29. What you *ought* to read are the words: "Whoever blasphemes against the Holy Spirit has not forgiveness *unto the age...*"

What you will actually read will not be so dramatically different. Only a few words will be changed. But they are sufficient to have perpetuated an entirely false doctrine about the nature and duration of God's potential forgiveness.

It is not hard to see how "has not forgiveness unto the age," comes to be rendered *"will never be forgiven."* Translators assume "unto the age" means *forever.* They then convert "not... forever" to *never.* What in the original indicates a *present* condition that may NOT last forever is changed to a future condition that WILL last forever.

With a few strokes of a translator's pen, the meaning has been *completely* changed.

To probe yet further into this mystery, we need to look at the root of the word *age*, from the phrase "unto the age." If the condition of unforgiveness lasts "unto the *age*," what does that mean? How long is it? We will consider that question momentarily.

ενοχοζ—LIABILITY NOT GUILT, SIN NOT DAMNATION

First, however, let us examine the word the NIV translates *guilty*— ενοχοζ... ENOCHOS—which the King James renders far more accurately as *in danger.* The truer sense of *enochos* is *liable*, being subject to a charge that has been brought—*indicted* but not yet found *guilty.*

The sense of the Greek is that an indictment has been issued and justice will ultimately be rendered. But as everyone deserves his day in court, the verdict is still out.

Liability implies only that a charge has been brought. Most translators, however, dispense with the rest of the proceedings and jump straight to the verdict, passing sentence and pronouncing guilt before a final determination is made. They turn the indictment into *guilty*...case closed.

At every point, the liberties taken by the translators lead to huge consequences. When Jesus spoke these words, he was not pronouncing sentence, he was pronouncing "liability," the danger of *potential* judgment. In a sense he was saying, "A case will be brought against those who blaspheme against the Holy Spirit."

We also need to expunge from our considerations once and for all "damnation" of the King James, It is an atrocious rendering and a *complete* mistranslation of the Greek. What Mark actually wrote at the end of the 29th verse are these words:

"...is liable for *sin.*"

The distinction is staggering. "Damnation" is nowhere to be found in what Jesus said. The KJV mistranslation is horrendous. Being *liable* for a *sin* is a far different thing than being sentenced guilty and permanently condemned.

αιων—AION

We now encounter the most serious difficulty in this passage—the word rendered in most translations *eternal.*

The word in question from the Greek is αιωνιος—AIONIOS—whose form AIONIOU appears in the text of Mark 3:29, and whose form AIONION appears in Matthew 25:46.

In αιων we encounter one of the most fascinating words in all New Testament Greek, intriguing yet enormously complex and fraught with controversy. It is a word with myriad nuances that simply "do not compute" into English.

You will notice that its root is exactly the same as that for one of the three missing words above. Yet that repetition has been removed from what we read in English. What does remain has been mistranslated. In consequence, we never see Mark's repeated use of the word "age" in the text at all.

The root for these two words is αιων—AION—a word with a long history in the Greek language. Its literal meaning is *age*, or *era*, from which we quickly recognize the similarity to "eon." Its adjectival form AIONION, literally "having to do with AION," is usually given as *of* or *unto* or *for* "the age." That its forms are often repeated contributes to the various "eternal" translations, as in Jude 25 ("before all the AIONOS and now and unto all the AIONAS"…translated in the RSV as *before all time and now and ever*); and in Rev. 1:6 ("unto the AIONAS of the AIONON"…usually rendered *for ever and ever*).

The depth and complexity of AION is illustrated by the remarkable fact that it can be translated in *opposite* ways, making the attempt to unravel its meaning infinitely more difficult. "Unto the age," or "lasting for the age," can mean *temporary* (lasting until the age ends), or it can mean permanent or *eternal* (lasting for *all* the ages.)

This ambiguity is especially pronounced in Mark 3:29, where the translators make the unforgiveness *eternal*, but where other factors indicate that Jesus actually meant potentially *temporary*.

Furthermore, AION contains two interrelated components, one of *duration* and another of *quality*. In this second sense, it is sometimes rendered *life*.

The etymological history of the word AION is far reaching. Examples are numerous in the Greek classics of the use of AION and its derivative forms, from Aristotle to Homer to Plato, intermingling the sense of *life* and *time*. The word signifies a continuous period lasting for a certain epoch (of that particular epoch's life-quality or characteristic), but which eventually gives way to *another* "aeon" of *different* characteristics. In Greek literature, the word rarely implies "forever."

We are reminded of the word "paradise." Obviously the chief sense is of a perfect *quality* of life. Yet there are hints of *timelessness*, of perfection where time stands still...yet which might not last for *all* time.

Of this dual complexity of *life* and *age*, W.E. Vine comments that AION, "signifies a period of indefinite duration, or time viewed in relation to what takes place in the period. The force attaching to the word is not so much that of the actual length of a period, but that of a period marked by spiritual or moral characteristics." [128]

Vine's words when applied to Mark 3:29 completely alter Jesus' meaning.

It will surprise many to learn that AION, AIONION, and its forms are used over 150 times in the New Testament, approximately the same number of times as the forms of AGAPE. Yet AION is a word scarcely studied or mentioned even by knowledgeable students of the Bible.

Several more passages further illustrate how variable are the renderings, and how many of them have been altered by translators in ways that cause the nuances and subtleties of the word to vanish altogether.

Luke 1:33—AIONAS ("unto the ages")... rendered *forever*.

John 9:32—AIONOS ("from the age")... rendered *Since the world began* (KJV); *has ever* (NIV).

1 Corinthians 2:7—AIONON ("before the ages"); 10:11— AIONON ("ends of the ages")... rendered *before the world* (KJV); *before time began* (NIV), and; *ends of the world* (KJV); *fulfillment of the ages* (NIV).

Ephesians 2:7—AIOSIN ("in the ages"); 3: 9—AIONON ("from the ages"); 3:11— AIONON ("of the ages"); 3:21— AIONOS ("of the age") and AIONON ("of the ages")...rendered *in the ages to come* (KJV), and; *from the beginning of the world*

(KJV); *for ages past* (NIV), and; *eternal purpose* (NIV), and; *throughout all ages* (KJV); *for ever and ever* (NIV).

Hebrews 1:8—AIONA ("unto the age") and AIONOS ("of the age"); 6:5—AIONOS ("a coming age"); 9:26—AIONON ("completion of the ages")...rendered *for ever and ever*, and; *the world to come* (KJV); *the coming age* (NIV), and; *the end of the world* (KJV); *the end of the ages* (NIV).

2 Peter 3:18— AIONOS ("unto the day of an age")...rendered *forever.*

ATTEMPTS TO SHINE THE LIGHT OF ACCURACY ON MARK 3:29

Consider the following renditions of Mark 3:29 as indication that at least some bold translators have attempted to address the complexities involved.

"...but whoever blasphemes against the Holy Spirit, he remains for ever unabsolved: he is guilty of a sin of the Ages." *(New Testament in Modern Speech,* R.F. Weymouth [129])

"...yet whoever should be blaspheming against the holy spirit is having no pardon for the eon, but is liable to the eonian penalty for the sin." *(Concordant Literal New Testament* [130])

"...but whoever may speak evil in regard to the Holy Spirit hath not forgiveness—to the age, but is in danger of age-during judgment." *(Young's Literal Translation of the Bible* [131])

"But whoever shall revile against the Holy Spirit hath no forgiveness, unto times age-abiding,—but is guilty of an age-abiding sin." *(The Emphasized Bible,* Joseph B. Rotherham [132])

These vague efforts to render the complexities of AION and its forms into English are understandably obscure. It is perhaps not surprising that gradually over the course of time the word "eternal" would be found as the simplest way to avoid the ambiguities of translation.

But it is a seriously incomplete solution, especially where it conveys a wrong idea about God's forgiveness. The meaning in this verse *may* be temporary, or it *may* be eternal. How long the condition will last is up to the blasphemer.

WHY BLASPHEMY CLOSES THE DOOR TO FORGIVENESS

Let us now turn again to the beginning of the verse to ask what it means to "blaspheme" against the Holy Spirit.

Is it an *act*, or a *condition*?

At this point in Mark's gospel, the scribes and Pharisees have called Jesus' miracles the work of Satan. This Jesus terms "blasphemy against the Holy Spirit": Reviling the work of God by calling it the work of the devil. It is more than a childish string of cursing. It is the non-recognition of the Holy Spirit's work.

When properly understood, Mark's words explode with new meaning. Jesus is not speaking of a single word or outburst, but of a *condition of heart.*

That is the indictment—the heart condition. As long as such an attitude persists, forgiveness cannot find a home. Not recognizing the work of the Spirit closes the only door through which forgiveness can enter. This unforgiveness will continue for the AION, as long as the door of recognition is shut, for the duration of that age defined by an antagonistic heart. Forgiveness cannot enter through a closed door.

The verdict resulting from the sin of non-acknowledgment is thus a *self-imposed judgment*—rendered, not by God, but against *oneself* by attributing God's work to Satan. For that wrong judgment the sinner is liable. He is not yet *condemned*, only indicted. Unless such condition is changed, he *will* be condemned—but *self*-condemned.

The situation, as Jesus utters it, is one of *present* moral condition, the heart condition existing *now*, but not what may be the condition of that heart in the future. Final judgment has not yet been passed. There remains time to alter the outcome and reverse the indictment.

To repeat: The jury is still out. The blasphemer is in the enviable position not accorded to the prisoners of most judicial systems of being his or her own jury. The blasphemer will ultimately decide his or her *own* fate!

THE SOURCE OF FORGIVENESS

Forgiveness cannot fulfill itself until its Source is recognized. This entire passage has been occupied with the theme of sin and forgiveness...and the *Source* of forgiveness.

When Jesus said to the paralytic, "Your sins are forgiven," he was making a claim in front of the Pharisees' very eyes—"I am the Source of forgiveness. In Mark 3:29 we come to the climax of what has been building for two chapters in Mark's narrative—the ultimate consequences of the Pharisees' denial of that Source.

The consequence is unforgiveness. *Forgiveness requires that its Source be recognized.*

That unforgiveness is *age-enduring.* The AION of unforgiveness *may* be eternal if he who refuses to acknowledge the Spirit's work *never* opens his eyes. That is not a judgment *God* will pass. The duration of that era of unforgiveness will be determined solely within the will of the man himself. Eyes can open at any time. If and when the Source is acknowledged, then the "age" of that condition comes to an end. The door opens and forgiveness flows in.

Unforgiveness lasts *to the age*...but not beyond. The moment recognition dawns, a *new* era of healing and spiritual recognition—indicating both a new *time* and a new *quality* of life—has come!

A new moral and spiritual AION dawns!

If I were rendering Mark 3:28-29 interpretively, I would paraphrase it thus: "I tell you the truth, men will be forgiven all their sins, careless words, and thoughtless attitudes. But whoever does not acknowledge the work of God's Spirit in men's lives, and in his own heart, cannot experience the fruit of the Spirit's work, which is forgiveness, as long as that blindness persists. He is liable for a condition of heart that prevents him from recognizing the truth. The sin of that willful blindness will remain with him for as long an age as he refuses to open the door of his understanding and humbly acknowledge God for who he is."

It is not that the word "never" should be stricken from the divine lexicon. There are indeed some things that God will *never* do:

God will *never* cease the relentless knock of his Fatherly love on the stubborn heart's doors of his wayward children as long as a single one remains lost. God is not capable of "never" forgiving. To *never forgive* contradicts his very nature.

He is not a God who will arbitrarily and endlessly punish to all eternity, *refusing* to forgive, *will-ing* and choosing "never" to forgive. Rather he is a God who is *anxious* to forgive, and who seeks all opportunities for the entry of his Spirit into the wayward human heart.

Verily, he is not the unforgiving Almighty of erroneous orthodoxies. He is the *always* forgiving, the *ever*-forgiving, the *ceaselesly* forgiving God and Father of Jesus Christ!

At last we can place the entirety of Mark 3:29 into its proper context, and see more deeply into the Greek text as it ought to have been represented to us.

ος	δ	αν	βλασφημηση		εις	το	πνευμα
os	d	an	blasphemese		eis	to	pneuma
but whoever			blasphemes		against	the	Spirit

(does not acknowledge the work of/
closes the door in his own heart to /
is in a moral condition of rejecting the work of)

το	αγιον,	ουκ	εχει	αφεσιν	εις	τον	αιωνα,
to	hagion	ouk	echei	aphesin	eis	ton	aiona
-	Holy,	has	not	forgiveness	unto	the	age,

(forgiveness cannot find an   (as long as such state persists/
opening to enter)   as long as such heart
condition exists)

αλλα	ενοχος	εστιν	αιωνιου	αμαρτηματος.
alla	enochos	estin	aioniou	hamartematos
but	liable	is	of an age-lasting	sin.

(indicted/   (for the duration
self-condemned)   of that condition)

PROBLEM PASSAGE 2—MATTHEW 25:46:
A HORRENDOUSLY DAMAGING MISTRANSLATION

More than any other single verse, Matthew 25:46 sits as an anchoring foundation for the doctrine of eternal punitive hell. A millennium or more of both Catholic and Protestant hell-theology is based as much as anything on this verse.

The fact is, however, most translators of this all-important passage have rendered the Greek inaccurately. What is most disturbing, they have done so *knowingly*. The translators have not attempted to give the words *correctly*, but have been more concerned to insure that their translations support the prevailing orthodoxy.

The result of an investigation into the true meaning of the Greek text drops an atomic bomb into the midst of our preconceptions about hell.

We quickly see the doctrine of punitive, punishing, everlasting hell jumping off the page when we read most of the well-known translations of Matthew 25:46.

And they will go away into eternal punishment, but the righteous into eternal life. (RSV)

And these will go away into eternal punishment, but the righteous into eternal life. (ESV)

And they will go away into eternal punishment, but the righteous into eternal life. (NIV)

And they will go away to eternal punishment, but the righteous will enter eternal life. (NEB)

And they will go away to eternal punishment, and the virtuous to eternal life. (Jerusalem Bible)

Even a cursory perusal reveals an astonishing uniformity given the nuances present in the Greek original. We will soon see that the frequent claim by every new translation to be "based on the oldest and most reliable manuscripts" is not necessarily a claim backed up by truth.

Let us read this verse once more, from the King James Version, highlighting in brackets the two significant Greek words we noted at the beginning of this chapter. The second of these—*aionion*—we have already looked at in connection with Mark 3:29.

"And these shall go away into <u>everlasting</u> [αἰώνιον/aiōnion] <u>punishment</u> [κόλασιν/kolasin]; but the righteous into life <u>eternal</u> [αἰώνιον/aiōnion]."

KOLASIS

To get to the bottom of the meaning of κόλασιν/kolasin—we again draw upon the contrast between a courtroom and a family. Punishment is often required in both settings. But it may be very different in nature. This contrast is suggested by five Greek words, all of which may be rendered "punishment" but which are distinctive in meaning.

> EKDIKĒSIS—vengeance. (1 Peter 2:14)
> EPITIMIA—penalty imposed by judge. (2 Corinthians 2:6)
> DIKĒ—execution of a legal sentence. (Jude 7)
> TIMŌRIA—also a legal penalty or punishment. (Hebrews 10:29)

It is not difficult to see the retaliatory, penal, tooth-for-tooth characteristics of these four. But the fifth word comes at "punishment" from a different angle altogether.

> KOLASIS—remedial, corrective discipline.

This last definition examples the punishment of a wise father whose objective is not vengeful, retaliative, retributive, nor the imposition of a sentence. Rather it is *restorative*—with the objective of growth into obedience and righteousness. The distinction is obvious between family discipline and a *quid pro quo* legal sentence. A more accurate rendering of *kolasis* than "punishment" would be *disciplinary chastening*.

This is the intended discipline of Matthew 25:46. It is not punishment meted out as the punitive sentence of a court of law. It is the chastening of remedial and corrective discipline exercised by a Father, with the end in view of repentance, healing, and restoration within the hearts of his children.

No *court of law* exists in Matthew 25:46, but a foundation for *family reconciliation*.

AION

The second significant word in Matthew 25:46 is one we have already considered: αἰώνιον—*aiōnion*.

As noted, *aion* is one of the remarkable terms in New Testament Greek whose shades of variation are almost nowhere preserved in translation. This single word represents one of the best kept secrets in biblical scholarship.

The two biblical scholars Andrew Jukes and Thomas Allin amplify this point:

> "...the language of the New Testament, in its use of the word which our Translators have rendered 'for ever' and 'for ever and ever,' but which is literally 'for the age,' or 'for the ages of ages,' points not uncertainly to...the glad tidings of the 'ages to come'...Would it not have been better therefore, and more respectful to the Word of God, had our Translators been content in every place to give the exact meaning of the words, which they render 'for ever,' or 'for ever and ever,' but which are simply 'for the age,' or 'for the ages of ages'...But even more remarkable are the words, in St. Peter's Second Epistle, which our Version translates 'for ever,' but which are literally 'for the day of the age'...These and other similar forms of expression cannot have been used without a purpose. It is, therefore, a matter of regret that our Translators should not have rendered them exactly and literally; for surely the words which Divine Wisdom

264

has chosen must have a reason, even where readers and translators lack the light to apprehend it." [133]

"*Let us consider the true meaning of the words aion and aionios. These are the originals of the terms rendered by our translators 'everlasting,' 'for ever and ever': and on this translation, so misleading, a vast portion of the popular dogma of endless torment is built up. I say, without hesitation, misleading and incorrect; for aion means 'an age,' a limited period, whether long or short, though often of indefinite length; and the adjective aionios means 'of the age,' 'age-long,' 'æonian,' and never 'everlasting.'"* [134]

A FEW COURAGEOUS TRANSLATORS HAVE ATTEMPTED ACCURACY

It will be clear that more doctrinal bias is at work in the translation process, as well as in the marginal notes of most Bibles, than is comforting. The doctrine of eternal punitive hell has been such a solidly entrenched pillar of orthodoxy for so long that translators have skewed their word options to substantiate it. In this particular case, Matthew 25:46 has been rendered without a hint of the pruning, corrective, and age-lasting aspects which the Greek original conveys.

As we saw in the case of Mark 3:29, there have been a few translators through the years with the honest courage to communicate this meaning implied by the Greek text.

And these shall go away into the Punishment of the Ages, but the righteous into the Life of the Ages. (*Weymouth New Testament,* original version [135])

And these shall go away into age-abiding correction, but the righteous into age-abiding life. (*The Emphasized Bible* [136])

And these shall go away to punishment age-during, but the righteous to life age-during. (*Young's Literal Translation* [137])

And these last will go away into aeonian punishment, but the righteous into aeonian life. (*The Twentieth Century New Testament* [138])

*And these shall be coming away into chastening eonian,
yet the just into life eonian. (Concordant Literal New
Testament* [139])

As a side-note of interest, subsequent editions of Richard
Weymouth's *New Testament in Modern Speech* (first published the year
after his death in 1903) do not read as indicated above. Long after the
translator was dead and could not object, the publishers of the fourth
edition of his work (1924) changed several controversial passages so as to
bring the Weymouth translation more in line with traditional
interpretation. The above rendition of Matthew 25:46 became:

*And these shall go away into everlasting punishment, but the
righteous into eternal life.*

Dr. Weymouth's attempt to capture the meaning of the Greek original
(which he did in his rendering of John 3:16 as well, and which was also
changed) thus disappeared from sight for the sake of "doctrinal
correctness."

BETWEEN THE LINES OF MATTHEW 25:46—
DOES HELL HAVE REDEMPTIVE PURPOSE?

By omitting the nuances of the Greek meanings of the two words
commonly translated *everlasting* and *eternal* "punishment," the translators
of this verse have erected a horrendous stumbling block to an accurate
knowing of God's intent.

A.R. Symonds and A.T. Robertson place the problem into
perspective.

*If the Greek word rendered 'everlasting' in the
English version does not support the notion of endless
suffering, much less does the word which is translated
'punishment.' The distinctive meaning of this word,
κόλασις [kolasis] is corrective punishment, being
derived from a verb which means to prune. I say its
distinctive meaning is this, in relation to another word,
τιμωρία [timōria] which signifies vindictive punishment.
In τιμωρία the vindictive character of the punishment is
predominant; it is the Latin ultio, vengeance,
punishment as satisfying the inflictor's sense of outraged
justice, as defending his own honour and that of violated
law. In κόλασις on the other hand, it is more the notion*

of punishment as it has reference to the correction and bettering of him that endures it; it is castigatio, chastisement, and has naturally for the most part a milder use than τιμωρία [140]

> *The word kolasin comes from kolazo, to mutilate or prune. Hence those who cling to the larger hope use this phrase to mean age-long pruning that ultimately leads to salvation of the goats, as disciplinary rather than penal. There is such a distinction as Aristotle pointed out between moria (vengeance) and kolasis...We can leave all this to the King himself who is the Judge...The word aionios (from aion, age, aevum, aei) is a difficult idea to put into language. Sometimes we have 'ages of ages' (aiones ton aionon).* [141]

The fundamental question raised is as simple as it is profound: Is hell a prison of permanent retribution and vengeance against sinners? Or does it have a purpose beyond mere incarceration, a purpose with defined length and restorative intent?

If *kolasin* is the word that fell from Jesus' lips, what did he mean?

Is hell truly intended for the *kolasin* of sinners—their discipline, their pruning, their correction, their healing, their redemption?

Is the chastening correction of hell not intended as permanent, but to last only for an *eon*, for an *age*, for the aion necessary to achieve its redemptive objective, at which time a new eternal aion will begin?

At that time "all things will be united in Christ," as Paul states in Ephesians 1:10 is the "mystery of God's will?"

William Barclay addresses these questions powerfully and personally:

> *I want to set down not the arguments of others but the thoughts which have persuaded me personally of universal salvation.*
>
> *First, there is the fact that there are things in the New Testament which more than justify this belief. Jesus said: 'I, when I am lifted up from the earth, will draw all men to myself' (John 12:32). Paul writes to the Romans: 'God has consigned all men to disobedience that he may have mercy on all' (Rom. 11:32). He writes to the Corinthians: 'As in Adam all die, so also in Christ shall all be made alive' (1 Cor. 15: 22); and he looks to the final total triumph when God will be everything to*

everyone (1 Cor. 15:28). In the First Letter to Timothy we read of God 'who desires all men to be saved and to come to the knowledge of the truth', and of Christ Jesus 'who gave himself as a ransom for all'(1 Tim. 2.4-6). The New Testament itself is not in the least afraid of the word all.

Second, one of the key passages is Matthew 25:46 where it is said that the rejected go away to eternal punishment, and the righteous to eternal life. The Greek word for punishment is kolasis, which was not originally an ethical word at all. It originally meant the pruning of trees to make them grow better. I think it is true to say that in all Greek secular literature kolasis is never used of anything but remedial punishment. The word for eternal is aionios. The simplest way to put it is that aionios cannot be used properly of anyone but God...Eternal punishment is then literally that kind of remedial punishment which it befits God to give and which only God can give. [142]

THE FATHERHOOD PRISM

Even the above evidence and testimony from reputed biblical scholars, however, is not conclusive. The debate rages on. It is fascinating in the extreme that two individuals can look at the same evidence and draw opposite conclusions. Many read the frequent uses of ALL in the New Testament in reference to the salvation of mankind yet find no inconsistency in concluding that all mankind will NOT be saved. Others read "all" and assume that all means *all*.

This highlights what might be a useful observation—the light that scatters upon the pages of Scripture gives off disparate interpretive images according to what prism we are using to illuminate the words. You may not be aware of it, but as you are reading at this moment, the light shining on the page in front of you is actually *colored* light. Your eyes don't see it, but it is there. In the same way, to understand what the words of the Bible mean, we have to see and *apprehend* what is really there. We have to look through the right glasses to bring the meaning into proper focus.

That prism by which the pages of Scripture are properly illuminated is Fatherhood.

The Fatherhood-prism scatters the radiant rainbow colors of light differently upon the pages of Scripture than for those who are looking through old-covenantal glasses. Inevitably, George MacDonald viewed truth more expansively than those of his era who came to the Bible looking through the glasses of rigid Calvinism. You or I may read a passage and see in it all the colors of the rainbow. Another may read the same passage and perceive only black and white.

Some will say that we are reading into the Bible what isn't there. Would they say that the light falling on this page contains no color? Because they do not see the seven colors on the page does not mean those seven colors do not exist. Inevitably, many read Scripture and see only black and white without perceiving the full rainbow Truth that God has hidden in his Word for us to discover.

Most truth *isn't* black and white. Reality is not always visible to the naked eye. The component nuances of truth, like the component colors of light, have to pass through the right kind of prism to be seen. It is my opinion that the Fatherhood-prism is the only light matrix that enables us to read Scripture accurately.

DEBATE REMAINS HEATED OVER TWO OPPOSITE CONCLUSIONS

Though validating the meaning of *kolasin* as prune, evangelical scholar A.T. Robertson is also quick to reject universal salvation. He makes the convincing argument, whatever the meaning of *kolasis*, that the two identical uses of *aionion* in Matthew 25:46 cannot be interpreted one way (eternal and permanent) for the righteous and another way (temporary and lasting only for an age) for the unrighteous.

Robertson's point is basically, "You can't have it both ways. If *aionion* is eternal for the righteous, it must likewise be eternal for the unrighteous."

> *The genuine universalist...can apply this signification to "eternal punishment" in Matt. 25:46 only if he is willing to give exactly the same sense to "eternal life" in the same verse. As F.D. Maurice said many years ago now, writing to F.J.A. Hort: "I did not see how aionios could mean one thing when it was joined with kolasis and another when it was joined with zoe" (quoted, J.O.F. Murray, The Goodness and the Severity of God, p. 195). To admit that the two phrases are not parallel is at once to treat them with unequal seriousness. And that a true universalist must refuse to do.* [143]

Millard Erickson parallels Robertson's reasoning.

> *To be sure, the adjective* κόλασις *may on a few occasions have reference to an age, that is, a very long period of time, rather than to eternity...In the cases we have cited, nothing in the contexts justifies our understanding* κόλασις *as meaning anything other than "eternal." The parallelism found in Matthew 25:46 is particularly noteworthy: "And they will go away into eternal punishment, but the righteous into eternal life." If the one (life) is of unending duration, then the other (punishment) must be also. Nothing in the context gives us warrant to interpret the word* κόλασις *differently in the two clauses...* [144]

Robertson's and Erickson's point about the translation of "eternal" are compelling. The honest believer in universal reconciliation must look at this perspective fairly and recognize—as must those on all sides of any scriptural conundrum—that legitimate validation exists for opposing viewpoints. The dilemma of hell is a "great debate" for precisely this reason.

Even as we take the above arguments into account with all seriousness, however, we are also reminded that *aion* often points in Scripture to *multiple* eons of time, even within the same passage. The word *aionion* ("for/of the age") illuminates the multiple distinction of time utilized repeatedly by the minor prophets: *I will punish them forever for the age...until the age of restoration is come.*

It is therefore possible that the two uses of *aionion* within the single verse of Matthew 25:46 indicate distinctive aeons of purpose. The text itself tells us nothing for certain.

We are left where we are often left, having to resolve the scriptural puzzle for ourselves.

καɩ	απελευσονται	ουτοι	εɩς
kai	apeleusontai	outoi	eis
And	will go away	these	into

κολασιν	αιωνιον,	οɩ
kolasin*	aionion,	hoi
chastening ("punishment")	of/for the age ("eternal")	but

δε	δικαιοι	εɩς	ζωην	αιωνιον.
de	dikaioi	eis	zoen	aionion.
the	righteous	into	life	of/for the age

PROBLEM PASSAGE 3—PHILIPPIANS 2:10-11:
THE TRIUMPH OF THE CROSS EXPLAINED AWAY

In six verses of unparalleled scope in the second chapter of Philippians, Paul sets forth several principles that go beyond anything else found in the New Testament.

If we take these words as revelations inspired by the Spirit of God, the implications are staggering. For contained within this passage are two verses, though familiar, whose obvious meaning has been swept under the doctrinal carpet by Christian theologians for centuries.

The passage from Philippians 2:6-11 contains two parts. The first establishes a foundation from which an entire "doctrine of Christ" has been formulated. With stunning brevity, Paul sets before us a breathtaking progression of truths—the preexistence of Christ, his equality with God, his manhood, his chosen submission, his obedient servanthood, his willing death, and, as a result of these, the Lord's exultation throughout the universe.

Paul then takes his vision of God's eternal purpose to the loftiest heights possible as he reflects on the ultimate and final response of mankind to the lordship of Christ.

"...Christ Jesus, who, though he was in the form of God, did not count equality with God a thing to be grasped, but emptied himself, taking the form of a servant, being born in the likeness of men. And

being found in human form he humbled himself and became obedient unto death, even death on a cross. Therefore God has highly exalted him and bestowed on him the name which is above every name... (2:5-9, RSV)

William Barclay writes of these verses, "It would be true to say that in many ways this is the greatest and most moving passage that Paul ever wrote about Jesus." [145]

Probably more than anywhere else in Scripture, Paul here sets the incarnation of Jesus into the context of his divinity. In harmony with *Colossians*, these verses provide a basis for the later development of the doctrine of the trinity.

The most controversial portion of this towering passage, however, is yet to come. Building upon what he has just said about the bestowing upon Jesus of the name above all names, Paul continues to the triumphant climax. The significant Greek words we will look at are shown in brackets.

> *...that at the name of Jesus every knee should <u>bow</u>* [κάμπτω—KAMPTO], *in heaven and on earth and under the earth, and every tongue <u>confess</u>* [ἐξομολογέω—EXOMOLOGEO] *that Jesus Christ is Lord, to the glory of God the Father. (2:10-11, RSV)*

Those schooled in the orthodox theology of everlasting torment immediately recognize a big problem. Paul's words in this passage clearly say that a day will come when the rebellion will end and when, in Paul's words from Ephesians 1:10, "all things" will be brought into a unity in Christ.

EXPLAINING AWAY THE OBVIOUS

We come to one of fundamentalism's most intriguing responses to Scripture. Widespread within evangelical scholarship is an unabashed pride in reading the Bible "literally," never rationalizing or dismissing what the Scriptures say.

Yet this perspective is based on *selective* literality. No evangelical reads the Bible literally in every case any more than do liberal scholars. When they need to in order to preserve their doctrine, the evangelical will "explain away" the literal meaning of a given passage as readily as a thoroughgoing skeptic. [146]

The dilemma posed to evangelical theology by Philippians 2:10-11 is one where such explanations become so convoluted they would be humorous if it weren't heartbreaking to see Christians going to such lengths to deny the obvious truth of what Paul wrote.

The common interpretation goes like this:

The bending of the knee of verse 10 will be the *forced* bowing of a vanquished and humiliated enemy.

The confession of the tongue of verse 11 will be the *unwilling* but inexorable admission of those who remain rebellious to the end. Through clenched teeth and recognizing defeat, they have no alternative but to acknowledge the victory of Christ.

The simple fact is, however, these rationalizations are false. This is not what the words mean at all.

A far larger question raised by these explanations is a glaring one: How does a *forced* and *unwilling* acknowledgment bring glory to God?

BOW AND CONFESS—WHAT DO THEY REALLY MEAN?

The two words of extreme interest are clearly—*bow* and *confess*.

As is often the case, different Greek words can be translated by the *same* English word, making differences of meaning disappear altogether.

For "bow" we have two Greek words to examine:

SUNKAMPTO—συγκάμπτω (to bend by compulsory force.)

KAMPTO—κάμπτω (to bend the knee in religious worship and veneration.)

For "confess" we likewise are presented with two Greek words:

HOMOLOGEO—ὁμολογέω (to admit oneself guilty of a proven accusation.)

EXOMOLOGEO—ἐξομολογέω (to speak out openly and gladly in public acknowledgement of sin, and/or to celebrate and give praise.)

In both cases, the difference between willingness and compulsion is obvious. There exists a *chosen* bowing of the knee and an *unwilling* act of forced homage. There is a chosen and *happily given* confession, and there is a *reluctant* confession.

It does not take a Greek scholar to confirm that it is both the *latter* two words that Paul uses in Philippians 2:10-11. Anyone desiring to understand this passage more fully can discover these usages easily enough by looking the verses up in a Greek/English interlinear Bible, or by consulting a book such as *Vine's Expository Dictionary of New Testament Words.* You don't need to take my word for it. Go to *Vine's,* look up "bow" and "confess," and you will see these exact meanings clearly illuminated.

A proper reading of these verses reveals why Paul climaxed this poetic passage with the triumphant words, *to the glory of God the Father.* The bowing of the knees and the confession of Christ's lordship are given *willingly, eagerly, and worshipfully.*

Every knee will <u>worshipfully</u> bow...*every* tongue will confess <u>with joy and praise</u>...to the glory of God the Father!

When the day arrives that Paul envisioned, the rebellion will be over. The restoration of the universe will be complete!

The cross of Christ will have triumphed indeed!

TWENTY-TWO

AT THE EDGE OF THE PIT

An Excerpt From Hell and Beyond [147]

by
Michael Phillips

TO THE EDGE OF THE FIRE

I left the City of Debt and the pool of the Waters of Forgiveness with a great feeling of buoyancy and freedom. To be debt-free in this place was mightier than any supposed financial freedom in my former life! How can words describe the joy of forgiveness, working upon the heart inward and outward together, forgiving and being forgiven. I felt so light and happy and unencumbered that for some time I completely forgot about the fire.

I walked jauntily along thinking of nothing but how good forgiveness felt...Was my journey at last reaching its climax?

Indeed, it was. Yet how could I have forgotten what lay between here and there? Then I noticed again the pillar of smoke rising out of the earth ahead. A chill swept through me.

Unconsciously, my step slowed. Ahead I saw a precipice disappearing over a vast chasm. Intense heat drifted up from it, greater by far than that from the fire that had purified the Tree of Gold. My brain flooded with images from Dante's vision of hell...

The pit of fire, which had seemed almost small from a distance, now stretched endlessly in front of me to the right and left. There was no possible way *around* it. Like millions of others, I knew that I could choose to make my home on this side. I could avoid the fire and put off the imperative of the flames...perhaps indefinitely. No one would *force* the fire upon me.

Knowing what I was thinking, a voice spoke from behind. I turned to see a bearded man approaching, dressed impeccably in a deep blue suit with tails, sporting a bright red waistcoat. The radiance of his countenance was the most obvious reflection of life on the other side...

"He has means of compelling you, if you do *not* choose it," said the man in answer to my silent thoughts. He spoke in a thick brogue. I knew instantly that at last I was face to face with the Scotsman. "You will choose it," he went on. "You must choose it. But it is always best to choose his way before extreme measures become necessary."

"I...I don't know if I can," I said.

"Do you want to be whole?"

"Yes, with all my heart."

"Then you will be made whole. You must be made whole. You must *choose* to be made whole."

He paused and gazed deep into my eyes.

"Do you want to be cleansed?" he asked.

I nodded.

"Then you will be cleansed. You must be cleansed. You must *choose* to be cleansed."

Still, a third time he put the probing question to me.

"Do you want to be purified?"

"Yes," I answered again.

"You will be purified. You must be purified. He is easy to please, but hard to satisfy. Therefore, you must *choose* to be purified."

"But who could ever choose...the fires of *hell?*" I said.

"Is that what you think?" he said with the hint of a smile, glancing in the direction I had been walking. "That you have come to the edge of hell?"

"Isn't it?"

"Perhaps. But no more than the rest of what you have come through."

"You mean to say I have been in hell all along?" I exclaimed.

"Perhaps," he repeated.

He saw the look of confusion on my face.

"For those who turn back," he went on, "for those who choose to remain in one of the Towns of Death, for those who refuse to acknowledge their debts and become imprisoned by that refusal in the City of Debt, all this will have been hell from the beginning. They will have chosen it as their hell. They will never come out of it until they pay the uttermost farthing. Some may choose to remain in their hell. To them, it will always have been hell.

"But none of that concerns you," he went on. "Everyone else's choices do not bear on your story. I have been sent to help you with *your* choice. So whether you are in hell or on your way to Beyond, that all depends on the choices that still lie ahead. The imperative lesson you have just learned has prepared you for the work of the fire."

"What lesson?"

"That Fatherhood is the heart of the universe, the doorway into the heart of God. We walk in the air of an eternal Fatherhood," the Scotsman went on. "Fatherhood is the oxygen of life. Not knowing that central truth, what can the fire be but a supreme terror. We must first know who God is before we can understand the fire."

"And I had to learn it by seeing my own father truly."

"It is not the only way into the high truth of Fatherhood," the Scotsman replied. "But it is the preferred method."

"I can't believe how blind to it I was before."

"You were not alone. That essential connection between the two fatherhoods is difficult for many to apprehend until their eyes are opened."

"It is not easy to see...you know, back on earth."

"Perhaps. But we should see it. Earthly fatherhood is the preeminent doorway into that discovery. In God's economy, the opening of one's eyes to one's own father—however good or bad a father he might have been— miraculously also opens one's eyes to perceive heavenly Fatherhood more clearly. That is why, for all who come here, the encounter with all that *Father* means is intrinsic to the preparation. We *must* understand who God is."

"At last I am beginning to see that," I said.

"And now," he went on, "you have seen your father through God's eyes, you have confronted your denial, you have paid your debts, you have forgiven and been forgiven. Your preliminary preparation is complete. You are now ready to face the sin that is closer than your own flesh, the sin that is *inside* you."

I shuddered.

"The fire of Malachi's Furnace is at hand," he continued. "It will be more painful than anything you have ever known. As it burns, you will feel the pain in your innermost soul. For the sin it must burn away is *inside* you."

All the while we had been slowly walking closer toward the chasm. The Scotsman did not seem in the least afraid of the fire.

"How deep is it?" I said in a trembling voice as I peered over the cliff.

"As deep as is required. Have you not yet realized that all things here are eternal? The fire is endless in all directions. Its depths are inside *you*."

"Are...are the old stories true—that there is no coming out?"

"The fire is meant to accomplish God's purpose," he replied. "The only coming out is by yielding to the refining and purifying of Malachi's

Furnace, being burned clean, and coming through it without spot or blemish."

"What lies at the bottom?"

"The All-Consuming Fire where every remnant of sin is destroyed forever."

"What is the...*all* consuming fire?"

"What else but what the ancients told us—the heart of the Father."

"You don't mean...that God is...down *there*?" I said in astonishment.

"Of course. He is everywhere. The psalmist stated as clearly as can be said, *If I make my bed in hell, you are there.* The fire of God, which is his essential being, his love, his creative power, is a fire unlike its earthly symbol in that it is only at a distance that it burns. The farther from him we are, the worse it burns. When we approach close to him, the burning changes to comfort. Old King David, bless him, he knew about the heart of God...

"All is God's," he added. "Heaven is God's home. Hell is his workshop. Why else do you think he invented the fire than to cleanse his creation from sin...the fire is on God's side, not the devil's. So entirely does God love, yea, *is* love, that hell itself must be subservient to that love and must be an embodiment of it...Every pain, every anguish you feel, he feels with you and a thousand times deeper than you feel it. He bears all your suffering with you so that you might endure it. Even the suffering of the fire he takes upon himself that it might purify those who yield to it. What is put before us is to *trust* him. With Job we say, *Though he slay me, yet will I trust him.* Let God's will be done and all is well."

THE ESSENTIAL SCHOOL OF CHILDNESS

I stared out over the seemingly bottomless expanse that yawned below. Flames a mile high swirled out of its depths. The heat was scorching and intense.

Even as I beheld the terrifying sight, a picture arose in my mind's eye. I recalled the many times I had been "witnessed" to, as they called it, by zealous Christians anxious to get me saved out of my atheism. I was reminded of the images they invariably presented of a great bridge stretching over the chasm of flames allowing the saved to walk across unscathed. It was a peculiar mental picture to come into *my* mind at such a time.

The Scotsman knew my thoughts.

"For those who did not become children before death, there is no way across it," he said, "only *through* it. There is no bridge. The cross never functioned like that. It was only those who misunderstood the Son's work, thinking that he came to protect us from the Father and save us from his wrath and from hell, who devised such simplistic images. But bridges over great chasms with flames licking up at their edges, the elect walking over safely to the sounds of the damned wailing in endless torments below..."

He paused and shook his head in frustration. He was unable to say more for several seconds. Then he drew in a deep sigh.

"It was never so," he went on. "The only way to enter into God's Kingdom is by childness, as he taught us and as he exampled to us. Childness can only be achieved at the altar of relinquishment, as he also showed us. On the other side of the Portal, that altar is faced a dozen times a day. That was the school where God intended childness to be learned. Those still alive there are taught childness by yielding the self-centered motions of the fleshly nature and taking for themselves God's will rather than their own...

"For that very purpose, Jesus came as Teacher and Prophet and King, and Headmaster of that school—to teach childness, to example the relinquishment of his will into the will of his Father. There were certain ways and means and methods used there to accomplish that purpose that do not apply to you in the same way now that you are here... truth functions on a high plane here. The equations have changed. The spiritual mathematics has different ways and means now. Everything here is fulfilled, enlarged, and imbued with higher meaning. For those who refused to learn childness before, the fleshly nature can no longer be the tool of self-abjuration. On this side the altar is the fire."

He saw that again I was confused.

"My apologies," he said... "One of the most common misperceptions about the work of Christ," he went on, "is that God *makes* us righteous without our *choosing* to be righteous many times a day. Even on this side, righteousness must be *chosen*, as you have chosen it throughout your pilgrimage. We must take our chosen share in the Father's work and the Son's sacrifice. *Their* work, with *our* wills, accomplishes childship..."

"Is that heaven over there—the Mountains?" I asked, pointing across the chasm.

"Perhaps," answered the Scotsman, exactly as he had answered my question about hell. "From where you presently stand, you cannot yet understand all...In a certain sense, heaven and hell are both retrospective, as one of my good friends here called it in his book on the subject. To those now living in the Mountains of God's country, all this was heaven from the beginning, stretching all the way back to their lives on earth. Both heaven and hell spread forward and back. Damnation extends back and defiles everything that came before. Repentant childness *glorifies* all that has come before with the radiance of heaven's slow-dawning Light. Surely you have seen glimpses of it already. As you paid your debts of forgiveness, your past as well as your present began to change. Your forgiveness worked in both directions. But for those who refuse the call of forgiveness, the hell of Self where they lived their earthly lives becomes the fully realized hell of eternity. As my Irish-born friend says, the blessed will say they always lived in heaven, the lost will say that they were always in hell."

"It is difficult, I must say, to get my head around the way things work here."

"Yes," he nodded. "But you were only an atheist."

"*Only* an atheist!" I said in surprise. "That was bad enough, wasn't it?"

"Oh, not so bad really. Atheism is not the great sin. For the honest-hearted, it may be a sincere response to the conundrums of the universe. Although from being appraised of your file, I know that your atheism contained within it an unhealthy dose of self-righteousness."

"You are right," I said. "I was *not* an honest-hearted atheist in any sense of the word. It is mortifying to see with clarity what I was."

"If atheists looked at the evidence of existence with fair and unbiased objectivity," the Scotsman went on, "they would become believers in an instant. I suppose, however, that is too much to ask...But wrong belief about God can do more damage than atheism. Once you woke up on this side, saw that you had been wrong, that was it—you *knew* you were wrong. There was the Lord walking toward you. Your atheism was undone in the blinding light of his Presence. But imagine what it is like for Muslims, to wake up and discover that nearly *everything* about their religion was false from beginning to end...

"Even a good many Christians have a similar difficulty, though perhaps not quite so severe. Yet many of them resist what they are told here because it so conflicts with what they always believed. It is true that most Christians, when they arrive and are startled at what they find, have little difficulty embracing it. When their eyes are opened, they immediately fall in with the deep purposes with joyful obedience because their hearts are pure, and blessed are the pure in heart...They were seekers of truth in spite of the fact that they had been wrongly taught about some of God's ways."

I reflected on his words for some time...

THE OUTER DARKNESS

"Will *everyone* eventually get to the High Mountains," I asked, "even if it takes a million years?"

The Scotsman became more thoughtful than I had yet seen him.

"Honestly...I don't know," he replied slowly. "I have thought and prayed on the mystery of that question for years. I used to be reasonably certain of it. But you have seen here that free will is no less the law of this place than it was in our former lives. Since being here I have been amazed at the positive stubbornness that exists in mankind. Yet, there is all eternity for God to accomplish his work.

"And therein lies a great truth—even a *million* years is but the blink of an eye to him. All eternity has not played itself out yet. Of this I *am* certain—there will *never* be an end to the opportunity for God's infinite love to probe the corners of his universe, searching for cracks even into the most hardened of hearts. But whether opportunity becomes reality...what will be the final outcome...whether some will eternally and everlastingly choose to retain the sin that is in them rather than cast it from them, resisting repentance aion unto aion...I do not know."

He smiled. I could sense that he was thinking back to his former life.

"Many called me a universalist back then," he said at length.

"You mean one who believed that all people would get to heaven in the end?"

He nodded.

"I may have been—I am not really sure. I always disdained such labels. But the Don may be right, and some will *never* make the imperative choice...

"I tried to believe that there was some remnant of good in every human being. But the Neros of antiquity and the Hitlers of your time, not to mention the inhuman cruelties of primitive man and all the Molechs of history certainly challenge that view. The Calvinists weren't altogether wrong when they spoke of the depravity of man. I know that God loves all his creation. But I simply don't know what will be the result of that love at the *very* end."

"The Hitler conundrum lay at the root of such questions in my time," I went on. "The most horrific aspect of it is that they must have *chosen* their evil, chosen it over and over...It is difficult to imagine what *he* would say to *them* at their first meeting. Do you think there are degrees of sin? How will God meet absolute, amoral, diabolical evil...What then about those who choose their evil by intent and design?"

"For the *intentionally* cruel, those who were dismissive of human life and the suffering they inflicted on others...for such I presume that

Malachi's Furnace of purification yet lies aions in the distance. They may indeed be met with an altogether different kind of fire—the fire kindled by the wrath of a righteous and angry God who will chastise and sorely punish their wickedness with a vengeance we can scarcely fathom. There are no doubt places on this side that I have never seen. I can only imagine that the guides for those regions must be severely broken souls whose aions have been painful indeed."

"You are not saying, are you…that there exist *two* hells?"

"There are different degrees and different purposes of the fire," the Scotsman answered. "Whether the wrath I speak of will merely punish their devilry against his creation, or whether it will be the cleansing punishment that hopes to wake some spark of life within them, I cannot say. Being on this side, one sees both good and evil more for what they truly are."

"How do you mean, that both are magnified?"

"More that both gain absolute clarity of motive and end result…Some evil is so repellant and debased that it would seem to deserve nothing but the fire of retribution…But of course, God is not ultimately bound to punish sin, but to destroy sin–destroy *sin*, not *sinners*. How he will accomplish that in the face of utter evil, these are mysteries still cloaked within the heart of the Godhead and not revealed to the rest of us. How could one such as myself possibly see to the end of it—my heart is not near as big as his."

"So are there different kinds of fire?"

"Malachi's Furnace is God's tool of purification for those who have made themselves ready for it. But it may be that his righteous wrath will have to be poured out in the Black Fire of the Outer Darkness to make some ready to begin being made ready. I speak in contradictions because I speak of mysteries into which no one can see…All we can know is that everyone will receive God's full justice, his full mercy, that he will give every man and every woman fair play, that each will receive exactly what they deserve, and that he will always love every one of his created children and will never cease doing his very best for them. God is good. God's love is infinite. And all is well."

He turned and walked away. I gazed after him until he was lost to my sight.

How long I stood at the edge of the chasm staring at the flames coming up from the abyss, I do not know. I stood as at the rim of an open volcano. I knew that the fire opening before me would not bring the relief of death, the relief of unknowing, but would bring the agony of greater knowing.

Again my life passed before me—my former life, and my life since coming through the Portal of Light. At last I was utterly alone. I knew that

I would meet no others. I was alone with my own will. Somehow I knew that no more guides would be sent. They had done their work. I was alone with myself and with my choice....

I glanced up at the Mountains beyond, so close now.

What did I want? Who did I want to be? What did I want to become? What kind of man did I want to be for the rest of eternity? Did I truly want to be whole? Was I prepared to undergo the suffering it would require to burn the burrowing worms and parasites of sin from out of the innermost depths of my being? Did I want to be pure, clean, perfect, and incapable of sin again?

Did I want to become capable of seeing God?

Did I want to be a child...a repentant and obedient son? No one in all the universe could answer the questions for me.

I stood for an aion...alone with my own free will. The thought of throwing myself into the fire was terrifying, too utterly horrifying to contemplate. Yet I recalled what the Scotsman had said. *The fire of God, which is his essential being, his love, his creative power, is a fire unlike its earthly symbol in this—that it is only at a distance that it burns. The farther from him we are, the worse it burns. When we approach close to him, the burning changes to comfort.*

The answer was yes...at last I wanted to be God's child.

I drew in a breath, then plunged headlong into the infinite chasm.

TWENTY-THREE

THE LAST FARTHING

by
George MacDonald

From *Unspoken Sermons, Second Series* [148]

Edited by Michael Phillips

"Verily I say unto thee, thou shalt by no means come out thence,
till thou have paid the last farthing."
—St. Matthew 5:26

There is a thing wonderful and admirable in the parables, not readily grasped, but specially indicated by the Lord himself—their unintelligibility to the mere intellect.

They are addressed to the conscience, not to the intellect, to the will, not to the imagination. They are strong and direct but not definite. They are not meant to explain anything, but to rouse a man to the feeling, "I am not what I ought to be, I do not the thing I ought to do!"

Many maundering interpretations may be given by the wise, with plentiful loss of labour, while the child who uses them for the necessity of walking in the one path will constantly receive light from them.

UNDERSTANDING COMES ONLY FROM DOING

The greatest obscuration of the words of the Lord, as of all true teachers, comes from those who give themselves to interpret rather than do them. Theologians have done more to hide the gospel of Christ than any of its adversaries. It was not for our understandings, but our will, that Christ came. He who does that which he sees, shall understand. He who is set upon understanding rather than doing, shall go on stumbling and mistaking and speaking foolishness. He does not have in him that which can understand that kind of truth.

The gospel itself, and in it the parables of the Truth, are to be understood only by those who walk by what they find. It is he that runneth that shall read, and no other. It is not intended by the speaker of the parables that his listeners should know intellectually what, known but intellectually, would be for his injury— what knowing intellectually he would imagine he had grasped, perhaps even appropriated.

When the pilgrim of the truth comes on his journey to the region of the parable, he finds its interpretation. It is not a fruit or a jewel to be stored, but a well springing by the wayside.

Let us try to understand what the Lord himself said about his parables. It will be better to take the reading of St. Matthew 13:14-15, as it is plainer, and the quotation from Isaiah (6:9-10) is given in full. In its light should be read the corresponding passages in the other Gospels. In St. Mark's (8:18) it is so compressed as to be capable of quite a different and false meaning. In St. John's reference (12:39-41), the blinding of the heart seems attributed directly to the devil:—the purport is, that those who by insincerity and falsehood close their deeper eyes, shall not be capable of using in the matter the more superficial eyes of their understanding. Whether this follows as a psychical or metaphysical necessity, or is to be regarded as a special punishment, it is equally the will of God, and comes from him who is the live Truth. They shall not see what is not for such as they. It is the punishment of the true Love, and is continually illustrated and fulfilled.

If I know anything of the truth of God, then the objectors to Christianity, so far as I am acquainted with them, do not. Their arguments, not in themselves false, have nothing to do with the matter. They see the thing they are talking against, but they do not see the thing they *think* they are talking against.

This will help to remove the difficulty that the parables are plainly for the teaching of the truth, and yet the Lord speaks of them as for the concealing of it. They are for the understanding of that man only who is practical—who does the thing he knows, who seeks to understand vitally. They reveal to the live conscience, otherwise not to the keenest intellect— though at the same time they may help to rouse the conscience with glimpses of the truth, where the man is on the borders of waking.

Ignorance may be at once a punishment and a kindness. All punishment is kindness, and the best of which the man at the time is capable: "Because you will not do, you shall not see; but it would be worse for you if you did see, not being of the disposition to do."

Such are punished in having the way closed before them. They punish themselves. Their own doing results as it cannot but result on them. To say to them certain things so that they could understand them, would but harden them more, because they would not do them. They should have only parables— lanterns of the truth, clear to those who will walk in their light, dark to those who will not. The former are content to have the light cast upon their way. The latter want to possess it in the eyes of their intellects, but are prevented: if they had, it would but blind them. For them to know more would be their worse condemnation. They are not fit to know more, more shall not be given them yet. It is their punishment that they are in the wrong, and shall keep in the wrong until they come out of it.

"You choose the dark. You shall stay in the dark till the terrors that dwell in the dark make you afraid, and cause you to cry out." God puts a seal upon the will of man. That seal is either his great punishment, or his mighty favour: "Ye love the darkness, abide in the darkness:" "O woman, great is thy faith: be it done unto thee even as thou wilt!"

DO WHAT YOU MUST BEFORE IT IS TOO LATE

What special meaning may be read in the different parts of magistrate, judge, and officer of this parable of the last farthing, beyond the general suggestion, perhaps, of the tentative approach of the final, I do not know. But I think I do know what is meant by "agree on the way," and "the uttermost farthing."

The parable is an appeal to the common sense of those that hear it, in regard to every affair of righteousness: Arrange what claim lies against you. Compulsion waits behind it.

Do at once what you must do one day.

As there is no escape from payment, escape at least the prison that will enforce it.

Do not drive Justice to extremities.

Duty is imperative. It must be done.

It is useless to think to escape the eternal law of things.

Yield of yourself, do not compel God to compel you.

THE COMPULSION OF ETERNAL GOODNESS IS A JOY TO THE TRUE

To the honest man, to the man who desires with all his heart to be honest, the word is of right gracious import. To the untrue, it is a terrible threat.

To him who is of the truth, this is sweet as a most loving promise. He who is of God's mind in things rejoices to hear the word of the changeless Truth. The voice of the Right fills the heavens and the earth, and makes his soul glad. It is his salvation.

If God were not inexorably just, there would be no rest for the soul of the feeblest lover of right. "Thou art true, O Lord: one day I also shall be true!"

"Thou shalt render the right, cost you what it may," is a dread sound in the ears of those whose life is a falsehood. Yet what but the last farthing would those who love righteousness more than life gladly pay?

It is a joy profound as peace to know that God is determined to require such payment, is determined to have his children clean, clear, pure as very snow. They rejoice to know that he is determined that not only shall they with his help make up for whatever wrong they have done, but at length be incapable, by eternal choice of good, under any temptation, of doing the thing that is not divine, the thing God would not do.

THE NECESSITY OF CHOOSING GOODNESS

There has been much cherishing of the evil fancy, often without its taking formal shape, that there is some way of getting out of the region of strict justice, some mode of managing to escape doing *all* that is required of us. But there is no such escape. A way to avoid any demand of righteousness would be an infinitely worse way than the road to the everlasting fire, for its end would be eternal death.

No, there is no escape. There is no heaven with a little of hell in it—no plan to retain this or that of the devil in our hearts or our pockets. Out Satan must go, every hair and feather!

Neither shalt thou think to be delivered from the necessity of *being* good by being made good. God is the God of the animals in a far lovelier way, I suspect, than many of us dare to think, but he will not be the God of a man by making a good beast of him.

You must *be* good. Neither death nor any admittance into good company will make you good. Though, doubtless, if you are willing and try, these and all other best helps will be given you. But there is no clothing in a robe of imputed righteousness, that poorest of legal cobwebs spun by spiritual spiders. The doctrine seems to me like an invention of well-meaning dullness to soothe insanity. And indeed it has proved a door of escape out of worse imaginations. It is apparently an old "doctrine," for St. John seems to point at it where he says, "Little children, let no man lead you astray; he that doeth righteousness is righteous even as he is righteous."

Christ is our righteousness, not that we should escape punishment, still less escape being righteous, but as the live potent creator of righteousness in us, so that we, with our wills receiving his spirit, shall like him resist unto blood, striving against sin. He is our righteousness so that we shall know in ourselves, as he knows, what a lovely thing is righteousness, what a mean, ugly, unnatural thing is unrighteousness. He *is* our righteousness, and that righteousness is no fiction, no pretence, no imputation.

One thing that tends to keep men from seeing righteousness and unrighteousness as they are, is, that they have been told many things are righteous and unrighteous, which are neither the one nor the other. Righteousness is just fairness—from God to man, from man to God and to man. It is giving every one his due—his large mighty due. He is righteous, and no one else, who does this.

Any system which tends to persuade men that there is any salvation but that of becoming righteous even as Jesus is righteous—that a man can be made good, as a good dog is good, without his own willed share in the making, that a man is saved by having his sins hidden under a robe of imputed righteousness—that system, so far as this tendency, is of the devil and not of God.

Thank God, not even error shall injure the true of heart. It is not wickedness. They grow in the truth, and as love casts out fear, so truth casts out falsehood.

RIGHTNESS IN ALL LIFE'S RELATIONS

I read, then, in this parable, that a man had better make up his mind to be righteous, to be fair, to do what he can to pay what he owes, in any and all the relations of life—all the matters, in a word, wherein one man may demand of another, or complain that he has not received fair play.

Arrange your matters with those who have anything against you, while you are yet together and things have not gone too far to be arranged. *You will have to do it*, and perhaps under less easy circumstances than now. Putting off is of no use. You must.

The thing has to be done. There are means of compelling you.

Do you complain: "In this affair, however, I am in the right."

"If so, very well," I answer. "Perhaps in this case you *are* right. But I have reason to doubt whether you are capable of judging righteously in your own cause:—do you hate the man?"

"No, I don't hate him."

"Do you dislike him?"

"I can't say I *like* him."

"Do you love him as yourself?"

"Oh, come! come! no one does that!"

"Then no one is to be trusted when he thinks, however firmly, that he is all right, and his neighbour all wrong, in any matter between them."

"But I don't say I am all right, and he is all wrong. There may be something to urge on his side: what I say is, that I am more in the right than he."

"This is not fundamentally a question of things. It is a question of condition, of spiritual relation and action, towards your neighbour. If in yourself you were all right towards him, you could do him no wrong. Let it be with the individual dispute as it may, you owe him something that you do not pay him, as certainly as you think he owes you something he will not pay you."

"He would take immediate advantage of me if I admitted that."

"So much the worse for him. Until you are fair to him, it does not matter to you whether he is unfair to you or not."

"I beg your pardon—it is just what does matter! I want nothing but my rights. What can matter to me more than my rights?"

"Your duties—your debts. You are all wrong about the thing. It is a very small matter *to you* whether the man give you your rights or not. It is life or death to you whether or not you give him his. Whether he pay you what you count his debt or no, you will be compelled to pay him all you owe him. If you owe him a pound and he you a million, you must pay him the pound whether he pay you the million or not. There is no business-parallel here. If, owing you love, he gives you hate, you, owing him love, have yet to pay it.

"A love unpaid you, a justice undone you, a praise withheld from you, a judgment passed on you without judgment, will not absolve you of the debt of a love unpaid, a justice not done, a praise withheld, a false judgment passed: these uttermost farthings—not to speak of such debts as the world itself counts grievous wrongs—you must pay him, whether he pay you or not."

THE ETERNAL DEBT OF LOVE MUST BE PAID

We have a good while given us to pay, but a crisis will come—come soon after all—comes always sooner than those expect it who are not ready for it—a crisis when the demand unyielded will be followed by prison.

The same holds with every demand of God: by refusing to pay, the man makes an adversary of him who will compel him—and that for the man's own sake. If you or your life say, "I will not," then he will see to it. There is a prison, and the one thing we know about that prison is, that its doors do not open until entire satisfaction is rendered, the last farthing paid.

The main debts whose payment God demands are those which lie at the root of all right, those we owe in mind, and soul, and being. Whatever in us can be or make an adversary, whatever could prevent us from doing the will of God, or from agreeing with our fellow—all must be yielded. Our every relation, both to God and our fellow, must be acknowledged heartily, met as a reality. Smaller debts, if any debt can be small, follow as a matter of course.

GOD WILL HELP THE WILLING HEART,
BUT A PRISON OF DARKNESS AWAITS THE UNWILLING

If the man acknowledge, and would pay if he could but cannot, the universe will be taxed to help him rather than he should continue unable. If the man accepts the will of God, he is the child of the Father, the whole power and wealth of the Father is for him, and the uttermost farthing will easily be paid.

If the man denies the debt, or acknowledging does nothing towards paying it, then—at last—the prison!

God in the dark can make a man thirst for the light, who never in the light sought but the dark. The cells of the prison may differ in degree of darkness. But they are all alike in this, that not a door opens but to payment.

There is no day but the will of God. He who is of the night cannot be for ever allowed to roam the day. Unfelt, unprized, the light must be taken from him, that he may know what the darkness is. When the darkness is perfect, when he is totally without the light he has spent the light in slaying, then will he know darkness.

THE OUTER DARKNESS

I think I have seen from afar something of the final prison of all, the innermost cell of the debtor of the universe. I will endeavour to convey what I think it may be.

It is the vast outside, the ghastly dark beyond the gates of the city of which God is the light—where the evil dogs go ranging, silent as the dark, for there is no sound any more than sight. The time of signs is over. Every sense has its signs, and they were all misused. There is no sense, no sign more—nothing now by means of which to believe.

The man wakes from the final struggle of death, in absolute loneliness—such a loneliness as in the most miserable moment of deserted childhood he never knew. Not a hint, not a shadow of anything outside his consciousness reaches him. All is dark, dark and dumb—no motion, not the breath of a wind! never a dream of change, not a scent from far-off field, nothing to suggest being or thing besides the man himself...no sign of God anywhere. God has so far withdrawn from the man, that he is conscious only of that from which he has withdrawn. In the midst of the live world he cared for nothing but himself. Now in the dead world he is in God's prison, his own separated self. He would not believe in God because he never saw God; now he doubts if there be such a thing as the face of a man—doubts if he ever really saw one, ever anything more than dreamed of such a thing. He never came near enough to human being, to know what human being really was. So he may well doubt if human beings ever were, if ever he was one of them.

Next after doubt comes reasoning on the doubt: "The only one must be God! I know no one but myself: I must myself be God—none else!" Poor helpless dumb devil!—his own glorious lord god! Yea, he will imagine himself that same resistless force which, without his will, without his knowledge, is the law by which the sun burns, and the stars keep their courses, the strength that drives all the engines of the world. His fancy will give birth to a thousand fancies, which will run riot like the mice in a house but just deserted: he will call it creation, and *his*. Having no reality to set them beside, nothing to correct them by—the measured order, harmonious relations, and sweet graces of God's world are nowhere for him—what he thinks, for lack of what God thinks, will be the man's realities: what others can he have! Soon, misery will beget on imagination a thousand shapes of woe, which he will not be able to rule, direct, or even distinguish from real presences—a whole world of miserable contradictions and cold-fever-dreams.

But no liveliest human imagination could supply adequate representation of what it would be to be left without a shadow of the presence of God. If God gave it, man could not understand it. He knows neither God nor himself in the way of the understanding. For not he who cares least about God was in this world ever left as God could leave him. I doubt if any man could continue following his wickedness from whom God had withdrawn.

The most frightful idea of what could, to his own consciousness, befall a man, is that he should have to lead an existence with which God had nothing to do. The thing could not be, for being that is caused, the causation ceasing, must of necessity cease. It is always in, and never out of God, that we can live and do. But I suppose the man so left that he *seems* to himself utterly alone, yet, alas! with himself—smallest interchange of thought, feeblest contact of existence, dullest reflection from other being, impossible.

In such evil case I believe the man would be glad to come in contact with the worst-loathed insect. It would be a shape of life, something beyond and besides his own huge, void, formless being! I imagine some such feeling in the prayer of the devils for leave to go into the swine. His worst enemy, could he but be aware of him, he would be ready to worship. For the misery would be not merely the absence of all being other than his own self, but the fearful, endless, unavoidable presence of that self.

Without the correction, the reflection, the support of other presences, being is not merely unsafe, it is a horror—for anyone but God, who is his own being. For him whose idea is God's, and the image of God, his own being is far too fragmentary and imperfect to be anything like good company. It is the lovely creatures God has made all around us, in them giving us himself, that, until we know him, save us from the frenzy of aloneness—for that aloneness is Self, Self, Self. The man who minds only himself must at last go mad if God did not interfere.

Can there be any way out of the misery? Will the soul that could not believe in God, with all his lovely world around testifying of him, believe when shut in the prison of its own lonely, weary all-and-nothing? It would for a time try to believe that it was indeed nothing, a mere glow of the setting sun on a cloud of dust, a paltry dream that dreamed itself—then, ah, if only the dream might dream that it was no more! that would be the one thing to hope for.

Self-loathing, and that for no sin, from no repentance, from no vision of better, would begin and grow and grow. To what it might not come no soul can tell—of essential, original misery, uncompromis-ing self disgust! Only, then, if a being be capable of self-disgust, is there not some room for hope—as much as a pinch of earth in the cleft of a rock might yield for the growth of a pine? Nay, there must be hope while there is existence. For where there is existence there must be God. And God is for ever good, nor can be other than good.

But alas, the distance from the light! Such a soul is at the farthest verge of life's negation! No, not the farthest—a man is nearer heaven when in deepest hell than just before he begins to reap the reward of his doings—for he is in a condition to receive the smallest show of the life that is, as a boon unspeakable.

All his years in the world he received the endless gifts of sun and air, earth and sea and human face divine, as things that came to him because that was their way, and there was no one to prevent them. Now the poorest thinning of the darkness he would hail as men of old the glow of a descending angel. It would be as a messenger from God. Not that he would think of God! it takes long to think of God. But hope, not yet seeming hope, would begin to dawn in his bosom, and the thinner darkness would be as a cave of light, a refuge from the horrid self of which he used to be so proud.

A man may well imagine it impossible ever to think so unpleasantly of himself! But he has only to let things go, and he will make it the real, right, natural way to think of himself. True, all I have been saying is imaginary. But our imagination is made to mirror truth. All the things that appear in it are more or less after the model of things that are. I suspect the imagination is the region whence issues prophecy, and when we are true it will mirror nothing but truth. I deal here with the same light and darkness the Lord dealt with, the same St. Paul and St. John and St. Peter and St. Jude dealt with. Ask yourself whether the faintest dawn of even physical light would not be welcome to such a soul as some refuge from the dark of the justly hated self.

WAKING INTO LIGHT

And the light would grow and grow across the awful gulf between the soul and its haven—its repentance. For repentance is the first pressure of the bosom of God. And in the twilight, struggling and faint, the man would feel, faint as the twilight, another thought beside his, another thinking Something nigh his dreary self—perhaps the man he had most wronged, most hated, most despised. And he would be glad that some one, whoever, was near him. The man he had most injured, and was most ashamed to meet, would be a refuge from himself—oh, how welcome!

So might I imagine a thousand steps up from the darkness, each a little less dark, a little nearer the light—but, ah, the weary way! He cannot come out until he has paid the uttermost farthing!

Repentance once begun, however, may grow more and more rapid! If God once get a willing hold, if with but one finger he touch the man's self, swift as possibility will he draw him from the darkness into the light.

For that for which the forlorn, self-ruined wretch was made, was to be a child of God, a partaker of the divine nature, an heir of God and joint heir with Christ. Out of the abyss into which he cast himself, refusing to be the heir of God, he must rise and be raised.

To the heart of God, the one and only goal of the human race—the refuge and home of all and each, he must set out and go, or the last glimmer of humanity will die from him.

Whoever will live must cease to be a slave and become a child of God. There is no half-way house of rest, where ungodliness may be dallied with, nor prove quite fatal.

Be they few or many cast into such prison as I have endeavoured to imagine, there can be no deliverance for human soul, whether in that prison or out of it, but in paying the last farthing, in becoming lowly, penitent, self-refusing—so receiving the sonship, and learning to cry, *Father*!

TWENTY-FOUR

LILITH'S REPENTANCE [149]

by
George MacDonald

From *Lilith*

Lilith's hour has been long on the way, but it is .come! Everything comes. Thousands of years have I waited—and not in vain...This woman would not yield to gentler measures; harder must have their turn. I must do what I can to make her repent...

"Will you hurt her very much?"...

"Yes; I am afraid I must; I fear she will make me...It would be cruel to hurt her too little. It would have all to be done again, only worse...She loves no one, therefore she cannot be with any one. There is One who will be with her, but she will not be with Him..."

"Will you turn away from the wicked things you have been doing so long?' ...

"I will not," she said. "I will be myself and not another!"

"Alas, you are another now, not yourself! Will you not be your real self?'"...

"I will do as my Self pleases—as my Self desires.'"...

"Then, alas, your hour is come!"

"I care not. I am what I am...Another shall not make me!"

"But another has made you, and can compel you to see what you have made yourself. You will not be able much longer to look to yourself anything but what he sees you..."

"No one ever made me. I defy that Power to unmake me from a free woman! ...You may be able to torture me...but you shall not compel me to anything against my will!"

"Such a compulsion would be without value. But there is a light that goes deeper than the will, a light that lights up the darkness behind it: that light can change your will, can make it truly yours and not another's... Into the created can pour itself the creating will, and so redeem it!...—See your own self!"...

A soundless presence as of roaring flame possessed the house...I turned to the hearth: its fire was a still small moveless glow. But I saw [a] worm-thing come creeping out, white-hot, vivid as incandescent silver, the live heart of essential fire. Along the floor it crawled...going very slow...The shining thing crawled on to a bare bony foot...Slowly, very slowly, it crept along her robe until it reached her bosom, where it disappeared among the folds.

The face...lay stonily calm, the eyelids closed as over dead eyes; and for some minutes nothing followed. At length, on the dry, parchment-like skin, began to appear drops as of the finest dew: in a moment they were as large as seed-pearls, ran together, and began to pour down in streams...from the poor withered bosom...But...no serpent was there—no searing trail; the creature had passed in...and was piercing through the joints and marrow to the thoughts and intents of the heart. [She] gave one writhing, contorted shudder, and I knew the worm was in her secret chamber...

[She] bent her body upward in an arch, then sprang to the floor, and stood erect. The horror in her face made me tremble lest her eyes should open, and the sight of them overwhelm me. Her bosom heaved and sank, but no breath issued. Her hair hung and dripped...and poured the sweat of her torture on the floor...

"She is far away from us, afar in the hell of her self-consciousness. The central fire of the universe is radiating into her the knowledge of good and evil, the knowledge of what she is. She sees at last the good she is not, the evil she is. She knows that she is herself the fire in which she is burning, but she does not know that the Light of Life is the heart of that fire. Her torment is that she is what she is...No gentler way to help her was left. Wait and watch."

It may have been five minutes or five years that she stood thus—I cannot tell; but at last she flung herself on her face...

"Will you change your way?"

"Why did he make me such?" gasped Lilith...

"But he did not make you such. You have made yourself what you are.—Be of better cheer: he can remake you.'

"I will not be remade!"

"He will not change you; he will only restore you to what you were…Are you not willing to have that set right which you have set wrong?"

She lay silent…

The strife of thought, accusing and excusing, began afresh, and gathered fierceness. The soul of Lilith lay naked to the torture of pure interpenetrating inward light. She began to moan, and sigh deep sighs…

"Those, alas, are not the tears of repentance…The true tears gather in the eyes. Those are far more bitter, and not so good. Self-loathing is not sorrow. Yet it is good, for it marks a step in the way home, and in the father's arms the prodigal forgets the self he abominates. Once with his father, he is to himself of no more account. It will be so with her."…

Gradually my soul grew aware of an invisible darkness, a something more terrible than aught that had yet made itself felt. A horrible Nothingness, a Negation positive infolded her…

With that there fell upon her, and upon us also who watched with her, the perfect calm as of a summer night. Suffering had all but reached the brim of her life's cup…—What was she seeing?

I looked, and saw: before her, cast from unseen heavenly mirror, stood the reflection of herself, and beside it a form of splendent beauty. She trembled, and sank again on the floor helpless. She knew the one what God had intended her to be, the other what she had made herself…

She rose…and said, in prideful humility,

"You have conquered. Let me go into the wilderness…"

"Begin, then, and set right in the place of wrong."

"I know not how," she replied with the look of one who foresaw and feared the answer…

A fierce refusal seemed to struggle for passage, but she kept it prisoned.

"I cannot," she said…

"You must…"

"I have told you I cannot!"

"You can if you will—not indeed at once, but by persistent effort. What you have done, you do not yet wish undone…"

"I will not try what I know impossible. It would be the part of a fool!"

"Which you have been playing all your life! Oh, you are hard to teach!"

Defiance reappeared on [her] face…

"I know what you have been tormenting me for! You have not succeeded, nor shall you succeed! You shall yet find me stronger than you think! I will yet be mistress of myself! I am still what I have always known myself—queen of Hell, and mistress of the worlds!"

Then came the most fearful thing of all...I knew only that if it came near me I should die of terror! I now know that it was Life in Death—life dead, yet existent...

She stood rigid...I gazed on the face of one who knew existence but not love—knew nor life, nor joy, nor good; with my eyes I saw the face of a live death! She knew life only to know that it was dead, and that, in her, death lived...She had killed her life, and was dead—and knew it... Her bodily eyes stood wide open, as if gazing into the heart of horror essential—her own indestructible evil...

"I yield," [she] said... "I am defeated..."

"I will take you to my father. You have wronged him worst of the created, therefore he best of the created can help you."

"How can he help me?"

"He will forgive you."

"Ah, if he would but help me to cease...I am a slave! I acknowledge it. Let me die.'

"A slave thou art that shall one day be a child...Verily, thou shalt die, but not as thou thinkest. Thou shalt die out of death into life..."

Lilith lay and wept...

Morn, with the Spring in her arms, waited outside. Softly they stole in at the opened door, with a gentle wind in the skirts of their garments. It flowed and flowed about Lilith, rippling the unknown, upwaking sea of her life eternal...She answered the morning wind with reviving breath, and began to listen. For in the skirts of the wind had come the rain—the soft rain that heals the mown, the many-wounded grass—soothing it with the sweetness of all music, the hush that lives between music and silence. It bedewed the desert places...and the sands of Lilith's heart heard it, and drank it in...

When we reached the door, Adam welcomed us...

"We have long waited for thee, Lilith!" he said.

She returned him no answer....

"She consents to...restore: will not the great Father restore her to inheritance with His other children?"

"I do not know Him!" murmured Lilith, in a voice of fear and doubt.

"Therefore it is that thou art miserable," said Adam..."Come and see the place where thou shalt lie in peace....And now Death shall be the atonemaker; you shall sleep..."

"I shall dream...?"

"You will dream."

"What dreams?"

"That I cannot tell, but none he can enter into. When the Shadow comes here, it will be to lie down and sleep also.—His hour will come, and he knows it will."

"How long shall I sleep?"

"You and he will be the last to wake in the morning of the universe."...

I grew aware of existence, aware also of the profound, the infinite cold. I was intensely blessed—more blessed, I know, than my heart, imagining, can now recall. I could not think of warmth with the least suggestion of pleasure...

How convey the delight of that frozen, yet conscious sleep!...

Then the dreams began to arrive—and came crowding.—I lay naked on a snowy peak. The white mist heaved below me like a billowy sea. The cold moon was in the air with me, and above the moon and me the colder sky, in which the moon and I dwelt. I was Adam, waiting for God to breathe into my nostrils the breath of life.—I was not Adam, but a child in the bosom of a mother white with a radiant whiteness. I was a youth on a white horse, leaping from cloud to cloud of a blue heaven, hasting calmly to some blessed goal. For centuries I dreamed...time had nothing to do with me; I was in the land of thought—farther in, higher up than the seven dimensions, the ten senses: I think I was where I am—in the heart of God....the wind and the water and the moon sang a peaceful waiting for a redemption drawing nigh...the solemn, æonian march of a second, pregnant with eternity.

Then, of a sudden, but not once troubling my conscious bliss, all the wrongs I had ever done, from far beyond my earthly memory down to the present moment, were with me. Fully in every wrong lived the conscious I, confessing, abjuring, lamenting the dead, making atonement with each person I had injured, hurt, or offended. Every human soul to which I had caused a troubled thought, was now grown unspeakably dear to me, and I humbled myself before it, agonising to cast from between us the clinging offence. I wept at the feet of the mother whose commands I had slighted; with bitter shame I confessed to my father that I had told him two lies, and long forgotten them: now for long had remembered them, and kept them in memory to crush at last at his feet. I was the eager slave of all whom I had thus or anyhow wronged. Countless services I devised to render them!...Love possessed me! Love was my life! Love was to me, as to him that made me, all in all! ...

Now I knew that life and truth were one; that life mere and pure is in itself bliss; that where being is not bliss, it is not life, but life-in-death.

Every inspiration of the dark wind that blew where it listed, went out a sigh of thanksgiving. At last I was! I lived, and nothing could touch my life...we were on our way home to the Father!...

It was a glorious resurrection-morning. The night had been spent in preparing it!

Twenty-Five

Into the Heart of the Consuming Fire

An Excerpt From Hell and Beyond [150]

by
Michael Phillips

The moment my feet left solid ground, rather than experiencing terror at my fall, a great warmth enveloped me, as if I were floating through a cloud of sunshine. The warmth grew. I knew that the fire had begun to burn. It singed my hands and feet and fingers. My extremities were aflame, but my flesh was not blackened.

Slowly, the heat mounted in intensity...hotter and hotter until the excruciation was of one being burned alive over every inch with pain unendurable. Suspended in live fire, I had no voice to cry or scream. Mouth and tongue and throat were blistered from the penetrating flame. Arms, fingers, and legs glowed red as hot iron. The fire surged through my chest, lungs, heart, stomach, and bowels. It probed and examined, wriggling flame-worms of horrific heat. I had become the tree on the mountain, caught in the midst of a wild, turbulent, hounding fire. I heard howls of torment. Whether it was my own voice or whether others were nearby, I cannot say.

I continued to fall through tumultuous scorching flames at the speed of light...falling...falling...deeper and deeper into the abyss, further down and further in...into the depths of my own Self, into the fires of cleansing.

From somewhere a mighty voice resounded, or were they words made alive in my brain? Somehow I knew that it was the great prophet Malachi of old calling over the centuries, across the millennia, calling to all who had chosen it what the fire meant, and why it had to be:

Behold, I send my messenger to prepare the way before me. For he is like a refiner's fire and like fuller's soap. He will sit as a refiner and purifier of silver. And he will purify the sons of Levi and refine them like gold and silver, till they present right offerings to the Lord. For behold, the day comes, burning like an oven, when all the arrogance and all the evildoing will be stubble. The day that comes shall burn them up, says the Lord of hosts. But for you who fear my name, the sun of righteousness shall rise, with healing in its wings. And he will turn the hearts of fathers to their children and the hearts of children to their fathers.

I fell and I burned and the flames probed my soul for what seemed to be a thousand years. How long and how far I fell, who can say? It was an aion of cleansing. The fire burned as if it must eradicate everything within me and ultimately destroy me. Yet I was not destroyed, and my awareness of being remained.

Below a great sound began to echo, a rhythmic pounding and throbbing. With every pulse, the fire rushed deeper, shot as pure blasts of white energy into my depths...Each new throb sent searing fingers of flame probing into me with renewed force.

Whatever the source of the pulsing echo, it came from the infinite below, from the depths into which no eye could see...The torrid vibrations grew deafening. I knew that I was entering the very Source of the fire, the Heart of the volcano, the Eye of the fiery tempest, descending into the beating core of the universe. I was being swallowed into the Consuming Fire.

And I was gathered into it. The sensation of falling ceased. I was inundated in pure Light. The throbbing continued...I *felt* its reverberations in rhythm to my own heart. The tumult silenced. Light and the energy of the great Pulse absorbed me into itself.

I floated through the silence, a silence of utter bliss, for I was at the Center of the Fire.

Words—mighty echoes of truth heard not by my ears but vibrating in my inner parts as giant invisible harp strings tuned to the measure of my being—resounded over and above and through me. A great Voice proclaimed the truth of the ages. And as the Voice spoke, time was turned inside out, and I knew that I was at the Center of creation itself.

All around me was darkness.

I floated in the midst of empty nothingness, formless and void...The pulsating Heart was inside me because I was inside it. Nothing existed but the live Heart that was the Origin of all things.

Let there be light! thundered the silent Logos into my soul and into the soul of the universe.

Whiteness exploded everywhere. Light consumed the darkness, and the darkness fled from the universe, for it could not withstand the power of the Light. And I was not just at the center of the Light in my imagination—my true being, my very essence was birthed in the moment of the mighty *Let there be*. For the Voice had not just created Light. He had created *me*...From the infinite beginnings, he had *known* me because he had fathered me out of his own Being. And he knew my name though I did not know it yet—my true name known only to him...

Out of the midst of the whiteness came the figure of a Man. But he was more than a man, for he had always been and would always be, for he was the live beating Heart made visible to mortal eyes, and he was One with creation...

I am the Alpha! resounded the great thunder of pure Light. *I Am because I Am, and I will draw all creation to myself. I Am your Creator and your God and your Father, and you shall be my sons and daughters because you are my created children.*

I fell and bowed my face low, for I could not gaze upon him.

Awake, awake, you who sleep. Let the flame awake your soul that it not destroy you. I will refine you like silver and test you like gold. I will refine you and test you and purify you by the fire. Then you will call upon my name and I will answer. I will say, "They are my people," and all the nations will rise as one and proclaim, "The Lord, our Creator and Father, is our God."

At last, I was compelled to look up. Around me as far as the eye could see in every direction I beheld the vast, teeming humanity of creation, surging and marching through the millennia from antiquity to modernity...rich and poor, kind and cruel, masters driving their slaves before them, slaves lusting after their masters' wealth, the intellectual and the ignorant, those who lived in squalor beside those who had enjoyed the opulence of luxury, rulers and peasants, kings and serfs.

And I saw into their hearts, for I had been given eyes to probe the mind and soul of everyone who had ever lived. And I was overwhelmed by the goodness that lay in the heart of mankind. Yet I was crushed to despair by the cruelty and greed and ambition and selfishness that lay deep alongside the goodness, for it spoiled the goodness and turned brother against brother and mother against daughter and son against father...

Still the teeming nations of humanity surged through the aions, forward, ever forward, rising on the progress of the past ever to new heights. Yet with its progress the mighty throng of humanity grew unseeing and unhearing, for the Voice that was above all and within all had grown silent. They could no longer hear its still small whispers reminding them from whence they had come and whence originated their life. None knew their names, or the name of the I Am, for their sin had hardened their hearts and dulled their understanding...

I turned away, and did not know if the throng I had seen was bound in the same direction. I only knew that I must continue and not look back. And the fire returned upon me.

I was walking now, my whole being glowing red...I was moving alongside a great river, glowing red like everything around me, red with liquid fire. The river flowed into a red flaming lake of limitless expanse...

I gazed into the distance whence came the river at my feet. Worlds away, as if I were again peering backward to time's beginnings, rose the blinding red of a great Heart of Fire, a mighty Sun hanging above the horizon and shooting out flames of light in all directions. It was a live Heart, pulsating with thunderous silent echo.

Across the Heart were emblazoned the letters *A-B-B-A*. From it gushed a torrent of blood, spewing from the mortal wound of an invisible sword. But the piercing did not kill the Abba-Heart. In the throbbing agony of its sacrifice of itself, its own Life was resurrected with yet greater power. For the Heart beat with the Life that enlightens every man...The torrent of life-giving blood rushed forth from the Wound of Life and fueled the river of fire, and it flowed across the aions toward me and tumbled into the lake beside me.

And I knew I was beholding the great life-birthing Heart of Father and Son, whose love together had created the world, and whose sacrifice together was redeeming it. They were redeeming me and giving me power to join my own sacrifice with theirs, that I might be one with them as they were one.

Many were around me, a vast swarm of men and women. Some were throwing themselves into the river as I had plunged into the abyss above, to be cleansed by sacrifice and purified by fire. Others were climbing up and out of the lake to join those alongside the river. On their faces was no torment but expressions of wonder. Their bodies were of gold and the lake of fire could not touch them. And thousands were plunging into the lake and rising up out of it.

Voices came from somewhere. It was not the One Voice, but the voices of a throng of heavenly hosts. And they were chanting in unison: *And the dead were judged. Death and Hades gave up the dead that were in them. Then death and Hades were thrown into the lake of fire.*

Then from above came the sound as of a mighty rushing wind. A great meteor, huge as a moon, engulfed in fierce flames, came hurling out of the sky and plummeted with a violent explosion into the lake of fire and disappeared into its depths.

Again spoke the Voice of the One, the Voice of the Light and of the Logos, ominous and mighty with command and judgment. And the Word declared: *Hell below is stirred up to meet you when you come. Your greatness is brought down to your own grave. How you have fallen from heaven, O Lucifer, son of the morning! In your heart you said, "I will ascend to heaven. I will make myself like the most High." But you shall be brought down to hell, into the depths of the Pit.*

Still the multitude walked beside the river of fire and blood. From each one, ashes of white floated up and disappeared, dead reminders of what had been burned out of them. Again I felt the fingers of fire, the probing worms of revelation, searching my innermost places. It burned deeper, ever deeper into my being, separating the bone from the marrow, separating the essential me from the sin at my core.

I must death my sin forever. I must relinquish all that I had held dear, my very self. I could not die, I must *become*, that I might *be*...and *live*.

I felt many things giving way inside me, releasing, emptying me of all but the me that had been birthed in the Light. With each release I felt a stab as from a white-hot knife plunging into my chest and then pulled from my depths. A thousand releasings were accompanied each by a stab of agony...

Still the fire probed. Deeper and deeper death reached inside me, that life eternal might emerge...Rain began to fall. Huge drops popped and sizzled as water met fire landing on the river and those who were glowing red. Yet the rain and the fire were one and came from the same Source.

Layer after layer of the hiddenmost pestilence of my sin floated away, burned off as from an onion of Self...And I knew that God's heart felt every pain with me. He loved me as the Father who had birthed me in the Light of Creation. I was his son! How could he not suffer with me? Again around me came the echo of rhythmic pulsating over all and in all and through all. Everywhere was inside the Great Heart.

And I knew that the falling rains were his own tears. He was suffering with his world as its sin was eradicated from the universe.

I listened. Far away—as in the heart of a silence too full for sound, I heard the clear jubilant notes as of the harps of many angels.

And then, in the midst of the fire and the rain and the music, I heard the Scotsman singing the eternal song of creation. The words that filled my being were his words, spoken long ago, yet timeless and spoken anew to every generation: *Hark the herald of the Sun of Righteousness, rising with healing in its wings, the auroral wind, softly trumpeting an Approach!*...

The latter rains that fell now splashed upon my face with unspeakable comfort, for they were the refreshing rains of the dawn of a new spring. And the agony of the fire turned to comfort...

I was aware of the joy of existence and knew that I was blessed— more blessed than I deserved or could imagine. The gentle rain of God's tears soothed every care, dissolved every anguish, comforted every pain. All sorrow was swallowed up in the life. I was at peace.

The throbbing of the great Heart entered my soul, for I was one with it. It vibrated in resonance with the strings of my own heart, for at last I had come home, into the Father's heart, the heart of him who had created me to be his son.

TWENTY-SIX

WIN, LOSE, OR DRAW?

God's Ultimate Victory—Complete or Partial?

by
Michael Phillips

I return to where I began, to the courtroom speaking on behalf of my client.

Though I have eschewed the courtroom image of judge and condemned prisoner to explain the atonement, I retain the authorial privilege of using the analogy of an attorney representing a client he believes in. A writer, you know, must be allowed the prerogative of mixing his metaphors and changing his analogies on a whim!

I have made my case. I now leave the evidence in your hands. You are a jury of one.

One point perhaps requires clarification. Throughout this journey of exploration, I have done my best to fairly and accurately represent the ideas of George MacDonald. But calling him my client is not technically true.

My client is God our Creator, the Father of Jesus Christ. He is the One whom George MacDonald and I and many others have given our lives to represent accurately according to what Jesus told us. In a sense, Jesus' mission was exactly the same—to represent accurately to mankind his own dear Abba and divine Daddy and Father.

In the final analysis, I write neither on my own behalf nor even on George MacDonald's behalf. I share these ideas, thoughts, writings, and make public this discussion, on behalf of Jesus Christ's Father, his Life and our Life, his God and our God.

With that said, I proceed to my closing arguments.

GOD MUST BE MORE AND HIGHER IN EVERY WAY

The common sense of true spirituality is often too much for the theologically minded to take in. If *our* human sensibilities would call a thing unfair, it defies reason to devise contorted theological legalisms in order to explain how *God* is capable of injustice, and yet at the same time be infinitely just. God cannot love justice, and yet act *unjustly*.

This folly reaches the height of absurdity with the nonsensical claim that it is precisely contradictions such as this, and our inability to understand them, because God's ways are higher than our ways, that proves them true. It is one more example of the orthodoxy talking in circles.

In one of George MacDonald's simplest and profoundest arguments, he insists that God most be more and higher than man in every way. We cannot explain away this imperative. God *must* be more than we. If we perceive an action or a judgment unjust, how much *more*, not less, will God see it as unjust.

As God himself created our imaginations, it is impossible for them to imagine him better, *more* loving, *more* forgiving, than he is. It would be for the created to rise above its creator.

It is such a straightforward argument. Yet the further one probes into the sense of it, the more it simply has to be so. If our imaginations can conceive a *higher* Goodness, a more *far-reaching* Forgiveness, a more *infinite* Love than our theologies can account for, then by definition that theology is not infinite.

The "god" of such a non-infinite theology is not truly *God* at all.

MacDonald writes: "More is required of the Maker, by his own act of creation, than can be required of men. More and higher justice and righteousness is required of him by himself, the Truth—greater nobleness, more penetrating sympathy..." [151]

With disarming simplicity, MacDonald has plunged straight to the heart of the infinitude of Love that must define the Godhead. Anything less than *infinite* love, *infinite* goodness, and *infinite* forgiveness cannot define our *Almighty* God.

CAN MAN BE MORE MERCIFUL THAN GOD?

Therefore, in an oft-repeated theme in many of his books, MacDonald asks: *Shall a man be more merciful than God* [152]

If man recoils from the idea of a hell of retribution and torment, how much more must God recoil from it?

Indeed, the only individuals who seem comfortable with the evil idea are those Christians bound to pagan notions of God's vengeance. Of all those who through the centuries should have insisted that God is larger than such low theologies, it is Christians. Yet *they* have been the most reluctant to see it. Scarce wonder that MacDonald's strongest language is reserved for the unbelief of so-called believers. "Oh ye hidebound Christians..." he writes, "some of you need the fire." [153]

God, then, must be infinitely more, higher, better, *more* loving, *more* forgiving, *more* merciful, than the best man who ever lived could imagine. MacDonald places this conviction poignantly in the mouth of *What's Mine's Mine's* Ian Macruadh:

> *"'The whole idea of such atonement is the merest subterfuge, a figment of the paltry human intellect to reconcile difficulties of its own invention. Once, when Alister had done something wrong, my father said, 'He must be punished—except some one will be punished for him!' I offered to take his place, partly that it seemed expected of me, partly that I was moved by vanity, and partly that I foresaw what would follow.'*
>
> *"'And what did follow?' ...*
>
> *"'He scarcely touched me, mother,' answered Ian. 'The thing taught me something very different from what he had meant to teach by it. That he failed to carry out his idea of justice helped me afterwards to see that God could not have done it either...'"* [154]

Though its dark and sometimes weird imagery is not to the taste of everyone, George MacDonald's third to last book, *Lilith*, which we read from in Chapter 24, offers an intriguing imaginative interpretation of the post death repentance of Adam's mythical first wife Lilith. In it MacDonald's imaginative interpretation of "the worm that dieth not" is both chilling and remarkable.

MACDONALD AND LEWIS—TWO POTENTIAL CONCLUSIONS

There is, however, an alternate conclusion to the end of all things as portrayed imaginatively in *Lilith*. It carries great weight because it was espoused by C.S. Lewis and doubtless represents his own personal view as well as his interpretation of MacDonald's. Lewis says that MacDonald "hopes" all will be saved, but he then also imputes to MacDonald the belief that "omnipotence cannot save the unconverted," calling such an "eternal impossibilit[y]." [155]

Whether Lewis is right, or is mistaken in his assessment of MacDonald's perspective, is a point that will continue to be debated. It seems likely from much in his writings that MacDonald's view extended beyond mere "hope."

Lewis's fictionalized postulation, as one possibility derived from *The Great Divorce*, is that sinners will be *capable* of repenting after death, and perhaps be *allowed* to...but that most simply won't want to. They will prefer to remain below. Basing too much of Lewis's view on *The Great Divorce* may be as inappropriate as to doctrinalize *Lilith* on George MacDonald's behalf. Yet the two fantasies illuminate at least the potentiality of a divergent perspective between master and protégé, highlighting what may be Lewis's belief that many will forever "choose" to remain separated from God's love—thus making an eternal hell inevitable. [156]

Of MacDonald—and perhaps reflecting his own "hopeful" but not altogether optimistic view—Lewis sums the matter up: "I know hardly any other writer who seems to be closer, or more continually close, to the Spirit of Christ Himself. Hence his Christ-like union of tenderness and severity. Nowhere else outside the New Testament have I found terror and comfort so intertwined...Inexorability—but never the inexorability of anything less than love—runs through it like a refrain: 'escape is hopeless...compulsion waits...the uttermost farthing will be extracted.'...MacDonald shows God threatening...terrible things if we will not be happy...He hopes, indeed, that all men will be saved; but that is because he hopes that all will repent. He knows (none better) that even omnipotence cannot save the unconverted. He never trifles with eternal impossibilities." [157]

MACDONALD'S PRAYERFUL ASIDE, AND FINAL WARNING

The summation to George MacDonald's sermon "The Consuming Fire" offers an intriguing window into its author's heart concerning the potential ultimate redemption of all men.

After quoting, *And Hell itself will pass away,* MacDonald writes, "For then our poor brothers and sisters, every one, shall have been burnt clean and brought home."

To all appearances, this statement presents MacDonald's view plainly and definitely: *Every one...burnt clean...brought home.*

Yet in mid-sentence, as an intensely personal aside, MacDonald suddenly bursts forth in prayerful plea. Does the brief nine-word soliloquy reveal his trusting *conviction* that all will be brought home, his "hope," as Lewis calls it, or perhaps a faint whisper of remaining *uncertainty*? It is impossible to know for certain.

The passage reads:

"Then indeed wilt thou be all in all. For then our poor brothers and sisters, every one—O God, we trust in thee, the Consuming Fire—shall have been burnt clean and brought home."

Then he adds the enormous questions. Perhaps soliloquizing with himself again:

Shall a man be more merciful than God?

Shall, of all his glories, his mercy alone not be infinite?

Would he not die yet again to save one brother more?

This surely represents one of the most tantalizing passages to flow from MacDonald's pen, climaxing this entire discussion in the single word *trust.*

In that trust we can rest. MacDonald thus concludes:

As for us, now we will come to thee, our Consuming Fire. And thou wilt not burn us more than we can bear. But thou wilt burn us. And although thou seem to slay us, yet will we trust in thee. [158]

Finally, two decades after writing the above, as always, MacDonald balances the scales with an observation and a warning:

> *In these days, when men are so gladly hearing afresh that "in Him is no darkness at all;" that God therefore could not have created any man if He knew that he must live in torture to all eternity; and that his hatred to evil cannot be expressed by injustice; itself the one essence of evil,—for certainly it would be nothing less than injustice to punish infinitely what was finitely committed, no sinner being capable of understanding the abstract enormity of what he does,—in these days has arisen another falsehood—less, yet very perilous: thousands of half-thinkers imagine that, since...hell is not everlasting, there is then no hell at all. To such folly I for one have never given enticement or shelter, I see no hope for many, no way for the divine love to reach them, save through a very ghastly hell. Men have got to repent; there is no other escape for them, and no escape from that.* [159]

CONCLUSION

We turn at last to the central query every reader of George MacDonald eventually confronts: Did George MacDonald believe, eternal aeons from now—through fire; through the purifying, chastening, refining, repentance-producing effects of God's hell; through free will compelled but not coerced; through the eye-opening power of loving, chastening, redemptive punishment to see the hideous self fully for what it is—that *all* creation—*every* creature, *every* sinner, *every* man, *every* woman, *every* child, would be restored and reconciled in the repentant humility of obedient and joyful childness, to God, the Father of the universe?

Did he believe in *universal* reconciliation?

A few closing words from MacDonald's pen must speak for themselves.

> He [Wingfold] was a servant of the church universal, of all that believed or ever would believe in the Lord Christ, therefore of all men, of the whole universe.... [160]

> Oh, the sweet winds of repentance and reconciliation and atonement, that will blow from garden to garden of God, in the tender twilights of his kingdom! Whatever the place be like, one thing is certain, that there will be endless, infinite atonement, ever-growing love...The light which is God, and which is our inheritance because we are the children of God, insures these things...God is; let the earth be glad, and the heaven, and the heaven of heavens! Whatever a father can do to make his children blessed, that will God do for his children. Let us, then, live in continual expectation, looking for the good things that God will give to men, being their father and their everlasting saviour. If the things I have here come from him, and are so plainly but a beginning, shall I not take them as an earnest of the better to follow?...God is, and all is well. [161]

> The whole history is a divine agony to give divine life to creatures. The outcome of that agony, the victory of that creative and again creative energy, will be radiant life, whereof joy unspeakable is the flower. Every child will look in the eyes of the Father, and the eyes of the Father will receive the child with an infinite embrace. [162]

Twenty-Seven

SILENCE IS GOLDEN

The Persuasiveness of Quiet Character

by
Michael Phillips

THE REDACTIVE ROLE OF THE LOVING CRITIC

The critic, the prophet, and the editor all share something in common—
a penetrating eye into what's *wrong*. Their job is often a thankless one
because it appears to the undiscerning eye as essentially negative.

How often do we read in the Old Testament of the Israelites
swarming the biblical prophets with gratitude for their hard words? How
often—something I know a little more about—do authors happily exclaim
to their editors: "Thank you for pointing out everything you didn't like in
my manuscript! Your red pen made my day!"

The function of such critics *isn't* negative but entirely positive. It only
looks negative to one who doesn't probe deep enough into the purposeful
nature of the thing.

In a sense those within Christendom who attempt to expose the flaws
in some of the church's traditionally held doctrines are like editors—or
more precisely *redactors*. They are trying to "edit" and "correct" mistaken
ideas that have infiltrated the gospel message.

The analogy, however, goes only so far. God is a *perfect* Author. His
work only needs editing because some of his spokesmen through the years
have garbled, and in some cases corrupted, his message. We are trying to
edit out the garble. We are trying to redact their human interpretations so
that they reflect the Author's original intent.

Carrying out such a high calling with balance, wisdom, and clarity,
however, is not easy. Any atheist can critique the church and point the

finger of judgment (perhaps with accuracy) at its hypocrisies.

Therefore, God sends among his people those who *love* the Church to help redact the church that it may in the end accomplish and fulfill what Jesus intended his Bride to be. It is not merely the "glad tidings" that must be published abroad, but *correct* belief about who God is.

We often call *history* "His story," and in truth we are the editors of that story. God's church needs redaction by those who grasp what is God's purpose. You and I and millions like us throughout history are part of that continual redaction process—enhancing and illuminating and clarifying how "his story" is communicated to the world.

Though it is occasionally necessary to explore the flaws of various ideas, the effort is born in love. The objective is to fulfill the purpose Jesus, the author of the Church, and God, the Author of "His story," intended from the beginning.

The gladdest tidings of all are that the Father of Jesus Christ is a good and loving and tender and patient and eternally forgiving Father, determined to work that eternal love, whatever it costs, to the fashioning of obedient sons and daughters.

Let the entire universe rejoice...the God who created us is a good Father!

THE *PEOPLE* OF GOD'S FAMILY

Two thousand years of Christendom has revealed all too clearly the effects of wrong teaching. Yet even wrong belief, in humble growing hearts generally pointed toward goodness, kindness, generosity, and selflessness cannot extinguish God's light from having its effect. When hearts are true, God's Fatherhood yet shines amid the most hideous of doctrines.

Though they often function surrounded by the dead stones of institutionalism, such true-hearted shiners of light are the living stones of the Church. Because they are true living organisms of Christ's body, they will in time see the Father of Jesus for who he is, just as I too will see him more clearly than I am able to now. On that day we will rejoice to leave behind the doctrines that have clung around our necks like millstones.

Judy and I recently shared meals with three families active in three different churches. They are among our dearest Christian friends in the world. All are predominantly Calvinist in outlook. As the last evening of the three drew to a close, the man of the family sat down at the piano and began softly playing one old hymn after another while the rest of us sang and hummed along and chatted informally. It reminded me of the Sunday evening sing-along services of my childhood as our beloved pastor exhorted us on with all the gusto of a tent-meeting revivalist...*Roll Jordan*

Roll, I Know Whom I Have Believed, What A Friend We Have In Jesus, Nearer My God To Thee, Wonderful Grace of Jesus.

As we left our friends' home in the glow of a warm Scottish twilight, I was struck again by a great truth—that in the end God's Church is made up, not of doctrines, not of buildings, theologies, budgets, books, music, programs, ministries, committees, nor of debates about hell or any other controversy or idea...but of *people*.

Millions of ordinary people the world over.

Though it may seem remarkable to those reading this book, most of my closest friends in the Spirit are what would probably be termed Christian fundamentalists. I never bring up differences of doctrine in our conversations. Hell, the afterlife, and the ideas of George MacDonald, never come up. Half of my friends have no idea who George MacDonald even is. I prize relationship far more than theology. Love for the people of God is paramount in my heart. Nothing could interest me less than foisting my perspectives off on them.

Not a single one of those dear friends with whom we enjoy rich fellowship know anything about the controversial side of my writing. To my knowledge, they are completely unaware of my theology. Devout Scottish Calvinists, the three men of the families we recently visited are among the most humble men I have met in my life. Daily their light shines into the world around them. It would not cross my mind to attempt to persuade them to change a single idea of their belief system. I am enriched around them knowing myself in the presence of Christlikeness. Their characters radiate goodness. I drink it in without the least thought they need anything from me other than the genuine friendship of Christian brotherhood. The unity between us in Christ is the only gauge of relationship that matters to me. Their characters are theology enough.

The ideas that have been intrinsic to our discussion here and that have informed my spiritual pilgrimage for the past four decades lie utterly outside the scope of my normal daily relationships and interactions. These are topics I wrestle with and study and read about and write about primarily in my prayer closet...with the door closed.

Of course, as a communicator I *write* about them. But that is a different thing. When approaching a book, everyone has to make a choice whether they are interested in a given topic or not. I am happy to address these things via the printed word with those who *choose* to engage me in conversation—as you have by reading this book. But I will push my ideas on no unwilling ear.

Therefore, when it comes to speaking out about hell and beyond or George MacDonald or the afterlife, my chosen code is ruled by silence. I relax that code only when someone *else* opens the door.

I let myself by guided by the old adage: *Silence is golden.* Or, if one prefers a more spiritual foundation for this conversational ethic, I would point to the command from the Lord's brother which succinctly summarizes many of Solomon's proverbs: *Let every man be quick to hear, slow to speak.* (James 1:19)

BE NOT SAY

Not everyone endorses this maxim. They feel it their duty to disseminate every idea that comes into their heads by *proclamation.* Christ's church is a church of talkers, singers, sharers, communicators, gossipers, witnessers, exhorters, expositors, teachers, and trumpeters. The entire blogging phenomenon is testimony to the fact that everyone is convinced that he or she has great things to *say* that the world needs to hear. Very few these days boast about having the gift of *listening.*

Many will therefore eagerly and excitedly want to share and talk about the ideas in this book with any and all who will listen, and with many who have no interest in listening. Others will want to talk about them to *dispute* them. Either option is fine, if one feels that is his or her calling. But I do not see that as *my* calling.

With all my heart I believe that the words "Silence is golden" represent far more than a cute cliché. There is "gold" here, a secret, a pearl of great price, a rare and prized mystery of the kingdom.

Our silence may, in fact, be the radiant jewel of character that will endure long after the wood, hay, and stubble of our multitude of words evaporate in the wind. Eternity may judge those silences to have been the most convincing and persuasive aspect of our lives. Our proclamations will fade as passing wisps of smoke. They will probably have persuaded no one to a single viewpoint or opinion. Our silences, however, may have exercised influence far beyond what we will ever see.

If we would convince, we must *be* not *say.*

It will not be our words, but it may rather be a quiet spirit of humility that will abide. In the wisdom of silence, the fruits of the Spirit find soil to send down roots, grow, and be seen.

Endless chatter obscures. Silence illuminates.

It is my hope, therefore, that you will be measured, cautious, and discriminating in your use of these high principles we have been discussing together. Truth is too holy to be bandied about lightly. The infinite Fatherhood of God is too mighty a truth to be made the subject of hasty and ill-chosen small-talk. Let us allow the gold of that Fatherhood to radiate from the depths of our hearts.

Another factor makes silence a worthy code of communication. As God gives every man time, so too must we. Everyone arrives at deepening levels of awareness according to a different timetable, on an individual pilgrimage of growth, led by God's Spirit along byways and quests of the heart completely unique and known to none other. We can neither interfere with nor rush that process. We may influence it, but we cannot hurry it along. The strongest trees grow slowly.

Words of attempted *persuasion* are singularly ineffective mediating influences in another's life journey. They may do more to impede that work than help it. Our words must be "fitly chosen" to do the most good, aimed with precision and purpose...and only when the time is right. God's work of revelation will unfold in others as it has unfolded within us—with the whispers of the still small voice initiating and informing the ever-deepening inner odyssey.

CHARACTER PERSUADES

One final factor urges me toward silence, patience, and great understanding toward those who may not embrace my perspectives about the afterlife.

Most Christians of all brands and stripes and beliefs and affiliations—obviously not all, but *most*—are good, honest, sincere men and women trying in their corners of the world to live moral, upright, conscientious, obedient lives. If they believe differently than I do about God and his ways in some of their doctrines, that intrinsic orientation toward simple Christian goodness and kindness is a higher and more important eternal influence for the gospel than any theology of theirs *or* mine.

Character persuades.

Wrong doctrines are not so serious a matter in those whose obedience is developing them into God's sons and daughters. Living the life of Christlikeness as one understands it and possesses the light to interpret it accomplishes more toward the eventual saving of the world than all the doctrinal correctness in the universe.

A time comes to all when they must confront the question whether God is a Father or a tyrant. But those times and seasons are not always for one's neighbors to know. Until then, God takes every man and woman where they are, and carries out the needful transformations within them that their obedience makes possible.

MacDonald writes:

"Good souls many will one day be horrified at the things they now believe of God. If they have not thought about them, but given themselves to obedience, they may not have done them much harm as yet; but they can make little progress in the knowledge of God, while, if but passively, holding evil things true of him. If, on the other hand, they do think about them, and find in them no obstruction, they must indeed be far from anything to be called a true knowledge of God. [163]

"God takes them where they are, accepts whatever they honestly offer, and so helps them to outgrow themselves, preparing them to offer the true offering, and to know him whom they ignorantly worship." [164]

We must keep focused on our true priorities. Though we have given great attention to many doctrinal ideas in our discussion together, in one sense, alongside the great swelling tide of Christlikeness within Christ's body, this entire discussion and "debate" will fade into insignificance.

Indeed, I marvel how the people of God, in the midst of many dubious notions about God, continually seed a fallen earth with goodness, kindness, gentleness, and self-sacrifice. It is true that we could do so more effectively by grasping the love of the Father aright. That represents the challenge before us. Yet the theological flaws within the body of Christ—though they need to be addressed—do not prevent the life-changing impact of salt and light spreading into the world.

It is truly wonderful to behold. Christendom in all its forms has filled every corner of the world with miraculous life and sacrificial love, and countless expressions of human kindness toward its kind.

Despite all that needs to be changed, therefore, despite what doctrine and institutionalism has done to corrupt the originating intent of Jesus, the people of God are yet a people of light in a world that is lost. The power of God's love changes lives in a way that lightens men's paths and leavens the world with truth and love and service and compassion. Incomplete as it is, God's church is full of *goodness*—good people who are taking cups of cold water to the thirsty around them.

And the Spirit of Truth continues his work among us.

APPENDICES

EXHUMING MACDONALD'S VISION OF GOD

My Redactive Work With George MacDonald

by
Michael Phillips

It has now been over thirty years since my first redacted ("edited") editions of George MacDonald's books were published.[165] Many of you who have picked up this book will know nothing of those efforts of three decades ago to bring back into print a message and a vision of God that was perilously close to being lost.

At that time, there was *nothing* of MacDonald's available other than his fairy tales. For anyone interested in MacDonald's theological ideas and vision, it was a barren desert. Few in Christendom had heard of George MacDonald. Except for isolated enclaves among those who knew of his connections with C.S. Lewis and those aware of his contribution to the imaginative legacy of 19th century *fairie* lore, MacDonald's name and reputation had vanished from the spiritual landscape.

RESURRECTING GEORGE MACDONALD'S WRITINGS

To resurrect MacDonald's reputation and bring his books again into print required what some viewed as drastic measures. My work over the span of two decades was twofold: One, to redact, edit, and simplify his novels so that they would be sale-able to a contemporary publisher, and, as many contained heavy doses of Doric, to make this Scottish dialect understandable to modern readers. The second parallel priority was to publish a new line of facsimiles of MacDonald's original works for those readers who preferred full-length editions.

Within several years MacDonald was being read on every continent, in several foreign languages (including Chinese!), and his name was again, if not exactly a "household name," certainly a recognized one. Nor could it be helped that this explosion of interest was accompanied by criticism of MacDonald for those of his views that lay outside the orthodox mainstream.

That all took place a long time ago. Eventually the internet and digitalization changed the entire perspective of what the word "book" even meant. MacDonald's works became so easily available that they are now in widespread circulation everywhere.

However, one of the reasons prompting my "editing" of his work in the first place remains. Some of MacDonald's writing is simply hard to understand. Those readers comfortable with his original writings have no need either of my previously published edited editions or what I bring to the table in this new book. Others, however, I hope to help by making MacDonald's thought more accessible. Our objective together is not to debate this or that edition of one book or another, but to get at the heart of MacDonald's meaning. We all must find the best means to do that. Editions matter nothing, our vision of God matters everything.

Those of you who would prefer MacDonald in his original editions will no doubt want to read the sermon selections that are included in this book from other sources, even perhaps from our own Sunrise Centenary editions of MacDonald's original works.[166] For those of you, however, who may benefit from having the way through the thickets of MacDonald's thought smoothed out a bit, I offer this brief explanation of what I have done and why.

This will also explain a little more regarding the numerous selections from MacDonald used throughout this book. I quote extensively from both edited and original editions—whichever in a given instance I feel most easily conveys MacDonald's intended meaning. The priority is to get at MacDonald's *ideas* and to make them understandable. When quoting from my edited editions, the endnotes will specify both edited and original sources.

Finally, in my "editing" of MacDonald's sermons, both here and in the two volumes *Your Life in Christ* and *The Truth in Jesus,*[167] some of MacDonald's work is presented so straightforwardly that little "editing" is necessary other than simplifying the punctuation, making the sentences and paragraphs shorter, and here and there rewording an archaic mode of construction or word use. In other instances, where the meaning is truly obscure, I have made greater use of my editorial pen to bring MacDonald's meaning to light. The sermons which appeared in the above two compilations have been reproduced in this book from those earlier works. Because those publications were directed primarily toward readers of MacDonald's novels, I exercised slightly more editorial latitude where I felt it appropriate in an attempt to make them more readable. Those of MacDonald's sermons in this book that did not appear in those compilations I have here taken directly from their originals, with relatively minor modifications of punctuation and sentence and paragraph length, with the occasional rewording of archaisms. These distinctions are highlighted in the footnotes. Some of the sermons here may thus "sound" a little more weighty and are presented in a more distinct 19th century style, whereas others will be more contemporary in flavor. Again, readers are encouraged to seek MacDonald's originals to accompany the selections in this volume.

This is neither the time nor the place for an extensive apologetic for my editorial work. That has been done elsewhere. My work has been analyzed to death—and both praised and condemned from all sides. As you continue in this volume, however, you need to know what the words "Edited by" mean in connection with the sermons of MacDonald that are included. You need to know what you are reading and why it appears in the particular form and format it does.

Toward that end, I will share the following two selections. The first is from the Introduction to the 1982 edition of *The Fisherman's Lady*, my edited edition of MacDonald's wonderful novel *Malcolm*. It was this book that inaugurated, in a sense, the "MacDonald renaissance" of the 1980s and paved the way for everything else I have done. I there explained how and why I had undertaken the redaction of MacDonald's novel. The second is from the Introduction to the 2005 edition of *Your Life in Christ,* the first compilation of edited sermons.

The reprints of these portions of the two Introductions will give you a clear idea of the nature of my redactive work and whether you think it will benefit and enhance your reading of MacDonald. I share them in hopes that this will help you understand the nature of the selections from MacDonald included in this book.

ON THE EDITING OF MACDONALD'S FICTION:
FROM THE INTRODUCTION TO *THE FISHERMAN'S LADY*

"There is a peculiar quality in a MacDonald novel that has great power to move its reader. For MacDonald...had a powerful vision of the meaning of life; his spirit was in close union with the Spirit of God; and he had unusual insight into the application of spiritual principles in daily life situations. And it is this wisdom and spiritual perspective which set his stories apart from those of his contemporaries...To understand MacDonald at all, one needs to experience his novels.

"When the reader does, however, two problems are immediately encountered in MacDonald's writing style. First of all, MacDonald frequently used lowland Scots dialect for the dialogue between his characters, which few now understand at a glance. And, secondly, MacDonald's tendency toward preaching and rambling often erupts without warning, and he lapses into off-the-subject discourses which slow up the story line considerably.

"For the loyal MacDonald follower, such idiosyncrasies lend a certain charm and flavor...MacDonald's novels are enhanced by spiritual truths woven in and throughout the characters whose lives open before us. MacDonald was so thoroughly a Christian that God's wisdom simply came forth from his pen almost in spite of the story line. It is as though he were continually weaving two parallel stories—that of the 'plot,' and that of the partially submerged spiritual journeys being traveled in a parallel plane by those characters involved in the story. And MacDonald moved freely from one level to another...

"The novels of George MacDonald are therefore intriguing to the modern Christian reader. Nearly every one contains in the narrative a strong vision of a loving God gradually revealing himself in the lives of men and women through nature and daily circumstances. As the various facets of the plot unfold, MacDonald carries on a commentary of spiritual observation (level two) through the characters, their growth and interaction, and the action of the drama itself (level one). The characters responding to their circumstances provide a rich source of insight into why people think and behave as they do. The plot is the skeleton around which the characters and truths come to life...

"The difficulty, however, as mentioned before, is that MacDonald's novels...are long and many times unintelligible to the fast-paced reader. My proposal with this reprinted edition of one of my favorites is to once again open this world of George MacDonald to modern-day readers. What I have done is to cut the original by about half by removing disgressions from the story and by condensing some of the 'wordy' portions. In addition I have 'translated' the Scots' dialect, an example of which follows, into English:

> *'Ye hae had mair to du wi' me nor ye ken, an' aiblins ye'll hae mair nor yet ye can weel help. Sae caw canny, my man.'*
>
> *'Ye may hae the layin' o' me oot," said Malcolm, "but it sanna be wi my wull; an gien I hae ony life left i' me, Is' gie ye a fleg.'*
>
> *'Ye may get a war yersel': I hae frichtit the deid afore noo. Sae gang yer wa's to Mistress Coorthoup, wi' a flech i' yer lug.'"* [168]

ON THE EDITING OF MACDONALD'S SERMONS:
FROM THE INTRODUCTION TO *YOUR LIFE IN CHRIST*

"The editing of these selections is as minimal as I have been able to make it. However, to extract the ore from MacDonald's writings does require some effort...Thus my goal is to make MacDonald's wisdom and prophetic insight about God readable and grasp-able to anyone willing to put in the effort to understand his ground-breaking, unorthodox, and sometimes revolutionary ideas. It is my hope that the minimal editing I have employed with these writings will help you discover these rich veins within MacDonald's thought.

"This is not to say, even now, that this will be a light read. MacDonald's ideas and processes of thought are occasionally so profound that nothing makes them easy. We are not used to having to think quite so hard for our spiritual food. We live in a superficial age where doctrinal formula provides the parameters by which spirituality is judged. MacDonald saw things differently. Doctrinal formula was nothing to him. His unique perspective takes some getting used to. I find that many passages require two or three readings. But I also find spiritual gold awaiting me, sometimes buried deep but always ready to shine out brilliantly from the page when suddenly I *see* it. Theologically, too, as imaginatively, I have discovered many doors of delight opening before me into new worlds of wonder about God and his work. In my life at least, I have found these non-fiction writings just as 'magical' and full of wonder as *Malcolm* and *Narnia*.

"I am aware that it is a high and holy calling to try to recast the words of another into a form that truly represents his intent. It is with prayerful trepidation that I undertake such a task with MacDonald's spiritual writings. When editing MacDonald's novels twenty years ago, my task was distinct from this. I was forced by the constraints of publication to shorten the originals. In many cases, because of the language employed, it was also necessary to 'translate' portions from the Scot's dialect of MacDonald's originals.

"With MacDonald's non-fiction writings, the case is different. There is no dialect. No need exists to shorten. Therefore, except for a few rare words and perhaps a very occasional phrase, I have removed little. What I have done, rather, is simply to shorten sentences and paragraphs, that I might order MacDonald's progression of thought in a more linear and straightforward fashion than is sometimes presented in the originals.

"Some will wonder why such editing is necessary. For two reasons: Because of the complex progression of MacDonald's ideas, and because of the elaborately entangled grammatical constructions in which he expressed these ideas.

"I would not presume to call MacDonald's logic other than straightforward. The operation of his mind is so far above mine that I would dare no such presumption. I think I am on safe ground to say, however, that as his logic progresses it brings in its train multitudinous tangential modifiers and explanations and offshoot points that it often becomes very difficult to follow the primary sequence of ideas. Once or twice a page, it seems, I have to stop to read a lengthy section four or five times simply to 'get it.'

"Additionally, MacDonald's grammar and syntax can become extremely involved and can itself impede understanding. Sentences of 100-120 words are common, and occasionally reach 160 or 180. These often contain a half dozen semi-colons, several dashes, numerous commas, and a colon or two. MacDonald can use *every* punctuation mark in a single sentence! Likewise, his paragraphs are extremely long and can run to five or six pages.

"MacDonald's ideas are here expressed, for the most part in the words in which he wrote them, or, if some change has been necessary, in something very close to them. Where MacDonald's originals are straightforward and clear, they are reproduced without change. Where the word-thickets are complicated and the sentences long, then structural editing has been done but most of his actual *words* kept intact.

"Clarity sometimes requires brevity. We live in a time when we are not adept at working our way through theologically dense sentences. Simplifying the complexity of the originals in these two areas—thought progressions and grammatical constructions—enables MacDonald's meaning and his wonderful expressiveness to rise to the surface with more radiance. Breaking up the progressions of thought into smaller chunks is an enormous aid to understanding. One of the chapters which follows contained a mere eighteen paragraphs. As I have rendered it, it now contains approximately seventy. I am confident that you will find, as I do, that the ideas are much easier to grasp with a little more white space on the page.

"Most of what I have done, therefore, is more 'structural' than *editorial*...I have not shortened for shortening's sake. Clarity, not brevity, has been the goal.

"Finally, the sub-headings within the text are my own additions, again, provided as an aid to understanding without materially altering the text.

An example or two may help illustrate this structural complexity I have tried to address.

"The following 140 word sentence appears in the original of 'The Creation in Christ'":

> *I worship the Son as the human God the divine, the only Man, deriving his being and power from the Father, equal with him as a son is the equal at once and the subject of his father—but making himself the equal of his father in what is most precious in Godhead, namely Love—which is indeed, the essence of that statement of the*

evangelist with which I have now to do—a higher thing than the making of the worlds and the things in them, which he did by the power of the Father, not by a self-existent power in himself, whence the apostle, to whom the Lord must have said things he did not say to the rest, or who was better able to receive what he said to all, says, "All things were made" not by, but "through him."

"Obviously we can 'understand' what MacDonald is saying. It is nothing like the Scottish dialect of his novels. Yet it takes a little mental work to unsnarl the complexity of the construction.

"Another sentence [from the sermon entitled "The Temptation in the Wilderness] of 218 words comes to us with three semi-colons, five dashes, and twenty-four commas:

But I will ask whether to know better and do not so well, is not a serving of Satan;—whether to lead men on in the name of God as towards the best when the end is not the best, is not a serving of Satan;—whether to flatter their pride by making them conquerors of the enemies of their nation instead of their own evils, is not a serving of Satan;—in a word, whether, to desert the mission of God, who knew that men could not be set free in that way, and sent him to be a man, a true man, the one man, among them, that his life might become their life, and that so they might be as free in prison or on the cross, as upon a hill-side or on a throne,— whether, so deserting the truth, to give men over to the lie of believing other than spirit and truth to be the worship of the Father, other than love the fulfilling of the law, other than the offering of their best selves the service of God, other than obedient harmony with the primal love and truth and law, freedom,—whether, to desert God thus, and give men over thus, would not have been to fall down and worship the devil.

"Both these examples, it should be pointed out, are embedded in the midst of paragraphs of greater length yet. Therefore, if MacDonald's meaning can be preserved, even enhanced, by reducing the sentence length and presenting his ideas in more a 'straight line,' it only makes sense to do so...

"Along with this, we must remember that these selections were all written over one hundred years ago. Methods of communication have changed. Words themselves have changed. For the sake of clarity, where meanings and connotations have shifted, some of these issues have also been addressed...

"After all this, MacDonald's language may still sound somewhat laborious to some. While untangling lengthy sentences and paragraphs into more straightforward progressions, I have yet tried to retain the essential character and flavor of MacDonald's modes of expression...

"It seems only fitting, in preparing us at last to move on to MacDonald himself, that we listen again to Lewis as he describes what made these writings so unique and powerful in his own spiritual development:

"'In Macdonald it is always the voice of conscience that speaks. He addresses the will: the demand for obedience, for 'something to be neither more nor less nor other than *done*,' is incessant...The Divine Sonship is the key-conception which unites all the different elements of his thought. I dare not say that he is never in error; but to speak plainly I know hardly any other writer who seems to be closer, or more continually close, to the Spirit of Christ himself. Hence his Christ-like union of tenderness and severity. Nowhere else outside the New Testament have I found terror and comfort so intertwined...All the sermons are suffused with a spirit of love and wonder.'" [169] [170]

APPENDIX 2

BIBLIOGRAPHY

GEORGE MACDONALD (1824-1905), Victorian novelist, preacher, poet, theologian, and man of letters, penned more than 50 books during the latter half of the 19th century before his reputation gradually faded from public view. His imaginative ideas, however, seized a student named C.S. Lewis and eventually led the young atheist to Christianity. Since then, an impressive roster of admirers (including Lewis, G.K. Chesterton, Dorothy Sayers, W.H. Auden, J.R.R. Tolkien, Madeleine L'Engle, and many others) have kept alive the flame of MacDonald's bold and uncommon vision of God. Admired primarily for his novels, short stories, fairy tales, and fantasies, it is mostly his theological writings through which MacDonald articulated the controversial and tantalizing perspectives of the afterlife that are the subject of this book.

MICHAEL PHILLIPS (1946-), MacDonald's biographer and redactor, is the man whose more than 50 republished editions of MacDonald's writings brought the Scotsman's work back from obscurity in the 1980s, and led to the renaissance of interest in the man C.S. Lewis called his "master." A best-selling novelist and devotional writer in his own right, Phillips has authored more than 80 books in addition to his work with MacDonald. Recognized as possessing special insight into MacDonald's heart, he is singularly qualified to illuminate the theological ideas addressed in this volume, and to bring valuable light to the question many have asked through the years: "What did George MacDonald really believe about hell?"

Further information about George MacDonald and Michael Phillips, biographical details, contact information, and book ordering details can be found at the website: FatherOfTheInklings.com.

The Works of George MacDonald

Categorizing and chronologizing George MacDonald's writings is difficult for several reasons. Nearly all MacDonald's books were released in different editions by a variety of publishers. *David Elginbrod, Alec Forbes of Howglen*, and *Robert Falconer*, for instance, were issued in at least twelve editions between 1865 and 1900, *Annals of a Quiet Neighborhood* in fifteen. Even his more obscure novels were released in four or five varieties.

MacDonald also had a passion for polishing and reediting. He constantly reworked his poems, with the result that every new edition of poetry contained newly worded poems by the same title. The book *Adela Cathcart*, a loose grouping of short stories in the guise of a novel, contained whole different collections of stories from one edition to another.

He not only reworked his material, title changes were frequent. Thus *Orts* became *A Dish of Orts* and was released in the U.S. as *The Imagination and Other Essays. The Gifts of the Child Christ* became *Stephen Archer and Other Tales*. The magazine parable released as *A Double Story* became *The Wise Woman* when first published in book form, only to later be released by two other publishers as *Princess Rosamond* and *The Lost Princess*—four titles in all. *The Twelve Spiritual Songs of Novalis* were expanded to fifteen (nine new and six from the 1851 edition) and added to other German and Italian translations to make up *Exotics*. Later *Rampolli* was released, which combined *Exotics* and *Diary of an Old Soul*. With every successive publication of poetry, changes were made until the 1893 release of *The Poetical Works of George MacDonald* (2 Volumes), which contained his longer poems *Within and Without, The Disciple*, and *A Hidden Life*, with a complete collection of 435 remaining poems of varying length.

When all is set down and assessed, George MacDonald produced 53 books (37 fiction and fantasy, 2 distinctive collections of short stories, 3 literary books, 5 volumes of sermons, and 6 distinctive volumes of poetry), though in his lifetime the number of separate editions of this material no doubt exceeded four hundred.

A CHRONOLOGICAL LISTING OF GEORGE
MACDONALD'S ORIGINAL PUBLICATIONS

1851   *Twelve of the Spiritual Songs of Novalis*—Privately Printed
1855   *Within and Without: A Dramatic Poem*—Longman, Brown, Green
1857   *Poems*—Longman, Brown, Green
1858   *Phantastes: a Faerie Romance for Men & Women*—Smith, Elder
1863   *David Elginbrod*—Hurst & Blackett
1864   *The Portent:* A Story of the Inner Vision of the Highlanders Commonly Called the Second Sight—Smith, Elder
        Adela Cathcart—Hurst & Blackett
1865   *Alec Forbes of Howglen*—Hurst & Blackett
1867   *Dealing With the Fairies*—Alexander Strahan

	The Disciple and Other Poems—Alexander Strahan
	Annals of a Quiet Neighborhood—Hurst & Blackett
	Unspoken Sermons—Alexander Strahan
1868	*Robert Falconer*—Hurst & Blackett
	Guild Court: a London Story—Hurst & Blackett
	The Seaboard Parish—Tinsley Brothers
1870	*The Miracles of Our Lord*—Strahan & Co.
1871	*At the Back of the North Wind*—Strahan & Co.
	Ranald Bannerman's Boyhood—Strahan & Co.
1872	*The Princess and the Goblin*—Strahan & Co.
	Wilfrid Cumbermede, an Autobiographical Story—Hurst & Blackett/Scribner
	The Vicar's Daughter—Tinsley Brothers
1873	*Gutta Percha Willie: the Working Genius*—Henry S. King
1874	*England's Antiphon*—Macmillan
1875	*Malcolm*—Henry S. King/Lippincott
	The Wise Woman: A Parable—Strahan & Co.
1876	*Exotics*: A Translation of the Spiritual Songs of Novalis, the Hymn Book of Luther and Other Poems from the German and Italian—Strahan
	St. George and St. Michael—Henry S. King
	Thomas Wingfold, Curate—Hurst & Blackett
1877	*The Marquis of Lossie*—Hurst & Blackett/Lippincott
1879	*Sir Gibbie*—Hurst & Blackett/Lippincott
	Paul Faber, Surgeon—Hurst & Blackett/Lippincott
1880	*A Book of Strife, in the Form of the Diary of an Old Soul*—Privately Printed
1881	*Mary Marston*—Sampson Low/Lippincott
1882	*Warlock O' Glenwarlock*—Sampson Low/Harper
	Weighed and Wanting—Sampson Low/Harper
	The Gifts of the Child Christ, and Other Tales—Sampson Low
	Orts—Sampson Low
	The Princess & Curdie—Lippincott/Chatto & Windus
1883	*Donal Grant*—Kegan Paul/Harper
	A Threefold Cord: Poems by Three Friends—Privately Printed
1885	*The Tragedie of Hamlet*—Longmans, Green
	Unspoken Sermons, Second Series—Longmans, Green
1886	*What's Mine's Mine*—Kegan Paul/Harper
1887	*Home Again, a Tale*—Kegan Paul/Appleton
1888	*The Elect Lady*—Kegan Paul/Munro
1889	*Unspoken Sermons, Third Series*—Longmans, Green
1890	*A Rough Shaking*—Blackie & Sons/Routledge
1891	*There and Back*—Kegan Paul
	The Flight of the Shadow—Kegan Paul, Appleton
	A Cabinet of Gems, cut and polished by Sir Philip Sidney, now for their more radiance presented without their setting by George MacDonald—Elliot Stock
1892	*The Hope of the Gospel*—Ward, Lock, Bowden

1893	*Heather and Snow*—Chatto & Windus/Harper
1895	*Lilith*—Chatto & Windus/Dodd, Mead
1897	*Salted With Fire*—Hurst & Blackett/Dodd Mead
1898	*Far Above Rubies*—Dodd, Mead

SOME PROMINENT 19TH-CENTURY
REPRINTS AND COLLECTIONS

1864	*A Hidden Life and Other Poems* (formerly Poems) —Longman, Green
1871	*Works of Fancy and Imagination* (10 Volumes)—Chatto & Windus
1883	*Stephen Archer and Other Tales* (formerly *The Gifts of the Child Christ, and Other Tales*)—Sampson Low
1876	*Dramatic and Miscellaneous Poems*—Scribner
1893	*A Dish of Orts* (formerly *Orts*)—Sampson Low
1883	*Imagination & Other Essays* (American edition of *Orts*) —Lothrop
1886	*Cross Purposes & The Shadows* (reprinted from *Dealings with the Fairies*)—Blackie & Sons
1890	*The Light Princess and Other Fairy Stories* (reprinted from *Dealings*
with	*the Fairies*)—Blackie & Sons
1897	*Rampolli: Growths from a Long-planted Root, being translations chiefly from the German, along with A Year's Diary of an Old Soul* (*Exotics* with a few additions plus the *Diary of an Old Soul*) — Longmans, Green
1893	*Poetical Works of George MacDonald*, 2 Volumes (some new, mostly reprints) —Chatto & Windus
1893	*Scotch Songs and Ballads* (reprinted from *The Disciple and Other Poems*)—John Rae Smith
1894	*Beautiful Thoughts from George MacDonald* (Selected readings) — James Pott & Co.

A LISTING OF GEORGE MACDONALD'S SERMONS

Unspoken Sermons (First Series, 1867): The Child in the Midst/The Consuming Fire/The Higher Faith/It Shall Not Be Forgiven/The New Name/The Heart with the Treasure/The Temptation in the Wilderness/The Eloi/The Hands of the Father/Love Thy Neighbor/Love Thine Enemy/The God of the Living.

Unspoken Sermons, Second Series (1885): The Way/The Hardness of the Way/The Cause of Spiritual Stupidity/The Word of Jesus on Prayer/Man's Difficulty Concerning Prayer/The Last Farthing/Abba, Father!/Life/The Fear of God/The Voice of Job/Self-Denial/The Truth in Jesus.

Unspoken Sermons, Third Series (1889): The Creation in Christ/The Knowing of the Son/The Mirrors of the Lord/The Truth/Freedom/Kingship/Justice/Light/The Discipleship of Jesus/Righteousness/ The Final Unmasking/The Inheritance.

The Miracles of Our Lord (1870): The Beginning of Miracles/The Cure of

Simon's Wife's Mother/Miracles of Healing Unsolicited/Miracles of Healing Solicited by the Sufferers/Miracles Granted to the Prayer of Friends/The Casting Out of Devils/The Raising of the Dead/The Government of Nature/Miracles of Destruction/The Resurrection/The Transfiguration.

The Hope of the Gospel (1892): Salvation from Sin/The Remission of Sins/Jesus in the World/Jesus and His Fellow Townsmen/The Heirs of Heaven and Earth/Sorrow the Pledge of Joy/God's Family/The Reward of Obedience/The Yoke of Jesus/The Salt and the Light of the World/The Right Hand and the Left/The Hope of the Universe.

RECENT REPRINTS FROM BETHANY HOUSE
PUBLISHERS (EDITED BY MICHAEL PHILLIPS)

Malcolm (retitled *The Fisherman's Lady*, 1982)
The Marquis of Lossie (retitled *The Marquis' Secret*, 1982)
Sir Gibbie (retitled *The Baronet's Song*, 1983)
Donal Grant (retitled *The Shepherd's Castle*, 1983)
David Elginbrod (retitled *The Tutor's First Love*, 1984)
Robert Falconer (retitled *The Musician's Quest*, 1984)
Alec Forbes of Howglen (retitled *The Maiden's Bequest*, 1985)
Thomas Wingfold, Curate (retitled *The Curate's Awakening*, 1985)
Paul Faber, Surgeon (retitled *The Lady's Confession*, 1986)
There and Back (retitled *The Baron's Apprenticeship*, 1986)
What's Mine's Mine (retitled *The Highlander's Last Song*, 1986)
Weighed and Wanting (retitled *The Gentlewoman's Choice*, 1987)
Warlock O'Glenwarlock (retitled *The Laird's Inheritance*, 1987)
Mary Marston (retitled *A Daughter's Devotion*, 1988)
Salted With Fire (retitled *The Minister's Restoration*, 1988)
Heather and Snow (retitled *The Peasant Girl's Dream*, 1989)
The Elect Lady (retitled *The Landlady's Master*, 1989)
Home Again (retitled *The Poet's Homecoming*, 1990)

The Works of Michael Phillips

Caledonia—Epic Scotland (1999-2000):
Legend of the Celtic Stone
An Ancient Strife

The Destiny Chronicles—
Contemporary U.S.A. (2002):
Destiny Junction
King's Crossroads

Shenandoah Sisters and Carolina
Cousins—U.S. Civil War (2002-2007):
Angels Watching Over Me
A Day to Pick Your Own Cotton
*The Color of Your Skin Ain't the
Color of Your Heart*
Together Is All We Need
A Perilous Proposal
The Soldier's Lady
Never Too Late
Miss Katie's Rosewood

American Dreams—
U.S. Civil War (2005-2008):
Dream of Freedom
Dream of Life
Dream of Love

Contemporary Scotland (2011):
Angel Harp
Heather Song

The Green Hills of Snowdonia—
19th Century Wales (2012):
From Across the Ancient Waters
Treasure of the Celtic Triangle

Fantasy (1998, 2013):
The Garden at the Edge of Beyond
Hell and Beyond

DEVOTIONAL AND NON-FICTION

A Christian Family in Action, 1977
Growth of a Vision, 1977
Does Christianity Make Sense?, 1978
Blueprint For Raising a Child, 1978
A Survival Guide For Tough Times,
1979
Control Through Planned Budgeting,
1979
*Building Respect, Responsibility, and
Spiritual Values in Your Child*,
1981
A Vision For the Church, 1981
Getting More Done in Less Time, 1982
In Quest of Gold, the Jim Ryun Story,
1984
*George MacDonald, Scotland's
Beloved Storyteller*, 1987
Good Things to Know, 1992

Good Things to Remember, 1993
A God To Call Father, 1994
A Tribute, 1997
Best Friends For Life (with Judy
Phillips), 1997
Universal Reconciliation, 1998, 2013
Raise Up a Standard, 1998
God A Good Father, 2001)
Jesus An Obedient Son, 2002
Make Me Like Jesus, 2003
*Is Jesus Coming Back As Soon As We
Think*, 2003
Leben (Vols. 1-12), 2004-2006
The Commands, 2013
Bold Thinking Christianity, 2013
*George MacDonald and the Late
Great Hell Debate*, 2013

GEORGE MACDONALD'S WORKS EDITED BY MICHAEL PHILLIPS

Adult Fiction

The Fisherman's Lady, 1982
The Marquis' Secret, 1982
The Baronet's Song, 1983
The Shepherd's Castle, 1983
The Tutor's First Love, 1984
The Musician's Quest, 1984
The Maiden's Bequest, 1985
The Curate's Awakening, 1985
The Lady's Confession, 1986
The Baron's Apprenticeship, 1986
The Highlander's Last Song, 1986
The Gentlewoman's Choice, 1987
The Laird's Inheritance, 1987
A Daughter's Devotion, 1988
The Minister's Restoration, 1988
The Peasant Girl's Dream, 1989
The Landlady's Master, 1989
The Poet's Homecoming, 1990

Youth Fiction

Wee Sir Gibbie of the Highlands, 1990
Alec Forbes & His Friend Annie, 1990
At the Back of the North Wind, 1991
Ranald Bannerman's Boyhood, 1991

Devotional Non-Fiction

Discovering the Character of God, 1989
Knowing the Heart of God, 1990
A Time to Grow, 1991
A Time to Harvest, 1991
Your Life in Christ, 2005
The Truth in Jesus, 2006

Compilation of MacDonald Quotes
Wisdom to Live By, 1996

Many of the above titles can be purchased through bookstores, various retailers, on Amazon, or at www.fatheroftheinklings.com. More information about Michael Phillips and George MacDonald and their works can also be found at that site. Visit Michael Phillips at www.facebook.com/michaelphillipschristianauthor, and at his blog www.daretothinkbigaboutgod.com.

ENDNOTES

Notes about notes. The books of George MacDonald and C.S. Lewis appear in so many different formats, each with distinct pagination, and now with ebooks giving no pagination at all, we have sourced quotes from their writings by chapter number and title only. We realize this makes looking up specific quotes difficult. To attempt greater specificity, however, would only potentially add yet more confusion. In cases where no ambiguity exists, and for Phillips-edited volumes of MacDonald's work, page numbers have been given. In the case of quotes used from the Phillips editions, the location from the original MacDonald title is also given. Though not cited below, many such quotes from MacDonald are also found in the two volumes *Discovering the Character of God* and *Knowing the Heart of God.* We have intentionally not used the *ibid, ob cit, loc cit* terminology for the simple reason that readers will presumably be using these footnotes to look up quotes. While perhaps not technically *de rigueur* by scholarly standards, the easiest means to this end is for the title and location of the quote to be listed in full in every instance where a given title is cited, rather than forcing the reader continually having to remind themselves, "Now what does *ibid* mean again?" Finally, as much care as an author, compiler, or publisher takes in researching sources, footnotes are notoriously subject to the inadvertent intrusion of error. For any inconvenience this causes, we sincerely apologize. We will be grateful if you would call our attention to these so that they can be corrected.

Introduction

[1] These were published by Bethany House Publishers, Minneapolis, Minn. Between 1982 and 2006.

[2] Published by Sunrise Books, Eureka, CA in 1998.

Chapter 1

[3] Both quotes from George MacDonald, *At the Back of the North Wind*, chapter 7.

[4] George MacDonald, *There and Back*, ch. 40; edited edition *The Baron's Apprenticeship* (1986, Michael Phillips, ed.), p. 151.

[5] George MacDonald, *Unspoken Sermons, Third Series*, "Justice."

[6] Andrew Jukes, *The Restitution of All Things*, pp. 155.

[7] St. Thomas Aquinas, *Summa*, Part iii, quoted in *The Restitution of All Things*, by Andrew Jukes, pp. 153.

[8] Peter Lombard, *Sentent*, lib. iv, quoted in *The Restitution of All Things*, by Andrew Jukes, pp. 154.

[9] St. Augustine, *De peccatorum meritis*, lib. i cap. 16, 21, quoted in *The Restitution of All Things*, by Andrew Jukes, pp. 153.

[10] Martin Luther, *De servo arbitrio*, 23, 1557, quoted in *The Restitution of All Things*, by Andrew Jukes, pp. 154.

[11] Jonathan Edwards, *Miscellaneous Discourses,* "The Final Judgment: Sinners in Zion Tenderly Warned," Sec. III.

[12] He makes this statement in the final summation of his sermon "Justice" from *Unspoken Sermons, Third Series.*

[13] John Piper, *The Pleasures of God*, pp. 66-67, 75.

[14] George MacDonald, *Unspoken Sermons, Third* Series, "Justice."

Chapter 2

[15] See the author's book, *Bold Thinking Christianity.*

[16] George MacDonald's original sermon "The Truth in Jesus" appeared in *Unspoken*

Sermons, Second Series, published in 1885 by Longmans, Green & Co. Reprints of that volume are available online. Printed editions of this and many of MacDonald's originals were reprinted by Sunrise Books in the 1980s and 1990s as collector editions in the "Sunrise Centenary Editions of the Works of George MacDonald." Most of the Sunrise titles are still available through the website FatherOfTheInklings.com, in "The Bookstore, the George MacDonald Alcove." These titles are listed in the Bibliography. An edited edition of "The Truth in Jesus" was published in 2006 by Bethany House Publishers in the volume entitled *The Truth in Jesus* (Michael Phillips, editor.) The selection here included is reprinted from Chapter 3 of that book.

[16] See Appendix 1 for an explanation of the editing of the MacDonald selections.

Chapter 3
[18] Cited in *George MacDonald, Scotland's Beloved Storyteller* by Michael Phillips, p. 143.
[19] Jonathan Edwards, "The Eternity of Hell Torments" a sermon from April 1739.
[20] Exodus 32.
[21] Amos 7: 2, 5.
[22] George MacDonald, *Unspoken Sermons, Third Series*, "Justice."
[23] TULIP: Total Depravity, Unconditional Election, Limited Atonement, Irresistible Grace, Perseverance of the Saints ("Once saved, always saved.")

Chapter 5
[24] George MacDonald, *Unspoken Sermons, Second Series,* "The Voice of Job."
[25] George MacDonald's original sermon "Light" appeared in *Unspoken Sermons, Third Series*, published in 1889 by Longmans, Green & Co., and reprinted by Sunrise Books in 1996. This and most of the "Sunrise Centenary Editions of the Works of George MacDonald" are available through the website FatherOfTheInklings.com, in "The Bookstore, the George MacDonald Alcove." An edited edition of "Light" was published in 2006 by Bethany House Publishers in the volume entitled *The Truth in Jesus* (Michael Phillips, editor.) The selection here included is reprinted from Chapter 7 of that book.

Chapter 6
[26] George MacDonald, *Your Life In Christ* (Michael Phillips, ed.), pp. 205-06, 208-08, from *A Dish of Orts, "*A Sermon."
[27] George MacDonald, *Your Life In Christ* (Michael Phillips, ed.), p. 35, from *Unspoken Sermons, Third Series*,"The Creation in Christ."
[28] George MacDonald, *Unspoken Sermons Third Series,* "Justice."
[29] George MacDonald, *The Truth in Jesus* (Michael Phillips, ed.), pp. 77-78, from *Unspoken Sermons, Second Series, "The Truth in Jesus."*

Chapter 7
[30] George MacDonald's original sermon "The Consuming Fire" appeared in *Unspoken Sermons, First Series*, published in 1867 by Alexander Strahan, and reprinted by Sunrise Books in 1988. This and most of the "Sunrise Centenary Editions of the Works of George MacDonald" are available through the website FatherOfTheInklings.com, in "The Bookstore, the George MacDonald Alcove."

Chapter 8
[31] John 12:32.
[32] Philippians 2:10-11.
[33] Though a detailed analysis of the Greek of Mark 3:29 lies outside the scope of this book, those interested may find that analysis by the author in the article entitled "The Great Sin" in *Leben 7*, available with the author's other books at FatherOfTheInklings.com.
[34] "Lord, do you want us to bid fire come down from heaven and consume them?" (Luke

9:54, RSV.)

[35] Adlai Loudy, *God's Eonian Purpose*, pp. 336-38.

[36] "And these shall go away into everlasting punishment: but the righteous into life eternal. (Matthew 25:46, KJV.)

[37] "But he that shall blaspheme against the Holy Ghost hath never forgiveness, but is in danger of eternal damnation:" (Mark 3:29, KJV). As pointed out in the text, the word "never" does not appear in the Greek original, but was an erroneous addition by the King James translators.

Chapter 9

[38] *Leben 4*, October, 2004.

[39] The topic of goodness, sin, and universal Fatherhood as they relate to Genesis 1-3 is treated at length in Chapters 15-17 of *A God To Call Father* (Michael Phillips, 1996), and in Chapters 19-22 of *God A Good Father* (Michael Phillips, 2001).

[40] George MacDonald, *Unspoken Sermons, Second Series,* "Abba, Father!"

[41] George MacDonald, *Unspoken Sermons, Second Series,* "The Truth in Jesus."

[42] The Westminster Confession of Faith, 1646.

[43] George MacDonald, *The Maiden's Bequest* (Michael Phillips, ed.), p. 47) from *Alec Forbes of Howglen,* Chapter 12.

[44] George MacDonald, *The Gentlewoman's Choice* (Michael Phillips ed.), p. 24, from *Weighed and Wanting,* Chapter 3.

[45] George MacDonald, *The Musician's Quest* (Michael Phillips, ed.), p. 62, from *Robert Falconer*, Chapter 12.

[46] George MacDonald, *David Elginbrod,* Chapter 58.

[47] George MacDonald, *Your Life In Christ* (Michael Phillips, ed.), pp. 116-18, from *Unspoken Sermons, Second Series,* "Self Denial."

[48] George MacDonald, *The Truth in Jesus* (Michael Phillips, ed.), pp. 157, 159-160, from *Unspoken Sermons, First Series,* "The Child in the Midst."

[49] George MacDonald, *The Truth in Jesus* (Michael Phillips, ed.), p. 161, from *Unspoken Sermons, First Series,* "The Child in the Midst."

[50] George MacDonald, *Unspoken Sermons Second Series,* "The Voice of Job."

[51] Letter from George MacDonald to a concerned reader, quoted in *George MacDonald, Scotland's Beloved Storyteller* by Michael Phillips, pp. 310-11.

Chapter 10

[52] George MacDonald's original sermon "Abba, Father!" appeared in *Unspoken Sermons, Second Series*, published in 1885 by Longmans, Green & Co., and reprinted by Sunrise Books in 1995. This and most of the "Sunrise Centenary Editions of the Works of George MacDonald" are available through the website FatherOfTheInklings.com, in "The Bookstore, the George MacDonald Alcove." An edited edition of "Abba, Father!" was published in 2005 by Bethany House Publishers in the volume entitled *Your Life in Christ* (Michael Phillips, editor.) The selection here included is reprinted from Chapter 9 of that book.

Chapter 11

[53] George MacDonald, *Unspoken Sermons, First Series,* "The Hands of the Father."

[54] George MacDonald, *Unspoken Sermons, Second Series*, "The Last Farthing."

[55] George MacDonald, *Unspoken Sermons, First Series,* "The Consuming Fire."

[56] In "The Final Unmasking," from *Unspoken Sermons, Third Series,* MacDonald writes: "A man may sink by such slow degrees that, long after he is a devil, he may go on being a good churchman or a good dissenter, and thinking himself a good Christian."

[57] George MacDonald, *Your Life In Christ* (Michael Phillips, ed.) p. 106, from *Unspoken Sermons, Second Series,* "Self Denial."

[58]   George MacDonald, *The Musician's Quest* (Michael Phillips, ed.), pp. 199-200), from *Robert Falconer*, Chapter 55.

Chapter 12
[59]   George MacDonald's original sermon "Salvation From Sin" appeared in *The Hope of the Gospel*, published in 1892 by Ward, Lock, Bowden & Co and reprinted by Sunrise Books in 1989. This and most of the "Sunrise Centenary Editions of the Works of George MacDonald" are available through the website FatherOfTheInklings.com, in "The Bookstore."

Chapter 13
[60]   George MacDonald, *Unspoken Sermons, Second Series*, "The Last Farthing."
[61]   George MacDonald, *Unspoken Sermons, First Series*, "The Child in the Midst."
[62]   George MacDonald, *The Hope of the Gospel*, "Sorrow the Pledge of Joy."
[63]   George MacDonald, *Unspoken Sermons, Third Series*, "Justice."
[64]   George MacDonald, *The Hope of the Gospel*, "Salvation From Sin."
[65]   George MacDonald, *Unspoken Sermons, Third Series*, "Justice."
[66]   C.S. Lewis, *Mere Christianity*, "What Lies Behind the Law."
[67]   George MacDonald, *Unspoken Sermons, Third Series*, "Justice."
[68]   George MacDonald, *Robert Falconer*, Chapter 28.
[69]   Francis Schaeffer, *The Mark of the Christian*, originally published as Appendix II of *The Church at the End of the 20th Century*. Schaeffer wrote: "All men bear the image of God. They have value, not because they are redeemed, but because they are God's creation in God's image...Very often the true Bible-believing Christian, in his emphasis on two humanities—one lose, one saved—...has given a picture of exclusiveness which is ugly. There are two humanities. That is true. Some men made in the image of God still stand in rebellion against him; some, by the grace of God, have cast themselves upon God's solution. Nonetheless, there is in another very important sense only one humanity. Al men derive from one origin. By creation all men bear the image of God. In this sense all men are of one flesh, one blood." (pp. 133-35.)

Chapter 14
[70] Michael Phillips, *George MacDonald, Scotland's Beloved Storyteller*, p. 145-6. So correct of orthodoxy was Louisa's family that the story was told of an aunt who said she could not lie in bed at peace at night were it not for her belief in the everlasting pains of torment suffered by the wicked in hell.
[71]   George MacDonald, *Unspoken Sermons, Third Series*, "Justice," and also in *Unspoken Sermons, Second Series*, "The Fear of God."
[72]   George MacDonald, *Unspoken Sermons, Third Series*, "Justice."
[73]   George MacDonald, *Unspoken Sermons, Third Series*, "The Creation in Christ."
[74]   George MacDonald, *Your Life In Christ* (edited by Michael Phillips), pp. 42-44, from *Unspoken Sermons, Third Series*, "The Creation in Christ."
[75]   George MacDonald, *Your Life In Christ* (edited by Michael Phillips), p. 49, from *Unspoken Sermons, Third Series*, "The Creation in Christ."
[76]   George MacDonald, *The Hope of the Gospel*, "The Heirs of Heaven and Earth."
[77]   George MacDonald, *Unspoken Sermons Second Series*, "Life."
[78]   George MacDonald, *The Truth in Jesus* (edited by Michael Phillips), pp. 221-224, from *Unspoken Sermons, Third Series*, "Righteousness."
[79]   George MacDonald, *The Truth in Jesus* (edited by Michael Phillips), p. 234, from *Unspoken Sermons, Third Series*, "Righteousness."
[80]   George MacDonald, *The Highlandetr's Last Song* (edited by Michael Phillips), pp. 83-86, from *What's Mine's Mine*, Chapter 40.
[81]   George MacDonald *Alec Forbes of Howglen*, Chapter 28.

Chapter 15
[82] George MacDonald's original sermon "Justice" appeared in *Unspoken Sermons, Third Series*, published in 1889 by Longmans, Green & Co., and reprinted by Sunrise Books in 1996. This and most of the "Sunrise Centenary Editions of the Works of George MacDonald" are available through the website FatherOfTheInklings.com, in "The Bookstore."

Chapter 16
[83] The topics in this chapter are discussed more extensively, as noted in connection with Chapter 15, in Appendix 1.
[84] The Shorter Catechism of *The Westminster Confession*, answer to question 35, "What is Sanctification?"
[85] J.I. Packer, *Concise Theology*, Tyndale House, 1993, p. 169.
[86] George MacDonald, *Unspoken Sermons, Second Series*, "The Last Farthing."
[87] George MacDonald, *Unspoken Sermons, Third Series*, "Justice."
[88] C.S. Lewis, *Mere Christianity*, "Faith (2)."
[89] George MacDonald, *Your Life In Christ* (edited by Michael Phillips), pp. 42-44, from *Unspoken Sermons, Third Series*, "The Creation in Christ."
[90] George MacDonald, *Your Life In Christ* (edited by Michael Phillips), p. 49, from *Unspoken Sermons, Third Series*, "The Creation in Christ."
[91] George MacDonald, *Your Life in Christ* (edited by Michael Phillips), pp. 79-81, from *Unspoken Sermons, Second Series*, "Life."

Chapter 17
[92] This incident and its ramifications is recounted in detail in Michael Phillips' *George MacDonald Scotland's Beloved Storyteller*, Chapter 14, entitled "The Heresy Hunt."
[93] George MacDonald, *Unspoken Sermons Third Series*, "The Final Unmasking."
[94] The entire premise of Lewis's *The Great Divorce* is that opportunity in many forms may potentially exist after death. The underlying conclusion that we may infer both from this book and other of his writings, is that Lewis believed that while repentance after death might potentially be "possible," many will not choose that repentance and will remain in a hell of their own making to all eternity. Beyond that, it is impossible to conjecture whether Lewis believed that some sinners and unbelievers *would* repent after death and be united with God in heaven. We simply don't know. The intriguing question of Lewis's beliefs on the afterlife is discussed in the interview between Robin Phillips and Michael Phillips on *Hell and Beyond* conducted by Robin Phillips on his blog "Robin's Readings and Reflections." Lewis also remarks that "the job will not be completed in this life; but He means to get us as far as possible before death," in *Mere Christianity*, "Counting the Cost," an obvious allusion to the ongoing nature of the sanctification process.
[95] George MacDonald, *Unspoken Sermons Second Series*, "The Hardness of the Way."
[96] George MacDonald, *The Truth in Jesus* (edited by Michael Phillips), p. 127, from *Unspoken Sermons, Third Series*, "Light."
[97] George MacDonald, *The Truth in Jesus* (edited by Michael Phillips), p. 129, from *Unspoken Sermons, Third Series,* "Light."
[98] George MacDonald, *Unspoken Sermons, First Series*, "It Shall Not Be Forgiven."
[99] George MacDonald, *Unspoken Sermons, First Series*, "The Heart With the Treasure."
[100] George MacDonald, *The Hope of the Gospel*, "The Salt and the Light of the World."

Chapter 18
[101] Malachi 3:2-4.
[102] Malachi 4:2.
[103] Zephaniah 3:8

[104] Zephaniah 3:9

[105] Amos 9: 11, 14, NIV.

[106] These ideas are developed in more detail in Michael Phillips' book *Is Jesus Coming Back As Soon As We Think?*

[107] George MacDonald, *Unspoken Sermons, Second Series*, "The Fear of God."

[108] George MacDonald, *Unspoken Sermons, First Series*, "The Consuming Fire."

[109] George MacDonald, *Unspoken Sermons First Series*, "It Shall Not Be Forgiven."

[110] George MacDonald, *David Elginbrod*, Chapter 59, "A Sunday With Falconer."

Chapter 19

[111] George MacDonald's original sermon "The Fear of God" appeared in *Unspoken Sermons, Second Series*, published in 1885 by Longmans, Green & Co., and reprinted by Sunrise Books in 1995. This and most of the "Sunrise Centenary Editions of the Works of George MacDonald" are available through the website FatherOfTheInklings.com, in "The Bookstore."

Chapter 20

[112] George MacDonald, *Unspoken Sermons, Third Series*, "Justice."

[113] George MacDonald, *Unspoken Sermons Third Series*, "Righteousness."

[114] George MacDonald, David Elginbrod, Chapter 59.

[115] George MacDonald, *The Hope of the Gospel*, "Salvation From Sin."

[116] George MacDonald, *Unspoken Sermons, Second Series*, "The Last Farthing."

[117] George MacDonald, *Lilith*, Chapter 39, "That Night."

[118] George MacDonald, *Unspoken Sermons, Second Series*, "The Last Farthing."

[119] George MacDonald, *Poetical Works of George MacDonald*, "Thanksgiving for F. D. Maurice."

[120] George MacDonald, *Robert Falconer*, Chapter 12.

[121] George MacDonald, *Unspoken Sermons, Second Series*, "The Cause of Spiritual Stupidity."

[122] George MacDonald, *Unspoken Sermons, Second Series*, "Man's Difficulty Concerning Prayer."

[123] George MacDonald, *Unspoken Sermons Third Series*, "The Final Unmasking."

[124] George MacDonald, *Unspoken Sermons Third Series*, "The Final Unmasking."

[125] George MacDonald, *Unspoken Sermons Third Series*, "The Final Unmasking."

Chapter 21

[126] William Strunk and E.B. White, (*The Elements of Style*, p. 58.

[127] Young's Literal Translation of the Bible, 1898.

[128] W.E. Vine, *Vines Expository Dictionary of New Testament Words*, p. 41.

[129] *Weymouth New Testament*, original version, published in 1903.

[130] Concordant Literal New Testament, published in 1926.

[131] Robert Young, *Young's Literal Translation*, published in 1898.

[132] Joseph B. Rotherham, *The Emphasized Bible*, published in 1902.

[133] Andrew Jukes, *The Restitution of All Things*, pp. 57, 61-3.

[134] Thomas Allin, *Christ Triumphant*, p. 258.

[135] *Weymouth New Testament*, original version, published in 1903.

[136] Joseph B. Rotherham, *The Emphasized Bible*, published in 1902.

[137] Robert Young, *Young's Literal Translation*, published in 1898.

[138] *The Twentieth Century New Testament*, published in 1901.

[139] Concordant Literal New Testament, published in 1926.

[140] A. R. Symonds, *The Ultimate Reconciliation and Subjection of All Souls to God Under the Kingdom of Christ*, 1878, pp. 130-31.

[141] A.T. Robertson, *Word Pictures in the New Testament, Vol. 1*, pp. 201-02.

[142] William Barclay, *A Spiritual Autobiography*, 1975, pp. 58-60.

[143] A.T. Robertson, *In the End, God*, p. 131, n. 8, quoted from *Christian Theology*, Millard Erickson, p. 1239.

[144] Millard J. Erickson, *Christian Theology*, Baker, pp. 1238.

[145] William Barclay, *The Letters to the Philippians, Colossians, and Thessalonians*, p. 42.

[146] I have detailed this hermeneutical incongruity in detail, with more examples, in the book *Is Jesus Coming Back As Soon As We Think?*

Chapter 22
[147] Taken from Chapters 19, 20, 22 of *Hell and Beyond* by Michael Phillips.

Chapter 23
[148] George MacDonald's original sermon "The Last Farthing" appeared in *Unspoken Sermons, Second Series*, published in 1885 by Longmans, Green & Co., and reprinted by Sunrise Books in 1995. This and most of the "Sunrise Centenary Editions of the Works of George MacDonald" are available through the website FatherOfTheInklings.com, in "The Bookstore."

Chapter 24
[149] Excerpts taken from what many consider to be George MacDonald's masterpiece, the next to last book he wrote, published in 1895, *Lilith*, selections from chapters 38-45.

Cha;ter 25
[150] From Chapter 23 of *Hell and Beyond*.

Chapter 26
[151] George MacDonald, *Unspoken Sermons, Third Series*, "Justice."

[152] George MacDonald, *Unspoken Sermons, First Series*, "The Consuming Fire."

[153] George MacDonald, *Unspoken Sermons, Third Series*, "Freedom."

[154] George MacDonald, *What's Mine's Mine*, Chapter 15.

[155] C.S. Lewis, *George MacDonald, An Anthology*, "Introduction."

[156] Lewis's most detailed exposition on hell appeared in Chapter 8 of *The Problem of Pain*, published in 1940, in which he vigorously defended the orthodox position. What must be born in mind, however, is that this was his first "religious" non-fiction book and was written not many years after Lewis's conversion. To what extent might his perspectives have expanded during the next twenty years of his life will forever remain unknown. This intriguing question is discussed at length in "Hell and Beyond, The Interview," found at "Robin's Readings and Reflections," as well as on Michael Phillips's blog, "Dare To Think Big About God."

[157] C.S. Lewis, *George MacDonald, An Anthology*, "Introduction."

[158] These quotes all taken from the last page of George MacDonald's sermon "The Consuming Fire," from *Unspoken Sermons, First Series*.

[159] From George MacDonald's Preface to *Letters From Hell*, by Valdemar Thisted, 1885, p. viii.

[160] George MacDonald, *There and Back*, Chapter 31.

[161] George MacDonald, *Unspoken Sermons Third Series*, "The Inheritance."

[162] George MacDonald, *Unspoken Sermons, Second Series*, "Life."

[163] George MacDonald, Unspoken Sermons, Second Series, "Self Denial."

Chapter 27
[164] George MacDonald, Unspoken Sermons, Second Series, "The Fear of God."

Appendix 1

[165] *The Fisherman's Lady*, an edition of George MacDonald's *Malcolm* edited by Michael Phillips was published in 1982 by Bethany House publishers of Minneapolis, Minn. Over the next nine years Bethany House released a total of twenty-six Phillips-redacted editions of MacDonald's work—eighteen adult novels, four young-reader editions, four devotional compilations—as well as Phillips' biography *George MacDonald, Scotland's Beloved Storyteller* (1987). Two volumes of redacted Sermons, *Your Life in Christ* and *The Truth in Jesus*, followed from Bethany House in 2005 and 2006.

[166] The Sunrise Centenary Editions of the Works of George MacDonald, published by Sunrise Books, Michael Phillips, series editor, facsimile editions of the original works of George MacDonald, P.O. Box 7003, Eureka, CA 95502.

[167] These two volumes of edited George MacDonald sermons were published by Bethany House Publishers in 2005 and 2006.

[168] From the Introduction to *The Fisherman's Lady*, redacted edition of George MacDonald's *Malcolm* edited by Michael Phillips, 1982, Bethany House publishers.

[169] C. S. Lewis, Introduction to *George MacDonald, An Anthology*, pp. 18-20.

[170] From the Introduction to *Your Life in Christ*, a compilation of sermons by George MacDonald on The Nature of God and His Work in Human Hearts, edited by Michael Phillips, 2005, Bethany House publishers.

Appendix 2

[171] Availability of the works of George MacDonald and Michael Phillips has curiously shifted almost exactly 180 degrees from twenty years ago. At the time of this writing, most of George MacDonald's corpus, once nearly lost from public view, is widely available in many formats, much of it online for free. The books of Michael Phillips, on the other hand, are mostly out of print and becoming increasingly difficult to find. Most of his titles, however, can usually still be obtained, either used or from what limited stock remains. As the Phillips titles that follow are not in the public domain and still copyright protected, they have been slower to appear in digital form. This availability is slowly increasing as well. Print editions of available MacDonald and Phillips titles can be ordered in "The Bookstore" at the website FatherOfTheInklings.com. in the *George MacDonald Alcove* and the *Michael Phillips Aisle*.

Michael Phillips may be contacted through FatherOfTheInklings.com,
at P.O. Box 7003, Eureka, CA 95502,
or through Alive Communications,
7680 Goddard St., Suite 200, Colorado Springs, CO 80920.

THE COMMANDS

Michael Phillips considers THE COMMANDS the most important book he has ever written. Available on Amazon, from any bookstore, or from FatherOfTheInklings.com. For quantity discounts, see "The Michael Phillips Aisle" in "The Bookstore" of www.fatheroftheinklings.com.

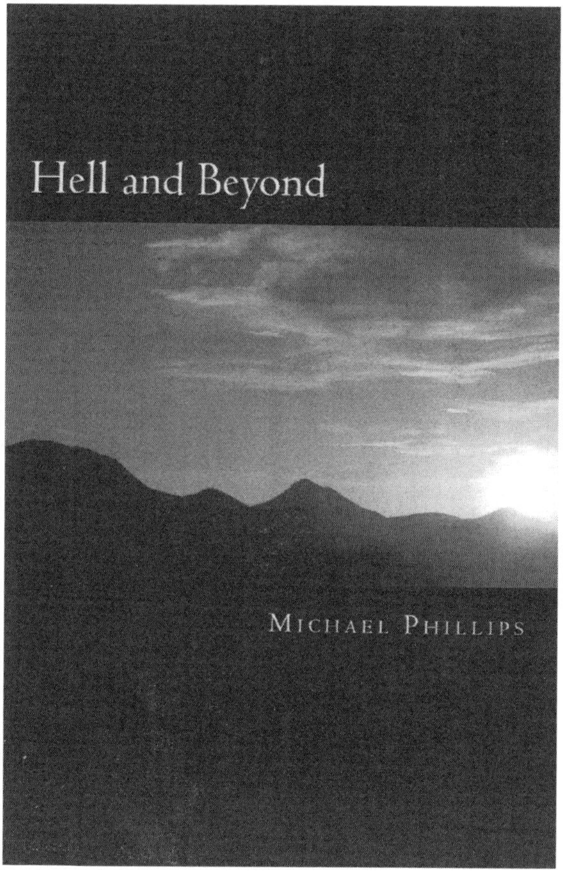

Hell and Beyond

The magnitude of the endorsements alone recommend this astonishing book as a new classic in Christian allegory. Read why Paul Young calls Hell and Beyond "breathtaking and important...beautiful beyond describing and stunning in its impact." C. Baxter Kruger writes: "Michael Phillips has done the impossible—written a thriller on hell."

21920317R00204

Made in the USA
Middletown, DE
14 July 2015